DOGS

THE ULTIMATE CARE GUIDE

GOOD HEALTH, LOVING CARE, MAXIMUM LONGEVITY

PREVENTION FOR PETS

Edited by Matthew Hoffman

Medical Adviser: Lowell Ackerman, D.V.M., Ph.D., is a veterinarian in private practice in Scottsdale, Arizona, and Ontario, Canada. He specializes in veterinary dermatology and nutritional counseling, and is the author of numerous books, including *Owner's Guide to Dog Health*.

RODALE®

© 1998 by Weldon Owen Inc.

Library of Congress Cataloging-in-Publication Data

Dogs : the ultimate care guide : good health, loving care, maximum longevity / edited by Matthew Hoffman ; medical adviser, Lowell Ackerman.

p.   cm.

Includes index.

ISBN 0–87596–532–6 hardcover

ISBN 1–57954–244–1 paperback

1. Dogs.   2. Dogs—Health.   I. Hoffman, Matthew.   II. Ackerman, Lowell J.

SF427.D57   1998

636.7'088'7—dc21   97–46600

Distributed to the book trade by St. Martin's Press

6   8   10   9   7   5   hardcover

2   4   6   8   10   9   7   5   3   paperback

WE **INSPIRE** AND **ENABLE** PEOPLE TO IMPROVE
THEIR LIVES AND THE WORLD AROUND THEM

DOGS
THE ULTIMATE CARE GUIDE

CONTRIBUTING WRITERS
Lowell Ackerman, D.V.M., Ph.D., Kim Campbell Thornton,
Bette LaGow, Kristine Napier, Jacqueline O'Neil,
Audrey Pavia, Elaine Waldorf Gewirtz

RODALE HEALTH AND FITNESS BOOKS
***Prevention for Pets* Editor:** Matthew Hoffman
Vice-President and Editorial Director: Debora T. Yost
Executive Editor: Neil Wertheimer
Design and Production Director: Michael Ward
Research Manager: Ann Gossy Yermish
Copy Manager: Lisa D. Andruscavage
Book Manufacturing Director: Helen Clogston
Design Coordinator: David Q. Pryor
Manufacturing Manager: Mark Krahforst
Manufacturing Coordinator: Melinda B. Rizzo

WELDON OWEN PTY LTD
Chairman: John Owen
Publisher: Sheena Coupe
Associate Publisher: Lynn Humphries
Project Editors: Bronwyn Sweeney, Madeleine Jennings
Copy Editor: Lynn Cole
Proofreader: Elizabeth Connolly
Editorial Assistants: Vesna Radojcic, Shona Ritchie
Art Director: Sue Rawkins
Designers: Matt Gavin-Wear, Kylie Mulquin, Mark Thacker
Cover Design: Matt Gavin-Wear
Picture Research: Karen Burgess
Illustrators: Janet Jones, Keith Scanlon
Cartoonist: Jim Chan
Indexer: Garry Cousins
Production Manager: Caroline Webber
Production Assistant: Kylie Lawson

Film separation by Colourscan Co Pte Ltd, Singapore

> *"We never really own a dog*
> *as much as he owns us."*
>
> GENE HILL
> *Tears and Laughter*

Contents

Introduction

There is really something quite remarkable about two distinctly different species forming a bond that can only be described as love. You wouldn't imagine that a pig could love a cow or a chicken would be enamored of a hedgehog, but somehow there is something very natural about the affection we share with dogs.

Today, more than ever, dogs are much more to us than just pets. They are family members. They share our hearts as well as our homes, and we often afford them the same status as our children (although they never whine for designer labels or ask to borrow the car). They are content with the knowledge that their ultimate care rests entirely in our hands. They implicitly trust our judgment and our commitment to them. After all, they love us. Meeting their needs is how we show them that we love them too and that they are important in our lives.

The concept of ultimate care may seem like a huge responsibility (and it is), but it is also a labor of love. When you take responsibility for a dog, you naturally want to do the best job you can. It's not that difficult and it has a lot of perks. After all, there are lots of snuggles and kisses, and your canine friend will rarely turn down an opportunity to accompany you on any outing. Once you have a dog, it's hard to be lonely, unless you need to leave home without him.

As a veterinarian, I've observed an extremely positive trend in dog ownership over the years. Although veterinarians and pet-related businesses can accept part of the credit for this, most of the advances have been made because dog owners

have demanded the best for their pets. Dog foods have improved dramatically and there is now more selection than ever before. New vaccines are constantly being formulated and many devastating canine diseases have been controlled or eliminated. And there's a lot of information available. In *Dogs: The Ultimate Care Guide*, you will find everything you need to know about training, grooming, first aid, basic health care and all the other topics that you will need to raise a dog in the best environment possible.

Dogs today live longer than ever before. This is partially due to better medicines and vaccines, but it's mostly due to owners caring for their dogs with the same attentiveness they give to other family members. The result is a healthier dog and a deeper connection between the dog and his owner. Both parties seem to benefit from this. Although your veterinarian is important, it is your day-to-day care that has the most impact on your dog's ultimate health and happiness.

In the last decade or so, there has been much celebration of the human–animal bond as researchers learn what dog owners have known for centuries—that forging a relationship with a dog can do us a lot of good. Dogs give us total support, companionship, acceptance and love. Dogs aren't judgmental or fickle. They don't find a need to rationalize a relationship or measure it against some imaginary scale. They are content in the knowledge that, for whatever reason there may be in Heaven or on Earth, it is their destiny to be with us. And we, their owners, have come to realize what a blessing this really is.

As you read through this book, keep your dog close by and feel good that you're giving him the best care. Your dog may not congratulate you for your efforts, but he'll repay you with many years of loving companionship. Treasure them!

Lowell Ackerman, D.V.M., Ph.D., Scottsdale, Arizona, and Ontario, Canada.

PART ONE

Getting Acquainted

With a new dog in your life, it's going to be love at first sight. Take your time to get to know each other, to understand each other and to become best friends.

1 THE PERFECT MATCH

pages 2–41
Big or small, boy or girl, youngster or grown-up, purebred or mystifying mix—this is the guide to choosing the dog for you.

2 JOINING THE CLAN

pages 42–53
It's time to welcome your new dog to your family. Greet him with open arms so he'll know that your home is his home now.

3 BRINGING UP PUPPY

pages 54–67
Everything you need to help your precocious pup grow into a polite and poised pooch that you will be proud of.

4 CANINE COMMUNICATION

pages 68–79
You can learn a lot about your dog from the things he does, the faces he pulls and the noises he makes.

1 THE PERFECT MATCH

A dog is wonderful, loving, entertaining and loyal. He will also demand a lot of you, because you're his owner and he's dependent on you. The responsibilities of ownership are great, but the love and friendship you will receive in return are priceless. Just ask the millions of happy dog owners who couldn't imagine life without their canine friends.

Choosing the Right Dog
pages 3–7
Spend time thinking about the kind of dog that will really suit you and your lifestyle

Why a Purebred?
pages 12–16
A purebred could be perfect if you're looking for a specific kind of dog

Make Mine a Mixed Breed
pages 35–37
A mixed breed dog will be devoted and loving—he will also be unique

Puppy or Adult?
pages 8–11
Do you have the time to start from scratch with a pup, or would an adult dog be best?

The 50 Most Popular Breeds
pages 17–34
A chart to help you choose the dog that's truly right for you

Where to Get Your Dog
pages 38–41
The best places to check out to find the dog of your dreams

Choosing the Right Dog

A dog will do his utmost to keep you laughing, and he won't mind if you drop a few tears on his coat when you're feeling down. He'll play as hard as you want, for as long as you want, or happily curl up at your feet when you need some serious relaxation. And a dog is so forgiving, allowing us silly humans our frequent mistakes, yet never holding them against us later. In short, a dog is just about the perfect friend.

However, he also relies on you for nearly everything—food, water, shelter, veterinary care, exercise, companionship, training, grooming and protection. "Know what you're getting into," says Steve Diller, a dog trainer in Elmsford, New York. "Take a serious look at what you expect from a dog, and what he will need from you. Remember the training and grooming and all the other responsibilities that are connected with owning a canine friend."

Family Matters

The decision to add a dog to your family needs careful thought, so it will work out well for everyone. First, consider your family as it is right now. Are you single? A young couple with no kids? A couple with kids? Are your children toddlers, school-age or older? Are you looking to fill your empty nest with a four-legged companion? Do you already share your home with another dog or perhaps a cat?

Maybe you don't have children—yet. Or a cat—yet. You must think ahead to the possibility of who else might join your family in the next 10 to 15 years, because that's a fair estimate of the time commitment you'll be making. And consider members of your extended family or neighboring children who might come in contact with your dog. While you certainly don't need to get a dog that's great with kids if you don't have any and don't plan to, you do need to know how your dog is likely to react when confronted with the boisterous children of friends.

Each family has its own needs, personalities, medical requirements, space limitations and busy schedules. If you take a careful, honest look at these, it will help you to decide on the type of dog that will enrich everyone's lives, rather than make them more awkward or difficult.

Is anyone in your family allergic to dog hair? Even if no one is allergic, how bothered are you by dog hair on everything from your pants to your toast? During certain periods of the year, some breeds shed profusely. Others don't shed so much,

The greatest pleasure this Boxer can think of is the love and approval of his owner. He watches intently for the sign that he has done well.

Many breeds will join in all the family activities and make wonderful pets for young children. Make sure you keep everyone's needs and wishes in mind when making the big decision.

but there will be regular vacuuming of dog hair and sweeping of leaves and dirt tracked in on doggy feet. Some dogs are low maintenance, but no dog is no maintenance.

The good news is there's a dog out there that's a perfect match for you and whoever else you share your life with. The time you invest in finding that perfect match will be well spent. Choosing a dog whose needs don't really suit your lifestyle and that of your family can mean heartache for both of you if the match doesn't work out. Take the time to make sure you get it right, for the sake of both you and the dog.

Time and Timing

A dog needs care and love and attention. You or another adult in the family will need to have enough time to walk, groom and feed him. And if he's a pup, parenting duties will be doubled, and housebreaking will be added to the list.

While children and dogs can be inseparable, the primary responsibility for your dog's care must rest on adult shoulders. "I'm wary when someone says they want a dog for the children to take care of," says Louise Sanders, a Bullmastiff breeder from Largo, Florida. "No child is really responsible enough to take on the total care of a dog."

Different dogs will need varying amounts of your time. Some need at least two long walks a day, while some can get most of their exercise inside the house. Dogs with long, double coats will require daily brushing, while dogs with short, wiry coats can get by on a lick and a promise. Different breeds housebreak at different rates, too, which will affect how much time you need for a puppy. And as adults, toy breeds will still need frequent trips outside, since they have tiny bladders and need to go out every two or three hours.

Make sure you're in a fairly settled situation before adopting a dog. It will take a while for him to adjust to the rhythms and routines of your family. Plan to get him when you know your life will be relatively stable. If career moves are imminent, or you are going to be traveling a lot for business or pleasure, wait until things settle down before adding a dog to the family.

The holidays might seem like a good time to get a dog. But such decisions tend to be impulsive and might be regretted later on. There are better times to introduce a new dog to a strange new environment and lots of strange new faces than the hectic, noisy holiday season.

Consider the Costs

Owning and caring properly for a dog takes money. Not only are there the monthly food bills, as well as heartworm and flea prevention medication, but there is the initial outlay for the things that every dog needs. You'll need a crate, bedding, toys, grooming tools and dishes.

Then there are vaccinations, vet visits, licenses and perhaps obedience training. That's the day-to-day and year-to-year costs you'll have.

There's also the amount you will have to pay to purchase your dog. You might opt for a shelter animal over a purebred from a breeder, in which case the price of your precious pooch will be minimal. But if you decide on a purebred dog, you could be looking at more than $1,000.

Will He Suit Your Environment?

Most dogs, even some of the smaller breeds, require a fair amount of exercise to stay happy and healthy. There are breeds that will adapt easily to apartment living, but others will need a house in the suburbs with a yard and a garden and something more substantial than a white picket fence to stop them from wandering.

Don't equate the size of the dog with the size of the living space he requires. "Just because a Beagle is small does not mean he's a great apartment dog," says Diller. "In fact, the opposite is true. Yet a Great Dane and some of the other working breeds don't require all that much space." Giant breeds, such as Newfoundlands and Great Pyrenees, can be real couch potatoes.

Some smaller dogs, including many of the terrier types, not only like plenty of exercise and space, they are also some of the barkiest dogs—not necessarily a good thing in an apartment where your neighbor is only a thin wall away.

If all you have is a postage-stamp of lawn and you had your heart set on a dog that likes a lot of exercise, don't give up on the idea. Instead, consider your entire neighborhood. Most likely there are parks, schoolyards and miles of sidewalks that the two of you can enjoy.

Be careful, though, about getting a cold-weather-loving breed if you live in a hot climate.

A large dog like this Great Dane doesn't necessarily need a big house or yard to accommodate his size. So long as he gets a good walk once a day, he'll enjoy apartment living.

Malamutes, Saint Bernards and the like have coats and thermostats set for snow and sub-zero temperatures. While they can be perfectly happy in an air-conditioned house in Arizona, they will be uncomfortable outside and at greater risk of heatstroke than some other breeds.

On the other hand, many shorthaired dogs do not like the cold. This is more easily remedied, though, by putting them in doggy sweaters or coats and making their bathroom trips "strictly business" on the coldest days.

More Than Just a Pretty Face

The key to choosing your perfect match is to investigate the various breeds to find out a little bit about their personalities and behaviors—their strengths as well as their quirks. Don't go for looks—that usually works only in the movies. Even if you're planning on getting a mixed breed from the shelter, an understanding of the different groups of dogs will give you some inkling of the personal style of the dog you have in mind.

Some people just rub you the wrong way and there are some dogs that may do the same. Dogs from certain breeds may have personality traits that you simply can't live with. Terriers, for instance, dig. And it's a particularly tenacious

This Australian Shepherd pup will be attentive and easy to train, but he will need lots of space and plenty of exercise to stay in shape. After all, these dogs were originally bred to work hard herding livestock on ranches.

trait that crops up even in a dog that you suspect has only a touch of terrier in his genes. You may be able to persuade your plucky little terrier mix to dig only in a specific area, but if you love your garden, don't be too surprised or upset when he shows that he has a special interest, too.

Hounds, such as Beagles and Foxhounds, bark. A lot. Again, they're supposed to, since they were traditionally used to track game. The jowl-flapping breeds, such as the Saint Bernard and Bullmastiff, can drool excessively. And if you thought dog hair on your pants was bad, wait until your shoes get soaked with saliva.

You need to know the good and the not so good, to make an informed decision. Some people would go nuts with a very active dog

It will be hard to cure this Boston Terrier of digging holes in that lawn you like to keep looking good. After all, he's just doing what he was bred for, even though there's no quarry for him to dig out.

inside the house, while others can think of nothing better for their equally active ten-year-old child. You might think vacuuming twice a day to pick up your Chow Chow's shed coat is good exercise, but your spouse may not. Select a breed that's right for everyone in the house.

"Picking a dog is like choosing a spouse, except you don't get to date for a while to see if you're compatible," says Diane Bauman, a dog obedience trainer in Sussex, New Jersey.

"When people ask me what kind of dog they should—or shouldn't—get, I sit down and find out about their personality, hobbies, what they expect of a dog, what experience they have, and how much dog hair they can tolerate," she explains. "Their answers to these questions give me a much better idea of the breeds that will be best suited to them and their lifestyle."

A Personal Decision

An eight-week-old pup with the cheekiest of expressions might seem like the perfect gift for a friend who's feeling a bit low at the moment. But chances are your friend won't think it's such a great idea when she opens that gift box with the airholes punched in the lid. After all, it will be her, not you, who will be doing the feeding and cleaning and caring for the next ten years or so—and she might have had other plans.

Never buy a dog for another person without their knowledge, consent and input. The decision is far too personal and important for you to make it for someone else. If you want to buy a puppy as a gift, wrap a stuffed dog and give it with the promise that you will help to locate the perfect real thing. That way, the dog will be their dog, and their choice, from the start.

A Male or a Female?

Before you start decorating your puppy's basket in pastel pink or sky blue, there are a couple of things you should consider when deciding whether you will purchase a male or a female pet. As a rule, a male will grow bigger than a female. If, for instance, you're thinking of getting a Newfoundland, bear in mind that males can grow to 150 pounds, whereas females don't usually top 125 pounds. With the smaller breeds, especially the toys, this size disparity is not such a big deal.

There are also some behavioral differences between the sexes. For instance, males can be more dominant, aggressive and territorial than females, but they may also be a bit more playful and active. While you might find a female easier to housebreak, she can also be more demanding of your attention and affection. Females, however, are easier to train, they are cleaner and seem more in tune with their owners, says Diane Bauman, an obedience trainer in Sussex, New Jersey. "Males often seem to have something else on their mind besides what you're trying to accomplish."

Dominance aggression, when a dog tries to be the boss, can be a problem in any dog, but is usually worse in males, says Kathalyn Johnson, D.V.M., who specializes in animal behavior at Texas A&M University's College of Veterinary Medicine in College Station. "Intact males are the worst, then neutered males, followed by spayed females, then intact females." By neutering your dog, especially a male dog, you can reduce or in some cases eliminate such gender-related behavior problems.

Puppy or Adult?

There's nothing cuter than a puppy, except maybe two puppies. And maybe cute is just the right thing for you, or maybe all the things that go along with cute, such as puddles on the floor or chewed up shoes, aren't high on your list of the most desirable attributes in a new dog. You'll need to think about whether a puppy or an adult is the right choice for you. Many of the same issues you thought about when you decided to adopt a dog are also ones you need to examine when deciding what age he should be.

Puppy Heaven

If you get a puppy, you're starting with a clean slate. "You can make a pup what you want him to be," says Diller. The drawback, of course, is that his training has to start from scratch, as does housebreaking. A puppy is a baby, and he'll need more of your time and patience than an older dog. Do you have enough of both to housebreak and train him, as well as the sense of fun and adventure to play with him? Puppies tend to be destructive when they're bored, so they need a lot of exercise and supervised play.

An ideal match for puppies is a family where one adult is home for much of the day. Working from home, you can also adjust your schedule to accommodate housebreaking trips and some of the playtime that he craves. If all the adults of the household have to go to work, it is still possible to get a puppy. Plan to acquire him when you have some vacation time and spend that time bonding with him and getting him established in a regular routine of exercise and feeding—not a vacation routine but the kind of schedule you are both going to have to live by once you're back at work. And when the honeymoon is over, if you can visit him during your lunch hour or hurry home straight after work to spend lots of quality time with him, he'll grow up to be a happy and well-adjusted dog.

What to Look for in a Puppy

Once you've decided you have the time and patience to raise a puppy, you want to make sure you get one

Nothing is off-limits to a puppy, especially when he wants a good chew. You will need time and patience to teach him what is and is not allowed.

that is healthy, social and compatible with your personality and experience. So what's the best indicator of a sound, reliable pup?

Early Influences

"Look at the puppy's relatives, as many as you can meet—the father, the mother, the brothers and sisters," says Suzanne Hetts, Ph.D., an applied animal behaviorist in private practice in Littleton, Colorado. "They will all give you some indication of the characteristics the puppy will grow into having."

"The best guidelines are the parents," agrees Bauman. "Are they high-energy? Low-energy? Obedient? This should give you an idea of what you're getting." Bauman cautions against getting a puppy too young. He should certainly not leave his mom before he's eight weeks old. "The longer a puppy stays with his mom, the more she will teach him about how to behave, which means less work for you, the new owner," she says.

If the litter of puppies you are looking at is purebred, consider letting the breeder choose the right match from the litter for you. "The breeder has been with the puppies since they were born and will have a good idea of what the different personalities are like," says Diller.

"But when in doubt, pick the middle-of-the-road female puppy in a litter—she'll be a bit more easygoing, not too shy, not too pushy," advises Diller. Particularly when you're selecting your puppy from a mixed breed litter, err on the side of caution by opting for a female, especially if you think the pups are going to grow up big.

Temperament Testing

Many breeders and trainers are in favor of evaluating a puppy's temperament at six to eight

Choosing among a litter, such as these Rottweiler puppies, is difficult. The breeder, who has observed them since birth, may be better able to choose the pup that will best suit you and your family's needs.

weeks of age by putting him through a series of tests designed to determine his level of dominance. For instance, one test involves holding a puppy on his back to see if he fights to get away (a dominant personality), if he accepts the situation after a small effort to escape (a normal personality), or if he gives in right away, licking the tester's hands (a submissive personality).

The goal here is to try to match the dog's personality to the prospective owner's. "I would not want a dominant male going to a family with small kids," explains Sanders. "And you have to be careful with any puppy that's very timid. He can turn into a fear biter later on."

While this sort of testing can be a helpful guide for any litter of puppies, whether purebred

Getting a Healthy Puppy

It's always important to choose a pup that's going to be fit and healthy. While there's no way to guarantee that he will never fall ill, you can reduce the chances by checking for certain signs when making your choice. Here's what to look for:

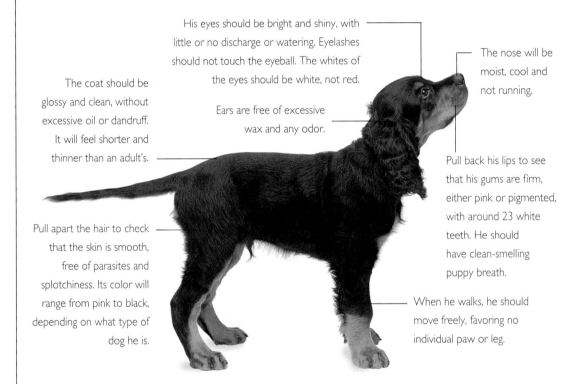

His eyes should be bright and shiny, with little or no discharge or watering. Eyelashes should not touch the eyeball. The whites of the eyes should be white, not red.

The nose will be moist, cool and not running.

The coat should be glossy and clean, without excessive oil or dandruff. It will feel shorter and thinner than an adult's.

Ears are free of excessive wax and any odor.

Pull back his lips to see that his gums are firm, either pink or pigmented, with around 23 white teeth. He should have clean-smelling puppy breath.

Pull apart the hair to check that the skin is smooth, free of parasites and splotchiness. Its color will range from pink to black, depending on what type of dog he is.

When he walks, he should move freely, favoring no individual paw or leg.

Reputable breeders make tremendous efforts to ensure that the dogs they sell are healthy and not prone to long-term problems. In most cases, the parents will be certified by a health registry, which reduces the risk of inherited diseases being passed along to the puppies. These registries include:

- Orthopedic Foundation for Animals: keeps a record of dogs whose hips and elbows have been x-rayed and show no sign of dysplasia.

- Canine Eye Registration Foundation: keeps a log of dogs whose eyes have been checked by a canine ophthalmologist and are free of progressive retinal atrophy or cataracts.

When buying a purebred puppy, make sure that the parents have been tested for von Willebrand's disease, a serious blood-clotting disorder that is present in some bloodlines. Reputable breeders will also have their dogs checked for possible heart problems.

The way this English Springer Spaniel puppy reacts when his feet are held off the ground can help you figure out what kind of temperament he has.

or mixed breed, it will not be the perfect crystal ball for predicting the adult behavior of all puppies. "I have seen different behaviors at six weeks, nine weeks and four months—all in the same pup," says Bauman.

"Try to meet the pup's relatives and examine what the breed was originally intended to do," advises Dr. Hetts "Don't be surprised by the natural herding instincts of Shetland Sheepdogs and Australian Shepherds," she says. "An Akita, originally a fighting dog, may have a low threshold of aggression toward other dogs."

If you're adopting a mixed breed pup, use the same thinking. A Shepherd mix is likely to retain some herding instincts; terrier mixes will dig and bark; and a dog with a bit of Doberman or Rottweiler will probably try to strut his macho stuff. Your dog's behavioral instincts are unlikely to cause problems. Just keep such potential traits in mind when you set about training him.

The Dog that Wasn't Born Yesterday

If the house is empty for much of the day and a new dog will be alone with just his toys, his water bowl and his bed, you might want to consider getting an adult dog. It could be easier on you and him, because the more mature dog will be better at keeping himself entertained, and he won't miss your company quite so much. Also, he won't need your absolute and undivided attention when you are home.

What's more, he may already be house-trained. He might also know what you're talking about when you start using basic obedience commands. One possible disadvantage is that he will be shaped and molded by his life experiences to a certain extent, experiences beyond your control and about which you may know nothing.

Then again, there's a good chance you might know a great deal about him if you are in the lucky position of "inheriting" an adult dog from a family member or friend. Adopting a dog this way is the perfect solution for all involved.

In the event that your adult dog has a few unappealing habits, be assured that an old dog can be taught new tricks, once he has unlearned the old ones. With the help of obedience classes, a professional trainer, or maybe just a good book on dog training, the two of you can be on your way to beautiful and mature friendship.

An older mixed breed dog can be an excellent choice, even if he needs a bit of retraining to fit in with your lifestyle. You will form an impression of his personality by observing him at the animal shelter, and you can also check with shelter staff for their opinion of his character.

Why a Purebred?

Your heart can't tell if the dog in your arms has a pedigree a mile long or a lineage that wouldn't make it to the end of your street. So why should you care if he's purebred? Because they're more predictable. Purebreds have certain specific traits, so you'll know what you're getting. If you decide on a quiet, large, non-shedding dog that's good with children, then you know that a Standard Poodle will fill the bill perfectly.

The Predictable Pooch
The various dog breeds have been monitored for generations, and their ancestry has been recorded and studied. All that history means that when you decide on a purebred dog, you've got a good idea of what kind of dog you'll be getting. "You buy a purebred for the predictability factor," says Christine L. Wilford, D.V.M., a veterinarian in private practice in Seattle, and regular columnist for the *American Kennel Club Gazette*. "You also have a good indication of his

If you choose a German Wirehaired Pointer, you can be sure he will be clean and well-behaved.

eventual size and behavior." Once you know your needs and you know your breeds, you can set about doing the matchmaking.

If you want a dog to accompany you on your daily five-mile jog, you'll want to rule out a Bulldog, whose physical characteristics lean toward strength, not stamina. Opt instead for a canine athlete, perhaps one of the sporting breeds.

Of course, environment and training both play a vital role in molding the adult dog. Nevertheless, certain breeds are genetically predisposed to certain behaviors. The key is to find out what these behaviors are.

The Seven Purebred Groups
Purebred dogs are divided into various groups, according to the breed's original purpose. And although the purebreds of today no longer lead the same lives that their ancestors did, they still retain certain qualities and behaviors.

Sporting Dogs
This group includes the larger spaniels, pointers, setters and retrievers. The Vizsla and Weimaraner also belong to this group. These dogs are alert and intelligent. They have been, and continue to be, used by hunters to find and retrieve game. Not surprisingly, they like lots of regular, energetic outdoor exercise.

Hounds
These are dogs that once used either their noses to track small game (scenthounds, such as the Basset Hound and Foxhound) or their keen sight

The Shar-Pei has a personality that belies his mournful appearance, but be prepared to handle him firmly.

and speed to run down prey (sighthounds, such as the Borzoi and Scottish Deerhound). This is a diverse group and includes some of the lesser-known breeds, such as the Otterhound and Harrier. They tend to have great stamina, although they differ in their exercise requirements. Most enjoy room to run and sniff.

Working Dogs

This diverse group includes guard dogs of both livestock and property (the Mastiff and Kuvasz, for example), sled or cart dogs (Samoyed and Bernese Mountain Dog), rescue dogs (Saint Bernard and Newfoundland), as well as dogs that serve the military (Doberman Pinscher). They are capable and quick to learn, and make dependable companions. Because of their size and strength, it is important that they be properly trained. People new to owning a dog might be wise to choose a female from this group, as she will not grow quite so large and will be less likely to exhibit dominance traits.

Terriers

These are dogs that "go to ground"—the name "terrier" is derived from "terra," Latin for earth.

Some terriers, such as Fox Terriers and Norfolk Terriers, were bred to dig burrowing animals from their dens. Others, such as the West Highland White Terrier and Miniature Schnauzer, were bred to kill troublesome vermin. They are feisty and very active, and need owners who are a match for their strong personalities.

Toys

Toy dogs include traditional lap-sitters favored by nobility (Pekingese, Japanese Chin and Maltese). Irresistibly cute because of their diminutive size, they can have quite determined personalities. They are ideal for people with limited living space.

Non-Sporting Dogs

This began as a catch-all group for dogs that were recognized by the American Kennel Club but didn't quite fit any of the other groups. Bulldogs, Dalmatians, Lhasa Apsos, Tibetan Terriers and Tibetan Spaniels are included.

Herding Dogs

These intelligent dogs were bred to herd sheep or cattle, and many still do. The Old English Sheepdog, Collie and Briard belong to this group, as does, surprisingly, the German Shepherd. They make excellent companions, but the instinct to herd is strong and sometimes they can't resist rounding up your children.

Getting Some Friendly Advice

As with any important decision, it's a good idea to get some input from people in the know. Talk to vets about the breeds that interest you. Vets have probably seen just about everything, and can give you general impressions. They can also probably put you in touch with breeders of that

A breeder takes his Cavalier King Charles Spaniel puppies out for a romp. These hardy little dogs are an excellent choice for apartment dwellers.

particular dog. "Some people think vets aren't fair judges because they see a dog when he's under stress, and therefore more likely to misbehave or show troublesome behavior," says Diller. "I think that's the best time to get an impression. If a dog is steady and reliable under the worst circumstances, it's a good dog."

Trainers can tell you how easy it is to train certain breeds, which they've had the most trouble with, and which breeds are better-suited to first-time owners or to people with more experience.

To see various breeds in action, visit dog shows or events, such as obedience trials or herding tests. Talk to the owners, who will often also be breeders. They will be happy to tell you about their canines. But be aware that you'll be talking to a real fan of that breed and may not get an objective opinion. "Someone who lives with, breeds and shows Doberman Pinschers is going to love them and may be a little one-sided on the topic," says Bauman. "Be sure to ask about what aspects of the breed they don't like."

Purebred Health Problems

Creating breeds involves concentrating genetic material to obtain certain physical characteristics, appearance, behavior or personality. The downside of this is that a smaller gene pool can increase a purebred dog's inherited predisposition to certain illnesses. Unfortunately, diseases or defects may show up only when the dog is several years old and has perhaps been bred himself.

Ten Questions to Ask About a Breed

 Here are some questions to ask when finding out about a particular breed:

- How big do adults grow?
- How much do they eat?
- How much exercise do they need?
- How much work is involved in keeping their coat, nails and ears clean?
- What is the breed's traditional function? (Even if a dog is no longer expected to do what his ancestors did, instincts remain an influence on his behavior.)

- Would you recommend these dogs for a family with small children? If not, why not?
- How playful are they likely to be? Are they reserved or outgoing?
- How much room do they need as a puppy? And as an adult?
- How much does the breed shed?
- What health problems are common to them?

You'll have other questions specific to your family's needs. Be sure to ask whatever you want to know.

Do Different Breeds Get Along?

A German Shepherd out for a walk passes a Yorkshire Terrier and decides to go take a sniff. But as he sidles up, he's not thinking, "Hey now, I've always liked terriers." He doesn't care what breed she is, and any future relationship between the two is going to be based on their temperaments and not their bloodlines.

Putting dogs of very different sizes together can be tricky, says Kathalyn Johnson, D.V.M., who specializes in animal behavior at Texas A&M University's College of Veterinary Medicine in College Station. "Toy breeds could be at risk," she explains. "Just one disciplinary bite or shake from the larger dog could really damage the smaller one."

Then there are dogs that don't get along with other dogs, whatever their pedigree. Some breeds can be extremely possessive of their owners and will get more than a little put out when another dog tries to grab a share of the attention. Terriers such as American Staffordshire Terriers (also known as Pit Bulls) tend to be best suited to one-dog homes, says Dr. Johnson.

Male guard-type working dogs won't always have an easy relationship with other males. Akitas, Rottweilers, Chow Chows and Mastiffs, for instance, can be aggressive. More often than not, a male from one of these breeds will do better with a female for company.

Every breed is susceptible to some ailment or disorder. Most large breeds are prone to a joint disorder called hip dysplasia. Cocker Spaniels, Akitas and Siberian Huskies, among others, have a higher incidence of progressive retinal atrophy and hereditary cataracts. And a blood-clotting disorder known as von Willebrand's disease has shown up in many breeds, including Doberman Pinschers and Scottish Terriers. Newfoundlands are prone to heart defects. Deafness can be common in Dalmatians. And dogs with pushed-in faces, such as Pugs and Pekingese, are prone to respiratory problems and heatstroke.

There are ways to lessen the chance that your purebred pup will suffer from a disease to which his breed is genetically predisposed. Purchase him from a reputable breeder, who will have carefully matched the parents based on their genetic backgrounds to breed out inherited problems. Make sure that the parents have received a clean bill of health. The pup should also have been checked carefully by a vet.

It's also wise to find out how old the pup's grandparents lived to be and ask if any of his relatives succumbed to diseases or conditions common to the breed. Long-lived relatives are often a good indicator of a healthy line of dogs.

Be careful when choosing a companion for your pet pooch. If there is a big difference in size, the smaller dog might be hurt during rough play.

Worth the Price

You can pay a lot for a beautiful purebred dog. But if you go to a reputable, knowledgeable breeder, you'll get your money's worth. You're paying for that person's years of experience with dogs in general and with that breed in particular. You're also paying for ongoing help and advice. Any breeder who cares about her dogs will gladly answer your questions, before you buy the dog and in the years to come. "A breeder is responsible for the puppy she has bred, whelped and weaned," says Janet Lalonde, D.V.M., a veterinarian in private practice in Alexandria, Ontario, and a Whippet breeder. "Responsibilities include day-to-day attention, socialization and health care, and also a commitment to selecting the proper home for the puppy."

Litter size is a factor that determines how much your pup will cost. Toy breeds may have only one or two pups per litter, so it

Pugs make captivating companions and are ideal if space is limited.

costs the breeder more per puppy to recoup stud fees and vet bills. The difficulty a dog experiences when whelping is another factor. Breeds with large heads, such as Bulldogs, must often have cesareans, which adds to the breeder's costs.

There's also the question of "show quality" versus "pet quality." Not every pup in a litter will live up to the ideal standard determined by a national breed club. Pups that do are "show quality," and can be exhibited in dog shows. Those that do not are often dubbed "pet quality." Don't assume there's anything wrong with a puppy just because the breeder hasn't chosen to show the dog. It's often just a case of a small kink in the pup's tail—a serious fault in the show ring but of no consequence to a loving family. "However, if you buy from show litters," advises Bauman, "you'll know that the health and quality of the pups was the breeder's main consideration."

Kennel Club Registration

A dog with "papers" is a purebred dog registered with a particular registry. The American Kennel Club (AKC) is the largest breed registry in North America. Others include the United Kennel Club (UKC), the Canadian Kennel Club and the newer Continental Kennel Club, which registers more than 400 breeds.

If a puppy has his papers, it means that he is eligible for registration because his parents are registered, purebred dogs. You'll need to fill out the appropriate paperwork and submit it with the designated fee to the registry. The dog's breeder will help you do this. If you are buying an older puppy or adult dog that has already been registered, then the breeder must give you the dog's AKC registration certificate, which transfers ownership to you.

Be aware that "AKC," "UKC" or any similar tag that goes with a dog or kennel is not a guarantee of health, temperament or soundness. A dog's registration means only that the dog is a purebred from a verifiable line of purebreds. You still need to do your homework to find a reputable breeder with good, healthy pups.

The 50 Most Popular Breeds

With so many different breeds to choose from, you want to get the one that's best for you. The following chart lists important features of 50 of the most popular breeds, beginning with the standard height and weight measurements for each breed, along with a personality description. A dog's height is measured from the ground to his withers, or shoulders. The personality description outlines a breed's basic temperament and includes information such as whether they are easy to train or suitable for a family with young children.

The color descriptions indicate coat color. Terms used for color are often common ones, but some may be unfamiliar. These are explained in the box to the right.

The grooming requirements tell you what kind of coat each breed has and how much brushing and bathing it needs. The exercise section indicates how much and what kind of exercise is best for the breed. If you want a low-maintenance dog, these are important sections to help you choose appropriately. The environment entry indicates if a breed is suitable for apartment dwelling or needs plenty of space. The health section gives a rundown of the health problems that each breed tends to be prone to.

You'll also find the group to which each breed belongs: sporting, non-sporting, hound, working, terrier, toy and herding. Each breed gets a star rating for trainability, city living and whether or not it's good with children. One star is poor,

two is fair, three is good, four is very good and five is excellent. You'll also see a photo of each of the 50 breeds, as well as a to-scale diagram so you can see what you're getting into. Good luck in finding the purebred dog that is ideal for you.

The Canine Color Chart

If someone says, "Look at that harlequin spaniel," and you're trying to find a dog dressed up in a clown suit, then you need some help. Here are the more unusual canine color terms:

Bicolor: a coat of two distinct colors.

Brindle: an even mixture of dark colors with lighter colors, usually as a striped, tigerlike coat.

Grizzled: a roan pattern that is usually a mixture of black, bluish-gray, iron gray, or red with white.

Harlequin: black or blue patches on white.

Merle: a mottled, marbled effect (usually red or black, sometimes blue).

Parti-colored: variegated patches of two or more colors.

Piebald: black and white or two other colors in patches.

Roan: an even mixture of white and another color.

Sable: black tips on silver, gray, gold, fawn or brown hairs.

Ticked: small areas of black or other dark colors on white.

Tricolor: a coat of three distinct colors, usually black, white and tan.

Wheaten: pale yellow or fawn colored.

AIREDALE TERRIER

HEIGHT: 22–24 in.
WEIGHT: 40–50 lb.

COLOR: Black or dark grizzled body, and tan head, ears and legs.

PERSONALITY: These playful, faithful and sometimes stubborn dogs are protective of their family members and wary of strangers. With a strong personality, they need firm and consistent training.

GROOMING: The wiry coat doesn't shed much, but needs frequent brushing and combing.

EXERCISE: A daily walk or other exercise is essential, even more so if these dogs live in the city.

ENVIRONMENT: These dogs are adaptable to any climate and enjoy being outdoors.

HEALTH: A generally hardy breed, these dogs have a tendency to develop gastroenteritis and hip dysplasia. Eczema can be a problem if they are kept indoors.

GROUP: Terrier

TRAINABILITY ★★★
KID'S PET ★★★
CITY LIVING ★★★★

AKITA

HEIGHT: 24–28 in.
WEIGHT: 85–110 lb.

COLOR: Cream, red, blue, gold, white, brindle or pinto.

PERSONALITY: This ancient breed of Japanese dog is known for its strength, alertness and courage. Aggression can be a problem. Akitas are not suitable for first-time owners.

GROOMING: The dense coat sheds heavily and needs weekly brushing to keep it in shape.

EXERCISE: These athletic dogs need extensive exercise. Avoid aggressive games like tug-of-war.

ENVIRONMENT: These dogs can be quiet, reserved apartment dwellers or equally happy with a large yard to roam around in.

HEALTH: This breed can have problems with hip dysplasia, thyroid disorders and progressive retinal atrophy.

GROUP: Working

TRAINABILITY ★★★
KID'S PET ★★
CITY LIVING ★★★

ALASKAN MALAMUTE

HEIGHT: 23–25 in.
WEIGHT: 75–110 lb.

COLOR: Light gray to black, with white underbody and markings.

PERSONALITY: A strong personality makes this breed good for the experienced dog owner. Malamutes need early, consistent training and should be watched around other pets. They enjoy an active lifestyle.

GROOMING: The thick, double coat needs brushing at least once a week.

EXERCISE: Known for endurance, these dogs need daily exercise.

ENVIRONMENT: These dogs are not suited to apartment living—a sedentary, bored Malamute can become very destructive. They prefer a cool climate.

HEALTH: Hip dysplasia and skin and thyroid problems can affect Alaskan Malamutes.

GROUP: Working

TRAINABILITY ★★★
KID'S PET ★★
CITY LIVING ★

AUSTRALIAN SHEPHERD

HEIGHT: 20–23 in.
WEIGHT: 45–65 lb.

COLOR: Blue merle, red merle, red or black.

PERSONALITY: These highly intelligent dogs can either be friendly or aloof with strangers. They are easy to train but have strong herding instincts.

GROOMING: The long coat needs to be brushed thoroughly several times a week.

EXERCISE: Running in a field is the kind of frequent exercise these dogs require.

ENVIRONMENT: These dogs are not suited to city living. They should be kept in the country, or at least in the suburbs with a large yard to roam in.

HEALTH: Progressive retinal atrophy, hip dysplasia and cataracts can be a problem for this breed. Merles are prone to deafness.

GROUP: Herding

TRAINABILITY ★★★★★
KID'S PET ★★★★
CITY LIVING ★★

BASSET HOUND

HEIGHT: 13–15 in.
WEIGHT: 50 lb.

COLOR: Black, white and tan, or lemon and tan.

PERSONALITY: These amusing, mild-mannered dogs are renowned for being peaceful and sweet. However, they are one of the hardest breeds to house-train. They can also be stubborn, so owners will need to be patient.

GROOMING: The smooth coat is easy to maintain but the ears need regular cleaning inside.

EXERCISE: One or more short walks a day will keep these dogs happy and trim.

ENVIRONMENT: These low-activity dogs are fine in the city, but their howling can be a problem in an apartment.

HEALTH: With their noses often to the ground, they easily pick up bacteria and viruses. They are also prone to glaucoma, spinal disk problems and bloat.

GROUP: Hound

TRAINABILITY ★★★
KID'S PET ★★★★
CITY LIVING ★★★★

BEAGLE

HEIGHT: 10–15 in.
WEIGHT: 20–30 lb.

COLOR: Black, white or tan combinations.

PERSONALITY: These dogs are known for their stamina and high energy. A good-natured breed, they are happy with kids and other pets, but are difficult to house-train. If left alone a lot, their barking can become excessive.

GROOMING: To get rid of dead hair the coat needs weekly brushing. The ears need regular cleaning.

EXERCISE: They need daily walks and some on-leash running in an open area every once in a while.

ENVIRONMENT: While their small size may make them seem perfect for indoor living, bored, sedentary beagles can become destructive.

HEALTH: Beagles are prone to heart disease and epilepsy, and to skin, eye and bleeding disorders.

GROUP: Hound

TRAINABILITY ★★★
KID'S PET ★★★★
CITY LIVING ★★

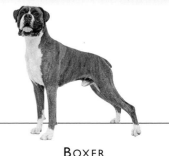

BICHON FRISE

HEIGHT: 9–12 in.
WEIGHT: 7–12 lb.

COLOR: White with buff, cream or apricot shading.

PERSONALITY: Good for first-time dog owners, these dogs are generally even-tempered and sociable among family and strangers. If they have been socialized early on, they should get on well with young children.

GROOMING: The fine, silky coat sheds lightly and requires daily brushing to avoid getting matted.

EXERCISE: Happy to play inside an apartment, they don't need regular outdoor exercise.

ENVIRONMENT: They are primarily indoor dogs and so are suited to any climate.

HEALTH: These dogs are prone to clogged tear ducts and need to have their eyes cleaned regularly. The condition of the coat needs to be carefully monitored.

GROUP: Non-sporting

TRAINABILITY ★★★★
KID'S PET ★★★
CITY LIVING ★★★★★

BOSTON TERRIER

HEIGHT: 12–14 in.
WEIGHT: 15–25 lb.

COLOR: Brindle or black with white markings.

PERSONALITY: These are sensitive, affectionate and sometimes stubborn dogs that are nevertheless good for first-time owners. They adapt well to both an active family or a more retiring owner.

GROOMING: Brushing and rubbing daily with chamois cloth will keep the short and smooth coat shiny.

EXERCISE: These dogs appreciate daily walks and love to fetch balls.

ENVIRONMENT: Well-suited to an indoor life, these dogs can make fairly good watchdogs.

HEALTH: Boston Terriers are susceptible to respiratory diseases and eye injuries and ailments.

GROUP: Non-sporting

TRAINABILITY ★★★
KID'S PET ★★★
CITY LIVING ★★★★

BOXER

HEIGHT: 21–25 in.
WEIGHT: 55–75 lb.

COLOR: Fawn or brindle, with white markings.

PERSONALITY: Playful and patient with children, Boxers are also courageous and devoted watchdogs. While good for first-time owners, they need firm training and early socialization with other animals and people.

GROOMING: The short, smooth coat requires simple brushing. The teeth need regular attention.

EXERCISE: Given their boundless energy, these dogs need plenty of exercise.

ENVIRONMENT: These dogs are clean and relatively quiet and can make good house pets if they are properly trained and given adequate exercise.

HEALTH: A short-lived breed, at about ten years, Boxers are prone to skin problems, stroke, heart disease, cancer and bloat.

GROUP: Working

TRAINABILITY ★★★
KID'S PET ★★★★★
CITY LIVING ★★★

BRITTANY

HEIGHT: 17¹/₂–20 in.
WEIGHT: 30–40 lb.

COLOR: Orange and white or liver and white.

PERSONALITY: These hardworking and tenacious sporting dogs are favored by hunters. They are good-natured and make happy family pets. They are fairly easy to train and are a good choice for first-time dog owners.

GROOMING: The medium-length coat needs brushing twice weekly and washing a few times a year.

EXERCISE: Happiest working in the field, these energetic dogs need plenty of regular walks.

ENVIRONMENT: Like most sporting dogs, Brittanys become bored if confined in small spaces for long periods, and may become noisy and destructive.

HEALTH: These dogs are prone to ear infections, glaucoma and spinal paralysis.

GROUP: Sporting

TRAINABILITY ★★★★
KID'S PET ★★★★
CITY LIVING ★★

BULLDOG

HEIGHT: 14–16 in.
WEIGHT: 40–55 lb.

COLOR: Red and other brindles, white, red, fawn or piebald.

PERSONALITY: These are loyal, reliable and gentle dogs with none of the ferocity of their forebears. They don't bark a lot and are known for their sweet temperament. They make fine pets but are not so easy to train.

GROOMING: This breed drools a lot. The short coat doesn't shed much and needs little brushing.

EXERCISE: Regular, easy walks will keep Bulldogs happy.

ENVIRONMENT: These dogs enjoy a cooler climate. They are happy indoors and are well suited to small houses and apartments.

HEALTH: A short-lived breed, at about ten years, these dogs are prone to breathing difficulties and heatstroke, along with eye, skin and heart problems.

GROUP: Non-sporting

TRAINABILITY ★★★
KID'S PET ★★
CITY LIVING ★★★★

CAIRN TERRIER

HEIGHT: 10–12 in.
WEIGHT: 13–16 lb.

COLOR: Cream, wheaten, red, sand, gray, brindle or black.

PERSONALITY: These plucky and curious little dogs are devoted to their owners, sometimes to the point of jealousy. Because of this they are best suited to homes with older children. Some Cairns bark a lot.

GROOMING: Brush the coat several times a week. Nails and ears need regular attention.

EXERCISE: Regular walks are advised. Because of their curiosity, these dogs are best kept on a leash.

ENVIRONMENT: Cairn Terriers adapt readily to apartments, farms and anything in between.

HEALTH: This hardy breed is prone only to skin allergies.

GROUP: Terrier

TRAINABILITY ★★★
KID'S PET ★★★
CITY LIVING ★★★★

CHESAPEAKE BAY RETRIEVER

HEIGHT: 21–26 in.
WEIGHT: 55–80 lb.

COLOR: Dark brown to light tan.

PERSONALITY: Bold and energetic, these dogs are devoted to their family. While not excessive barkers, they will alert their owners to strangers. A stubborn streak makes them best suited to experienced dog owners.

GROOMING: Brush away dead hair regularly. Bathe infrequently to keep the coat's waterproof oils.

EXERCISE: This breed needs lots of strenuous exercise, like running and swimming, to keep in shape.

ENVIRONMENT: These dogs are best suited to an environment where they can spend plenty of time outdoors.

HEALTH: These dogs are susceptible to hip dysplasia, progressive retinal atrophy and cataracts.

GROUP: Sporting

TRAINABILITY ★★★
KID'S PET ★★★★
CITY LIVING ★★

CHIHUAHUA

HEIGHT: 6–8 in.
WEIGHT: 2–6 lb.

COLOR: Blonde, white, fawn, patched, or black and tan.

PERSONALITY: These intelligent and lively dogs prefer their owner's company to other dogs. They can bark a lot and be difficult to house-train. Their tiny physique makes them unsuitable pets for energetic young children.

GROOMING: Clean the smooth coat with a wet cloth and bathe the long-haired variety monthly.

EXERCISE: A short, daily walk in pleasant weather will make these little dogs very happy.

ENVIRONMENT: Chihuahuas are perfect apartment or house dogs that enjoy accompanying their owners on outings.

HEALTH: These dogs are prone to dry and bulging eyes, as well as heart disease and tooth and gum problems.

GROUP: Toy

TRAINABILITY ★★★
KID'S PET ★
CITY LIVING ★★★★★

CHINESE SHAR-PEI

HEIGHT: 18–20 in.
WEIGHT: 40–50 lb.

COLOR: Any color, such as fawn, black, cream, chocolate or red.

PERSONALITY: While devoted to their family, these dogs can show aggression toward strangers and other dogs. They need firm training and are better suited to experienced owners.

GROOMING: The harsh coat needs weekly brushing, but shedding isn't a big problem.

EXERCISE: Daily walks are adequate, but a good run every so often will be appreciated.

ENVIRONMENT: Because they are such clean dogs they are suited to city living, but will readily adapt to a more rural setting.

HEALTH: Chinese Shar-Peis are prone to skin and eye problems, as well as hip dysplasia.

GROUP: Non-sporting

TRAINABILITY ★★
KID'S PET ★★
CITY LIVING ★★★★

CHOW CHOW

HEIGHT: 17–20 in.
WEIGHT: 50–70 lb.

COLOR: Black, blue, red, cream or cinnamon.

PERSONALITY: These are aloof, powerful and reserved dogs, particularly with strangers. Some are very territorial and prone to aggression. They need firm handling during training and are not suited to first-time owners.

GROOMING: These heavy shedders need regular brushing; weekly for smooth coats and daily for rough.

EXERCISE: A daily, but not necessarily strenuous, walk is essential for these dogs.

ENVIRONMENT: Their thick coats make them uncomfortable in the heat. Chow chows are clean and quiet indoors.

HEALTH: These dogs are prone to eczema and joint and eye problems.

GROUP: Non-sporting

TRAINABILITY ★★
KID'S PET ★★
CITY LIVING ★★★

COCKER SPANIEL

HEIGHT: 14–15 in.
WEIGHT: 24–28 lb.

COLOR: Black, any other solid color or parti-colored.

PERSONALITY: Energetic and playful, these dogs can also be aggressive. English Cockers are slightly larger and retain more of their sporting instincts than their American counterparts. Both breeds are easy to train.

GROOMING: The long, silky coat sheds moderately and needs extensive brushing and clipping.

EXERCISE: Both varieties need regular walks, but the English variety needs a little more.

ENVIRONMENT: As long as they get out frequently to run off their energy, these dogs are suitable as house pets.

HEALTH: Eye problems are the biggest concern. Heart disease, ear infections, hemophilia and epilepsy are also apparent in the American variety.

GROUP: Sporting

TRAINABILITY ★★★★★
KID'S PET ★★
CITY LIVING ★★★★

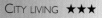

COLLIE

HEIGHT: 22–26 in.
WEIGHT: 50–75 lb.

COLOR: Sable and white, blue merle, white or tricolor.

PERSONALITY: Recognized by millions as "Lassie," these dogs are easy to train and affectionate with their family. However, they can be high strung and anxious around strangers. Some Collies bark a great deal.

GROOMING: These heavy shedders require frequent brushing.

EXERCISE: Daily jaunts are necessary to keep these dogs happy.

ENVIRONMENT: Collies are not well suited to hot and humid climates. They are better suited to an outdoor lifestyle due to their heavy shedding.

HEALTH: Collie-specific disorders include Collie nose (sunburn on the nose). They are also prone to progressive retinal atrophy and deafness in the blue merles.

GROUP: Herding

TRAINABILITY ★★★★
KID'S PET ★★★
CITY LIVING ★★★

DACHSHUND

HEIGHT: 5–9 in.
WEIGHT: 10–26 lb.

COLOR: One or two colors of red, black, tan or brown.

PERSONALITY: Clever, tenacious and sometimes stubborn, these dogs love to dig. They can be a little snappish around young children. Dachshunds can be tough to house-train and if bored become destructive.

GROOMING: Brush long- and wire-haired coats several times a week, and smooth-haired coats weekly.

EXERCISE: Frequent exercise will prevent these dogs from becoming overweight.

ENVIRONMENT: Their small size makes them highly suitable for apartment dwelling.

HEALTH: Keep a look out for hereditary eye problems and paralysis of the hind quarters, as well as disk disease, diabetes and skin problems.

GROUP: Hound

TRAINABILITY ★★★
KID'S PET ★★
CITY LIVING ★★★★★

DALMATIAN

HEIGHT: 21–24 in.
WEIGHT: 48–55 lb.

COLOR: White with black or liver spots.

PERSONALITY: These protective dogs have incredible energy and a boisterous nature. When bored, they become destructive, so keep them busy. They are not recommended for first-time dog owners.

GROOMING: Brush daily to maintain the dog's smooth coat. These dogs are heavy shedders.

EXERCISE: Athletic by nature, they need to run as much as possible to keep in shape.

ENVIRONMENT: If they get regular outdoor exercise, they are happy indoor dogs. They don't like to be outside in the cold.

HEALTH: They are prone to deafness, bladder stones and hip dysplasia.

GROUP: Non-sporting

TRAINABILITY ★★★
KID'S PET ★★★
CITY LIVING ★★★

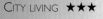

DOBERMAN PINSCHER

HEIGHT: 24–28 in.
WEIGHT: 60–85 lb.

COLOR: Black, red, fawn, brown or blue with red markings.

PERSONALITY: These are the quintessential guard dogs. They need to be with people and can be good with children if raised among them. They are best suited to experienced owners.

GROOMING: The smooth coat doesn't shed much. It needs brushing several times a week.

EXERCISE: They need plenty of vigorous exercise, but avoid aggressive games.

ENVIRONMENT: These dogs don't like to be in cold weather. They can be fine house dogs if they are given daily exercise.

HEALTH: Prone to bloat, hip dysplasia and heart problems. They are also prone to a bleeding disorder called von Willebrand's disease.

GROUP: Working

TRAINABILITY ★★★★★
KID'S PET ★★★
CITY LIVING ★★★

ENGLISH SPRINGER SPANIEL

HEIGHT: 19–20 in.
WEIGHT: 45–55 lb.

COLOR: Black and white, liver and white, tricolor, blue or liver roan.

PERSONALITY: Most of these dogs are cheerful, playful and happy to be around people. However, be careful when choosing a breeder—some breed lines have unacceptable levels of unpredictability and snappishness.

GROOMING: Brush the soft, water-repellent coat weekly and pay close attention to the ears.

EXERCISE: These dogs are active and need plenty of exercise.

ENVIRONMENT: If they are given brisk walks daily, they are fine to have in the city.

HEALTH: These dogs are prone to progressive retinal atrophy, hip dysplasia and ear and skin conditions.

GROUP: Sporting

TRAINABILITY ★★★★★
KID'S PET ★★★★
CITY LIVING ★★★

GERMAN SHEPHERD

HEIGHT: 22–26 in.
WEIGHT: 65–100 lb.

COLOR: Black and tan, bicolor, gray or golden sable, or solid black.

PERSONALITY: These intelligent and confident dogs are good for families but need an experienced and strong hand for training. They can be aggressive toward other dogs.

GROOMING: The dense, double coat sheds heavily and needs to be brushed several times a week.

EXERCISE: Without daily walks, these dogs can become restless and destructive.

ENVIRONMENT: German Shepherds are perfect for the suburbs. If they get adequate exercise, they can cope in the city.

HEALTH: Common problems include bloat, hip dysplasia, skin and eye disorders and spinal paralysis.

GROUP: Herding

TRAINABILITY ★★★★★
KID'S PET ★★★
CITY LIVING ★★★

GERMAN SHORTHAIRED POINTER

HEIGHT: 21–25 in.
WEIGHT: 45–70 lb.

COLOR: Liver with white ticking.

PERSONALITY: These incredibly energetic dogs love people. They can overwhelm young kids so are better suited to older children. They can be flighty and hard to train, and need an experienced owner.

GROOMING: The short, hard coat needs occasional brushing. Check ears and feet often for parasites.

EXERCISE: These dogs need plenty of vigorous exercise, such as running.

ENVIRONMENT: Because of their high activity needs, these dogs are not at all suited to apartment living.

HEALTH: German Shorthaired Pointers are a hardy breed, but are susceptible to hip dysplasia.

GROUP: Sporting

TRAINABILITY ★★
KID'S PET ★★★
CITY LIVING ★

GOLDEN RETRIEVER

HEIGHT: 21½–24 in.
WEIGHT: 55–75 lb.

COLOR: Various shades of gold.

PERSONALITY: Golden retrievers are one of the most popular breeds, especially for families. Playful, energetic and not big barkers, they are fairly easy to train and are suitable for first-time owners.

GROOMING: The dense, water-repellent coat needs brushing several times a week.

EXERCISE: They need regular daily exercise. As their name suggests, fetching is a favorite game.

ENVIRONMENT: These dogs will adapt easily to most living situations, but city-dwelling dogs must have daily walks.

HEALTH: Prone to progressive retinal atrophy and other eye ailments, as well as hip dysplasia, heart and skin problems, and von Willebrand's disease.

GROUP: Sporting

TRAINABILITY ★★★★★
KID'S PET ★★★★★
CITY LIVING ★★★

GREAT DANE

HEIGHT: 28–32 in.
WEIGHT: 120–150 lb.

COLOR: Brindle, fawn, blue, black or harlequin.

PERSONALITY: These gentle giants love people and, when properly trained and socialized, can make wonderful family pets. They can be territorial and aggressive with other dogs, but they are good with kids and other animals.

GROOMING: The short, thick coat needs weekly grooming and infrequent bathing.

EXERCISE: These dogs need regular daily walks. Don't play tug-of-war or wrestle with them.

ENVIRONMENT: Although these dogs can adapt to city living, owners with a yard will find exercising easier.

HEALTH: They are prone to bloat, bone cancer, hip dysplasia and heart disease, and have a short life span of about ten years.

GROUP: Working

TRAINABILITY ★★★
KID'S PET ★★★
CITY LIVING ★★★

GREAT PYRENEES

HEIGHT: 25–32 in.
WEIGHT: 95–125 lb.

COLOR: White with tan or gray markings.

PERSONALITY: Traditionally used as guards, these calm and regal dogs have retained their protective nature. While they make good family pets, they need consistent and early obedience training by an experienced owner.

GROOMING: The double coat needs frequent brushing. These dogs are big seasonal shedders.

EXERCISE: They need plenty of exercise to stay fit.

ENVIRONMENT: They are not suited to indoor living and prefer a cool climate.

HEALTH: These dogs are prone to bloat, hip dysplasia and eye problems. They have a short life span of about ten years.

GROUP: Working

TRAINABILITY ★★★
KID'S PET ★★★
CITY LIVING ★

LABRADOR RETRIEVER

HEIGHT: 21½–24½ in.
WEIGHT: 55–75 lb.

COLOR: Black, yellow or chocolate.

PERSONALITY: These popular dogs are friendly and have a steady temperament. To keep their high energy focused, they need early training. They are suitable for first-time owners.

GROOMING: The short, weather-resistant coat needs brushing once a week.

EXERCISE: These dogs require lots of exercise and love to play fetch.

ENVIRONMENT: They adapt easily to almost any situation. Apartment dwellers need to be exercised frequently. Otherwise their boredom will lead to destruction.

HEALTH: Labradors tend to suffer from bloat, epilepsy, hip dysplasia, progressive retinal atrophy and other eye problems.

GROUP: Sporting

TRAINABILITY ★★★★★
KID'S PET ★★★★★
CITY LIVING ★★★

LHASA APSO

HEIGHT: 9–11 in.
WEIGHT: 13–15 lb.

COLOR: Gold, red, black, gray, brown, honey, white or cream.

PERSONALITY: The cuddly look of these ancient Tibetan dogs belies an independent and bold temperament. Despite their size, they require a firm, experienced hand in training. They are better for families with older children.

GROOMING: The dense coat needs almost daily brushing to prevent matting. The eyes water a lot.

EXERCISE: These dogs need only moderate exercise.

ENVIRONMENT: Lhasa Apsos are fine indoors, but if you have more than one provide each with their own toys as they can get possessive.

HEALTH: They are susceptible to skin and eye problems, as well as kidney ailments.

GROUP: Non-sporting

TRAINABILITY ★★★
KID'S PET ★★
CITY LIVING ★★★★

MALTESE

HEIGHT: 6–7 in.
WEIGHT: 4–7 lb.

COLOR: White.

PERSONALITY: For a toy breed, these dogs are particularly hardy. They are intelligent, energetic and good-natured dogs, but can get snappy when handled roughly. They are better pets for homes with older children.

GROOMING: The long, silky coat needs daily brushing with special tools to prevent damage.

EXERCISE: These dogs like walks but won't mind missing one every once in a while.

ENVIRONMENT: Because of their size and low exercise require-ments, these are perfect apartment dogs.

HEALTH: These dogs are prone to eye, tooth and gum disorders, as well as hypoglycemia and joint problems.

GROUP: Toy

TRAINABILITY ★★★
KID'S PET ★★★
CITY LIVING ★★★★★

MASTIFF

HEIGHT: 27½–30 in.
WEIGHT: 170–200 lb.

COLOR: Fawn, apricot or brindle.

PERSONALITY: These massive, ancient guard dogs combine docility with courage. They like being with people as much as possible, but need a firm and experienced hand in training.

GROOMING: The coarse, short coat needs brushing only once a week. These dogs drool a lot.

EXERCISE: To maintain good health they need to do plenty of running and stretching.

ENVIRONMENT: These dogs are best suited to the suburbs or country, where their size won't be a problem.

HEALTH: They are prone to hip dysplasia, eyelid abnormalities and have a short life span of about ten years.

GROUP: Working

TRAINABILITY ★★★
KID'S PET ★★★
CITY LIVING ★

MINIATURE PINSCHER

HEIGHT: 10–12½ in.
WEIGHT: 9–10 lb.

COLOR: Black or chocolate with rust markings, or red.

PERSONALITY: These are very self-possessed, bold and stubborn toy dogs. They act like big dogs and may get aggressive with other dogs. They are not so easy to train and require experienced owners.

GROOMING: The smooth, hard coat sheds very little and requires only weekly brushing.

EXERCISE: These active little dogs need regular walks.

ENVIRONMENT: They are well suited to apartment living and prefer not to be outside too much in the cold weather.

HEALTH: These dogs are a very healthy breed.

GROUP: Toy

TRAINABILITY ★★★
KID'S PET ★★
CITY LIVING ★★★★★

MINIATURE SCHNAUZER

HEIGHT: 12–14 in.
WEIGHT: 13–15 lb.

COLOR: Salt and pepper, black and silver, or solid tan.

PERSONALITY: These dogs are playful, smart and stubborn. They combine general terrier behavior (barking, excitability, digging) with general guard dog behavior (territorial, dominant) and are better for families with older kids.

GROOMING: The hard, wiry coat needs combing periodically and shaping about four times a year.

EXERCISE: These dogs are happy with regular walks. Provide toys for them to play with indoors.

ENVIRONMENT: They adapt very well to indoor living.

HEALTH: Miniature Schnauzers are prone to eye and bleeding disorders, kidney stones, heart and liver diseases, and diabetes.

GROUP: Terrier

TRAINABILITY ★★★
KID'S PET ★★★
CITY LIVING ★★★★★

NEWFOUNDLAND

HEIGHT: 26–28 in.
WEIGHT: 100–150 lb.

COLOR: Black, black and white, brown or gray

PERSONALITY: These are sweet, affectionate and protective dogs. Rather than a bark or growl, they use their massive body to deter strangers. Easy to train and house-train, they are great for first-time owners and children.

GROOMING: The thick, water-repellent, double coat sheds heavily and needs daily attention.

EXERCISE: These dogs enjoy walking and swimming whenever they get the chance.

ENVIRONMENT: They prefer cool climates to warm ones, and adapt well to an air-conditioned house or apartment.

HEALTH: These dogs are prone to heart problems, hip dysplasia and bloat.

GROUP: Working

TRAINABILITY ★★★★
KID'S PET ★★★★★
CITY LIVING ★★★

PEKINGESE

HEIGHT: 8-9 in.
WEIGHT: 9-14 lb.

COLOR: Red, fawn, sable, brindle, black and tan, white or parti-color.

PERSONALITY: These are the quintessential lap dogs. They are dignified, reserved with strangers and affectionate with their owners. They are hard to train and house-train, and are better for families without children.

GROOMING: The long, coarse coat needs daily brushing to avoid matting.

EXERCISE: A daily walk is fun, but not necessary for these low-activity dogs.

ENVIRONMENT: These are very good apartment dogs. They don't like cold or damp conditions.

HEALTH: A flat face makes this breed prone to respiratory ailments, heatstroke and eye problems such as lacerations, infections and prolapse.

GROUP: Toy

TRAINABILITY ★★
KID'S PET ★★
CITY LIVING ★★★★★

PEMBROKE WELSH CORGI

HEIGHT: 10–12 in.
WEIGHT: 25–30 lb.

COLOR: Red, sable, fawn, black or tan.

PERSONALITY: These happy and intelligent dogs fit the bill for those wanting a big-dog personality in a smaller package. They are easy to train and house-train, and are good with kids.

GROOMING: The thick, medium-length, weather-resistant coat needs weekly brushing.

EXERCISE: These dogs enjoy playing, walking and running daily with their family.

ENVIRONMENT: They need some running room but can adapt to apartment living if adequately exercised.

HEALTH: This breed is prone to progressive retinal atrophy, glaucoma, bleeding disorders, hip dysplasia and back trouble.

GROUP: Herding

TRAINABILITY ★★★★★
KID'S PET ★★★★
CITY LIVING ★★★

POMERANIAN

HEIGHT: 6–7 in.
WEIGHT: 3–7 lb.

COLOR: Red, black, white, blue, orange, cream or brown.

PERSONALITY: Although they are tiny, these dogs are bold, curious and make good watchdogs. They are also very intelligent and require confident owners for effective training. They are better for homes with older kids.

GROOMING: The long, dense coat sheds heavily and, along with the bushy tail, needs daily brushing.

EXERCISE: A walk every now and then is nice, but not necessary.

ENVIRONMENT: These are the perfect apartment dogs.

HEALTH: These dogs are prone to eye, skin, tooth and gum problems, and joint and heart disorders.

GROUP: Toy

TRAINABILITY ★★★
KID'S PET ★★
CITY LIVING ★★★★★

POODLE—TOY, MINIATURE AND STANDARD

HEIGHT: 9–10 in., 10–15 in., 22–26 in.
WEIGHT: 5–7 lb., 14–17 lb., 45–60 lb.

COLOR: Blue, gray, silver, brown, cafe-au-lait, apricot and cream.

PERSONALITY: From the tiny Toy to the large Standard Poodle, all varieties of this breed are intelligent and easy to train. The Standard and Miniature are particularly easy to house-train. The two smaller varieties are both very demanding of affection and can bark a lot. All three are fine for first-time owners, but families with young children should look toward owning the Standard first, then the Miniature. The Toy Poodle can be too snappish around active children.

GROOMING: Grooming requirements depend on the owner's taste. For the simple clip, brush once a week and have it shaped by a professional every few months. All varieties are low shedders.

EXERCISE: Toy Poodles require very little exercise. The Miniature variety can do with regular walks a few times a week. Standard Poodles are the most active and should be taken for a walk daily.

ENVIRONMENT: The two smaller varieties make good house pets. Standard Poodles will fare well indoors if they are given enough exercise.

HEALTH: All three varieties are prone to eye and skin disorders, including cataracts, glaucoma, infections and cysts. Standard Poodles can also be affected by progressive retinal atrophy, von Willebrand's disease, bloat and hip dysplasia. Heart disease can be a problem in the two smaller varieties.

GROUP: Toy, Non-sporting, Non-sporting

TRAINABILITY Toy ★★★★★ Miniature ★★★★★ Standard ★★★★★
KID'S PET Toy ★★ Miniature ★★★ Standard ★★★★★
CITY LIVING Toy ★★★★★ Miniature ★★★★★ Standard ★★

PUG

HEIGHT: 10–11 in.
WEIGHT: 14–18 lb.

COLOR: Silver, apricot-fawn or black.

PERSONALITY: Unlike some toy breeds, Pugs don't have a problem with excessive barking, snapping at children and excitability. They can be difficult to train but are suitable for first-time owners.

GROOMING: The fine, smooth coat doesn't shed much. It needs weekly brushing.

EXERCISE: These dogs don't have a great need for exercise but they do like walking and playing.

ENVIRONMENT: Pugs are good house pets, but need to be kept out of the extreme heat or cold.

HEALTH: This breed is prone to eye injuries, respiratory difficulties and heatstroke.

GROUP: Toy

TRAINABILITY ★★★
KID'S PET ★★★★
CITY LIVING ★★★★★

ROTTWEILER

HEIGHT: 22–27 in.
WEIGHT: 85–115 lb.

COLOR: Black with mahogany or rust markings.

PERSONALITY: These guard dogs are strong, confident and naturally protective. Some Rottweilers can become aggressive. They are suitable for experienced, confident owners.

GROOMING: The coarse, short coat needs weekly brushing.

EXERCISE: They require vigorous daily exercise. Aggressive tug-of-war games should be avoided.

ENVIRONMENT: These dogs are best suited to the suburbs or country.

HEALTH: Rottweilers are susceptible to bloat, progressive retinal atrophy, hip dysplasia, eye problems and spinal paralysis.

GROUP: Working

TRAINABILITY ★★★
KID'S PET ★★★
CITY LIVING ★★

SAINT BERNARD

HEIGHT: 25–28 in.
WEIGHT: 150–170 lb.

COLOR: White with red or brindle markings.

PERSONALITY: These dogs are gentle, calm and generally good with children and other animals. They do not bark a lot, but, like any of the giant breeds, need early and consistent training to quell dominant tendencies.

GROOMING: Both the long-haired and short-haired varieties need daily brushing when shedding.

EXERCISE: These dogs need daily walks or other forms of regular exercise.

ENVIRONMENT: Because of their coats, they prefer cooler climates. They are better suited to the suburbs and country.

HEALTH: They are prone to bloat, hip dysplasia and heart disease.

GROUP: Working

TRAINABILITY ★★★
KID'S PET ★★★
CITY LIVING ★★

SAMOYED

HEIGHT: 19–23 in.
WEIGHT: 45–70 lb.

COLOR: White, biscuit, cream or white and biscuit.

PERSONALITY: These energetic and playful dogs have high-pitched barks, which make them good watchdogs. Independent and strong, they are best suited to experienced owners.

GROOMING: The thick, double coat sheds heavily and requires daily brushing.

EXERCISE: They require robust outdoor exercise every day.

ENVIRONMENT: They prefer cooler climates and are much better suited to the suburbs or country.

HEALTH: Hip dysplasia, skin problems, progressive retinal atrophy and other eye disorders are common to this breed.

GROUP: Working

TRAINABILITY ★★★
KID'S PET ★★★★
CITY LIVING ★

SCHIPPERKE

HEIGHT: 10–13 in.
WEIGHT: 15–18 lb.

COLOR: Black.

PERSONALITY: These curious and fearless little dogs worked as watchdogs and ratters on Belgian barges. As long as they are treated with respect, they are good with children and suitable for new owners.

GROOMING: The dense, short hair doesn't shed much and only needs brushing once a week.

EXERCISE: Daily walks are fine for these dogs. Some will enjoy more if you are up to it.

ENVIRONMENT: With adequate exercise, these dogs can adapt to any living situation.

HEALTH: These dogs are a very hearty breed.

GROUP: Non-sporting

TRAINABILITY ★★
KID'S PET ★★★★
CITY LIVING ★★★★

SCOTTISH TERRIER

HEIGHT: 10 in.
WEIGHT: 18–22 lb.

COLOR: Steel, iron gray, black, sandy, wheaten or grizzled.

PERSONALITY: These very bold, self-possessed, and even stubborn dogs dig and bark. They are better for homes with older children as they can be snappy and dominant. They need gentle and consistent training.

GROOMING: The wiry, dense coat needs periodic brushing and regular shaping by a groomer.

EXERCISE: Regular walks and games of fetch are good for these dogs.

ENVIRONMENT: These dogs love to travel and adapt easily to any living situation.

HEALTH: These dogs are prone to von Willebrand's disease, allergies, jawbone disorders and "Scottie cramp," which makes walking difficult.

GROUP: Terrier

TRAINABILITY ★★
KID'S PET ★★★
CITY LIVING ★★★★

SHETLAND SHEEPDOG

HEIGHT: 13–16 in.
WEIGHT: 14–18 lb.

COLOR: Black, blue merle or sable with white or tan markings.

PERSONALITY: These dogs are intelligent, affectionate and easy to train. Many bark a lot and some can be a little nervous. They are better with older children.

GROOMING: The long and harsh double coat sheds heavily. It needs regular brushing.

EXERCISE: They need plenty of exercise and love to run and frolic outdoors.

ENVIRONMENT: If they are given enough exercise, these dogs can adapt to apartment living.

HEALTH: Prone to progressive retinal atrophy and other eye problems. Heart disease, epilepsy and deafness (in the blue merle) can also be problems.

GROUP: Herding

TRAINABILITY ★★★★★
KID'S PET ★★★★
CITY LIVING ★★★

SHIH TZU

HEIGHT: 8–11 in.
WEIGHT: 9–18 lb.

COLOR: All colors and blends of colors.

PERSONALITY: Unlike some toy breeds, Shih Tzus don't have a problem with snapping and excessive barking. They are feisty but not too difficult to train, and good for new owners.

GROOMING: The long, dense coat doesn't shed much, but needs daily attention to avoid matting.

EXERCISE: Most of these dogs will be happy with a walk every other day.

ENVIRONMENT: Their size and low activity levels make these dogs perfect apartment dwellers. Keep them out of cold and damp places.

HEALTH: The pushed-in face makes this breed prone to eye injuries, respiratory problems and heatstroke. Also watch for joint, tooth and gum problems.

GROUP: Toy

TRAINABILITY ★★★
KID'S PET ★★★
CITY LIVING ★★★★★

SIBERIAN HUSKY

HEIGHT: 21–23 in
WEIGHT: 35–60 lb

COLOR: All colors from black to white, usually with facial markings.

PERSONALITY: These energetic and playful dogs love to work. While they can make good family pets, they can be difficult to train and may attempt to dominate. They require confident, experienced owners.

GROOMING: The medium-length, double coat sheds heavily and needs brushing every two days.

EXERCISE: They need rigorous outdoor play. Without sufficient exercise they can be destructive.

ENVIRONMENT: Their thick coats make them better suited to cold climates. Because of their size, they shouldn't be kept in a small house or apartment.

HEALTH: These dogs can suffer from progressive retinal atrophy and other eye disorders, along with hip dysplasia and skin and thyroid problems.

GROUP: Working

TRAINABILITY ★★
KID'S PET ★★★
CITY LIVING ★

WEIMARANER

HEIGHT: 23–27 in.
WEIGHT: 55–90 lb.

COLOR: All shades of gray, from silver to mouse.

PERSONALITY: These are active and headstrong dogs. They need a firm and experienced hand to bring out their better traits (loyalty and intelligence) while controlling their tendency to dominate and be aggressive.

GROOMING: The short, sleek coat doesn't shed much and only needs brushing once a week.

EXERCISE: Weimaraners need plenty of exercise, both walking and running.

ENVIRONMENT: These dogs are far too active to be living in apartments, and are best suited to the country or suburbs.

HEALTH: These dogs are prone to bloat, hip dysplasia and various skin ailments.

GROUP: Sporting

TRAINABILITY ★★★	
KID'S PET ★★	
CITY LIVING ★	

WEST HIGHLAND WHITE TERRIER

HEIGHT: 10–11 in.
WEIGHT: 15–19 lb.

COLOR: White.

PERSONALITY: These lively and playful dogs are a little easier to train than most terriers. They may bark a lot and will certainly dig, but they are affectionate. This breed is better suited to homes with older children.

GROOMING: The hard, straight-haired coat needs brushing several times a week.

EXERCISE: A daily walk is fine, but these dogs also enjoy romping about in the yard.

ENVIRONMENT: These fine apartment dogs are very adaptable and love to travel.

HEALTH: They are prone to hernias, skin conditions, copper toxicosis, jawbone calcification and a hip joint disorder called Legg-Perthes disease.

GROUP: Terrier

TRAINABILITY ★★★	
KID'S PET ★★★	
CITY LIVING ★★★★	

YORKSHIRE TERRIER

HEIGHT: 7–9 in.
WEIGHT: 3–7 lb.

COLOR: Steel blue with tan markings.

PERSONALITY: If pampered, these dogs can become excitable and snappish. If respected for their cleverness and hardiness, their spirited Terrier temperament shines through. They are better for homes with older kids.

GROOMING: The long, silky coat doesn't shed much, but needs daily brushing.

EXERCISE: The exercise a Yorkshire Terrier gets inside the house is sufficient.

ENVIRONMENT: Keep these perfect apartment dogs out of cold, damp places.

HEALTH: This breed is prone to eye, gum and tooth problems, and to joint disorders.

GROUP: Toy

TRAINABILITY ★★★	
KID'S PET ★★	
CITY LIVING ★★★★★	

Make Mine a Mixed Breed

The mixed breed, better known as the mutt, is a lovable hybrid whose ancestry can be the basis of a long-running guessing game. This is your ordinary, sometimes quirky-looking, everyday kind of dog.

You'll see flyers posted outside your supermarket offering "Cockapoos" or "Peekapoos" or any number of "Lab" or "Shepherd" mixes free to a good home. And for sure you will have known, or even owned, at least one adorable mixed breed in your time.

Because mixed breed puppies are almost by definition unplanned, a disproportionate number of them tend to wind up in shelters or for sale from cardboard boxes outside supermarkets. This could be an advantage because they're often free or close to it. But despite your lower investment, you're not sacrificing quality. And all the remaining costs will be exactly the same as those for a purebred dog. Regardless of their pedigree, all dogs need to be loved, valued and cared for in just the same way.

The Element of Surprise

Mixed breeds are wonderful, loving and devoted, just like purebreds—they're all dogs after all. And one of the great things about a mixed breed is that he is truly his own dog. "He is unique; no other dog will look exactly like him," says Sue Sternberg, a dog trainer and obedience instructor in Accord, New York. "You really get a sense of individuality with a mixed breed."

In many cases, you won't know who this dog's mom and dad were, let alone his grandfolks, which means you're dealing with unknowns from a hereditary point of view. "Getting a mixed breed always brings some surprises, because you're never sure what breeds are in the mix," says animal behaviorist Dr. Suzanne Hetts. "Ten different people will look at the dog and tell you ten different things about its identity. And none of them is necessarily right."

Sternberg does have a method of guessing at a mixed breed puppy's eventual size. While admittedly unscientific, in her experience it has proved fairly successful. "At four months of age, a pup is roughly half of its adult size," she says. "But you can forget about looking at paw size. Some breeds, such as Collies or Shelties, have tiny feet in relation to their body."

Even if you can predict how large a mixed breed pup will grow, you will have a harder time predicting his personality, behavior and grooming needs— factors determined by his genes. The way in which his mixed bag of behavioral characteristics are

Who could resist this lovable mutt? Alert and attentive, he can be trained to behave as well as any aristocratic purebred.

manifested will not be as clear-cut as they would be if he were a purebred.

The "good" traits of his mixed lineage may be prevalent, such as the intelligence of the Maltese or the playfulness of the Shih Tzu. Or the "bad" traits may surface, such as the dominance of the Alaskan Malamute or the mouthiness of the Golden Retriever, leaving you with a dog who's going to be tempted to chew your new shoes no matter what you say.

Whatever bubbles up to the top of your four-legged melting pot, the odds are good that the end result will be a great companion. "Any dog is trainable if you find out what motivates him," says Sternberg, who is a strong advocate of adopting shelter dogs. All of her dogs, mixed breed and purebred alike, have come from shelters. Your new dog's looks will depend on various in-gredients in his gene pool. But his personality and man-ners will mostly depend on the dedicated and consistent way you train him.

One Tough Cookie

Chances are that a mixed breed dog and his brothers and sisters came into this world unplanned, and it's likely his dad wasn't around for the birth. He may not have received all the refined care and knowledge that might be lavished on a pure-bred, nor been given all the breaks. Some mutts have to survive a pretty tough start to

When choosing a mixed breed puppy, let your head rule your heart. He should be lively and friendly, and approach you confidently. Beware of timid puppies—they might later turn into fear biters.

life, a long way from easy street. Perhaps this is why people tend to think that mixed breeds are hardier and healthier than purebreds.

Certainly, the mix of genetic material in a mixed breed will lessen the likelihood of him developing certain hereditary problems. So he may be less likely than a purebred to suffer from some genetic diseases. However, Dr. Hetts feels this may be an oversimplification. "We hear about deafness in Dalmatians and hip dysplasia in giant breeds, but no one has tracked the specific disorders that affect mixed breeds," she explains. Mixed breeds can still get sick from the various non-hereditary illnesses that can affect any dog.

Choose a mixed breed because you like his personality and his looks, not because you think he'll be free from the hereditary diseases as-sociated with purebred dogs. Remember, mixed in any dog's genetic pool will be an assortment of genes—the good, and the not so good.

The Adult Mixed Breed

If you want to adopt a mixed breed, you may decide to get an adult from a shelter. Not that shelters are the exclusive domain of the mixed breed dogs of the world; they often have purebreds, too. Adopt-ing an adult is an excellent choice for people who don't want to train a puppy and the odds are great for getting a reliable, friendly dog at the local shelter. "Many shelter dogs are terrific dogs that

He may not win any ribbons, but this young adult mixed breed will win more than his fair share of hearts. He'll also need lots of grooming.

people just gave up on," says obedience trainer Diane Bauman. "It may have been the wrong match for their family or they just didn't have the time." Maybe the family's circumstances changed suddenly—a new baby that left them with no time to give their Shepherd mix all the exercise he needed; a job transfer to Alaska that their fine-boned, shorthaired pooch wasn't going to enjoy. There are all sorts of reasons why people have to give up their dogs.

"Adult dogs, say from nine months to five years, are a wise choice for the would-be dog owner," says Bauman. "What you see is what you get. You can tell the size they're going to be and how clean they are, and get a good idea of their social skills and temperament."

Breeding certainly isn't everything. Knowing a dog's breed or mix of breeds is only part of the equation. "I've known cupcake Rottweilers and Labs that wouldn't let you in the house," says Dr. Hetts. Any dog's early environment and life experiences will have affected him. So once you're at the shelter and have found a mixed

breed that looks like the right one for you, pay close attention before allowing yourself to become too smitten. Instead of trying to figure out his lineage, consider the individual dog, his behavior, and his reaction to you. Animal behaviorist Dr. Kathalyn Johnson suggests that you look at the following:

- Does the dog come rushing to the front of the enclosure to greet you in a friendly way, with ears up and tail wagging?
- Does he have the self-confidence to approach strangers, both men and women?

If the answer is yes on both counts and you've got a good feeling about him, then he could be the dog for you. It's best to avoid any dog that acts shy, cowering in the back while growling or showing his teeth. Bauman suggests that you take a trainer with you to the shelter to help you choose a good dog.

While these are helpful guidelines, keep in mind that a dog's behavior will differ depending on the environment, advises Dr. Hetts. "It may be friendly in the shelter and snappish at home."

It can take a shelter dog a few weeks to adjust and feel secure enough to relax, Bauman explains. Give him a little time and a gentle, reassuring approach. "But be prepared to take the dog back if he doesn't work out," she adds. "It's important to give both yourself and the dog the opportunity to find the right fit."

Where to Get Your Dog

Whether it's a show-quality Shar-Pei or a Heinz-57 with a personality and a look that just catches your eye, you want this to be a happily-ever-after affair. There are many ways to acquire the dog of your dreams, but if you want to maximize the chances of it being a perfect match, some ways are better than others.

Reputable Breeders

Breeders know just about everything there is to know about the breed of dog they raise, and they work to improve the quality of that breed with every litter. The money they spend on breeding a litter of puppies far exceeds the money they make from selling the pups. They are doing it for love, not money.

Breeders will screen potential puppy buyers very carefully, turning down those whom they feel will not provide the pups with the right lifestyle or environment. "Someone purchasing a puppy must make me feel that they are willing to commit to the lifetime of the dog and that they are going to be responsible dog owners," says Whippet breeder Dr. Janet Lalonde.

Don't take offense if a breeder suggests that you think about another breed. She has both the dog's best interests, and yours, in mind, because a bad match will leave everyone unhappy. In fact, responsible breeders will almost always take a puppy back if for some reason it doesn't work out, or your circumstances change. And a responsible breeder will happily answer your questions and give you tips and advice, even long after you've taken your new friend home.

A good breeder will offer a contract that explains the pup's health and neutering requirements. For instance, if you don't plan to show the dog, the breeder may ask you to sign a contract stating that you will have the dog neutered at a certain age. This is because the breeder feels responsible for the dog for the dog's entire life, and wants to make sure the dog doesn't end up in the hands of someone who will breed him without the benefit of knowledge or experience.

Breeders to Avoid

Backyard breeders breed their dogs and sell the puppies as a way of making money. They are unlikely to be involved with a local or national club dedicated to studying and advancing the breed, so their dogs aren't to the breed standard.

It's a good idea to visit several reputable breeders before making your choice. They will be happy to answer all your questions, both before and after your purchase.

Without a knowledge of the breed and the standard, they may not understand how to prevent unfortunate genetic traits from occurring in their pups. They may still, however, charge prices as high as a reputable breeder.

Many classified ads are placed by backyard breeders. Be wary if someone agrees to sell you a puppy with no questions asked. Chances are, he won't want you asking him any questions either, because he doesn't want to tell you about the health and temperament of the pup's parents.

Finding a Good Breeder

For advice on how to find a reputable breeder, contact the American Kennel Club customer service department for a list of national breed clubs. Or try their Breeder Referral Representative Hotline. In Canada, you can ring the Canadian Kennel Club and ask for the Breeder Referral Service.

If you have access to the Internet, there are several websites where you can start, including BreederLink Home Page, Dog Breeders Online Directory and A-1 Dog Breeders Showcase.

"Don't buy a pup until you've visited at least three good breeders," advises Bauman. "Then you'll have plenty of comparison points."

Pet Shops

When you walk by a pet shop and see all those sad little eyes, keep on walking. Pet shops are often supplied by puppy mills, which breed large numbers of purebred dogs of questionable lineage for profit, says veterinarian Dr. Christine Wilford. Puppy mill conditions may be poor, with female dogs being bred every time they come into season. Puppies are often taken from their mothers at four to six weeks, too young for

them to have received the socialization they need before leaving home. "Purchasing a pup from a pet store may seem like a humane act," says Dr. Wilford. "But in the long run, it just provides revenue to the puppy mills and encourages them to continue to breed indiscriminately."

Pet shops sometimes also take litters from backyard breeders. You might see a tag next to a puppy's cage with a breeder's name on it, but this isn't a guarantee of anything. Many experts feel that it's best to avoid puppies in pet shop windows, even though they look to be in need of a good home. "You should buy a purebred puppy only from the person who actually bred the dog," advises Dr. Wilford.

Animal Shelters

An animal shelter is a first choice for many would-be dog owners. You may feel the dogs to be found there deserve a second chance. Or since there are already so many dogs in the world, you'd prefer to get a dog that really needs a good home. Or maybe you simply want a unique, one-of-a-kind, mixed breed dog, and shelters have plenty to choose from.

The majority of dogs in shelters are adults. Some are young adults that outgrew the cute puppy stage and became a handful for their owners, who may have been unaware of the time needed to care for a dog. With love and proper training, many of these make happy, reliable family pets.

"Many of the dogs in shelters have stable temperaments, but are untrained and maybe a bit wild. If you teach them a vocabulary and the ability to love learning and training, they can be well-trained," says Sternberg. "A shelter dog can be regarded as special," she adds. "Because with a little training to scrub away some dirt and silt, he can emerge as a pearl."

Shelters are operated by various organizations, either local humane societies or the local chapter of a national group such as the American Society for the Prevention of Cruelty to Animals. They usually charge an adoption fee of $10 to $50.

Shelters are committed to encouraging the neutering of dogs. They may, therefore, arrange through a local veterinary clinic for free or reduced-cost neutering, so check their policy.

You can visit a local pet shelter. Or you could try the website of the Humane Society of the United States, with profiles of dogs for adoption from across the nation. The local shelter might not have what you're looking for, but one only 50 miles away may have.

There's a good chance of finding a fine friend at your local shelter. There are many reasons why he's come to be there, but with training and care, he'll make a great pet.

Breed Rescue

Purebred dogs have been showing up at shelters in increasing numbers in recent years. Alarmed that their beloved breeds are ending up there, purebred fanciers have formed breed rescue clubs to give these dogs a second chance. Volunteers who raise a particular breed open their homes and kennels to individual dogs that have ended up in a shelter or been abandoned. They also take in dogs from people who realize it isn't working out but who want to make sure their dog goes to a good home.

Once in their foster home, these dogs are evaluated for basic obedience, health, temperament and house-training. If a dog isn't quite up to speed, volunteers will often work with him until he meets the requirements to make a good pet. The last thing these groups want is for the dog to go through the cycle of abandonment all over again.

Rescue leagues are wonderful places to find a young adult purebred dog. If you find the purchase price of a purebred puppy prohibitive but have your heart set on, say, a Norwegian Elkhound or Papillon, breed rescue may be just the answer for you.

Local breeders will be able to refer you to rescue clubs, or you can access some terrific clearinghouses on the Internet. Try the Canine Connections Breed Rescue Information website or the Pro Dog Breed Rescue Network. Both of these sites will link you to hundreds of individual breed rescue clubs, categorized by breed.

Looking for a Good Home

Despite the efforts of owners to make sure their unneutered females don't come in contact with males when they're in season, the dogs still sometimes manage to get pregnant. The result is often a box of adorable puppies and a sign saying, "Puppies. Eight-week-old Lab mix. Looking for a good home."

If you've been thinking about including a dog in your life, have your heart set on a puppy, and prefer the pauper to the prince, this will

Finding the right dog will be easier if you know the right place to look. It will take time and thought, but the result will be a very happy twosome.

probably be your chance to make a match. But whatever you do, don't make it an impulse decision. You both deserve more than that, because this friendship is for life.

He deserves your honest and thoughtful consideration of all the implications of having a dog, and your absolute certainty that this is the right thing to do. You need to find out as best you can if this is the right pup for you. If it's a neighbor's litter, you will know the mother

and you might even guess who's the father—which gives you some idea of the family background. And you will also have the first eight weeks of their lives to get to know the puppies and decide on the one to suit you.

If your heart's been stolen away outside the local supermarket, take a deep breath. Question the person who's giving away the puppies to get as much background information as possible. Watch how the puppies interact with each other. Pick up the one that you like and check that he looks healthy and reacts well to you. Take your time to make your choice.

Choosing a "Used" Dog

You've decided you're going to adopt an adult dog. The biggest drawback is that his history is a mystery. If he's a mixed breed, you won't even know what kind of dog he is. Nevertheless, there are some steps you can take that should set your mind at rest.

- Check if the dog has been neutered. A neutered animal will generally be less prone to a variety of gender-related behavior problems. If possible, get his vaccination record, as this will tell you what shots, if any, you will need to have your vet administer when you take him home.
- Find out as much as you can about the dog's background, including his behavior around children, other animals and adults. If you are adopting from a shelter, people working there may be able to tell you something of his history from information his

previous owners provided when they brought him in. At the very least, they will have formed an impression of the dog while he has been under their care. If you are planning to adopt from a breed rescue club, the foster owner will be able to give you her impressions of the dog while she was looking after him.

- "Most shelter dogs are basically good dogs," says Sue Sternberg, a dog trainer and obedience instructor in Accord, New York. "But try to find a shelter that tests the temperament of its dogs." Some shelter personnel are trained to evaluate the behavior and personalities of their dogs in an effort to make more perfect matches.
- Once you get your new dog home, have your vet check him over thoroughly. In the unlikely event that he is seriously ill, you still have the option of returning him to the shelter for treatment.

2 JOINING THE CLAN

Your new dog is coming home—this is the beginning of the rest of your lives together. She'll possibly be nervous and unsure of herself at first. Her surroundings will be new to her, and there won't be any familiar faces. But with you making her feel welcome and safe, she'll soon know that she's come to the right place.

Dog-Proofing Your Home
pages 43–47

Check out your home from a canine point of view to eradicate doggy danger zones

Making the Introductions
pages 50–51

How to ensure the new friendship gets off on the right foot

The First Night
pages 48–49

Make the move smooth, and she'll soon be feeling like one of the family

Dogs and Children
pages 52–53

The things that kids need to know about getting on with dogs

Dog-Proofing Your Home

What do you do if you see something interesting on the floor? If you're a puppy, you sniff it, then pick it up in your mouth. This tactic works pretty well if the item happens to be an inoffensive chew toy or a piece of kibble. But what if it's a quarter, or a foam-rubber sponge, or a battery?

You may think your house is perfectly safe, but to a dog it's full of fascinating, yet potentially dangerous, attractions. This is particularly true when you get a new dog, since she'll be eager to explore—and taste—her new surroundings.

The majority of vets would recommend that you take a tour through your house, garage and yard from a dog's eye view. Get down on all fours and move around and you'll be amazed at the number of chewable everyday items you come across: electrical cords, children's toys, bars of soap, books, even jewelry.

"Use the same precautions for a dog that you would for children," says Robert Linnabary, D.V.M., an instructor at the University of Tennessee College of Veterinary Medicine in Knoxville. "But remember that dogs are better at breaking open bottles and boxes."

Home Safety

Whether you're getting a puppy or an older dog, you can be sure her first order of business will be checking out her new digs. Here's a room-by-room guide to the things to watch out for, so she doesn't get into something she shouldn't.

The Kitchen

Most families spend a lot of time in the kitchen and so will your new pet. While nosey dogs don't have hands to wrest open cupboard doors, they do have surprisingly agile paws and most determined muzzles, so it's important to lock cleaning supplies away where they can do no harm. You may even want to think about installing childproof locks on those cabinets where you store solvents and cleaning materials.

Since even the best behaved dogs enjoy making the occasional foray into the garbage, it's a good idea to keep it safely stored away. Or pick up a can with a tight-fitting lid.

You can further reduce her natural inclination to explore by placing especially appetizing—and dangerous—items, such as chicken bones, in the freezer until you're ready to take them out to the trash. Not only will this eliminate the danger of sharp, splintered bones, it will also protect your dog from illnesses caused by eating old, spoiled foods.

Another common canine hazard that often lurks around the kitchen is chocolate. This favorite people food contains a stimulant called theobromine, which can make dogs seriously ill.

Chocolate should be thought of as a poison to dogs, says Dr. Linnabary.

Choose a can with a tight-fitting lid—it will foil her efforts to get at the garbage.

"I've even seen a case of a dog getting very ill from a Snickers Bar, which seems mostly caramel and nuts and very little chocolate."

"The effect on dogs is both dose- and size-dependent," adds Jay Geasling, D.V.M., a veterinarian in private practice in Buffalo and president of the American Animal Hospital Association. "The smaller the dog, the less chocolate it needs to eat in order to overdose."

Even such innocent items as towels, throw rugs and dishcloths can be dangerous, because dogs do love to chew them. If your dog swallows a big enough piece, it could cause an obstruction in the intestine, resulting in serious, even life-threatening problems. So if your pet seems to be a material girl, find an out-of-the-way spot for all your kitchen linen.

The Bathroom

Dogs don't use the toilet or settle in for long steamy baths, but they'll often explore the bathroom just to see what's there. All too often, they discover enticing tastes that they can't resist—but that can make them seriously ill.

"Colorful, fun-smelling bottles and soaps sitting along the side of the tub are an open invitation to your dog to explore," says Priscilla J. Whittington, D.V.M., a veterinarian in private practice in Yorktown Heights, New York. An elevated shower caddy is a great way to keep shampoos, conditioners and soaps well out of harm's way. And don't forget to store cleaning powders and disinfectants out of dog reach in a cabinet—preferably one that has a tight-fitting latch.

Don't take any chances with your children's tub toys, either. They look very much like your dog's chew toys, but they aren't designed with her strong jaws and teeth in mind.

Sanitary napkins and tampons are highly absorbent, and that means they're a problem if your dog chews them and they get inside her intestinal tract. "Be on the safe side and make sure you don't let your dog have access to any trash that might contain items such as these," says Christine Wilford, D.V.M., a veterinarian in private practice in Seattle and a regular columnist for the *American Kennel Club Gazette*.

The Living Room and Den

We think of family rooms as comfort rooms, but for dogs they can be accidents waiting to happen. The number of dog-unfriendly objects in living rooms and dens is as varied as each family. Do you paint? Sew? Knit? Listen to music? Play chess? The materials used for many hobbies can be extremely dangerous to your dog.

The easiest and most practical solution is to store these items in their own special carriers and put them away when you're done. Keep a knitting bag instead of an open basket of needles and yarn.

Cushions are fun to play with, but if your new pet eats the filling, it could do her harm.

Put your paints in an art bin. Find a high nook for that ongoing game of chess. While you're at it, teach your kids to put away their toys when they're finished playing. (Once they've lost a favorite toy or two to sharp doggy teeth, this will become easier.)

"Some dogs have perverse appetites," says Dr. Linnabary. "They may eat something like cigarettes from boredom, and then get seriously ill." If anyone in your family smokes, empty ashtrays regularly. Be careful with chewing tobacco, too, which generally comes in cardboard canisters or bags—no problem for a prying pooch.

And don't forget electrical cords. If possible, coil cords and tuck them out of sight. Or cover cords hanging against a wall with metal covers, which you can get from lighting supply stores. At the very least, says Dr. Wilford, you may want to move lamps and other appliances until your dog outgrows that particular interest.

While chewing cords is mainly a problem with puppies, certain "mouthy" breeds, such as Labradors and Golden Retrievers, will be tempted by them all their lives. In this case, you may want to permanently rearrange your furniture to get all cords out of sight, says Dr. Wilford.

"Repellents like bitter apple are short-lived and often ineffective," she adds. "Taping the cord to the floor doesn't solve any problems, either. A dog will simply chew through the tape—and it takes only a second for her to be electrocuted."

The Bedrooms

Just because you sleep through the night doesn't mean your dog is similarly disposed. New dogs are particularly prone to being wakeful, and what better place to idle away the midnight hour than the family bedrooms.

Children's bedrooms are especially tempting to dogs because of all the toothsome toys lying about. Small rubber balls or even uninflated balloons are easy to swallow—and choke on. Every night before bed, take a few minutes to make sure toys are off the floor and out of the way.

Adult bedrooms harbor two top doggy dangers: nylon stockings and medications. Stockings are easily swallowed and can obstruct the intestine. And medications are as dangerous to dogs as they are to children. What's more, a small dose for a human may be an overdose for a dog. So keep all medications out of reach. And don't think that bottles with childproof caps will stop her.

It's also best not to leave your loose change and jewelry on the dresser. Your four-legged forager might give them a taste test the minute your back is turned. Instead, place your change in a narrow-necked bottle and put rings, cuff links and earrings in a safely stowed jewelry box.

The Garage

Even the best-kept garage can be a hazardous place for a dog. There are all those screws and nails that invariably wind up on the floor. Then there's the paint thinner, insecticide, fertilizer and other poisons lurking about.

A curious canine will investigate garden implements lying around the garage and in the yard. To avoid accidents, store tools safely.

"Antifreeze is perhaps the biggest danger to your dog," says Dr. Whittington. "First, because it's so sweet smelling and attractive to her, and second, because it's so deadly. If the antidote isn't given within 24 hours, the dog is likely to die."

When storing antifreeze, put it well out of reach. Also periodically check beneath the car: antifreeze leaking from a hose is just as dangerous as when it pours from a bottle. You may want to use a new, less toxic antifreeze. It's still poisonous, but not as much as the traditional kind.

When dog-proofing the garage, pay special attention to any poisonous substances lying about. Slug bait in particular can be big trouble. "It doesn't take much to harm even a large dog," says Dr. Linnabary. In fact, when it comes to dog-proofing your garage, the safest bet would be to make the whole area off-limits.

The Garden and Yard

For dogs, gardens and lawns offer a veritable smorgasbord of smells—and, all too often, tastes. More than a few plants, given a nibble or two, can turn your dog a little green.

Various common outdoor plants can harm your dog, as can some fruits and vegetables.

Dogs dig, so they may eat the poisonous underground parts of spring bulbs.

And don't overlook your indoor garden. Your dog won't, so it's

Keep potted plants out of reach, at least until your dog learns there are better ways to get her vitamins.

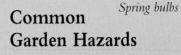

Common Garden Hazards

Spring bulbs

Almonds	Foxglove
Apricots	Jack-in-the-pulpit
Azalea	Kalanchoe
Black-eyed Susan	Lily of the valley
Boxwood	Mountain laurel
Buttercup	Oleander
Dumb cane	Peaches
English ivy	Philodendron
	Potatoes
	Rhododendron
	Rhubarb
	Spring bulbs
	Tomatoes
	Wandering Jew

Potato

a good idea to move all houseplants out of her reach. Hanging plants and those on window sills are probably safe, but it's best to move any plants off the floor or tables to higher shelves.

Incidentally, you need to be particularly careful around the holidays, since traditional plants, such as poinsettia and mistletoe, can be extremely poisonous. To be safe, you may want to use the artificial varieties instead.

For a complete list of the poisonous plants found in your neighborhood, Dr. Linnabary suggests contacting your county agent.

If you keep a compost pile or barrel, make sure your dog isn't able to get to the partially decomposed food inside. "We had to treat a West Highland White Terrier once who had eaten part of a corn cob, which then obstructed his digestive tract," says Dr. Whittington.

Then there are sticks. Everyone knows that dogs and sticks go together like peanut butter and jelly. Or do they? "Sticks can perforate the roof of a dog's mouth, its throat or intestine," says Dr. Wilford. "I had someone bring in a Doberman who hadn't eaten in days. I looked inside her mouth and found a small stick wedged between her back teeth."

A better alternative is to provide your dog with hard, splinter-free chews, such as Kongs or Nylabones. And while it may be difficult to remove every stick from your yard, it's a good idea to make a careful sweep of the area following a storm, and get rid of any new branches that may have blown down.

Home Security

Nothing could be more heartbreaking than to welcome your new dog into your family, only to lose her through a hole in (or under) your back fence. It's not that your dog necessarily wants to make a break. It's just that the outside world with all its smells and sounds is so enticing.

Before letting your new dog run, take a stroll around the yard. Are there any loose boards in the fence? Gaps that she could squeeze through? A soft place where she can dig?

Your dog will spot potential escape routes more quickly than you will. Dr. Geasling suggests putting her on a leash and strolling around the perimeter of the yard. "Let her explore with you. And chances are she might find something you missed—a loose board or small hole, for instance."

Stay with your dog while she makes herself familiar with her new yard, and praise her when she stays and plays where you want her to. If she becomes bored, she's more likely to go looking for excitement on the other side. When you're there to play with her, however, the temptation to find fun outside will diminish.

The outside world, with its fascinating smells and sounds, can prove an irresistible temptation if there's a hole in the fence.

Outdoor Safety

If your dog will be spending a good deal of time outdoors, you'll want to take a few additional steps to keep her safe and comfortable. Here's what vets recommend:

- Always leave adequate water. A heavy ceramic bowl is best, so she doesn't knock it over.
- If she has to be tied up, make sure that her rope or chain is long enough. That way, if she does manage to wrap herself around a tree, or jumps over a fence, she won't strangle herself. If her rope is too short, she might get into trouble.
- Remove a choke collar or dangling tags that can get stuck in fences, decks and other tight places.
- Provide shelter from rain and sun, preferably an insulated doghouse with cross ventilation. A shady haven during the warm months is a must.

The First Night

The arrival of your new dog is certainly a cause for celebration, but that doesn't mean that you should throw a surprise welcome-home party and invite everyone you know. Remember that from her point of view, she's in a strange place, surrounded by strange faces.

Your new dog, like all dogs, needs to feel that she's part of the pack. From now on, her pack consists of you and your family, so it's important to let her know she belongs from day one.

"Don't segregate the dog from the rest of the family," says Dr. Whittington. "She may view this as being ostracized and feel she's done something wrong. Keep her with you, play with her, cuddle her, just let her be with the family."

This is especially important for an adult dog. "Spend as much time as possible with her the first few days," advises Susan Bonhower, a Newfoundland breeder in Cornwall, Ontario. If possible, let your dog go wherever you go until she feels secure enough to be exploring on her own.

The Arrival

When you first walk in the door with your new friend on her leash, take her to the room where she'll likely spend a lot of her time, such as the kitchen. Keep distractions to a minimum as she explores her new world, sniffing and searching to her heart's content. Leave her leash on but let her drag it around. This way, if she tries to nibble a chair leg, you can gently distract her. But save the training for later. You want this first experience to be purely positive. Show her the food and water dishes you've got especially for her, also her toys and basket. Tell her how happy you are she's joined the family.

With all the excitement, your dog will likely have to go to the bathroom before long. Now's the time to introduce her to her designated toilet spot in the yard. It's important that you're okay with this spot as well, since she will return to it over and over again.

Something Old, Something New

She's feeling homesick, a bit lost and alone, maybe even wishing she was back in her old bed with her brothers and sisters. One way to soften the strangeness is to minimize the changes.

Feed her the usual. Changing her diet right away can upset an already nervous stomach, so feed her the food she's used to eating. A pup's digestive system, in particular, may not cope with the change, says Dr. Wilford. "Diarrhea commonly results. If you want to change her food, wait a week or two, then gradually introduce the new food." It's not likely that your new dog will refuse to eat.

Let her have a memento. "It's good to take something the puppy had when she was with her mother and littermates," suggests Bonhower. "Maybe it's a toy she played with, or even a towel that has the smell of home on it."

If you're adopting an adult dog, bring along one of her toys or her comfort pillow. If she's from a shelter, make her a present of a new toy when you pick her up. Let her sniff it, and when you get home put it alongside her bed.

Where to Sleep

Opinions vary over the best place for your new dog to bed down. Close to you will be especially reassuring on the first night. But if you get allergies, or she snores, you might need some distance.

"Start a puppy off in the room you eventually want her to sleep in," says Jeanine Murphy, a dog trainer in Somers, New York.

An adult dog might have her own ideas about where she'll sleep—a particular corner of the kitchen, for example. As long as it's okay with you, move her bed to her chosen spot.

Your Bedroom

This is one place where the newcomer will truly feel part of the pack. But should she sleep on your bed? As a pack animal, your dog follows a strict hierarchy—one in which you, and all the human members of your family, are considered "top dogs." Will letting her sleep on your bed give her the wrong idea about her status?

Your bedroom, even the bed, is quite acceptable, as long as it's okay with you, says Wayne Hunthausen, D.V.M., an animal behaviorist in Westwood, Kansas, and author of *Practitioner's Guide to Pet Behavior Problems*. "Ninety percent of dogs can sleep on the bed without showing any signs of dominance or aggression."

The Kitchen

The kitchen is a good place for your dog's bed. At night it's quiet, whereas it's usually the hub of household activity during the day—the perfect spot for lots of attention and socialization.

The Basement

A cozy basement can be a great spot to set up her bed—especially for a large dog, or a pup that's going to be a giant. But don't just put her there to sleep. Play with her there so she feels settled.

A Secure Bed

When it comes to your dog getting her shut-eye, the question is: crate versus basket? A crate may seem cruel, like a jail, but a roomy crate that's the right size for your dog can be a favorite place.

For a pup, a crate really is the best solution. "It dramatically reduces house-training problems and destructive chewing until the pup has grown into a dependable adult," says Janet Lalonde, D.V.M., a veterinarian in private practice in Alexandria, Ontario.

An older dog may not like being confined in this way. She might prefer a basket, an exercise pen, or a dog run set up in the basement.

"If you're adopting a shelter animal, who may not tolerate any kind of confinement well, you can, as a last resort, consult your vet about medication to calm her until she becomes accustomed to the new situation," says Dr. Hunthausen.

Crate or basket, be sure to put in a dog cushion with a washable cover and leave a toy nearby.

Sweet Dreams

Reassure your dog as you introduce her to her new bed. When it's time to sleep, put in her toy or blanket. Comfort her, then say goodnight.

An older dog might not sleep the night through at first. And a pup is likely to wake up and whine. Take her out in case she needs to go, says Dr. Whittington. If she keeps it up, try again 15 minutes later, then ignore her. Make her realize that nighttime is for sleeping.

Making the Introductions

Everyone is excited at the prospect of a new family member—your dog, the adults and the children. The idea is to take it slowly, just as when you introduce any stranger to your family. You might have an idea of what to expect, but your new friend will have none. Avoid alarming her with too much hugging and rough-housing.

Meeting the Human Residents

"Prepare everyone ahead of time," advises Dr. Hunthausen. "Get the children books about dogs and give them stuffed animals so they can practice the proper way to pick up a puppy." It's important that the adults take charge during the introductions, adds Murphy. "This will reduce the mayhem and make things safer for the dog."

If your new pet is an adult dog and you're not sure about her background, keep her on a leash while everyone pets her and she gets a sniff of each family member. If you hear a growl or you see any other signs of aggression, Dr. Hunt-hausen suggests calling your vet, who can refer you to a behaviorist. Chances are she's just over-whelmed, but you want to be sure.

Meeting Your Other Pets

Getting the new dog together with other pets doesn't have to become a fur-flying fiasco. The adjustment time for four-legged residents will depend on your new dog's level of socialization. Each animal's past experiences will also play a part in creating harmony in the pet household.

Adults and Puppies

"You won't have too many problems with an adult animal accepting a new puppy," says Gary Landsberg, D.V.M., an animal behaviorist in private practice in Thornhill, Ontario, and co-author of *Dog Behavior and Training*. "Older dogs don't see a puppy as a threat to their status or territory."

You may notice the adult "putting the puppy in its place" by swatting, barking or biting at it. But don't do anything about it. They must establish the pecking order. Otherwise, you could make matters worse. "You will send the message that your older dog will have to work harder to keep her spot in the pack," says Dr. Whittington. "She'll have to bark louder and snap more next time."

Introducing Adult Dogs

Who is going to be top dog? Two or more mature dogs will have to work it out between themselves. "It might be best to have them meet on neutral ground first, like a park. Let them get acquainted before bringing the new dog into the other's territory," says Dr. Landsberg.

Don't be surprised by some play-fighting between them—play-fighting that seems real. "What looks like aggression is just a challenge of authority," explains Dr. Landsberg. "One will likely emerge as the obviously dominant dog."

The outcome will depend on such things as the personality, breed, sex and age of the dogs. The main thing is to support the relationship the dogs have established. "Feed the leader first, greet her first, let her out first," says Dr. Landsberg.

Paws for thought

Are Dogs and Cats Natural Enemies?

"Dogs talk dog language and cats speak cat," says Gary Landsberg, D.V.M., an animal behaviorist in private practice in Thornhill, Ontario, and co-author of Dog Behavior and Training. *"Unfortunately when the dog is saying 'Let's play,' something often gets lost in the translation to cat."*

But just because they can't talk to each other doesn't mean that they're natural enemies. Much depends on their personalities and ages.

"Puppies love cats," says Dr. Landsberg. "They often just want to play. An adult dog, however, if not socialized with cats early on, may take a predatory stance."

Cats are not so keen to come to the party. They might be frightened (that's the cat that makes itself scarce) or stalwart (that's the one hissing or swatting). Kittens can be more accepting—they may even adore a dog and eat, sleep and play with her.

Meeting the Cat

"Bringing a puppy or dog into a cat's home can be very disruptive," says Murphy. "The dog must make the compromises. Dogs will take easily to a kitten, but cats are rarely as accepting of a puppy."

They don't have to fight like cat and dog, but your dog must learn to take it easy.

Owners can't expect that an adult cat is going to want to play."

Murphy advises keeping the new arrival on her leash for the introductions. Let the cat sniff your dog if he wants, but don't let your dog overpower the cat. Tug the leash every time your dog goes too close, says Murphy. "Make 'avoiding the cat' one of the rules your dog must learn," she adds.

Keep your dog on a leash when you're with her and the cat for the first few weeks. Correct her if she goes near the cat, praise her when she stays away. "Curb any predatory behavior—such as chasing squirrels—that may translate into anti-cat behavior in the future," says Dr. Hunthausen.

Also provide a way for the cat to escape if he wants, suggests Dr. Hunthausen. A high perch, a kitty door to a quiet room, or a baby gate to keep the dog away—all will give the cat an out.

The ideal situation, says Dr. Landsberg, is to get a new pup and a new kitten at the same time. An adult cat who has been around dogs will also be a good match for an adult dog.

Not a Good Mix

There are some dog and cat combinations that you should be careful about. "Some large dogs naturally see small animals as a kind of prey," says Dr. Landsberg. "Take a former racing Greyhound, which has been trained from day one to chase after rabbits. It would be pretty hard for her to live peacefully with a cat."

Dogs and Children

Who could be better at keeping pace with a wonderfully energetic young dog than an equally energetic young human? Growing up together, spending part of every day playing and hugging, keeping each other company, offering each other comfort in hard times, a friendship can be made that is remembered for a lifetime.

Preparing for the New Arrival

If you and your family don't have a dog, then chances are your children haven't had much exposure to dogs. That means they won't have much idea about what dogs do and don't like. They might also be a bit tentative and nervous around this hairy thing that pants and barks and seems almost as big as they are. Your children will need to be well prepared for the arrival of your new family member, so that they can be confident and careful dog lovers. Give them as much time as they need to get used to your dog.

They must learn how to behave around a dog, and the way to handle one properly, particularly if it's a pup. "Parents must teach their children how to carry a puppy and how to approach a puppy," says Dr. Lalonde. "Otherwise, aggression problems in the dog might develop."

A dog isn't a toy. Children need to be gentle, and not too rowdy to begin with, until your dog is used to them and they are used to your dog.

Always make sure there's an adult around to supervise whenever your new dog and the kids get together, advises Dr. Hunthausen. You'll then be assured of everyone's safety and enjoyment, until you are confident that they are all consistently doing the right thing.

Training: A Family Thing

Of course, it's not just the kids that need to learn how to behave. Your new dog should also be taking lessons. Find a training school that will let children take part, or if they are too young, at least where they'll be allowed to watch, suggests Bonhower. "Kids love it if they can tell a dog what to do and she does it," she says.

There are other benefits to making training a family affair, explains Dr. Lalonde. "While there's only one person holding the leash, the other family members are looking on," she says. "This way everyone learns the same commands, which provides the consistency the dog needs."

Young Pups

The line between canine and human can occasionally become blurred for young puppies. "Sometimes, kids act more like puppies than humans," explains Bonhower. "Running around and screaming—these things can get the puppy excited. If one of her siblings were playing in that way, the puppy would probably nip at him."

Explain to your children that when they play rough, the puppy can lose control in its eagerness to join in. "If this happens with your kids, teach them to squeal like a puppy, even if the nip didn't hurt much. This will teach the new pup bite inhibition." And the children are less likely to be unintentionally hurt.

Good Dogs for Kids

Dogs are as individual as we are. You'll come across gregarious, retiring, playful, lazy, silly and even crotchety creatures—all within the same breed. Yet there are several general axioms about the best breeds for kids.

"Often, the bigger the dog, the better," says Wayne Hunthausen, D.V.M., an animal behaviorist in Westwood, Kansas, and author of *Practitioner's Guide to Pet Behavior Problems*. "Big dogs tend to be more patient. Golden Retrievers, Boxers, Standard Poodles—all of these are great kid dogs. But the other side of this is they can also get really rowdy, unintentionally knocking over a child."

Small dogs can also be happy companions for kids, as long as the kids learn how to behave around them. "Small dogs face the real possibility of being squished by a child," says Susan Bonhower, a Newfoundland breeder in Cornwall, Ontario. Take special care with toddlers, whose balance and control leaves something to be desired.

What about dogs that families with small children would do best to avoid? "Most studies have shown terriers to be more reactive, and more likely to snap at children," says Dr. Hunthausen. That said, he would still recommend West Highland White Terriers and Cairn Terriers.

"Barring any serious behavior problems, almost any dog of any breed can be properly trained and socialized to be around kids," he adds. "Some breeds simply take longer than others."

It's best to encourage your children to play quieter games with the puppy, and to confine her when the children are playing hard.

Adult Dogs

What about adult dogs around children, especially those dogs from uncertain backgrounds? "Behaviorally, there's a risk when you don't know a dog's history," says Dr. Hunthausen. "Adopting a shelter dog is a courageous thing to do, since you can never be entirely sure what sort of animal you're dealing with."

He advises that you keep your new dog on a leash whenever she's around children. Make sure she remains under control until she exhibits consistent positive behavior. And with plenty of diligence and kindness, you'll likely end up with a terrific pet for the whole family.

A puppy and a child can forge a lasting friendship that's second to none, but adults need to show the youngsters how to behave so no one gets hurt. And always supervise them when they're playing together.

3 BRINGING UP PUPPY

With a puppy in your home, expect warm greetings and occasional warm
puddles. Be ready to learn how to play again, in case you've forgotten, as
you help him become a loving and well-behaved companion. All it takes
is patience and simple, consistent training. But don't rush it. You can only
raise him once, so take your time and enjoy it, and you will do it well.

What to Expect of a Puppy
pages 55–57
There's a new baby in your life,
and that means you've got
lots to look forward to

Raising Him Well
pages 58–59
Treat him with care and
common sense, and just
be yourself

What is Puppyhood?
pages 60–61
What to expect during the
first 24 months of your pup's
life, stage by stage

Socializing Your Puppy
pages 62–63
Your puppy needs to have new
experiences to become a
well-adjusted adult

The Polite Pup
pages 64–66
Giving your puppy lessons early
on will make life easier and
more pleasant for you both

The First Checkup
page 67
How to make this
necessary first visit to the vet
a positive experience

What to Expect of a Puppy

Puppies feel warm and solid when held and hugged. Born comedians, they make people play, and playing makes people feel younger and happier. Not all is fun and games, though. Like human babies, puppies eat sloppily, and need small amounts of food at frequent intervals. They make messes constantly and chew on everything that passes their taste test, with furniture and shoes being their favorite flavors. They also sleep a lot—but not necessarily to your schedule.

Be prepared for an ego trip. You will be the most important person in your puppy's life, and he will love you unconditionally. But remember that no matter how much he wants to please, he will sometimes do the wrong thing—because he is, after all, just a baby.

Dinnertime

If you think a dog is fond of food, wait till you see your puppy in action. He'll need frequent, small, but nutritious meals to grow up strong and healthy. Provide him with a good diet, and match the number of feeds and the amount you feed him to the needs of his age.

Beware the bargain. Use a reputable brand of puppy food. "It's best to avoid foods that cost a lot less than name brands," warns Bonnie Wilcox, D.V.M., a veterinarian in private practice in Preemption, Illinois, and co-author of *The Atlas of Dog Breeds* and *Successful Dog Breeding*. "You get what you pay for, and the quality of the protein, fat and other nutrients is important."

You and your puppy will form an instant mutual admiration society. Be prepared to love and laugh and care for him, even when he puts the wrong paw forward.

Switch foods slowly. When you pick up your new puppy, ask his former owners what brand of food he's been eating. Feed him the same thing for a few days, even if it isn't the brand you plan to use. "A young pup has a sensitive stomach, so make the transition from his old food to his new food gradually," says Dr. Wilcox. Give him time to settle before changing his food.

Start by mixing the old and new brands together in a ratio of three-quarters of the old with one-quarter of the new. After he's eaten this mixture for three days, go to half and half for another three days. Finally, feed him one-quarter of the old food with three-quarters of the new for three more days. By then, he'll be ready to eat the new food alone.

Be patient with table manners. He's going to make a mess until he learns to coordinate mouth, teeth and tongue with a little finesse. Minimize your cleaning chores by buying a food dish that doesn't tip over. Place it in a corner so he won't have to chase it all over the floor.

Snooze Time

Your pup is going to want plenty of shut-eye—the amount will vary with his needs. He'll sleep more when his body is going through a growth spurt and less during slower growth times. He won't need to be put down for daily naps. When he's tired, he'll sleep. And when he's not, he won't. So don't be surprised if he yawns and folds up into a small heap right in the middle of playtime.

No need to tiptoe, he'll learn to sleep through normal household noise. A young pup like this one will spend a lot of time snoozing, and he'll decide the time and place.

And do be patient when he shatters the night with a mournful whine because he is wondering where everyone is at two in the morning. When your puppy gets over being lonesome for his mother, sisters and brothers, he will sleep through the night. Help him to feel secure by giving him a soft, fluffy toy made especially for dogs. Put a wind-up clock (the kind that ticks loudly) right near his bed to sound like his mom's heart, or play a radio softly at night.

Placing his crate right beside your bed is another way to stop him from feeling lonely. Whatever you do, don't let him out of his crate as a way of getting him to stop howling. That will only teach him that if he complains loudly, he'll get what he wants.

Exercise and Playtime

When your puppy isn't eating, he's sleeping. When he isn't eating or sleeping, he's likely to be looking for ways to get rid of all the energy he was storing up while he was eating and sleeping.

Set the alarm, just in case he doesn't wake you. You will have to get up earlier than usual, because he'll need a good play and exercise session in the morning. This is particularly important if you work and he's going to be confined by himself for most of the day. Exercise should be fun. As soon as he's learned to walk on a leash, take him out for long, exploratory walks (provided he has been vaccinated). Play "chase me" games in the backyard. Ball games are especially good exercise for a pup that loves retrieving.

Accidents Happen

What goes in must come out. It's one of the basic rules of anatomy, and you'll know it all by heart after just a few days in the company of your new friend. Housebreaking your puppy is a lot like potty training a toddler, according to Dr. Wilcox. It depends on how diligent you are. When your puppy is young, he won't have the muscular control to hold his urine or bowel movements, and you'll have to anticipate his needs. But his control will gradually improve, and by three or four months old, he should be quite dependable—just be patient and persistent.

Knowing when your puppy needs to go is the key to housebreaking, so establish a routine. And prepare for an occasional accident by keeping an odor neutralizer and stain remover on hand. An odor-free floor is an important part of housebreaking. Dogs tend to eliminate where their noses tell them they went before, so quick clean-ups help prevent repeat performances.

The Chewing Blues

Some days, you'll feel as if your new pup is all teeth. Even though you confine him when you are away, and supervise him when you're home, he may still find a way to shanghai a shoe or pilfer a piece of underwear. Your dogged devourer chews because he needs to. Between four and six months of age, he'll be teething.

"Chewing helps his baby teeth to loosen and fall out, which makes room for the permanent teeth that are emerging," says Paul S. McGrath, D.V.M., a veterinarian in private practice in Kalispell, Montana.

Curiosity will also lead him to put things in his mouth. Since he can't pick objects up in his paws, he investigates new things through his sense of smell and taste. It also helps his jaw muscles and facial nerves develop. It's essential for puppies, and a healthy habit for adult dogs, too. "Gnawing on appropriate objects removes plaque from teeth and promotes good gums," explains Dr. McGrath.

Chew Toys

It's not chewing that's the problem, it's his choice of object that the two of you don't see eye to eye on. To protect your belongings, you need to get your puppy his own chew toys. Nylabones or their softer chew counterparts Gumabones, sterilized bones, and solid rubber toys for dogs make good chews. They are all available at pet supply stores. Don't get more than two. Planting chewies all over your home isn't a good idea, because if almost everything he finds on the floor is a chew toy, he may think anything he can reach is suitable for sinking his teeth into.

Easing Teething Pain

Puppies tend to be pretty stoic about teething pain, but loose teeth, inflamed gums, and sometimes even a lack of appetite will give the game away. Store-bought chew toys make excellent teething aids. Or you can try making your own. Wet and twist old washcloths and freeze them solid, recommends Amy Ammen, director of Amiable Dog Training, host of "Amiable Dog Training with Amy Ammen" on MATA Television in Milwaukee, and author of *Training in No Time* and *Dual Ring Dog*. Give one to your puppy to chew whenever he seems to be suffering from the new-tooth blues—the cold will help relieve the pain.

As soon as the washcloth thaws or your puppy has finished chewing, wash the cloth well, give it a twist, and put it back in the freezer for next time.

Chew Taboos

Resist the impulse to use worn-out leather loafers, old socks, clothing and purses as teething toys. "He doesn't know the difference between old and new things, so he'll think if one shoe is his, all shoes must be ripe for chewing," says Amy Ammen, director of Amiable Dog Training, host of "Amiable Dog Training with Amy Ammen" on MATA Television in Milwaukee, and author of *Training in No Time* and *Dual Ring Dog*.

Soft latex toys with squeakers or bells inside should be used only when you will be in the same room to supervise. He could shred and swallow the toy, squeaker and all. Also avoid rawhide or other edible chews for now. It's better if what he swallows is nutritious food.

Raising Him Well

Puppies are tiny, winsome and cute as buttons, but are they fragile? That all depends. Healthy, vaccinated puppies are vigorous, and the bigger they grow, the hardier they get. Before they're vaccinated, they are susceptible to certain diseases, says Dr. McGrath. So it's important to keep your puppy away from unvaccinated dogs until he's had his first shots. But there's no need to treat a healthy puppy as if he were fine crystal. Puppies are capable of playing, loving and learning—and are happiest when they have an opportunity to do all three.

How to Act Around Your New Pup

What should you do if your puppy dashes across the room in a madcap race, pounces on his toy and plays "kill" with violent shakes of his head? Laugh and enjoy it, says Dr. McGrath. "Be yourself. And incorporate his schedule into your regular household routine." If he is napping and you want to watch television or play the piano, do it. He will learn to sleep through normal household noises. If he's contentedly gnawing his chew toy and you have an irresistible urge to hug him, do so. Puppies understand spontaneity and can give us lessons in having impromptu fun.

Common Sense

In dealing with your puppy, let common sense be your guide. When the neighbor's kids want to share their nachos with him, let them give him a dog biscuit instead. If he wriggles to get off your lap, place him on the floor. A puppy can be hurt jumping or falling off your lap or the furniture, because it's a long way down. Be as cautious with him as you would be with any toddler.

Keeping an Eye on the Kids

When a friend wants to bring her toddler and three-year-old over to see your puppy, supervise closely. Hold your puppy, sit on the floor with the kids, and show them how to pet him before giving them a turn. Never let young children, no matter how gentle, walk around with a puppy

Puppies are experts at having fun and seem to understand that children are at a similar stage of life. Teach your children how to handle the puppy carefully from his very first day in his new home, and always supervise closely when other children visit.

in their arms. Squirmy puppies can easily slip out of chubby little hands. And if you have children, you'll need to supervise closely whenever their friends come over.

Not all people teach their children how to handle animals or that they have feelings. "Peer pressure is a potent force," warns Dr. McGrath. "Your child may be unable to stop friends from treating the puppy roughly." You don't want your puppy being hurt, either physically or emotionally, by any kind of rough treatment.

Hands-On Care

Your pup has to get used to being handled on all parts of his body. He'll need this for a lifetime of

Constant, gentle touching on every part of his body will allow your puppy to get used to the handling he will experience throughout his life.

grooming and paw checks, ear exams and all the other hygiene routines. To get him used to this, pet him all over, advises Dr. McGrath. "Touch him from the top of the nose to the tip of the tail and every place in between."

Lots of puppies are sensitive about having their feet touched, but he'll get over it if you deal with it the right way. Sit down to a good book or your favorite TV show with your puppy on your lap or beside you. Then stroke him in places he enjoys being petted until he relaxes so much he's nearly asleep. Continue stroking his body, but include his feet as well. If he tenses, go back to petting only his body until he's sleepy enough that you can try his feet again. After he falls asleep—and he will—gently massage the toes of all four feet. Soon your puppy will relax and let you touch his toes when he's awake too.

"When doing daily or weekly grooming, such as brushing or trimming nails, be gentle but matter of fact—not apologetic or cajoling," says Dr. McGrath. "Use just the amount of firmness it takes to stay in control and get the job done." If you stop brushing because he struggles, you're letting him control the situation. Next time, he will simply struggle sooner and harder.

The Puppy Pickup

Picking up a puppy needs two hands, so that you can support him at both ends, advises Paul S. McGrath, D.V.M., a veterinarian in private practice in Kalispell, Montana. "Scoop under him with your right hand pointing forward so it is under his chest, and use your left hand or arm to cradle his rear end," he says. Reverse this if you are left-handed.

Carry your puppy close to your body in both arms. Don't hold him away from you so his rear dangles. A pup should never be picked up by the nape of the neck or the front legs or armpits, as this can cause permanent damage to his joints.

What is Puppyhood?

Puppyhood is the period when your dog is immature, physically, mentally and emotionally. It lasts until he reaches adulthood at about 24 months, although this can be even later in some large breeds. Here's what to expect in those 24 months, and how to bring out the best in your pup.

Day 1 to 6 Weeks

A pup needs his mother's care and the company of his littermates. At four weeks, he needs about 10 minutes a day outside the puppy pen, being handled gently by a human to develop his individuality. At around six weeks, he will start to learn about his place in the pack pecking order. Mom teaches him to respect authority, which will make him more trainable later. Roughhousing with his brothers and sisters makes him less sensitive to body contact and noise, teaches him to behave socially in the pooch world, and also to keep his aggression in check.

7 to 8 Weeks

This is the ideal age for a pup to move into your home and start finding out what goes on beyond the puppy pen. "After he has had his temporary immunizations, take your pup to all sorts of places," advises Chris Walkowicz, a breeder of Bearded Collies in Sherrard, Illinois, author of *The Perfect Match* and co-author of *Successful Dog Breeding.* "Put him down, walk away and let him follow you." This will teach him that you're the leader of his pack and he's a faithful follower. Set up situations where he can follow every family member, including the kids. This is the critical time for human socialization, warns Walkowicz. It won't come again, so don't miss it.

Puppies this age can learn what simple commands such as "Sit" and "Come" mean. You can also start gentle leash training. But these lessons can wait a week or two, if necessary.

8 to 10 Weeks

More than anything, your puppy needs to feel secure right now. This is the "fear imprint period," when puppies can easily be traumatized and may never forget what frightened them. "Some pups are more affected than others," says Walkowicz, "but this isn't a good time to take your puppy to a rock concert in the park."

At this age, puppies love to learn, as long as the teaching is gentle and consistent. Knowing

These Shiba Inu puppies learn by playing with their littermates and by observing mom. The first thing to be established is the pecking order and control of aggression.

This mom still guides and teaches her 12-week-old Cavalier King Charles Spaniel pups to respect authority. She will assist you with the responsibility of bringing up the pups.

how to please you by coming when called will bolster his confidence, and sticking to a schedule will also make him feel safe. Continue socializing him: eight weeks is the ideal time to enrol him in puppy-training classes.

10 to 12 Weeks

Now's the time to add to your pup's social activities and continue gentle training. "If he has not been leash trained or learned his puppy 'Sit' and 'Come,' start now," says Walkowicz. He should accompany you to new places, both indoor and outdoor, meet friendly people of all ages, other puppies and gentle adult dogs.

12 to 16 Weeks

During these weeks, your bundle of fun will continue to need a heap of attention and plenty of social activities. Keep up the training with your puppy, but be gentle. Some pups go through an "avoidance" period at this age, peeping from behind your legs when you go out, or crawling under the couch when company arrives. If he's been okay around people and other dogs until now, his shyness will probably be short-lived. Keep his social life low-key but regular for a while if he keeps hiding.

16 Weeks to 6 Months

The juvenile period begins at 16 weeks. While your pup is fully developed mentally, he still has some physical and emotional growing to do, and he won't have an adult attention span. The name of the game is consistency—keep your expectations the same from day to day so he doesn't get confused. Take him out to meet humans and other dogs, and have short, upbeat training sessions. Integrate training into everyday life, for example, by having him sit while you prepare his dinner. He may be clumsy now, but that's just adolescence. He'll be graceful when he's grown.

6 to 12 Months

Your puppy reaches puberty, or sexual maturity, during these months, and male youngsters may try out being pushy. You'll notice that your pooch's attention span has improved. "Training of some kind should be ongoing, whether it's for obedience or just tricks for fun," advises Walkowicz. Some dogs go through a second avoidance period at around ten months of age, but they are usually happy-go-lucky again by one year old.

12 to 24 Months

This is when your youngster becomes an adult, although some dogs won't reach emotional maturity until they're about 30 months old. Congratulations to you both.

Socializing Your Puppy

Socializing your puppy means getting him used to people, places and things. "Every time your puppy does something he's never done, goes somewhere he's never been, or meets a new person or a friendly dog, he's being socialized," says Carolyn Brown, of Thayer, Missouri, who raises and shows American Staffordshire Terriers.

Between 7 and 16 weeks of age is a critical time in a dog's life. A dog will never forget what he learned in those 9 weeks, says Walkowicz. "His experiences, good and bad, will leave a

A walk in the park is a great learning adventure for your puppy. Exposing him to new experiences from the start will help him to grow up fully socialized, confident and outgoing.

permanent mark on his personality, making him outgoing or shy, happy-go-lucky or cautious, eager to learn or resentful of authority."

Your puppy needs to be exposed to the world outside so he can learn how to live happily with all that goes on around him. He will decide for himself what's safe and what isn't, but he needs your steady guidance. With you there to help him, he will be introduced to a friendly world and grow up confident and outgoing.

Out and About

Taking your puppy with you when you visit a friend socializes him. So does meeting a friendly stranger while out for a walk, playing with another puppy, or examining a soccer ball. Your puppy needs to meet senior citizens, toddlers, bearded men, women in sun hats, teenagers with skateboards and people pushing strollers. He needs to walk on carpet, linoleum, grass and pavement. He needs to learn to climb steps (start by placing him on the third or fourth step and letting him walk down) and to ride in the car.

Coping with His Fears

There are two cardinal rules for socializing a puppy, says Brown. Never pet him when he's afraid and always praise him for being brave.

"When your puppy seems fearful, do not reassure him with petting and soothing words because he will interpret your actions as praise," Brown explains. He will repeat what he is praised for over and over, so a hesitant stance could become his learned reaction to anything

How Old are Dogs in Human Years?

A popular old wives' tale claims that one year of a dog's life equals seven human years, but today we know better. "For example, dogs are capable of reproducing at around one year of age, but seven-year-old children are far from sexually mature," says Chris Walkowicz, a breeder of Bearded Collies in Sherrard, Illinois, author of The Perfect Match *and co-author of* Successful Dog Breeding. *Veterinarians have now come up with a much more realistic comparison between dog and human years, says Bonnie Wilcox, D.V.M., a veterinarian in private practice in Preemption, Illinois. Here's how it works:*

DOG	HUMAN
5 months	10 years
8 months	13 years
10 months	14 years
12 months	15 years
18 months	20 years
2 years	24 years

From here on, the scale goes up in a ratio of four dog years for every human year. That means a three-year-old dog is the equivalent of a 28-year-old person, a four-year-old dog is about 32 in human years, and so on.

new. On the other hand, never jerk him toward the object he fears. Treatment like that could turn a little trepidation into total terror.

Set an example. If your puppy is afraid to go near something, leave him where he is and go yourself, says Brown. "Handle the object as if it were a winning lottery ticket and invite your puppy to join you. Sitting down beside the feared object works well. Your puppy will probably start creeping over, but hold your praise until he at least touches the thing with his nose." If the object isn't breakable or too large, roll it away from, never toward, your puppy. This might awaken his chasing instinct and entice him to play with the object himself.

Ask a friend to help. If your puppy is afraid of people, have a friend toss a dog treat his way. She should then ignore the pup and chat with you. When your pup comes nearer, as he surely will, your friend should kneel down and make herself seem friendly and nonthreatening. When your puppy comes in for an exploratory sniff, your friend should hold her hand low, reach under the puppy's chin and tickle him on the chest, advises Brown. Reaching over the puppy's head could make him back up in fright. If your puppy doesn't approach, don't force him, but give him a lot more socialization. Get other friends in on the act and set up situations where your puppy will be enticed into approaching.

Link noise with niceness. If loud noises send your puppy behind the sofa, Brown advises announcing his favorite things with sound. If he loves to eat, mix his meal in a metal pan with a metal spoon before giving it to him. Don't make a racket; keep the volume realistic. Eventually, he'll learn that loud noises can mean nice things and be less likely to jump out of his skin.

The Polite Pup

Puppies learn by repetition and consistency, so the first step in establishing good habits is to set up a schedule you and he can live with. Dogs are creatures of habit. Stick to a routine right from the start to help your pup make sense of his new home and understand what you want from him.

A Regular Routine

"Your puppy should be fed, watered, exercised and taken outside to eliminate at pretty much the same times every day," advises Dave Wedum, a professional dog trainer and owner of Grizzly Dog Obedience School and Training Kennels in Choteau, Montana. "Besides being healthier for your puppy, feeding at regular times and using a crate makes housebreaking easier." For more information, see "Crate-Training" on page 98.

Ideally, when a pup is between seven and ten weeks old, his toilet needs should be tended to about every three hours from the time he wakes up until the time you put him to bed. He'll need to eliminate first thing in the morning, right after breakfast, mid-morning, right after lunch, mid-afternoon, right after dinner and again before bed. Remember that exercise and play-

time also act as "on" switches for puppy plumbing. "But don't worry," says Wedum. "Every three hours isn't a life sentence. As your puppy gets older, his holding capacity will increase and he'll need fewer trips outdoors."

Entertaining Training

"Start training your puppy as soon as you get him," advises Wedum. He'll love the attention and you can start with simple things such as "Sit" and "Come." Just keep the training sessions short (like puppy attention spans) and always be playful and upbeat. Never train your puppy when you are feeling grouchy. Young puppies are just learning how to learn, so your earliest lessons together will color his lifelong attitude toward training.

The Basic Commands

Bribery works wonders when teaching your puppy. When you want him to sit, hold a treat in front of his nose, say "Sit," and move the treat upward and back over his head. When his eyes follow the goodie upward, his head will tilt back and his rear will lower to the floor. Give the treat immediately, while he's still sitting, and praise him.

This yellow Labrador pup is all attention, head up, bottom down. It's not the most perfect "Sit" but it's his first step toward good manners and a cooperative attitude.

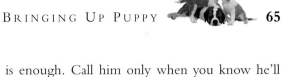

Although not nearly as tasty as a shoe or a slipper, this chew toy will satisfy a puppy's need to exercise his jaws. He'll soon learn what's okay to chew and what's not.

"Come" is a command that can be lots of fun, but it could also save your dog's life. At feeding time, say his name, then the word "Come" in a happy voice. Show him his dish, then walk a few steps holding it. Praise him when he follows, and let him eat. Do this every time you feed him and he'll get the general idea.

Chasing games are another good learning opportunity. Touch your puppy playfully, say his name followed by the word "Come," and run away a few steps while clapping, bending down and talking happily. Let him catch you. Play with him for a few seconds, then give him another playful tap and run away as before. Three times

is enough. Call him only when you know he'll want to come—not when he is sleepy or busy with food or a toy. And never sabotage your training by calling him over, then giving him a pill or chastising him. Make sure you go to him for the upsetting stuff.

Teaching Him What Not to Chew

Puppies love to chew—in fact, they have to chew—but they can't always distinguish chew toys from chew taboos. If he can walk on a leash, there's a great game he can play while learning what's okay to chew and what's not, according to Ammen. Decide on a command that means "Get that out of your mouth." (Most people opt for "Out" or "Drop it.") Then place some personal objects, such as a wallet or slippers, and some paper items, like napkins or a roll of toilet tissue, on the living room floor, along with your puppy's chew toys. Put your pup on his leash and let him explore the clutter. When he picks up a taboo item, give your "Drop it" command and jerk the leash. Then quickly move toward a toy and encourage him to play with it.

If you play this game two or three times a day your puppy will soon proudly lead you to the correct object. When he does, be sure to praise him and let him keep the toy. "Now that your puppy knows a command for releasing an object, be sure to use only that command on every occasion, whether he is holding a shoe, a finger, or a dead rabbit," says Ammen.

And if he holds tight to a taboo object even after you tell him to drop it and jerk the leash? Spray your finger with a drop of bitter apple, recommends Ammen. Then slide your finger along his gumline as you give your "Drop it" command. He'll soon learn to let go.

No More Nipping

Puppies use their mouths to check things out and to play, much as humans use their hands. But needle-sharp teeth hurt, so puppies have to be taught that nipping is out. "Lack of exercise is a frequent cause of nipping," says Marilyn Bain, breeder-handler of English Springer Spaniels and owner of Legacy Kennels in Kalispell, Montana. "Your puppy may be so energetic that he has trouble controlling himself."

If your puppy nips, try taking him on longer or more frequent walks and keep him on a leash in the house when you are home. As soon as he mouths you, make a high-pitched "Ouch" and jerk the leash. Then encourage him to play with one of his toys. If that doesn't make a difference in a few days, Bain recommends choosing a command that means "Don't bite" and saying it every time your puppy touches you with his teeth, while pressing firmly on his nose or gently pinching his upper lip. If that doesn't work, spray bitter apple on the part of you that he mouths. He'll think twice before taste-testing it again.

If your pup is one of the herding breeds and there are no sheep and cattle handy, he may try herding people, especially children, by nipping at their heels. Teach your children and their friends to stand still and say "No!" if he takes them for sheep. Running only makes matters worse.

A Training School for Pups

Puppy classes, often called Kindergarten Puppy Training, can be found in most metropolitan areas. You can take him to puppy school for help with housebreaking, crate-training, selecting toys and preventing destructive behaviors.

Other things you might learn about include teaching your pup to accept grooming, to ride

Help for Working People with Puppies

If a young pup should have attention every three hours or so, is it possible to work full-time and still be a good puppy parent? "Sure," says Dave Wedum, a dog obedience instructor in Choteau, Montana. "Just use common sense when you are planning your puppy's schedule and he'll adjust to your hours."

Acquire your puppy when you have some time off, Wedum advises, so you can get to know each other and form a strong bond. Introduce him to a schedule you can live with from day one and stick to it. "Don't confuse your puppy by feeding him and taking him outside on one schedule during your vacation and on weekends, and another schedule when you work," says Wedum. "Not only will that slow housebreaking, but not knowing what to expect can produce anxiety in puppies."

Try to come home at lunchtime when your pup is young, but if you can't, be sure to come home right after work. You could ask a neighbor to take him out, or hire a dog walker. "Eight or nine hours is a long time to leave a puppy unattended," says Wedum. "But thousands of puppies have grown up with working owners and grown into happy, well-adjusted dogs. If you make the effort, yours will, too."

in a car, walk on a leash and obey simple commands. Going to class is great fun and provides super socialization for your pup. He will be handled by other owners and will learn to get along with other dogs, accept restraint, and pay attention to you in spite of distractions. Eight weeks is the ideal age to enroll him, says Ammen.

The First Checkup

Your puppy should visit the vet within two days of your bringing him home, whether his vaccinations are due or not, advises Dr. Wilcox. Put him in his crate for the journey, and pack a roll of paper towels just in case he gets carsick on the way. If you have your puppy's health record, take it along. Also take a sample of his stool. (A quick tip: Turn a resealable plastic bag inside out, pick up a small section of your pup's stool with the bag, turn the bag right side out and close it.)

When you arrive at the clinic, give the health record and stool sample to the receptionist—it will be checked under a microscope to see if he should be treated for worms. Keep your puppy in your arms or in his crate while you wait for the vet to see him. It's easy for young pups to pick up germs, so don't let him sniff around on the floor or play with strange dogs.

Keeping Him Happy

When it's your puppy's turn in the examining room, be matter-of-fact about putting him on the table. Hold him in place gently, but as firmly as necessary, for the checkup. "Don't console or coddle him or he'll be sure something terrible is about to happen," says Dr. Wilcox. "Instead, talk to him in a happy, upbeat voice."

Even if needles make you nervous, don't let it show, because your puppy will take his cue from you. If you're tense, he will be fearful, but if you act naturally and seem to like the vet, he will feel more comfortable and like the vet, too.

The Checkup

On your puppy's first trip to the vet, he will be checked over thoroughly to make sure everything is okay. Your vet will take your puppy's temperature and listen to his heart, as well as examine his eyes, nose, ears, throat, stomach and skin, and check for swollen glands. Your pup will also be given any vaccinations that may be due. The whole examination is painless and will be over in five to ten minutes.

Any Questions?

If you've noticed anything about your puppy that you especially want to have checked, or if you have any questions, be sure to bring them up, advises Dr. Wilcox. You've already spent a day or two with him and may sense something unusual that your vet maybe won't see during a routine exam unless you mention it.

This is also a good time to discuss heartworm prevention, a vaccination schedule and neutering, and to find out how the clinic handles after-hours and weekend emergencies.

Having his eyes examined is just one of the routine health checks your puppy will learn is part of going to visit the vet.

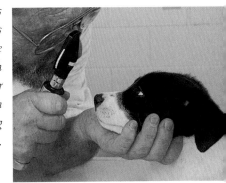

4 CANINE COMMUNICATION

Your dog doesn't speak human and you don't speak dog, but that doesn't mean you can't communicate. The key to a happy life together is to find a way to "talk" to each other—learn to read her behaviors, and be aware of how she interprets yours.

How Dogs Communicate
pages 69–71

Body position, facial expression, ear and tail movement, and all sorts of sound—that's how dogs express themselves

Reading Your Dog's Body Language
pages 77–78

The lowdown on all those poses that your dog likes to do

Why Does She Do That?
pages 72–76

A look at why your dog does the curious things she does

Getting Your Message Across
page 79

Your body, face and tone of voice are all sending signals to your dog

How Dogs Communicate

Communicating with a dog often comes naturally to kids, but adults find it harder, says Amy Ammen, director of Amiable Dog Training, host of "Amiable Dog Training with Amy Ammen" on MATA Television in Milwaukee, and author of *Training in No Time* and *Dual Ring Dog*. As we get older, we rely on more words and start to lose our nonverbal communication skills. And we seldom sit back and just look at what is going on. These are the very skills you will need if you want to know your dog and how she relates to you and her world.

Dogs aren't verbal, but their overall body position, their facial expressions, their ear and tail movements, and all sorts of sounds let other dogs and people around them know how they're feeling. "You can learn a lot about your dog by watching her," says Ammen. If you observe her and her body language, you'll soon know how things are with her. You'll even get to the point where you can tell what she'll be up to next.

Dog Watch

Some doggy signals are pretty universal and mean much the same whether the dog is communicating with a person or another dog. When a dog is play bowing, her rear end up, her front down and her tail wagging, you can be sure she is issuing an invitation, "Let's play," to whoever she's talking to.

Then there are the subtle differences among individual dogs. Sit back and observe your dog— watch how her posture changes, how she uses her ears, eyes, brows, lips, nose, mouth, tail and coat, advises Ammen. Also take a close look at how her body language changes, depending on her mood. Once you can work out how she expresses herself when she's happy, questioning, anxious, proud of herself, sleepy or whatever, you'll be able to "read" her.

"But don't assume you can 'read' a strange dog," warns Ammen. "Picking subtle differences in strange dogs is tricky, even for experts." A calm dog and a mildly apprehensive one can be easily confused, as can a dominant dog and an aggressive one. "To really grasp the nuances of canine body language, sounds and expressions, you need to be familiar with the breed's characteristics," says Ammen. If a dog's tail is low, for example, it generally means she's feeling insecure, but some sighthound breeds hold their tails this way simply as a matter of course. A Greyhound or a Whippet with its tail between its legs is probably feeling just fine.

These Labrador siblings are learning how to relate to one another during the rough-and-tumble of play.

What Her Body and Face are Saying

"Submissive dogs contract, while dominant dogs expand," Ammen explains. A frightened pooch makes herself as small as she can by moving everything inward. She shrinks slightly, tucks her tail, lays back her ears and averts her eyes. She may "surrender" by rolling over and exposing her belly. If she's so scared she wants to bolt for it, she'll pull back her lips and her weight will be back over her haunches.

A dominant dog makes herself seem larger by raising her hackles, carrying her tail straight out or up, and standing absolutely erect, says Ammen. She makes and holds eye contact and her mouth is usually closed. If the dog's body appears to be leaning forward (in contrast to an erect stance) and her ears point forward, she may be aggressive and about to attack. An aggressive dog may also have a hard stare, her mouth closed, top lip pulled up and bottom lip down to show lots of teeth, and a snarl that you'll *never* forget.

A relaxed pooch looks quite different. She wags her tail in a neutral position—not stiffly, or raised high or tucked under. Her mouth is often open, her ears are held half-back or relaxed, her weight is evenly distributed on all four legs, and there's no sign of tension or threat in her eyes.

Learning Her Vocabulary

Most dog owners know their dogs are capable of a variety of sounds: barks, whines, squeals, yelps and howls. But although dogs sometimes sound as if they are trying to talk, these noises aren't attempts to mimic our language, says Ammen.

Your dog knows that making a noise is a great way to get your attention, so of course she's going to use it to get you looking and listening her way. And dogs are not above using noises to

Do Dogs Smile?

"Sure, dogs can smile," says Judy Iby, a registered veterinary technician in Milford, Ohio. They generally use smiles on their human friends as a way of giving a delighted greeting. So how can you tell when your dog is giving you a grin? Her mouth will be relaxed and partly open, her eyes will have a happy gleam and her ears will be relaxed or held at half mast, depending upon what type of ears she has.

Some dogs have a special smile. Known as a submissive grin, it's an amusing expression in which the dog pulls her top lip up as high as she can, sometimes making her muzzle wrinkle. A few dogs can even give a half smile, Iby adds, by pulling up just one side of their upper lip.

A dog's toothy grin may be read as a snarl by a stranger, leaving the human terrified and the dog puzzled. "But there's a big difference between a smile and a snarl," says Iby. "Dogs usually bounce about or tap their feet in happy expectation when giving their best friends a grin. A snarler has a tense body and a hard, challenging stare."

manipulate and impress. Have you ever seen, in a two-dog household, how cleverly one dog can use sound and body language to invite her canine companion to come play, when he's snoozing in the best spot on the sofa? As soon as dog number two is on his feet, dog number one is jumping onto the sofa and snaffling the prime pooch position. Dogs will also often bark to distract an opponent, or they may whimper in fake surrender to throw another dog off guard.

"A growl, bark or whimper can mean different things at different times," says Ammen. As well as being terrific for getting noticed, a bark can signal alarm, happiness, frustration or surprise. In general, the faster and higher the bark, the more excited or agitated the dog. Growls can be deep and threatening, or more like moans of pleasure during a good back rub.

Listen to your dog and you'll soon know her verbal repertoire. "If you don't know the dog, don't take her owner's word that an alarming sound is actually harmless," cautions Ammen.

Visual Connections

Many people think that submissive dogs avert their eyes when you look at them, while dominant ones meet your eyes and stare straight back. But a dog may look directly at you, refuse to look at you or look sideways at you, whether she is feeling queen of canines or meek as a mouse.

When your dog stares at you, staring her down won't necessarily convince her that you're in charge, Ammen says. Besides, it's a mistake to assume that a stare indicates your dog is trying to dominate you. Sweet, submissive dogs often stare with melting adoration at their owners. To work out your dog's true intentions, you will also need to look at her facial expressions and at her body posture. It also helps to know

Relaxed but alert, with ears half-cocked, this German Shepherd mix knows she's on duty. Even when asleep, any strange noise will bring her to attention.

something about your dog's background.

So what should you make of intense eye contact? "It tells you the dog is interested in something that she may like, dislike or be afraid of," says Ammen. "If your dog is over-excited or she's easily distracted, pay close attention to her when she makes eye contact

The eyes of the Basset Hound puppy above are fixed on her owner in love and adoration.

elsewhere. She may be getting ready to pull on the leash, lunge, bark, attack or run."

Mixed Messages

You and your dog will probably have occasional misunderstandings, and sometimes you can misread dogs that you don't know too well. Not all dog messages have a single meaning. And dogs, like humans, give conflicting signals, sometimes by accident, sometimes not. "Contradictions will always exist among body language, eye contact, vocalizations, actions and actual intentions, in both humans and dogs," explains Ammen.

Watch your dog and note the mannerisms that precede excitable, fearful, silly or aggressive behavior. This will help you to anticipate sudden movements and to keep your dog under control if she gets excited. You will soon learn to interpret her feelings, and to know when she needs reassurance or to be kept from harm on a tight leash.

Why Does She Do That?

Your dog may be completely at home in your comfortable world, but not so many centuries ago, her ancestors probably belonged to a pack of wild, woolly canines living in the forest or out on the plains. From that world, she has inherited behaviors, such as submissive urination and rolling over belly up on the ground, that she still displays. These relate to her establishing her place in the pack pecking order, and to generally understanding and getting along in a world where the going was usually tough.

Dogs need a social structure with a leader and a clear pecking order. Every dog will act either submissive or dominant in relation to another dog or human. "Dogs can also be submissive around one person or dog and dominant around another," says Mary Burch, Ph.D., an animal behaviorist in Tallahassee, Florida, and author of *Volunteering with Your Pet* and *The Border Collie*.

For example, your dog may obey your every command but choose to ignore those that are given by your teenage child.

Contented Followers

Although the same dog is perfectly capable of being dominant in one situation and submissive in another, most dogs are born followers, says John Loomis, owner-instructor of Alibi Obedience and Agility Training School in Jacksonville, Arkansas. They don't really want to be boss. In fact, they are usually quite content to please their human family so that they can always get heaps of positive attention.

"While extremely submissive behavior involves shrinking and contracting, most well-behaved pets are submissive to some degree, although not to the extent such postures show," says Loomis. Your happy, submissive dog may follow you from room to room, stay fairly close to you when turned loose, and dote on your children. But if she's well socialized and has been consistently complimented during training, she'll also be brave if your family is threatened, provided being protective is part of her nature.

Going belly up like this mixed breed dog doesn't necessarily mean submission. She may be scratching an itchy back or inviting you to give her belly a rub.

Why Do Dogs Love Legs?

He's done it again. The whole family is gathered for the big annual reunion and your dog decides that now is a good time to start humping a leg—not a chair or a table leg, but one belonging to Aunt Emma. As you apologize and get him outside, you're going to be asking him, "Why?"

Rampaging male hormones are most often to blame. Dogs try to make love to legs out of frustration. They're also being dominant. "They don't have sexual inhibitions like humans do," explains Mary Burch, Ph.D., animal behaviorist in Tallahassee, Florida, and author of The Border Collie and Volunteering with Your Pet. *"So when the scent of a female dog in season wafts by and stimulates their libido, they settle for whatever is available. Since legs are close enough to the right height and width, many dogs will try to hump them."*

Neutering cures many males of trying to hump human legs and, by relieving their frustrations, makes them better pets in other ways, too, advises Dr. Burch. But if humping has been habitual, it may be a month or more after neutering before you notice a difference.

Submissive Urination

If your dog greets you happily but with a hint of shyness, while squatting and dribbling several drops of urine, don't assume that you have a housebreaking problem. "What you have is an anxiety problem," explains Loomis, and it's known as submissive urination. Be careful not to mistake it for something else.

Submissive behavior may be inherited, or it could have been caused by corrections that were too frequent or too harsh, or even by abuse that your dog suffered before you got her.

Among wolves in the wild, such submissive urination means, "Hi boss. I hope I didn't do anything to upset you, but if I did, I'm sorry." Though most common during a greeting, your pup may urinate in this way when you bend over to pick her up or when you chastise her. It's a conditioned reflex to dominant treatment and she isn't doing it on purpose. In fact, says Loomis, she's absolutely unaware of it.

Don't be upset with her because that will make things worse. Instead, make homecomings low-key. Silently toss a treat for your pup as soon as you come home, then ignore her until she approaches you. When she does, don't reach over her head to pet her. A very submissive dog will read this as an intimidating gesture. Instead, kneel down and give her a chest rub.

Better still, teach your puppy a few easy commands so she learns how to please you and earn praise, advises Loomis. Use a command such as "Stand, stay" when she greets you, so she can express her devotion to you in a non-submissive posture and earn your praise.

Who's Going To Be Boss?

A dominant dog may test her human family to see how high she can rise. A few actually reach the top and may aggressively demonstrate their dominance, says Dr. Burch. You can recognize them by their behavior. It's the dog that settles into her favorite spot on the sofa and growls if anyone tries to shift her. She's possessive of her toys or food bowl, and doesn't like it if anyone comes close. She barges through doors first, even steps on people to be first out to the car. Most dogs are born followers, but they need a social structure. So if no one in the human family takes the role of leader, the dog will fill the vacancy.

Demonstrating dominance isn't always a bad thing when it's in relation to another dog. If a friend visits with his dog, your dog will probably assert dominance. It's her house, her toys and her territory. It's normal for her to mount the other dog by standing over that dog's shoulders—that's how she lets her visitor know who is in charge. It's not unusual for the situation to be reversed when you take her to visit the other dog.

In the doggy world, sniffing out who's about is the way to keep tabs on the neighbors. When out for a walk, dogs seem compelled to leave little squirts of urine that can simply mean "This is my bit of ground" or "I was here."

Leaving Urine Messages

"Urine, or scent, marking is a characteristic of wolves and dogs and is often used to declare ownership of a territory," according to Carol Hopwood, a psychotherapist and the owner-instructor at Grizzly Dog Obedience School in Whitefish, Montana. When dogs are walked,

Dogs use play to establish the pecking order, but if no clear leader emerges, the game may escalate into a fight. Usually, one dog submits and the matter is quickly settled.

especially males that haven't been neutered, they sniff every tree, post and fireplug, looking for the scent marking of other dogs. And when they find one, they cover or add to the scent by urinating on it, to stake their claim. That's why a male dog leaves small spurts here and there instead of one big puddle—he keeps a little urine in reserve in case he wants to leave his signature on yet another upright object.

Not every dog that marks outdoors does it to establish territory or declare dominance. Many do it to get and leave information. "Marking is like leaving a calling card," Hopwood says. "It's how dogs read the newspaper." From what they sniff, they learn who was there before them, and by leaving their mark, they become headline news for the next dog passing by.

"Although it's usually considered a male trait, some female dogs also mark," explains Hopwood. "After all, they want to get in on the daily gossip, too."

Marking Inside

Urine marking can be a bit annoying but it's nothing to worry about, unless it starts happening indoors. Then, it's out of order. When male puppies stop squatting to urinate and begin lifting their legs like grown dogs, at anywhere between 6 to 12 or even 14 months of age, depending on the breed, they may decide to test their dominance by urinating on table legs, drapes or indoor walls. "These adolescents have not suddenly developed a housebreaking problem," explains Hopwood. "Dogs that urinate indoors are probably signaling they are boss and the area marked by their scent is their territory."

However, sometimes there may be a medical problem, such as a bladder infection, so have your dog checked by the vet right away. If you have him neutered, it will lessen his desire to dominate and his leg-lifting tendencies. Alternatively, work at giving him an attitude adjustment. There is no better way to handle a dominant dog than through obedience training, says Dr. Burch.

Signs of Aggression

You should never, ever, be afraid of your dog. Not for a minute. Not even for a heartbeat. Don't excuse or ignore any behavior that is threatening, not even if it ended quickly and without incident. Next time, her threat will probably be more forceful. And unless you do something about it, says Dr. Burch, there will always be a next time.

Some dogs display aggression as they reach puberty and try to establish their rank in the pack—your family. For example, your dog may recognize you as leader because you taught her to obey commands, yet still try to assert herself by growling at your spouse. That's the type of aggression that takes many people by surprise. The first time their dog growls a challenge at them, most owners are startled, but they try to rationalize their pet's behavior by saying, "She never did anything like that before." The truth is, she did challenge them before, says Dr. Burch. They just didn't notice the signs.

According to Dr. Burch, the first sign that your dog is vying for the position of pack leader or second-in-command is when she simply ignores a command. For example, you and your

This Border Collie is intent on something out of the ordinary. It's her job to alert her owner, so her stance is full of confidence, her eyes focused. She'll continue to bark until her owner assures her that everything is now okay.

spouse are setting out chips and dips in preparation for a party and your dog is underfoot and begging. One of you commands "Down," but she leaves the room instead. She's out of the way, which is what you wanted, so you don't bother to enforce the command and soon forget all about her minor disobedience. But she doesn't, explains Dr. Burch. After a few more unenforced commands, she'll test you at a higher level.

The next incident may occur a few days later. In a hurry to leave for a meeting, you reach down to pick up your dog's dish before she's eaten the last morsel. But you change your mind when she stands over the dish, her body rigid, her mouth closed and her eyes glaring into yours. "Okay, hurry up and finish it," you say, never realizing that you have just lost round two.

Round three will probably be a growl, says Dr. Burch. Startled and momentarily fearful, you'll finally realize that there's a problem.

Prevention is the best way to keep aggression from escalating, so socialize your dog well, and never urge her to be aggressive toward humans. While she's still a puppy, teach her to respond to commands, whether they come from you or

anyone else in the family, and use the commands during everyday activities: "Down" for petting, "Sit" for a treat, "Come" when it's time for dinner. And never give a command unless you are prepared to enforce it.

Your dog may be well-behaved for you but dominant or even aggressive with other dogs or strangers. Keep your eyes on her if she suddenly becomes alert and tries to make eye contact with an animal or a person. Defuse aggression by being confident, relaxed and softly spoken.

Stop your dog from concentrating on the object of her aggression by giving her a command, covering her eyes, or removing her from the situation. If she doesn't obey you, no matter what, obedience school is the answer. But why wait? Obedience school is also the best way to learn to train your dog and keep problems from occurring in the first place.

Fear Biting

In a frightening situation, any dog may bite, whether she's dominant or submissive, says Loomis. This usually results from mishandling a terrified dog. She's nervous and is trying to stop you from making her do something she is too scared to do. For example, if your dog cowers under the bed after a particularly loud thunder clap and you try to drag her out, she might snap. Instead, wait for her to calm down and emerge by herself. Don't punish a fear biter, advises Loomis. All you'll do is add to her terror. And check with your vet in case there's a serious reason for it.

You don't need a big dog to ward off intruders. Despite being small, this Jack Russell Terrier has more than her fair share of courage. This snarl is probably more nervous than aggressive, but it is still quite intimidating.

Reading Your Dog's Body Language

Dogs don't write poetry or speak in elegant sentences, but they can still be very eloquent. Here are some of the most common ways in which dogs express themselves, and what they are telling you by each particular behavior.

Play Bowing

When your dog is play bowing, her rear end goes up, her front end goes down, her tail wags like crazy and her eyes light up. She's saying, "I want to play," whether it's to another dog or to you. She may perform this friendly, attention-seeking maneuver when you're serious and she wants to change your tone. Accept her invitation to play if you're in the mood.

Tail Wagging

You're usually right if you assume that tail wagging indicates a friendly dog, but it's not always the case. Dogs also wag their tails when they are scared, agitated or unsure. A frightened dog may wag her tail low and between her legs as she weighs up her next move: "Should I fight, flee or go belly up?" An aggressive, angry dog may wag her tail high while she chases or even attacks. Look at what's going on—is the dog's best buddy just getting off the school bus, or is another dog eating out of her dish? Also check how the dog has distributed her weight, before being certain that the tail wagging is welcoming. If she's feeling aggressive, her body will be tense and the weight will be mainly on the front legs.

Rolling Over

When your dog rolls over on her back with her belly exposed and her legs in the air, she's being submissive. If done in front of another dog, she's saying, "You're the boss and I don't want to fight." When your dog rolls over for you, it could have more than one meaning. If done in anticipation of a scolding, it means, "I don't know how to please you and I'm afraid you're angry. Please accept my apology." Or she may be trying to avoid something she doesn't want to do. More often, rolling over is a sign that your dog is happy, trusts you and has a pleasant, submissive nature. It just means, "Please pet my belly."

This Samoyed is telling her owner, "You're the boss, I trust you implicitly and I will do my utmost to please you." Such behavior survives from when dogs traveled in packs, and were dependent on the leader of the pack.

Mounting

When your dog either mounts another dog or stands above another dog by putting her front paws on the other dog's back, she's saying, "I'm top dog and don't you forget it." Mounting other dogs isn't just a male characteristic, says Judy Iby, a registered veterinary technician in

Milford, Ohio, and author of *The New Owner's Guide to Cocker Spaniels* and *The Cocker Spaniel*. Dominant females do it, too. Owners wonder why male dogs mount other males or why females mount at all, but mounting is usually a dominance thing. It rarely has sexual overtones.

Humping

There's sexual intent in this behavior, even if the dog doing the humping is neutered. You can let them interact, as long as the subject isn't trying to hide (and, of course, providing your dog is not an unneutered male and the other dog a female in season). If he does it to a person, break his focus suddenly by making a loud noise to stop him in his tracks.

Tail Tucked and Ears Back

If your dog tucks her tail, lays her ears back, takes a few steps backward or hides behind your legs, you can be sure she's feeling apprehensive. It could be a person or an object that she's not sure of, and you'll need to gently lessen her fear by introducing her slowly and unthreateningly to what she's apprehensive about.

Tongue Flicking

If your dog repeatedly flicks her tongue up to lick her nose, she's uneasy, says Iby. She may be assessing a new situation or wondering if she should approach a guest. Or maybe she is concentrating hard to master a new obedience

This Golden Retriever may be listening intently, waiting for the next move in a game, or she may have discovered that this look is just too cute to ignore.

maneuver. While a dog may flick her tongue over and over and be friendly, don't approach a strange tongue flicker—the dog is obviously tense. Tongue flicking sometimes precedes biting.

Paw Lifting

If her lifted paw is accompanied by a relaxed, happy expression and a neutral position, your dog just wants attention. Maybe she's even been taught how to shake hands and she knows she can get positive attention that way. While paw lifting is most likely an invitation to play, your dog might be telling you something else. Maybe she has a burr between her toes or ice clumped around her pads that she'd like some help with.

Ears Back and to the Side

If a dog's ears are flat back, her head low and her eyes averted, she is afraid. If her ears are to the side and her brow is furrowed, she may be nervous. But if there are no wrinkles in her brow and her eyes don't seem worried, she may simply be a dog who holds her ears to the side when she's happy and relaxed.

Ears Pricked Up

Your dog is alert. She may be listening intently for your next command or the meow of the neighbor's cat. Pricked ears are also a sign of a well-adjusted, confident dog. But when combined with raised hackles, a stiffly erect stance and a penetrating stare, your dog is demonstrating dominance.

Getting Your Message Across

Dogs learn all about the meanings of sounds and body language when they're puppies by looking at their mom and littermates. So, your dog is going to get to know you by watching the way you move, by checking out your expressions and listening to the tone of your voice.

Body Language and Eye Contact

Your dog is naturally good at reading body language. Just test this by smiling, backing up a few steps and spreading your arms the next time you call her to come, and see how much faster she gets the message.

While most dogs are able to understand our body language, too much exuberance around pets can send them confusing or scary signals. "Don't talk baby talk to your dog or swoop down on her to pick her up or pet her," says Loomis. To the canine mind, swooping down from above is an extremely dominant gesture. If your dog looks a little leery when you bend over her, kneel down to her level and rub her chest rather than reach over her head to pet her.

The same goes for eye contact. Some dogs don't mind being looked straight in the eye, while others do. If it unnerves your dog, you'll know because she'll look away, wag her tail low and try to appear smaller.

Make eye contact with her briefly, and give her a gentle smile. Chances are she'll soon get used to human signals by watching you interact with family and friends. Then she won't care how you pet her as long as she gets attention, and she'll cheerfully return your admiring gaze.

Meeting Strange Dogs

Swooping down on a dog, bending over her, and making unwelcome eye contact should especially be avoided when meeting a strange dog, cautions Loomis. Improperly socialized dogs may take it as a threat or a challenge and answer with their teeth. If you want to make friends with a strange dog, make yourself inviting and nonthreatening by kneeling down at an angle to the dog and looking to the side of her, not directly into her eyes. Wait for her to come to you, then tickle under her chin or gently scratch her chest instead of raising your hand over her head.

When meeting a strange dog, be careful to take a nonthreatening position. Get down to her level and allow her to sniff your outstretched hand before touching or petting her. Then scratch her chin or chest to say hello.

PART TWO

Training

No matter what kind of dog you have, whether she's a young pup or an older dog, you can form a loyal and trustworthy partnership that lasts. All it takes is patience and a little practice.

5   STARTING FROM SCRATCH

pages 82–95
Dogs are natural students, so don't delay and start training as soon as possible.

6   BATHROOM BASICS

pages 96–103
With a few simple guidelines your dog will quickly understand where the bathroom is.

7   BASIC TRAINING

pages 104–121
To have a well-mannered and much-admired pet, teach her the basic commands.

8   ADVANCED TRAINING

pages 122–135
Once she has mastered the basics, you can encourage her to do graduate work.

9   CORRECTING UNWANTED BEHAVIOR

pages 136–167
A canine behavioral problem? Don't worry, there is an easy and practical solution.

5 STARTING FROM SCRATCH

Your dog is a loving and loyal creature by nature and wants nothing more than to please you. As soon as you learn how to harness his natural willingness, you can set about training him.

A Dog's-Eye View
pages 83–87
Get his view on learning, and you'll get training techniques that work for him and you

Leader of the Pack
pages 88–90
Take the lead in training and watch your dog follow

Rewards and Corrections
pages 91–92
Learn how to use these and you will get speedy results

Talking to Your Dog
page 93
Communicating effectively in doggy language is easy

Ready to Learn
pages 94–95
Young or old, your dog is ready to learn at any age

A Dog's-Eye View

Puppies are born with their eyes closed, they don't ask questions, and they don't get lessons from private tutors. They have to figure out the world the minute they take their first breaths.

Using their super-sleuth noses, puppies soon sniff out where mom keeps the food. All it takes is practice. Puppies are awkward and clumsy at first, but through trial and error, they pick up speed and sharpen their style. They get better each time they receive the goodies.

"When it comes to learning, if it feels good, dogs will do it," says John C. Wright, Ph.D., an animal behaviorist, professor of psychology at Mercer University in Macon, Georgia, and member of the adjunct faculty at the University of Georgia School of Veterinary Medicine in Atlanta. "If there's no payoff, they'll try something else."

How Dogs Learn

"Once their eyes are open, dogs learn in many ways," says Carol Lea Benjamin, a professional obedience trainer in New York City, and author of *Mother Knows Best: The Natural Way to Train Your Dog* and *Dog Training in 10 Minutes*. "They learn much as people do." Give your dog positive reinforcement, says Benjamin. "Most dogs want to make their owners happy." A reward helps them know that they've done the right thing, and you're pleased.

Dogs also learn to associate something they like with a particular object or behavior, says Benjamin. They do it naturally, without any for-mal training. For example, maybe you always feed your dog at the same time you run the vacuum cleaner. Try vacuuming when you're not going to feed him. He'll be drooling the minute the motor revs, and won't stop the fuss until he's fed. You've conditioned him to expect food as soon as the vacuum plug goes into the wall.

It's hard to believe that dogs notice these small details, but they're always watching what goes on around them. "Like their wolf ancestors who followed the leader of the pack, dogs pay attention to what their owners or the more aggressive pups in the litter are doing to pick up their cues," says Benjamin. So, if you dig in the garden, your dog will want to dig right beside you...only he'll be faster and messier.

There's yet another way that dogs unearth new knowledge. "Accidents happen," explains Benjamin. If your dog rubs up against the gate and it suddenly pops open, he's learned that he can get out of the yard. When you've got him back inside again, he'll remember the amazing opening gate and return to the scene of his last great escape, where he'll likely get pushy again.

It's not just the good times that your dog is going to store away for future reference. Unpleasant experiences have consequences too, says Deena Case-Pall, Ph.D., a psychologist and animal behaviorist in Camarillo, California. "Dogs remember the pain or displeasure they felt and avoid repeating the behavior."

This begins in puppyhood when a pup learns that mom's growl means "Keep your distance." If he ignores her warning, she'll give him a louder,

When your dog does something you tell him, a reward lets him know that he's done well. It can be something he likes to eat, a game, or simply pats and praise. It's a mighty motivator to get him learning in the fast lane.

meaner growl and snap at him for good measure, which usually works. Touching something hot, for example, will also be burned into his memory.

Reading Your Moods

If you train your dog when you're upset about something, he may not be as willing to work for you. "Often, dogs are reacting to our moods," says Dr. Case-Pall. "Some are more tuned in to us than others, which can affect their behavior."

In fact, owners often find that their dog's behavior—or misbehavior—mirrors their own moods. Have you been irritable? Very excited? Relaxed? A little down? Take a look at your dog. Is he running through the yard barking at everything that moves? Pacing back and forth in the house? Standing with his tail between his legs? You'll often find that your dog's behavior is an accurate barometer of how you're feeling that day. And since training works best when you're relaxed and confident, choose a time when you are not feeling stressed to work with him.

Different Breeds, Different Needs

Every characteristic of a breed, from the length of the coat to the width of the feet, is designed to help the dogs of that breed perform the task they were originally bred to do. So, different breeds have different personalities. A Miniature Dachshund doesn't look anything like a Poodle, nor does he react or learn in the same way.

When it comes to training, says Steve Aiken, the "Pet Shrink" on America Online and the owner of Animal Behavior Consultants in Wichita, Kansas, it helps to match your techniques and rewards to the natural passions and behavior of your dog's breed. "Since terriers were bred to dig out and kill underground rodents, it's natural that they will want to go excavating in your backyard," he says.

You don't have to like that instinct, he adds, but you can work with it. Let your dog know it's okay to dig—when you give permission. You can use his itch for a ditch as a reward after he's put in a good training session with you. Set aside a special area in the yard and hide something there in the dirt, then let him dig to his paws' content. Soon your eager beaver will be dragging you out to the yard so he can practice his heeling—and get the fun reward afterward.

To the terrier, dirt is a reward. But digging isn't as fun for a Portuguese Water Dog, bred to spend his life in the water. However, splashing in a creek or a wading pool is. Find out about the breed history of your dog and what his relatives did for a living. Match his rewards to this.

"If you have a mixed breed, look at the dog's body type for hints on what he might enjoy," says Dr. Case-Pall. If he resembles a Greyhound, reward him by letting him race around the house. Make a game out of it.

Consistency Counts

Dogs do their best learning when they know exactly what to expect. When you're teaching your dog the rules, you can't be wishy-washy. "The most common problem new owners have is not being consistent with either their training schedule or with telling their dog loud and clear what they expect him to do," says Tony Bugarin, an obedience instructor in Los Angeles.

If you're training your dog to heel, it's best to take him out every day for at least a half hour of practice, says Bugarin. "Don't go out three times the first week, skip the second week, then work only one time the third week." There are other ways of keeping things consistent.

Say the same thing. Your dog will learn faster when you're consistent with your commands. Give them in the same order when he's just starting out, and always use the same firm tone of voice. If you say "Stay here" one day and "Right here stay" the next, he'll be confused. Make a habit of calling his name first, then the command—it's a good way to grab his attention.

Set firm rules. Always be clear about what is and isn't allowed. If you let him get up on the couch one day and yell at him for doing the same thing the next, he won't know what to do the day after that. Dogs are not mind readers.

"Your dog will behave better if he can predict what can happen day in and day out," says Wayne Hunthausen, D.V.M., an animal behaviorist in Westwood, Kansas, and co-author of *Practitioner's Guide to Pet Behavior Problems*. "You'll get the best results that way."

Form a united front. Get everyone in the household to be consistent. "He'll feel more secure and apt to try new things if everyone follows the same plan," says Dr. Hunthausen.

Linking Actions to Commands

Imagine visiting a foreign country where you don't speak the language, and asking for street directions. If you thought the translation for "Turn right just before the bridge" really meant "Keep going straight over the bridge" you'd continue on ahead and never get to where you wanted to go.

Your dog can find himself just as lost and confused. You come home from work and he's jumping up all over you. You say "Sit!" but you don't make sure that he responds to your command. He then thinks the word "sit" means "jump all over me when I come home from work." He'll miss the correct meaning of the command altogether.

To make sure your dog does exactly what you want him to do, correct or reward him according to his response. "This shows your dog that his response matters," says Dr. Case-Pall. "He'll be more open to what is going on and the next

A happy dog is one who knows what you want him to do. Avoid mixed messages, let him know when he's got it right, and your dog will be devoted to you.

time will be even easier." Of course it's going to take practice if you're a beginner.

Timing is Everything

A dog can connect a word or reprimand only to what is happening at that moment. If you hesitate for even a few seconds, he'll get interested in other sights and smells and your window of correction opportunity has gone. Here's how to do it.

Match the word to the moment. Timing is really all about using the right word at the right time in response to your dog's action. He has to understand what he's done wrong—what you're correcting him about—and what you want him to do. If he's got that information, he can follow the directions correctly. It takes some practice, but if you act quickly, he'll learn almost instantly.

Read his mind. If you can be a few steps ahead of your dog and catch him before he misbehaves, you're really ahead of the game. Turn his potential error into his positive action in such a way that he thinks it was all his idea.

If you see your dog eyeing a piece of chicken sitting on the kitchen counter, anticipate one of two things happening. Either he'll try one giant leap for lean cuisine or he'll look around to see if you're watching. Be ready to reprimand him if he goes for the jump shot, or quickly reward him for not crossing the foul line. Dog training at its finest involves a little bit of reading and predicting the canine mind.

Correct Corrections

The best way to keep your dog on the straight and narrow is to correct him using praise, not punishment. You walk into the kitchen to find him moseying over to the garbage. Before he even has time to realize you're there, say his name. Then "Sit!" He does. What a good dog. Then say "Come!" And he runs over. Praise him lavishly. What a cute, clever, well-behaved dog. Pat him and play with him. He deserves it. He could take it all day. And he's learned that doing what you want him to do is where the good times are at—forget the trash.

Pile on the praise. "When your pup does what you want him to do, praise him immediately, using your happy tone of voice," says Dr. Hunthausen. "Using positive reinforcement will let your dog recognize he did the right thing, and build trust between you and him."

"Find out what turns your dog on or off—a rope toy, treats, a tennis ball, a hug, even dinner," says Dr. Case-Pall. "Use it to your advantage."

Don't be a pushover. When your dog does the wrong thing, just saying "No" works wonders, says Benjamin. "Many people are hesitant to tell their dog "No," but it has to be a small part of any dog-training program."

Catch him in the act. If he's in the middle of making a mistake, you can use something noisy to stop him in the act. Blow an air horn, use a motion-activated alarm that makes a loud sound, or put some pennies in an empty soda can and rattle them near the culprit the second he goofs. "The loud stimulus interrupts his behavior and gives him a chance to stop," says Dr. Hunthausen. Calling him to come to you in a happy, upbeat tone will also distract him from what he is doing. Remember to praise him lavishly for coming when you called.

Know when to ignore him. Another easy way to extinguish bad behavior while he's at it is simply to ignore it. If your dog steals your shoe and you chase him, he'll learn that it's a great way to attract your attention—not to mention

Do Dogs Really Recognize Their Names?

Even though people often spend days or even weeks coming up with the perfect names for their canine companions, it's very unlikely that dogs actually recognize their names—at least not in the same way that people do.

"Dogs don't have the same self-awareness that humans have," says Wayne Hunthausen, D.V.M., an animal behaviorist in Westwood, Kansas, and co-author of Practitioner's Guide to Pet Behavior Problems.

But because they hear their name every day—"Annabelle, it's dinnertime!" or "Sonja, get the ball!"—they soon learn that the sound of their name is a sign of nice things to come. For a start, they're getting attention, and that alone feels good. "No matter how old they are, dogs learn to respond to names in three days or less," says Deena Case-Pall, Ph.D., a psychologist and animal behaviorist in Camarillo, California.

How they respond to their name, of course, depends on your tone of voice when you call them. There's a big difference between a happy, upbeat "Sonja, come here!" and a stern "Sonja, did you eat those cookies?"

At the very least, your dog knows when she hears her name that you're trying to get her attention. And since she isn't applying for a credit card or expecting mail from Publishers Clearing House, that's really all a name has to do.

When training your dog, you have a split second to link everything together in his mind, plus squeeze in praise or a correction. Once he understands what you want, he'll try his utmost to please you and earn your praise.

lots of fun with you chasing him round the house—and keep doing it. If you don't react, he'll get bored and drop the shoe.

Respect his limitations. If you come home and discover the shoe in a million little leathery pieces, don't get mad. There isn't anything you can do after the fact, because he won't understand why you are angry. Just make sure your other possessions are out of reach next time.

Avoid the harsh correction. Physical punishment to "teach him a lesson" will only break the bond you have worked so hard to create with your dog. Hitting with either an object or your hand, chasing, yelling or rubbing his nose in unpleasant substances will only erode his confidence and may even change his personality for the worse.

Harsh correction may scare a dog so badly that he will become anxious and afraid. There are far better ways to correct him. And remember, you can never praise him enough for a job well done.

Leader of the Pack

In the dog world, you are either a follower or a leader. This pack mentality comes from dogs having wolves for ancestors. Wolves live in a pack and must rely on a leader to survive in the wild. Even if a wolf is not the head howler, he's an important link in the chain of command. It's the same for a dog. It doesn't matter if he's the only canine living with just one person, or if he shares space with other dogs in a large human household. His instinct is to find out where he stands in the hierarchy and to look for ways to move up a notch.

You're the Boss

It's cute, but definitely no accident when your dog sits on top of your feet. Or ignores you when you call him to heel, or grumbles when you insist he get off the couch. He's trying to show you that he's the boss and has the upper paw.

"These are mild signs of dominance," say Aiken. "A dog will try to be in charge. But if he can't, he'll be the follower because he sees himself as a member of a group." You have to make it clear from the very beginning that you're the one in charge of the household. If you don't, your dog will soon be doing more than just resting on your running shoes. He may start getting bossy with you and you'll be feeling like a guest in your own home.

Inconsistent messages from you will encourage pack behavior. "Dominance tension builds up when the owner is in charge one day but lets the dog be the leader the next," says Steve Lindsay, trainer and owner of Canine Behavioral Services in Philadelphia. If your normally obedient dog suddenly ignores your command to sit, and walks out of the room instead, don't let it slide. He will take this as a sign that your position can be challenged. Put him in his place firmly and consistently. And don't take your dog's behavior personally. He's not doing this because he's mean, but because he's been programmed to act in this way. You just have to make sure you don't let him get away with it.

Given half a chance, your dog will try to move up in the household's hierarchy until he thinks he's running the show. Unless you want to be sitting on the floor while he lounges about in grand style, you need to make it very clear to him, right from the start, that you're the one in charge.

"Without using force, you can easily guide your dog's pack behavior in a positive direction," says Lindsay. Act like the wolf leader who controls the food and feed your dog after you have finished eating. Wait until he's sitting obediently before you attach his leash to his collar and take him out for a walk. Lindsay also suggests playing follow-the-leader games with your dog, so that he knows where he is in the lineup.

"There are some dogs who don't like to be in charge and are very happy being number three, as long as they know that's where their place is," says Nicholas Dodman, B.V.M.S., professor in the Department of Surgery and director of the Behavior Clinic at Tufts University School of Veterinary Medicine in North Grafton, Massachusetts, and author of *The Dog Who Loved Too Much* and *The Cat Who Cried For Help*. Reinforce this position by letting the number one and two dogs enter the yard first or give dog number three more freedom in the house than the new puppy.

"Whatever the privilege, the owner must be the one to decide what it is and who gets it," says Dr. Dodman. Even if it's the front-row seat on your sandals!

Setting Limits

Rank has privileges and responsibilities. When you are the leader, no one tells you what to do. As leader, you need to set out the rules from day one so that your dog has someone to follow—unless he knows the rules, he won't be able to play the game.

"Dogs are creatures of habit who like to know what to expect," says Dr. Dodman. Giving him reasonable limits and sticking by them is the best thing you can do for your dog. When he knows how far he can go, he feels safe and secure and

The Small Dog in Charge

Cute, fluffy little dogs look like toys brought to life. They trot about in quick-step, jump up and down on you when excited, burrow into your neck when they're frightened, or hide in a corner of the room when someone unfamiliar enters. But no matter how amusing this behavior might seem, it's a sign of dominance and needs to be corrected.

Because of their size, some owners think they have to protect their small dog. Rather than correct his dominant behavior, they pick him up and cuddle him instead. This is exactly what the small dog wants. He may be the smallest family member, but he is the one calling the shots.

Don't let your small dog get away with behavior you wouldn't accept from a large dog. "Small dogs don't think they are small. They just act as any other dog would," says Steve Lindsay, trainer and owner of Canine Behavioral Services in Philadelphia. To prevent your dog from ruling the roost, don't reward this kind of behavior. When he jumps up on you or barks without stopping, don't pick him up. Command "Down" instead.

his confidence soars. "It's the dogs who are punished too harshly or given too much freedom that have problems," adds Dr. Dodman.

Taking Advantage

If you give in to your dog once, he won't forget it. See what happens if guests come to visit. Your dog barks and fusses and, instead of correcting him as you would normally, you give him a treat to quiet him quickly and graciously. Your dog will soon figure out that the minute company walks in your door, all he has to do is bark and you'll feed him.

Your dog gets away with more than most people do. He runs into you, sniffs your midnight snack and blocks your way to the bathroom. But you can prevent this by being clear about what is and isn't acceptable behavior, and by enforcing those limits. "A dominant dog will take more advantage of his owner and expect to get what

You are the one calling the shots. Your dog will be happy to please you and collect his reward. Let him know what it is you want from him. Be firm and consistent—if he doesn't know the rules, how can he play the game?

he wants when he wants it," says Dr. Dodman. If you let your dog walk all over you, he'll be running your life before you know it.

Taking Control

If your dog is dominating you, gather the leashes, set those boundaries and take back control. With a few corrections, it won't be long before your dog knows there will be no negotiating. The "no's" will be loud and clear.

For example, if your dog jumps all over you when you're getting ready to serve his dinner, make him take a seat and wait until his name is called. Do this every time for every meal and you'll have a well-behaved diner. Your dog will soon understand that he gets fed only when he does exactly what you say, when you say it.

First-Time Owners

One of the things that baffles new dog owners is how much of a correction to give. If you're too much of a softy, your dog will immediately trot all over you. If you overcorrect, he may become very cautious around you and not self-assured. Knowing when you're being too easy or too hard on your dog will take some trial and error, but don't give up. You'll soon find a level that is comfortable for both of you.

Decide in advance what your dog is capable of obeying and what you are going to feel comfortable correcting or ignoring. Be realistic in your expectations and consistent in your corrections. "Make sure you say what you mean and mean what you say," says Dr. Dodman. When you correct your dog, feel confident that you are doing the right thing by him. Remember, your dog needs guidance. By being firm and decisive with him, you are being kind and caring.

Rewards and Corrections

If someone told you to sit down and be quiet while you were in the middle of your favourite pastime, you'd think, "No way!" But if the person offered you a million dollars to do it, you'd plop yourself in a chair faster than you could say, "Show me the money." You can get your dog to obey just as readily but, luckily, it won't cost as much. You'll just need to know your dog's preferred reward, be it a tidbit, a toy, or a heartfelt, "Good boy!"

Food

If food is the way to your dog's heart, then use it for all it's worth when teaching him good manners. To inspire your food-motivated dog to park himself immediately, for example, attract his attention with dog food. You won't need a juicy steak—dry biscuits will work just as well if you've conditioned your dog to expect them.

The next time your dog has your left shoe for ransom, don't give chase. Instead, put some kibble into a metal cup, call him, then shake the container noisily. When he hears the clink, he'll drop the shoe and fly to you in a flash, especially if he knows you'll give him the yummies the minute he comes to you. "When both dog and owner can get what they want, it's a win–win situation for everyone," says Dr. Wright. "This elicits a happy mood while you're training him."

Toys

If food isn't important to your dog, use interesting playthings to grab his attention. Rubber shapes that make squeaky noises, tug or hug bears, rope tosses and even cardboard boxes and twigs are all tools of the trainer's trade. Try everything to see what will get the job done best.

For the chewer who obeys your "Down" command, give him something he can sink his teeth into the moment you tell him to get up. After your dog listens to your "No" command instead of jumping on the toddler at the park, take out a toy you've hidden in your pocket and wave it in front of him. "If your dog loves to play ball, a quick bounce when he does what you want him to works wonders," says Jill Yorey, training consultant at the Society for the Prevention of Cruelty to Animals in Los Angeles.

Attention and Praise

Other dogs care more about getting the attention of their owners and winning praise than they do about swallowing a tidbit or playing a game. Saying "What a good boy!" lets him know he's done what you've asked. It makes passing up the bone inside the trash can or standing still while getting his nails clipped all worthwhile.

"You are praising your dog's compliance with your wishes, so congratulate him as if it were his idea," says Dr. Wright. Gentle petting or a little scratch in just the right spot—behind his ears, on the chest or on top of the base of his tail—makes your dog want to go the distance for you.

"When it comes to training, you can never give your dog too much attention," says Sandy Myers, behavior consultant and trainer in Naperville, Illinois.

The Fine Art of Good Correction

With food, toys and kindness at your fingertips, dog training isn't a mystery. You just need to anticipate what your dog will do and seize the moment when he does it. If you correct him straight away and keep your corrections short, precise and positive, your dog will know right away what he did wrong.

"A correction must be only enough to startle a dog, not make him frightened," says Dr. Hunthausen. You should never use harsh techniques such as hitting, yelling or collar yanking. "These correction methods only damage the communication and respect you've tried so hard to build up between you and your dog," says Myers.

Ten Right Ways to Correct Your Dog

1 Build a good relationship with your dog before making any corrections.

2 Use a choke collar to make a correction— they make it easy to get his attention.

3 Use positive reinforcement.

4 Correct at the moment your dog makes a mistake, not a few minutes after.

5 Use food, toys, attention, praise or a combination of these to reward your obedient dog.

6 Be consistent with corrections.

7 Follow a correction with another opportunity for your dog to do it and get it right, and reward him when he does so.

8 Rattle a loud, noisy object or use a low tone in your voice to startle your dog just as he is about to do something wrong.

9 Use a collar and a leash when training outside.

10 Be comfortable correcting him around others.

Ten Wrong Ways to Correct Your Dog

1 Never hit your dog, either with your hand or an object such as a rolled-up newspaper or something he has chewed.

2 Never shout at your dog or blame him for not obeying your command.

3 Never chase after your dog.

4 Never corner your dog.

5 Never jerk your dog's leash upward. This could injure his neck.

6 Never leave your dog locked up in a small dark room.

7 Never punish your dog for doing something you did not see him do at that precise moment.

8 Never withhold food or water from your dog for long periods of time.

9 Never do anything anyone, including a trainer, tells you to do that you don't feel comfortable doing.

10 Never rub his nose in messes in the house.

Talking to Your Dog

Whisper your dog's name and watch him perk up as he recognizes it. But apart from his name, most of the words you use will sound Greek to him. That is, until you teach him to associate specific words with specific meanings. He will be able to understand what you say to him if you base your commands on his language. If you're comfortable talking happy dog talk, he'll be a joyous worker. Add your own different tones, emotions and movements, and you're ready to start training.

Attitude

The most successful training happens when you are enthusiastic and confident that what you're doing is right for you and him. "He'll try to copy you as much as he can, so being in a good mood will definitely affect him," says Myers. Don't doubt your own judgment when giving corrections, because your dog will sense your indecision. "If you're confused about what he should be doing, he'll be scratching his head, too."

Tone of Voice

"The pitch of your voice plays a big part in teaching your dog what you want him to do," says Janice DeMello, an obedience trainer in Somis, California. "It's not what you say but how you say it that counts." When you're excited and praise him with a light, upbeat tone, it reminds your dog of the whiny sounds he makes when he's excited. "Don't get too high-pitched

because that irritates most dogs, but don't let your voice go too deep either," says DeMello. With commands, it's okay to bark orders, because that's the range of tone your dog understands—matter-of-fact and filled with authority. To correct, keep the tone low, like a growl.

Emotion

"You have to keep your emotions out of training," says Myers. "When you're happy your dog did well, it's okay to be exuberant, but that's the only time." Negative feelings hinder productive training sessions. If a dog doesn't respond to your command there is no point in getting angry. Yelling and screaming will just scare him and make him feel insecure. Since he can't figure out why you're mad at him, he may repeat the act, or he might just shut down and do nothing.

Movement

Your dog is a constant meter-reader, registering everything about you—your body language, facial expression, and what your hands and legs are doing. If it moves, your dog watches it. This is how he guesses what will happen next. Where your body is in relationship to your dog is particularly important when you're training. If you tell your dog to "Stay" and move forward, it is likely that he will move forward, too. But if you stay, he will get the idea of what you want him to do from your behavior. The key to making all the right moves is to use all of your skills—body language, tone and attitude—and match them with the correct word commands.

Ready to Learn

Dogs can be trained at any age, but the best results are usually achieved with puppies. So start teaching your dog as soon as you bring him home. Dogs need routine and are keen to please their owners, so you should find yourself with an eager student. But remember, training takes patience and persistence—shortcuts won't get you anywhere.

Training Puppies

Puppies are learning all the time. "They're capable of doing anything from seven to eight weeks," says Amy Marder, Ph.D., animal behavior consultant to Angell Memorial Animal Hospital in Boston, and pet columnist for *Prevention* magazine. "Maybe they can't do perfect heels, but they can learn to sit at that age."

Coordinating their body parts is another story. "Puppies aren't very agile at that age," says Dr. Marder. So forget perfection and focus on play training. Since young pups are curious about everything, seize those moments to begin your lessons. If you're out in the yard together and a sudden breeze sends a leaf fluttering toward you, your puppy will naturally scamper after it. Tell him, "Get it, get it!" and when he catches it say, "Good puppy!" You've given his chasing a name that you can use again later when you want to teach him how to retrieve.

You can also train your puppy to "Come" long before he's four months old. Whenever you set his food dish down, call his name over and over again in an excited, happy voice—"Puppy, puppy!" After a few times he'll come flying to you when he hears this familiar call.

But it's important not to go overboard with a new pup. "Keep your other training sessions brief, perhaps several five-minute sessions a day," says Sharon Crowell-Davis, Ph.D., professor of veterinary animal behavior at the University of Georgia in Atlanta. "Puppies have a much shorter attention span than older dogs, and they'd rather play," she adds. You want to make training sessions a treat, not a chore, for your pup.

The Older Dog

Don't believe that you can't teach an old dog new tricks. Dr. Crowell-Davis says the only difficulty in training older dogs is having to untrain incorrect behavior they've already learned. "If you're teaching a new behavior, your older dog should pick it up right away. By age six to seven, a little earlier in larger breeds, a dog is in the prime of life and has the best attention span."

Some dogs older than eight become less responsive to commands. They still want to learn but lack the energy. Their reactions may slow down and their memory may be fading. If your new dog is a senior, have your veterinarian evaluate his health before beginning his training program.

Training Techniques for All Ages

Use the same training techniques with puppies as you do with older dogs. They work because no matter what the age, dogs want to please you and be rewarded. "Always use positive reinforce-

such as Bloodhounds, Labrador and Golden Retrievers, will probably be much better at learning how to lie down on command.

If you want quick results, match the tricks with the right dog. A Golden Retriever has been bred to fetch wildfowl, so teach him to bring back a ball. Don't bother him with sled dog racing. But if you want a challenge, try training a Chow Chow, whose ancestors were guard dogs, to bring back a dumbbell in record time. It's likely he will act as if it's beneath him to fetch anything. "If one dog excels in one area, he may not be quite so good in another," says Dr. Crowell-Davis.

Training a dog takes patience. It's important to remember that dogs have different strengths and weaknesses and they do not all learn at the same speed.

ment and if you need more help with an adult, try a choke chain for training," says Dr. Marder.

Different Learning Speeds

Every breed of dog has been bred to perform different tasks, and this affects how fast your dog will be able to learn. "There are real differences in the breeds' anatomy, the senses and natural levels of motivation," says Dr. Crowell-Davis. A narrow-chested dog, such as a Saluki, is extremely fast and has remarkable sight. He will have a hard time lying down and staying there, but if you ask him to run after an object he will be able to do that in a flash. More sedentary dogs,

Fast Learners

To discover which dogs are the easiest to train, a study of 56 of the most popular breeds was conducted by Benjamin Hart, D.V.M., Ph.D., a professor in the Department of Anatomy and Physiology at the University of California in Davis, and Lynette Hart, D.V.M., Ph.D., a sociologist and director of the Human-Animal Program at the University of California in Davis.

Shetland Sheepdogs, Shih Tzus, Miniature, Toy and Standard Poodles, Bichons Frises, English Springer Spaniels and Welsh Corgis are among the top pupils at training school.

Labrador and Golden Retrievers, Hungarian Vizslas, Brittany Spaniels, German Shorthaired Pointers, Newfoundlands, Chesapeake Bay Retrievers, Keeshonden, Collies and Australian Shepherds are also very trainable but react more slowly than the first group. A third group of medium to highly trainable dogs include German Shepherds, Akitas, Doberman Pinschers and Rottweilers.

6 BATHROOM BASICS

Whether she is just a young puppy or a more mature dog, good bathroom habits should be established from the first day you bring your new pet home. Because a dog is naturally a clean animal, once you get your message across, she'll be only too happy to oblige.

House-Training Puppies
pages 97–101

Puppies learn from their mothers, and since you have stepped into mom's shoes, it's up to you to take over the house-training

House-Training Adults
pages 102–103

Sometimes you might need to house-train an adult dog. Set about training her as you would if she were a puppy

House-Training Puppies

Bringing home a puppy means lots of fun but also lots of mopping up. Housebreaking is usually the first thing on the training list for new puppies and teaching her that your hardwood floors and Oriental carpets are not her personal restroom can be a challenge. A first-time owner might think his puppy has a plumbing problem, but usually it's just a case of her being in the wrong place at the wrong time. Once you teach her the bathroom basics, she'll quickly get the idea.

Natural Instinct

Dogs are naturally clean animals, following in the house-proud tradition of their ancestors, the wolves. They'll not dirty their eating or sleeping area, and their mothers teach them from day one how to be clean—and not just behind the ears.

"If you follow this instinct for cleanliness when your new puppy comes home, your pup can be house-trained within 48 hours," says Dennis Fetko, Ph.D., an animal behaviorist in San Diego and host of "Animal Talk with Dr. Dog" on KFMB radio in San Diego. This takes some pretty intensive working with your pup, and you might not be able to spend this much time with her. Using the same philosophy but working more slowly, you'll get the same result.

Starting Right Away

"If you take a preventive approach with your puppy right from the beginning, you'll be far more effective in your house-training," says Scott Line, D.V.M., an animal behaviorist at the Golden Valley Humane Society, and staff veterinarian at the University of Minnesota Veterinary Teaching Hospital in Minneapolis.

When you bring your puppy home at eight weeks, she is ready to learn that there is a time and a place for everything. "It's the optimum time to establish good bathroom habits," say Dr. Fetko. Your puppy wants to make you happy and, despite an accident here, there and everywhere, she will try hard to fit in with her new human owners, who already know how to use the lavatory.

The One-Stop Toilet Spot

It's easiest for your dog if you assign one particular area as her toilet spot. In most cases, this will be somewhere in your yard. For apartment dwellers this will be paper spread thickly on one area of the floor.

When dogs relieve themselves, they release scent chemicals that are passed with the waste. These are called pheromones, and when dogs smell them later on, they trigger a reflex that makes them want to eliminate again. This is why it's a good idea to take your puppy to the same place each time. The odor also lets other dogs know that this patch of ground is taken.

Your dog won't let this idea fade, either. She will keep freshening up her scent by going back to the same spot over and over again to relieve herself. "That is why you'll want to control the routine as much as possible," says Dr. Line.

Toilet Routines

Knowing when your puppy needs to relieve herself is the key to house-training. Puppies will always need to go first thing in the morning, last thing at night, when they wake up from a nap, when they leave their crate, after finishing a meal or after a playtime. If you establish a routine and keep your eye on her, you'll know exactly when she wants to go.

So, when you see her lick her lips after polishing off her dinner, it's time to visit her toilet spot. Take a walk with her to the area you want her to always use. If you are outside, don't leave your puppy there on her own—you're going to have to share the early morning chill with her to make sure she finishes what she set out to do.

Your pup may not go straight away when you get to the spot. "Once they're outside, puppies like to investigate and soon forget what they came out to do," says Janice DeMello, an obedience trainer in Somis, California. This explains why you can be outside for an hour waiting for your puppy to use the facilities, and the minute you come back in the house she piddles on the kitchen floor.

DeMello suggests hooking your puppy's three-foot leash to her before going into your yard. "Keep the puppy in one area on the leash and tell her, 'Get busy.' When she's bored checking out the spot, she'll proceed with the task. Then you can take the leash off."

When your puppy is successful, let her know she's done well. Praise her, pat her gently and bring her back inside the house. Never reward your puppy with food for eliminating outdoors. It just jump-starts her system all over again. If, after an hour, your puppy still hasn't eliminated, you can take her back inside the house, but don't let her run loose. Put her inside her crate where she won't make any messes.

Crate-Training

Putting your dog in a crate may seem cruel, but it's actually one of the kindest things you can do for her. This will be a cozy spot all of her own where she sleeps, rests and gets away from it all. And it is an excellent way to keep tabs on what she's up to. There's no worry she's going to destroy the place when she's home alone.

Tips for Full-Time Workers

Trying to house-train your new dog when you are at work five days a week can be difficult. It will take a little longer than if you were supervising all day, and you may have to juggle your schedule a bit, but it can be done.

Get up a little bit earlier in the mornings so you have some extra time before you leave for work to take your pup out in the yard once or twice.

Choose a safe area in your home where you can leave your pup while you are gone during the day. The kitchen, bathroom or laundry are the easiest rooms to puppy-proof and they can usually be blocked off from the rest of the house with a baby gate. Put her crate, some toys and a water bowl close to the gate, and spread some newspapers down on the floor at the back of the room.

Until she is six months old, someone will need to come and feed your puppy at lunchtime and take her outside afterward. If you don't have family or friends who can help, hire a puppy sitter to come by.

Since dogs won't soil where they sleep, a crate is indispensable for house-training. "Introduce the puppy to the crate gradually," advises Suzanne Hetts, Ph.D., an applied animal behaviorist in private practice in Littleton, Colorado. Tempt her inside by throwing in a few puppy biscuits, then let her explore. Praise her when she peeks in to retrieve the food but don't be in a rush to shut the door. Call the puppy out and praise her, then toss another biscuit in and praise her when she goes inside. Repeat the process until she goes in and out on her own.

Once your puppy seems confident about going into her crate, try closing the door for a short period. Open the door and compliment her again. When she goes back in, put an assortment of objects—a soft blanket, a brightly colored toy, some chew bones—into the crate to keep her company. You can even feed her dinner in there but don't allow whining or barking after she's done eating. "If it fits, put the puppy's crate near your bedroom so you can hear her when she wants to go outside at night," advises Dr. Hetts. And remember that the minute she's let out of her crate, the two of you have an appointment with the toilet spot.

"In the beginning, you don't want to crate a young puppy for more than three hours at a time," says Dr. Hetts. "Leaving a ten-week-old pup confined all day is totally inappropriate." And it should never be used as a

A Poor Punishment

Although it is a commonly heard piece of advice, holding your dog's nose to her feces is cruel and unnecessary. "You wouldn't rub a baby's diaper in her face, so don't do the same thing to a dog," says Dennis Fetko, Ph.D., an animal behaviorist in San Diego and host of "Animal Talk with Dr. Dog" on KFMB radio in San Diego. In any case, although your puppy will recognize that it's her mess, she won't be able to understand that she created it in the wrong place.

You want to punish the behavior, not the dog. Studies show that if there is more than a three-second delay between the naughty act and the the effectiveness of the punishment drops off. If you catch your dog eliminating in the house, you'll have more success taking her outside right away and praising her for going there.

punishment—your puppy's crate should be a place where she likes to spend time. Vary the objects you put in her crate so she looks forward to going there. Once your puppy is four months old, she can spend five hours in her crate after she has been exercised.

Paper-Training

Maybe there's a blizzard the week after you get your new friend

If you get her used to her crate kindly and gently, she'll soon come to regard it as her own special place.

home. Or she's a small dog who needs to go to the bathroom more often than a larger dog. Or you live in a high-rise building and you know that taking the elevator down 15 floors every time your dog needs to go is simply not feasible. Perhaps it's just that your schedule won't allow for such frequent trips outside. You may have to paper-train her.

Paper-training works because it lets your dog know that there is a special place in the house

you want her to use as her bathroom when she can't get outdoors. To teach her where this spot is, spread several layers of the newspaper over a large plastic sheet on top of the floor (don't put it on top of the carpet). Leave a slightly soiled paper underneath the fresh paper pile so she knows that this is place you want her to go. As the days progress, make the paper area smaller. When the time comes to move her bathroom training outdoors, take along one of her soiled papers for the first day or two. It will take some time for her to feel comfortable in the new environment and having the familiar scent will ease the transition.

Paper-training should be used only when you can't go outside with your pup. It should not be the first step in the house-training process. "You will be rewarding the dog for eliminating in the house, but you will still have to train her later to go outside," says Dr. Fetko. Whatever the difficulties, your pup should be introduced to the toilet in the great outdoors at least once in her first week or two at home.

Preventing Accidents

In the house, keep your puppy in your sight at all times, suggests Dr. Hetts. This way you'll minimize the number of accidents she has and she won't have a chance to develop preferences for going in areas that you consider off limits.

If you pick up the mess as soon as she makes it, your puppy will realize it's much nicer to be clean than it is to be dirty. Most dogs don't want to walk through urine any more than people do.

Training your puppy to go to the bathroom on newspapers may be a necessity if you don't have quick access to the outdoors, but only use it as an interim measure.

Handy Hints for Removing Stains

It's one thing for your dog to make a mess, but another when you can't get the stain out of the new carpet. Luckily, there are a number of cleaning products that have been created for this specific purpose. Some are colorless and odor neutralizing, and all will safely remove these types of stain. Commercial products made from concentrated orange peel work very well. You can also try adding a quarter of a cup of white vinegar and a few teaspoons of liquid laundry detergent to a quart of warm water. Spray the soiled area with this solution and let it sit for a few seconds before rubbing it in. Dry with a towel.

Sometimes it's impossible to give your puppy your undivided attention. "If you can't watch her, confine her to a safe area such as the laundry room or her crate," suggests Dr. Hetts.

You should also be careful not to overfeed your pup—the more she eats and drinks the more chance she has to mess up. Feed her a well-balanced commercial dog food on a regular schedule of three meals a day. Water should be offered three to five times a day. This builds a steady appetite and regulates your dog's digestion. "Avoid leaving the food out all day if you want to house-train your puppy quickly," says Patrick Connolly, D.V.M., a veterinarian in private practice in Thousand Oaks, California.

Caught in the Act

If you catch your puppy with a piddle in progress, create a commotion that will startle her. This could be clapping your hands, stomping your foot or shaking some keys. When she stops to listen, pick her up and take her to the right location. As soon as she completes her business, praise her lavishly. You should never yell at her, or hit her with your hand or a rolled-up newspaper. This will only teach her not to urinate when you can see her, and she'll go behind your back instead.

Common Problems and Solutions

Despite her best intentions, your pup may have a relapse and forget what she's learned. Just patiently repeat the process and it should all come back to her. It's not always possible to watch your dog carefully, especially when you're busy during the day. As a result, more accidents occur than would normally, according to Dr. Line. "Just try to not give your puppy opportunities to mess up in the first place," he says.

For pups who consistently use the wrong spots indoors, such as the bedrooms, stairs or the living room carpet, Dr. Fetko recommends feeding your dog in those locations. Dogs will not soil where they eat.

Another pet in the house, a new baby or a visitor can throw your dog's bladder control off. This is a sign of insecurity and can be prevented by giving her extra attention during this time.

Some dogs leak a little urine when you bend to pet them. "This isn't a house-training problem, but over-submissive behavior," says DeMello. A dog does this to show submissiveness to more dominant dogs or people in her human pack. If your dog is a submissive wetter, don't punish her as it will just make the problem worse. She needs more confidence. Obedience or agility training will help provide this.

House-Training Adults

If you welcome an adult dog into your home and she isn't house-trained properly, forget paper-training and go straight to the outdoors. Train her the same way you would a puppy—by routine and prevention. The only difference between an untrained adult dog and a puppy is that an adult dog can hold her bladder for much longer.

Take your adult dog to the same spot outdoors morning, night and after meals, and wait with her while she does her business. When she's indoors, keep your eye on her as much as possible. If you catch her sniffing about or just about to go, make a loud, distracting noise and take her outside. When you can't watch her, confine her to a small space, such as a crate, the laundry or bathroom.

New Home, Old Smells

If you bring a new adult dog to your home and you owned a dog before her, you might not be aware that your first dog leaked some urine on the carpet here and there, which soaked through to the padding underneath.

Despite your best house-training efforts, your new dog will be attracted to the odor only she can detect, and will think it's okay to use the living room rug as her bathroom. Inexpensive UV lights available at hardware stores can reveal urine spots you can't see but your dog can smell—under the lights they will glow bright green. To convince her that the carpet is off limits, keep her out of that room and call in a professional carpet-cleaning company to steam clean the carpet and replace the padding underneath.

Moving Confusion

A move to another house can sometimes confuse your adult dog. She hasn't established her scent there yet and may want to mark her territory by

Give your new adult dog plenty of opportunities to leave her calling card around the neighborhood by taking her for a walk at least four times a day. She'll soon get the idea that outdoors is the place to relieve herself.

Why Do Male Dogs Lift Their Legs?

Trees, walls, car tires and fence posts are just a few of the landmarks male dogs love to spritz. Take them for a five-mile walk and they'll happily lift their legs at every tall object along the sidewalk.

Although some males do it more than others, depending on their own testosterone level, it is a universal trait among male dogs. "It's just what they do," says Karen Martin, D.V.M., a veterinarian in private practice in Thousand Oaks, California. "They're males trying to impress other males and it's their way of saying, 'This is mine and that is mine and so's this. In fact, this whole street belongs to me, so stay away.' It's a kind of canine gang graffiti."

Lifting the leg is both a learned and instinctive posture, says Scott Line, D.V.M., an animal behaviorist at the Golden Valley Humane Society, and staff veterinarian at the University of Minnesota Veterinary Teaching Hospital in Minneapolis. Often pups see other males lifting their legs and copy the behavior, but a single male puppy will do this even if he's never seen another male in the act.

urinating in all the wrong places. If this becomes a persistent problem, put her food dish next to her favorite new spots. Dogs don't like to soil the places where they eat and sleep.

Occasional Mistakes

Sometimes a dog you've owned for years may suddenly have an accident in the house. Perhaps she was too distracted or excited when she was outside to concentrate on going to the bathroom. Maybe she wanted to get back in for her dinner or to greet a special visitor. Unless the act is repeated, consider it an isolated incident. If it continues, retrain her as you did when she was a puppy.

If visitors bring an adult dog over to play with your dog, this might trigger a urinating contest in the house and your dog may be prompted to return to those spots long after her playmate goes home. If possible, let the games stay outdoors. Don't let the visiting dog inside the house unless you can watch both dogs constantly, or they are crated.

Getting Older

Your senior dog is starting to leave puddles around the house. She's normally so fastidious, but now that she's getting on in years she's becoming a little incontinent and can't always wait to get outside to use the restroom.

The best thing you can do is to quietly mop up the mess and visit the vet for a checkup. If she could help it, she wouldn't be doing it, so this is not the time to reprimand her.

"There are several medical problems that might cause this," says Karen Martin, D.V.M., a veterinarian in private practice in Thousand Oaks, California. These include diabetes, gall stones, urinary tract infection and, more commonly, memory loss. "It's wise to have the dog evaluated by a veterinarian and be in a position to make choices regarding treatments or changes in diet that can help."

7 BASIC TRAINING

Every dog needs to be taught basic good manners. Not only does this ensure his safety and give you peace of mind, it also provides the framework for further training, allowing him to fulfill his canine potential.

Teaching Old Dogs New Tricks
page 118
Don't despair—you can correct bad habits in an older dog

Get into Training
pages 105–107
It's your job to make the rules and let your dog know what they are

Tasty Rewards
page 111
Edible treats will attract your dog's attention, but don't let him put on weight

Training a Therapy Dog
page 119
A well-behaved dog can work miracles visiting the sick and elderly

Leash Training
pages 108–110
A collar and leash will help your dog follow in your footsteps

The Five Basic Commands
pages 112–117
These five commands are the foundation of training, so teach them as soon as you can

Professional Training Schools
pages 120–121
If you need it, professional help is at hand

Get into Training

When you take your dog out in public and he walks confidently by your side, it's impressive. When he sits and stays on command, strangers will admire him and you will feel proud to be his owner. It's much easier for you, too, if your dog can take a trip to be groomed, boarded or to receive medical care all in his stride, and he can pass other dogs along the sidewalk without causing a commotion. You want a dog you can enjoy, and a confident, well-behaved dog is a lot of fun. On the other hand, a dog that constantly disturbs the peace and nearly knocks you over can be a challenge to live with.

It would be nice if all dogs were well-behaved right from the start. But dogs need to learn what you want them to do and not do. They need to be trained, and that's your job.

The rules for good canine manners are simple. Dogs should be quiet and not bark or howl at the neighbors. They should wait patiently, instead of jumping all over guests who come to visit. Respecting your possessions by not chewing them up is a good thing, too. A well-behaved dog will stay put when asked and come to you when you call his name. If the front door swings opens, he will watch the world go by, instead of running to catch it. At the dinner table, he will know to lie low instead of begging for leftovers.

Training is easy and rewarding—no fancy tricks or superdog intelligence are required. Just make a point to work with your dog on a

Make Your Dog a Canine Good Citizen

Your dog may not be able to vote, but he can still be a good, well-behaved citizen. So says the American Kennel Club (AKC), which designed the Canine Good Citizen Program for both purebred and mixed breed dogs. The program fosters responsible dog ownership by teaching and testing dogs' manners, but it is not a competition or a precision event. Besides being a good bonding activity for dogs and their owners, dogs can earn the AKC official title of Canine Good Citizen (CGC). Contact a local AKC office for more information.

The ten-step test includes sitting and staying in place, coming when called, letting a friendly stranger approach and pet him and walking through a crowd on a loose leash. His reactions to other dogs and to distractions are also evaluated.

regular basis, and don't give up until he does exactly what you want him to do.

When to Start

It's good to teach your new dog the rules of your house before he starts making his own. Training should start as soon as his paws first paddle through your door. If you bring home an adult dog, he may already know the basic commands of sit and stay. But he is not a mind reader and you will need to tell him when you expect him to do these things. This is what you can teach him as soon as he joins the household. If you want, you can also train your dog to obey more advanced commands, such as to retrieve, sit up, and walk through an obstacle course.

Most puppies go to their new homes at between seven and eight weeks of age and they, too, should be trained right away. Why wait until they are older, when you can prevent a bad habit from forming? While you can't expect a puppy to learn the advanced stuff right away, you can begin to lay the foundations.

How Often Should You Train?

Be consistent and spend some time training your dog every day, even if you have only a few minutes. Some people think that a dog will get tired and bored if you train him every day. That won't happen if you make your training sessions short and fun, and give him plenty of praise and rewards when he performs correctly.

A daily training routine builds good learning habits and gives him a chance to practice and perfect what he's learned earlier. As well as specific training sessions, find opportunities throughout the day to incorporate what he's learned. For example, once he understands "Sit," make him sit before you feed him or put his leash on when you take him for a walk.

By reinforcing the training in this way, his new behavior will soon become a habit. Your dog will be eager for opportunities to practice what he's learned because he wants to show off what you taught him the day before and get his treat.

How Long Should a Session Last?

Keep your training sessions short and sweet. Sessions that last between 10 and 20 minutes will work better than drilling out commands that go

Puppies have short attention spans and tire easily, so keep your training sessions short and sweet. Never persist in training a puppy if he becomes bored or distracted.

on and on. For a puppy, the training times should be shorter, say sessions of 3 to 5 minutes spaced throughout the day, with at least a half-hour break in between.

"The more often you can do it for shorter periods of time, the better the results," says Dan Estep, Ph.D., an animal behaviorist in Littleton, Colorado. "Three hours one day a week doesn't work as well because your dog gets tired and bored after just 30 minutes."

Shorter but more frequent training sessions will also fit in better with your schedule. If you suddenly find you have a spare ten minutes, you can use this time to work in an extra training session with your dog.

Because different dogs learn at different speeds, one session might be all you need to teach your dog one command. You can use other sessions that day to review what your dog has already learned, then go on to something new. Since there are five basic commands for your dog to learn, you won't run out of activities. Or it may be that he needs the same lesson repeated three or four times a day until he gets the idea. Just remember to stay flexible and remain upbeat. You want your dog to enjoy his training times, not to dread them.

Where to Train

Just as you wouldn't be able to concentrate in a noisy room if you were trying to understand a math lesson, your dog won't be able to learn under distracting circumstances, either. When teaching commands such as "Sit" and "Down," start your instruction in a quiet environment. Choose an area of the house where no other family members will be wandering in and out and a time when you won't be interrupted.

The Release Word

Your dog needs to learn one word that lets him know that school's out and that he can break from the position he was told to maintain. This magic word, which your dog wants to hear you say more than anything else, will mean, "You can relax now, you've done a good job training and you can come for praise."

The release word doesn't have to be anything special. In fact, most trainers use the very ordinary word, "Okay." But there are disadvantages to using "Okay" as a release word, says Dan Estep, Ph.D., an animal behaviorist in Littleton, Colorado. "People use it so often in regular conversation that your dog might not think it's magic."

Pick a word your dog isn't going to hear very often in regular conversation, suggests Dr. Estep. "Something like 'Bananas' works just as well." As long as you feel comfortable saying it and there's a happy, upbeat tone to it, you can use whatever word you want.

When you start teaching him to walk on a leash, you will need more space, so move to an outside area that has few distractions, such as your backyard or a quiet street or park.

"In the beginning, try and make things as easy as possible, then gradually add new and busier surroundings," says Dr. Estep. Once your dog obeys your commands in the house, take him to new and interesting areas, such as your garage or a neighbor's house, to work with him.

"These diversions are a good test," says Dr. Estep. But don't be surprised if at first he acts as if he's forgotten everything. It may take a few tries before he can ignore what is going on around him, but he will. And once he follows your commands, put him through his paces in even more challenging places, such as a shopping center, schoolyard or on a crowded sidewalk.

Who Should Train?

When you ride in a car, only one person at a time can sit behind the wheel. The same is true when training a dog. The person who will be spending the most time with the dog, and therefore needs to be in control of him the most, should be given the primary responsibility for training him, recommends Dr. Estep. That person can then show other members of the family what the dog is learning and how they can get him to respond to their commands.

If he's spending equal time with everyone, the whole family can be involved in the training process, but only one member at a time will be able to "steer" his leash. Children can take part in the training process, but they should be supervised by an adult at all times. A well-trained dog will know that the member of his family who is handling him at the time is the leader.

Leash Training

Every dog reacts differently the first time he hears the click of the leash and feels the tug on his collar. Some dogs are ready and willing to go with you, while others can't figure out why they want to go one way but their neck is going another. No one likes to be dragged somewhere, including your dog. If you train him correctly, you will have him walking politely on a leash in no time.

The Right Collar

The first step in leash training your dog is to make sure he has a comfortable collar. A good first collar for your dog to wear around the house is a nylon or leather buckle collar, or a snap-on type collar.

The collar should fit snugly around his neck without choking him. At the same time, don't go overboard and buy a collar a few sizes too big, thinking that your pup will grow into it. If the collar is too big, it will slip off easily and

be useless. An oversized collar can also catch on all sorts of objects.

To make sure your dog's collar fits properly, take him to the local pet supply store and try a selection on him. A good fit is when you can put two of your fingers comfortably between your dog's neck and the collar.

When you put a collar on a puppy for the first time, get ready for a show. He'll scratch, yelp, shake and roll on the ground to try and take it off. But don't be mistaken into thinking that it's hurting him—it's just something strange and new on his neck. Give him some time to get used to it and after a while he'll relax.

Training Collars and Leashes

When you start training your puppy you can use his regular collar, but by the time he is six to eight months old, you will need to switch to a special training collar, called a choke collar.

A choke collar is made up of a chain with a large ring at each end. By putting the chain into one of the rings, you can form a loop that slips over your dog's head. Make sure that the ring end attached to the leash comes over his neck, not under it. It's standard practice to stand to the right of your dog while he is wearing this collar.

Your dog will need a six- to eight-foot leash that fits comfortably in your hand. For a small dog a quarter inch may be wide enough; for

A puppy of a large breed, such as this Labrador Retriever, will outgrow several collars before he reaches adulthood. So check regularly to make sure his collar is not too tight.

Choke Collars— the Pros and Cons

Some people think that chain collars look like instruments of torture, and wonder how trainers can use them. But despite their name, they are actually very humane, and if put on the right way, they are also a very effective way to give a correction. "I would rather use a choke collar and get a dog's attention the first time than pull on his neck a dozen times with him wearing a buckle collar," says Kathy Marmack, an animal training supervisor at the San Diego Zoo.

A dog's neck is very sensitive and he can be controlled by the pressure he feels there when you're training him with a collar and leash. A buckle or snap-on type collar is good for day-to-day identification and handling your dog, but he won't feel anything when you need to let him know he goofed. With a choke collar, the rings at the end of the chain allow you to vary the amount of pressure that is exerted on your dog's neck.

For example, if you just want to guide him, a gentle tug will do. But if you want to communicate "Don't jump," you can make a quick jerk on the leash, which tightens the collar for a moment and then loosens it. For the collar to work effectively the ring end attached to the leash must come over your dog's neck, not under it. Don't leave the choke collar on your dog when you're not watching him, as the rings can become caught on all kinds of objects.

It's standard practice to stand to the right of your dog. This allows you to hold the leash in your right hand and use the left as a second grab, if necessary, or to reach down and pet or reassure your dog.

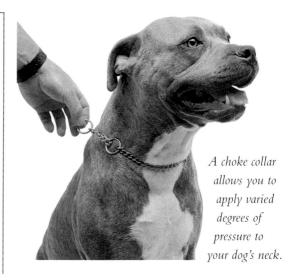

A choke collar allows you to apply varied degrees of pressure to your dog's neck.

a larger dog, choose one that is one-half to three-quarter inch wide. Don't use a chain or a flimsy nylon leash—they will cut into your hand.

Find a special place in the house to keep your dog's training collar and leash. Choose a location that's easy for you to get to, so you can just slip on his collar, hook up the leash and go.

Using the Leash

Just as he did when he first wore a collar as a puppy, your dog will need to become familiar with the leash. Start by putting on his training collar, then attaching the leash to this. Always take off his regular buckle or snap-on collar when you are using the training collar.

Instead of rushing outdoors right away, let him drag the leash around the house for a while so he can get used to the sound and feel of it. Keep your eye on him all the time so he doesn't get it caught up in anything.

Every few moments, bend down and pick up the end of the leash and gently call your dog to come to you. When he does, praise him. Once

Just like he did when he wore his first collar, your dog may need a bit of time to get used to the sound and feel of being on a leash.

Who's Walking Whom?

Your dog is supposed to keep pace with you when you're out for a walk. But sometimes, dogs will forge ahead, dragging their owners along. To change this habit, says Kathy Marmack, an animal training supervisor at the San Diego Zoo, you need to take them by surprise occasionally. "I simply change direction a lot and walk the other way while my dog hurries to catch up with me."

After a few surprise turns, your dog will start to watch you for signs of where you're going. If you notice that he's not watching, give the leash a quick, gentle jerk across and down without saying anything. Soon he will be paying attention to you constantly.

If he starts to pull ahead in front of you, abruptly turn around and start walking in the opposite direction again. This way, your dog learns that you are leading and that he has to follow.

he comes to your side while he's on the leash, you're ready to start taking steps with him. Holding the leash, walk away from your dog for a bit, then stop and call him to come. When he comes to you, reward him with a treat, either some food or praise.

Your dog might resist this exercise by trying to bite the leash or by digging his paws in and refusing to budge. These are all normal reactions. To discourage him from chewing the leash, you can spray it with bitter apple, a pet repellant. If he refuses to move, don't scold or pick him up because this just reinforces his reluctance. Be gentle and persistent, and try to entice him, with a toy or food, to move with you.

After performing this exercise successfully a few times, move to the outdoors. Gradually coax your dog into moving at a regular speed with you. As he begins to accept this and moves in the same direction and at the same pace as you,

stop and praise him. Keep repeating the exercise, making sure you have his full attention. If his concentration wanders, give a short correction on the lead. Your dog will soon get the message that whenever you put his leash on him you want him to pay attention to you and to walk at your pace beside you.

Tasty Rewards

Food is an excellent way to reward good behavior. Dogs love it and it gets results. "Food treats speed up the training process in a way that nothing else does," says Wayne Hunthausen, D.V.M., an animal behaviorist in Westwood, Kansas, and co-author of *Practitioner's Guide to Pet Behavior Problems.*

"It gets the dog's attention quickly, and when you link it to verbal praise, it's especially powerful," says Susan Anderson, D.V.M., a clinical instructor of outpatient medicine in the Department of Small Animal Clinical Sciences at the University of Florida College of Veterinary Medicine in Gainesville. Since most dogs like to eat, a bite-sized treat gives them an incentive.

Rewarding Intermittently

Once your dog understands what you want him to do, it's not a good idea to keep rewarding him with food, says Sandy Myers, a behavior consultant and trainer in Naperville, Illinois. If a dog knows he will get food all the time, he'll eventually skip the behavior you trained him to do and just wait for the food. "When I see puppies respond to commands because of food treats, I back off on the food," says Myers. "A dog should always be waiting and hoping that maybe a treat will come. Hand out a food treat less often and you'll maintain your dog's interest a lot longer."

Alternate verbal praise with tasty tidbits. Hand out goodies from different locations, such as from your other hand or your back pocket. Put

Tempting Tidbits

Most dogs like liver, ham, beef, turkey and chicken pieces, but there are always a few that can be tempted with carrots or cheese pieces. "Some dogs will eat anything you give them, others have favorite and not-so-favorite foods, and a few couldn't care less about eating," says Kathy Marmack, an animal training supervisor at the San Diego Zoo.

Vary the treats, but notice what your dog gets excited over. Cook him bits of soft, garlic-flavored chicken or really aromatic hot dogs, says Jill Yorey, a training consultant at the Society for the Prevention of Cruelty to Animals in Los Angeles.

the food directly in front of his mouth and let him gently take it from you. Don't let it drop to the ground. Gradually limit the treats to once every two or three times your dog performs correctly, eventually phasing out food altogether.

Go Easy on Overfeeding

If you use food as a reward in training, keep an eye on how much your dog is getting. Calculate how much you'll use for treats, then deduct that amount from his daily meals. There's no need to count calories fanatically, but an overfed dog is an unhealthy one who won't be able to perform at his best. "It's even okay if your dog is a little bit hungry, but not starving, when you're training," says Dr. Anderson. "He'll focus on his treats and be eager to do an excellent job for you."

The Five Basic Commands

To fit in with the family, every dog needs to learn five basic commands. Learning how to sit is the foundation of dog training, with all other behaviors building from there. So start by teaching your dog how to sit. Next, teach him to lie down. Follow this by teaching him to stay, then to come and heel. Once he has mastered these commands, your dog can be taught to do practically anything you want him to.

Always use positive reinforcement and reward your dog with lots of verbal and physical praise when he has done well. You can also use food and toys to reward him. Remember to keep training sessions short and frequent. Try to end each session on a positive note so that he looks forward to the next. With hard work, patience and persistence, you will have a well-trained dog in no time.

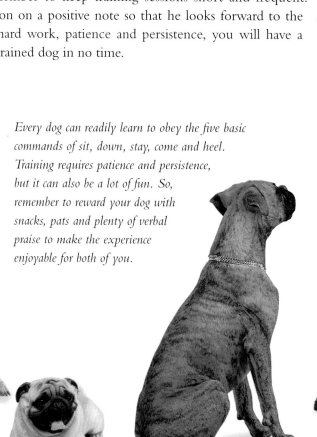

Every dog can readily learn to obey the five basic commands of sit, down, stay, come and heel. Training requires patience and persistence, but it can also be a lot of fun. So, remember to reward your dog with snacks, pats and plenty of verbal praise to make the experience enjoyable for both of you.

Teaching "Sit"

There are two ways to teach your dog to sit. One involves placing him in that position using your hands, and the other uses food. Both get the job done, but the tasty incentive is probably better to use for shy or very active puppies. You don't need the choke collar for either of these methods, but be sure to heap on plenty of verbal praise. Most dogs learn to sit very easily, but you have to keep them practicing until they can associate the command with the action.

Method 1

1 Begin by sitting or kneeling next to your puppy. Place one hand on the back of his rear legs and your other hand on his chest.

2 As you say his name and command him to "Sit," gently push back on his chest with one hand and press on his back legs with the other so that his knees bend inward. The minute he slips into position, praise him, then let him pop up if he wants to.

Method 2

1 Stand in front of your puppy and hold a small piece of food in front of his nose. Say his name, followed by the command "Sit."

2 Raise your hand slightly over his head. As his eyes follow your hand, he will lift his head up and drift into the sit position. Once he does this, give him the tidbit to nibble and praise him.

Teaching "Down"

Learning to rest comfortably is one of the most useful things you can teach your dog. If you want to stop and have a chat with a friend, commanding your dog to lie down so he can rest is much better than having him pull on the leash because he wants to get going. Remember, a dog must be able to sit before he can lie down, so teach "Down" after your dog can sit. As with the sit command, there are two methods. The second is usually easier to teach, but both need to be practiced until your dog can associate commands with actions.

Method 1

1 Command your dog to sit, then squat close behind him on your knees. If he needs some reassurance to stay in this position, reach out to him with one hand.

2 Reach forward for his front legs. At the same time, lean on his back very gently and say "Down" in a firm voice. Your dog may not like this position very much at first, but the minute he lies down—even with your help—praise him.

Method 2

1 Command your dog to sit, then sit in front of him. Hold a small piece of food in front of his nose.

2 As you command "Down," slowly move the food down to the ground so his nose follows it. If he needs help, put your hand on his shoulders and guide them down. When he is down, tell him how wonderful he is and give him the food treat.

Teaching "Stay"

This command means, "Don't even think of moving until I tell you it's okay—no matter what goes on around you." You'll need to teach this command with your dog's leash, so make sure he has his training collar on. At first, make him stay for only a few seconds before you release him. Gradually build this up to a minute. If he seems apprehensive, go back to a time limit he was comfortable with and gradually increase it again.

1 Standing in front of your dog, hold his leash in your right hand and rest it level with your stomach. Raise your left hand so your palm faces your dog. Look at him and command him to "Stay."

2 Slowly walk backward from your dog, all the while maintaining eye contact, telling him to stay.

3 Once you get to the end of the leash, drop it on the ground and put your foot on it. If he tries to move before you have given the release word, he'll soon figure out he can't go anywhere. Quietly praise him while he is keeping the stay. After about five seconds, say the release word and reward him with a food treat.

Teaching "Come"

A dog that responds to his owner's call to come, will always be in safe hands. Teach your dog to come to you indoors first. He will need to wear his training collar and be on a six- or eight-foot leash. It could take several weeks or months until he is well-trained to come. Until this time, he should never go outside without a leash on.

Always reward him for coming to you. If you want to correct bad behavior, don't call him. Go to him, instead. This way he will always associate "Come" with positive behavior.

I With his leash in your right hand, face your dog and slowly walk backward, telling him to come in a happy, upbeat voice. When he follows you, keep walking backward and tell him how wonderful he is.

2 After a few feet, stop walking. Tell him to come. Lean over, stretching your arms out to welcome him warmly.

3 When he is right in front of you, praise him lavishly and then repeat the process.

Teaching "Heel"

Heel means "stay by my side when we go walking." Some dogs are natural heelers, while others
require a lot of training. To teach your dog how
to go out for a stroll with you without taking
you for a mad dash, use his training collar and a
loosely held six- or eight-foot leash. Be prepared
to spend a lot of time outdoors because this
exercise can't be practiced inside.

1 Have your dog on a loose leash on your left side. You should be holding the leash with your right hand so that it crosses your body. Hook your right thumb into the loop of the leash. Keep your right hand at your waist.

2 As you start walking with your dog, say his name and the word "Heel." If he doesn't pay attention and follow you right away, use your left hand to grab the leash and give it a quick jerk.

3 If he starts to pull or lag, put your left hand on your right for extra strength and turn in the opposite direction. If you bump into him, don't apologize. It's his job to stay out of your way. He'll soon realize that it's more comfortable if he keeps a watchful eye on you.

4 When your dog is walk-
ing nicely by your side, look at him and praise him verbally. You can also reach down and give him a pat.

Teaching Old Dogs New Tricks

Bringing home an adult dog takes some adjustment for both parties. He might not be properly housetrained or might have been used to different rules in his former environment. Living in your fine home, he thinks he's arrived in doggy heaven. But he might be doing all sorts of unacceptable things—chewing the furniture, digging up the backyard or barking at the neighbors. Don't despair—a dog is never too old to learn new behaviors, says Kathy Marmack, an animal training supervisor at the San Diego Zoo. It just takes time and lots of patience to re-tool his canine thinking machinery.

Changing Bad Behavior

Take preventive measures to deter your new dog's undesirable behavior. Put the leash on him and attach it to your waist for a few days after you bring him home, suggests Marmack. "This gives both of you an idea of what to expect from one another. If you're watching TV, your dog can sit nicely beside you, or if you're going from room to room, he has to follow." This way, your dog can't get into the trash or go exploring in the other rooms of the house. You have total control over him until you both feel comfortable with one another. If you need a break from the tether of the leash, you can put him in his crate.

A Sudden Change of Behavior

If your dog has lived with you for a while and suddenly starts misbehaving, it's another story.

"Dogs usually don't act up without a reason," says Jill Yorey, a training consultant at the Society for the Prevention of Cruelty to Animals in Los Angeles. "Something is going on in the home and the dog is upset or wants attention."

Think about what's been happening lately at home. Is there illness, sadness or loud fighting? Lots of suitcases or moving boxes piled up? Are you renovating and the furniture is topsy-turvy? Dogs are sensitive creatures and become afraid if their world isn't orderly. Just like some people, dogs become set in their ways. When there's disorganization, they may express anxiety by urinating in the house, avoiding the family, chewing up objects they haven't touched since they were puppies or demanding more attention than usual. This is really a yelp for help.

Dealing with Persistent Misbehaviors

If your adult dog is getting impossible to live with, start treating him like a puppy. Be happy to see him each morning but keep him confined to a crate or the yard when you cannot watch him. Wherever possible, take him along when you go out of the house.

When you're at home, give him plenty of personal attention—a game of tug, or a soothing all-over grooming session. He will enjoy the extra company and reassurance.

Getting out in the fresh air can take your dog's mind off destroying your house. Take him for a walk in a different park or, if he enjoys a car ride, visit a friend. "New views help wake up a bored and tired adult dog," says Yorey.

Training a Therapy Dog

All dogs are special to their owners, but a therapy dog is special to everyone. These working dogs provide comfort and serenity to strangers. They visit hospital patients, the elderly in retirement villages or nursing homes, and other members of the community who are unable to own and care for a pet of their own.

A therapy dog doesn't need to learn a lot of fancy tricks. He just needs basic training like any family dog. The only difference is that because he comes into contact with many people, he needs to be very well-socialized and behaved. Once the basic commands of sit, down, stay, come and heel are thoroughly mastered, he'll need to learn to let strangers pet and love him.

Training your dog to be a therapy dog requires patience and a genuine desire to share your pet with others. Your dog must really like people, have a calm and predictable temperament, and be able to take loud noises, new sights, smells and surprises all in his stride. He has to enjoy being touched and fussed over for the time he'll be on visiting duty. Lots of dogs take to nurturing naturally, while others are too highly strung and are more interested in what's going on around them than the people they're with. A therapy dog needs to be able to sit quietly while a patient with Alzheimer's strokes his fur or a small child suddenly grabs him to give him a big hug.

To find out if your dog would make a good therapy dog, take him on a leash to hectic and noisy locations where people of various ages will be attracted to him—shopping centers or the post office, for example. When admirers pet your dog, observe his reactions. Check how well he listens to your commands of "Sit" and "Down" in a crowded environment.

If you think your dog would make a good therapy pet and you would like to share him, contact the National Delta Society, 289 Perimeter Road, East Renton, Washington.

A gentle animal that enjoys being petted and is confident with strangers will make a good therapy dog.

Professional Training Schools

Sometimes owners don't have the knowledge or confidence to train their own dog. They may not have the time or the inclination, or they may be physically unable to do so. Luckily, there are special training schools that you can take your dog to. Each school might use different training methods, but your dog should attend a program he enjoys. If his tail is wagging and his ears are up when you return for a second visit, you'll know that the program is a success.

A good training school will carefully evaluate each dog and recommend to his owner what kind of training is suitable. Many schools offer both private lessons or resident programs where your dog stays overnight. A private lesson lasts from 45 minutes to an hour and will take place once a week for a couple of weeks. A dog attending a resident program can receive as many as three to six 20-minute training sessions a day, with plenty of downtime in between. A hard-working dog will be able to learn the basics within about five days.

Choosing a Good School

If you've decided to get some training help, set about finding a reputable training school in your area. Ask other dog owners or your vet for recommendations. Take some time to visit schools that interest you. You don't have to be a super-sleuth to check out a training school, but a look behind the scenes wouldn't hurt. Have a look at the space your dog will be trained in. Does it seem big, clean and inviting? If you think you would like to learn something in this environment, chances are your dog will, too. If you feel uncomfortable, so might your dog.

Find out what your dog will be taught and ask to observe a training session. Watch how the dogs respond to the trainer. Do they seem happy? Do they want to please the trainer? How does the trainer react if a dog doesn't understand him? Ask what experience the trainer has. Anyone can call himself a dog trainer, but a serious trainer will usually be a member of the National Association of Professional Dog Trainers. The school should also provide a contract that includes follow-up lessons with the owner. Chatting with the people who

When you enroll your dog in obedience classes both you and your dog receive professional guidance, plus your dog will learn how to get along with other dogs.

Are Some Dogs Hopeless?

After the umpteenth correction, it might seem as if your dog will never learn to stop rummaging through the trash or forging ahead on the leash. Even though all dogs can learn, some are slower than others.

"You will have to keep trying different corrections until you find one that works," says Kathy Marmack, an animal training supervisor at the San Diego Zoo. "As long as you're persistent and consistent, most dogs can be trained."

But just because your dog isn't top of the training department, doesn't mean he is less of a pet. Most dog owners rate companionship and loyalty just as highly as obedience, if not more so. And when your pooch is snuggling beside you on a cold and miserable day, you won't mind that he hasn't quite mastered sit and come yet.

will be taking care of your dog while he's at the school will also reveal the school's general philosophy. Make sure there are provisions for adequate medical care in case your dog has a health problem. Only if it all seems satisfactory should you sign up.

Pros and Cons

The advantage of having a professional train your dog is that he gets trained faster. The trainer knows what works for your dog and will be able to teach you how to follow up the training. The

school might also be able to offer specialized training, such as search-and-rescue work.

The downside is that when someone else trains your dog, they automatically build up a bond. Your dog may respond perfectly to the school trainers, but when you get him back home, he may not respond to you. You'll need to spend time building up your own bond with him and learning, from the professionals, how to give consistent commands. And not everyone may be able to afford tuition at these schools, which typically costs from $100 to $1,000, depending on the amount of training involved.

Obedience Classes

If you can't bear to send your dog away, you can enroll him in obedience classes that you attend with him. This way you can participate in your dog's training, but still receive the help and guidance of professionals. Obedience classes also give your dog an opportunity to meet other dogs and owners, which helps to socialize him. Try to find a class that doesn't have more than ten dogs per instructor.

The instructor will demonstrate appropriate commands, rewards and corrections for you to follow with your dog. No dog will be a model student so don't be embarrassed if your dog misbehaves in class. Don't be shy about speaking up to your dog either. It doesn't matter if people are watching. Chances are he'll do the same thing in public, and if you're hesitant to correct him in class, where everyone shares the same goals, it will be even harder out in the big world.

Obedience classes usually meet once a week for six to eight weeks and last for an hour or 90 minutes. Some dogs might take two or three courses of instruction before they're well-trained.

8 ADVANCED TRAINING

As your dog's skills increase, it's likely that the two of you will both get hooked on learning more. And with every new skill she masters, your pride and joy in her will swell.

Higher Education
pages 123–125
When you're both having so much fun, why stop after she has learned the basics?

Working with Pros
page 126
Seek professional guidance to help with your dog's advanced training

Showing Off
pages 127–128
Organized dog shows give you and your dog the chance to exhibit your achievements

Tracking
pages 129–130
Teach her to follow a scent— you'll both enjoy the challenge

Tricks and Games
pages 131–135
It's not always easy to tell who's having the most fun when you teach your dog games

Higher Education

When you start training your dog, the two of you build up a special bond. You work hard together, so of course you can't help but feel pleased when she responds to your instructions. By the time your dog can obey the basic commands without a training collar and leash, you may not want to stop training—you'll be so excited by all that she is capable of and will look forward to doing more advanced work with her. And like a snowball picking up speed as it rolls downhill, the more you teach your dog, the faster she'll learn.

Because you've used positive reinforcement throughout your training, your dog will also be eager to keep going—she enjoys the challenges and rewards. Just from her expression, you can see how self-assured she is when you give her a command she knows and can execute. Her ears are alert, her eyes are bright and she holds her head up proudly. Who wouldn't want to keep the training ball rolling?

Canine Capers

Is there life after "Sit" and "Stay?" Definitely. In fact, there's another world of training skills that dogs can learn. Although there may be limitations, depending on her breed, your dog can be trained to do all kinds of things—retrieve an object without damaging it, pose with small children for a photo in a crowded auditorium, jump over hurdles, herd sheep, shoot through tunnels and chase small game. Once you get past

the fundamentals, there's a whole range of skills your dog is capable of learning. And with plenty of dogs working alongside their owners and helping out in the community, there are lots of opportunities for well-trained dogs to perform beyond their backyards.

"Well-trained dogs can save lives on land or in water, or help the physically disabled by opening and closing doors, getting the mail and picking up dropped objects," says Bob Jervis, an animal trainer and director of training at the National K-9 Dog Training School in Columbus, Ohio. "Others act as the eyes or ears of their human companions. They alert their hard-of-hearing owners by barking loudly when the doorbell or

Not everyone would be thrilled that their dog had mastered opening the refrigerator door. But this Labrador Retriever's owner thinks she's pretty cool. The tie on the handle makes it easier for her to do her owner's bidding.

the phone rings, and guide those with poor sight safely through busy traffic."

Famous Dogs and Their Tricks

Over the years, a number of highly trained dogs have graced our film and TV screens and wowed us with their presence. One of the most joyous canine actors in the 1950s was a rough-haired Collie who played the part of Lassie. Whenever Lassie's young owner got himself into trouble, he would ask Lassie to "go for help." Lassie would immediately know this was the cue to run and find someone who could help, and get the person's attention by barking furiously. Lassie would persuade that person to follow her and return to the spot where the youngster was in trouble.

But dog actors are not confined to just one particular breed. A 150-pound French Mastiff named Hooch played a detective in the movie *Turner and Hooch*, while a team of Saint Bernards

How Many Words Can a Dog Learn?

People often wonder how much a dog actually understands. More than you think, according to Stanley Coren, Ph.D., a professor of psychology at the University of British Columbia in Vancouver and author of The Intelligence of Dogs. *His own two dogs, a Cairn Terrier and Cavalier King Charles Spaniel, have responded to more than 60 different words. Add to that hand signals and other body language which your dog can learn to recognize, and there aren't many secrets you can hide from your dog.*

shared the limelight in the movie *Beethoven*. One of the lead canine actors in *Beethoven* was trained to dig on command and pull over a picnic table.

A Jack Russell Terrier called Moose plays the character Eddie in the television sitcom, *Frasier*. Moose jumps up and down on command and stares intently at the lead actor. Behind the scenes, the Terrier is really jumping up and down on a trampoline. In the movie, *Zeus and Roxanne*, a Portuguese Podengo was taught to ride on the back of a dolphin, and in the television show *Empty Nest*, the Saint Bernard/Golden

The instinct to retrieve is strong in breeds such as these Golden Retrievers. You just have to get the message across about what it is you want them to retrieve and teach them to handle the objects delicately.

Retriever mix was trained to raise and lower his eyebrows on command. In TV's popular *Mad About You*, a smart and well-trained mixed breed dog commands a high fee for playing dumb.

But the live-action remake of Walt Disney's *101 Dalmatians* takes the cake for being the most ambitious movie made with dogs to date. More than 300 Dalmatian puppies and several adult dogs appeared in the film. Small groups of six-week-old puppies were taught to run on command, sit and stay together in a group and dive into a haystack. An adult Dalmatian was trained to jump up on a kitchen sink, start the coffee maker, turn off the alarm clock and wake up his owner. A Standard Schnauzer was trained to jump up on his hind legs, and toss a burlap bag over his own head while hopping across the room. Not only are these performances amazing but so, too, are the trainers for having the enormous amount of patience required to achieve all of this.

How Dogs are Trained for TV and the Movies

It all seems so effortless, but dogs who appear on television and in the movies are very special creatures. They need a lot of training to be able to work so well off the leash and look happy and natural while they're doing it. For the professional trainers who train these dogs, it's a full-time and highly specialized occupation.

"For most television or movie roles we spend eight hours a day for 14 to 16 weeks, teaching a dog everything she needs to know," says Mary Kay Snyder, a professional animal trainer who trained the Dalmatian puppies in the movie *101 Dalmatians*.

Besides the basics of "Sit," "Stay," "Down" and "Come," acting dogs need to be able to respond to silent hand signals as well as verbal commands on the set. They must be able to retrieve an object and remember routine commands such as "On your side," which makes them look as if they're sleeping, and "Speak." When given a cue, acting dogs also have to be able to walk on or off the set with another actor they might have seen only once or twice before.

"Every script calls for different combinations of these behaviors, so we have to break them down into parts

and teach them to the dog in sections," says Snyder. Establishing a strong bond with the dog and using lots of positive reinforcement and food treats is the key to training a successful canine actor.

"We might also use toys if a dog isn't motivated by food," she adds. Acting dogs must be able to stay calm around the big equipment and strange sounds found in a studio or on location. Before one of her dogs goes on a film set, Snyder takes her everywhere she can to desensitize her to unfamiliar noises.

Working with Pros

Teaching your dog advanced skills is not easy to learn from books or mere observation. It takes a school or a teacher trained in the task to show you how to prepare your dog properly. To find a reputable training school or professional dog trainer in your area, ask your vet, other dog-owning friends and local kennel clubs for recommendations.

Advanced Training Schools

There are many types of advanced training schools. Some specialize in certain areas, such as competitive obedience, agility training, herding, search-and-rescue work or servicing people with disabilities. Others might teach a bit of everything.

A good school will help you train your dog or do the job for you. The school will evaluate your dog to make sure she has mastered the basics—sit, stay, down, heel and come—without the use of a leash. If she hasn't, brush-up courses are usually available. Advanced training schools will also tell you whether your dog is suited to the task you want her to perform. If you own a Greyhound, a breed known for not liking water, she probably won't want to rescue people drowning in the ocean or a pool.

Working with Private Trainers at Home

Some owners prefer to work on an individual basis with an experienced dog trainer in their own home. This is usually more expensive than taking your dog to a school, but you and your dog are guaranteed to be the star pupils and you won't have to share the time you pay for.

When hiring a professional, check that her experience is sufficient and that she has worked with other dogs of the same breed as yours. Ask what methods she uses and whether she suggests many different solutions to problems. You might like to ask if you can observe one of her lessons before you commit.

You'll want to hire someone who explains things in terms you can easily understand. A private dog trainer needs to communicate well with animals, but for you to progress in your ability, she also has to communicate well with you. Remember also that you should enjoy the time you spend with your trainer, as well as see results in your dog that you are pleased with. Your dog should really like the trainer, too.

A good professional dog trainer will give you the confidence you need to continue training your dog effectively on your own.

Showing Off

Dog shows are organized by licensed dog associations throughout the country on a regular basis. Besides the American Kennel Club there are the United Kennel Club and the American Rare Breed Association competitions. Held at both outdoor and indoor locations, dog shows give you the chance to see breeds you might not otherwise have the opportunity to see. If you are planning to get a dog, you can also approach breeders, who will be only too happy to discuss their dogs' merits with you.

For exhibitors competing at these events, dog shows provide the chance to show off their dogs and be rewarded for the countless hours they spend training, grooming and conditioning them. There's a camaraderie among exhibitors that enhances the fun of dog shows, and competitors loyal to the sport are keen for all to do well.

Obedience Trials

As the name suggests, these events test a dog's ability to follow a number of commands. If your dog can sit, stay, come, heel (with and without a leash) and remain in both a sit and a down position while you stand at the opposite side of the testing area, she will be awarded with the CD, or Companion Dog, degree.

Once the CD degree is obtained, you and your dog can continue training for the CDX, or Companion Dog Excellent, degree. Training can take almost a year to prepare for this. Your dog must be able to do all the exercises that she did

for the CD degree as well as more complicated behaviors. These include leaping over both high and low hurdles without hitting the bars and remaining in a sit and then down position while you go out of her sight range.

After your dog passes this level, she can train for the UD, or Utility Dog, degree. This award tests your dog's scent discrimination. She has to be able to find and retrieve a wooden dumbbell and a glove that you have handled among a pile of other wooden dumbbells and gloves.

Conformation Events

At these events your dog is judged for how closely she meets the standards set by each breed's national club. These standards include the

An owner accompanies his Akita around the show ring at the Westminster Kennel Club Dog Show in New York City as she shows off her paces. They are competing in the Working Dog category.

Dogs competing in agility events, such as this Australian Cattle Dog, must show no hesitation before tackling tunnels and other obstacles on the course. They must also respond to their owners' hand and voice signals.

length of her body, her coat color and thickness, her eye color, head shape, and her gait and temperament. In shows sponsored by the American Kennel Club, the conformation event is a process of elimination, with only one male and one female dog from each breed category being selected and awarded points. Once a dog earns 15 points, she is considered a "champion" of her breed.

Don't be fooled into thinking you can just give your dog a quick groom and be ready for the judges. A lot of training is required for this event. First, your dog has to learn how to stand very still for a few minutes to allow a judge to examine her. She must also be able to walk at a certain pace by herself, as well as with other dogs in front of and behind her. If your dog is a medium or large breed, you will need to run beside her in the ring, so make sure you're in good physical shape too. Most importantly, your dog must look as if she's loving every minute of the show and not be unsettled by loud noise or clapping spectators.

Agility Events

This is a fairly new dog sport that has become very popular in England and the United States.

In agility events, you will be required to direct your dog to complete a course filled with obstacles. The course usually requires your dog to walk over an A-frame, walk on a raised platform and go through tunnels. You will need to race alongside your dog, shouting commands and giving hand signals to let her know which part of the course is next. Dogs are individually timed and the one who completes the course in the fastest time wins.

To compete in agility events, your dog must not be afraid of any of the obstacles and be able to move quickly from one to another. She also has to be very proficient at basic obedience skills because the events are outdoors and she is off the leash the whole time. To prepare your dog to reach these levels of competition, you must be willing to put in many hours of training and also be in good physical shape yourself.

Tracking

When a dog follows a trail of scent left by someone, she is said to be "tracking." Some dogs have a natural ability to track, while others are trained to do it. Being able to track is a very useful skill and just one of the many ways in which dogs can help humans. Hounds track game, rescue dogs track lost children, police dogs track suspects and well-trained pets can find lost items for their owners. Having your dog sniff out and retrieve an item that has a person's scent on it can be a fun and rewarding hobby. It's also a great way to spend quality time with your dog outdoors.

Teaching Your Dog to Track

To be able to track, your dog needs to be in good physical condition. She needs to be able to obey the commands for sit, stay, lie down, heel and come, as well as know how to retrieve an object. You will need to buy a special tracking harness for your dog to wear and a long leash (between 20 and 40 feet) to attach to it. To stake out an area in some grassy, open fields, you'll need some wind flags or colored clothes pegs. You'll also need a couple of freshly washed socks with no odor, which can be "scented" and used as markers along the trail.

The idea is that your dog follows the exact path that someone has walked over a grassy area. Ask the person whose scent your dog is going to follow to place one of the socks inside his shirt for a few minutes. Take the scented sock and put it in your dog's mouth for a few seconds so she gets used to the tracklayer's scent. After she drops the sock, praise her and reward her with some food. Repeat this exercise a few times.

When you are confident your dog is familiar with the tracklayer's scent, give your dog the sit and stay command and place the same sock in the grass about 6 feet in front of her. Then give her the command to retrieve it. When she does, praise her. Repeat this a few more times, then place the sock about 30 feet away from her. Attach her harness and leash and command her

Your dog will be expected to follow the exact course taken by the tracklayer. Some breeds, such as Foxhounds, Bloodhounds, Basset Hounds, Beagles and Weimeraners, have natural tracking ability. Others must be trained by gradually increasing the difficulty of the task.

to fetch it, following her on the leash. When she succeeds in this exercise, ask another person to stand in front of the sock to distract your dog from the tracklayer's scent. This will make the exercise more challenging.

Soon you will be able to progress to more advanced tracking. Ask the tracklayer to scent a second sock and place it farther along the trail, making sure there is a right-angle turn in the trail so your dog is in different wind directions. Place food containers or other objects which have distracting smells along the track to further challenge your dog. Gradually get the tracklayer to cover a larger area in more complex terrain.

Tracking Competitions

If you think your dog has a keen sense of smell, enter her in tracking competitions. If she successfully completes a tracking test sponsored by the American Kennel Club, she will be awarded the TD, or Tracking Dog, title and this will be permanently recorded on her pedigree papers.

To earn the TD title, your dog must be able to find a dark-colored glove or wallet belonging to the tracklayer that has been left along the track. She either picks up the glove or leads you to it. The track must be 440 to 500 yards long, and the scent on the track should be between half an hour and two hours old. It's a pass or fail event and there's no time limit, as long as your dog is clearly following the scent.

If your dog receives a TD award, she can compete for the TDX, or Tracking Dog Excellent, award. The track for this award is a lot harder. It is between 800 and 1000 yards long and the scent must be between three and four hours old. The track also crosses over at two points and your dog has to find four objects instead of one.

Amazing Tracking Dogs

Kelly, a black Labrador Retriever, has been taking classes in "teeter-totter," ladder climbing and crouch and crawl. These are all exercises which help accustom Kelly to walking on unstable surfaces in treacherous conditions, for Kelly is training to be a disaster search dog with the National Disaster Search Dog Foundation. The training takes two years and after this period, Kelly will be certified to help search for victims of earthquakes, mudslides, avalanches or bombsites by tracking their scent amid rubble and barking at the point of strongest scent until her handler arrives.

"These dogs can quickly search a 12,000-square-foot building and tell you where to start digging, even through concrete," says Kelly's owner and handler, Captain Gary Smith, who is with the Ventura County Fire Department in Camarillo, California.

For half an hour every day, Captain Smith and Kelly practice hand-signal obedience, voice-command obedience, and freezing and barking when (and only when) she sniffs out a human scent, in order to hone her tracking skills. And so that she won't be distracted in an emergency situation, Captain Smith makes sure she practices around crowds, sirens and loud power tools.

Kelly is the second dog Captain Smith has trained as a search dog. His first, Eric, a German Shepherd, was a wilderness-area search dog. On one occasion, Captain Smith and Eric were called in to a mountainous area to help locate a teenage boy who had become separated from his mother during a hiking expedition. Eric took a good sniff of the boy's clothing and after just a few hours of tracking, located him on the trail, alive and well.

This Boxer enjoys a good stretch as he obeys his owner's command to roll over.

If your dog knows how to wave, he'll become the most popular pooch in the neighborhood.

Tricks and Games

 One of the best things about having a dog is being able to play with her and have a good time. Enjoying games with your dog and teaching her new tricks is an excellent source of fun and a good way to spend time together. You can learn what she likes and doesn't like to do and understand how she solves problems. These activities will also help to build her attention span and make life more interesting for her.

Make your dog the star of the show by teaching her how to jump through hoops and retrieve useful items.

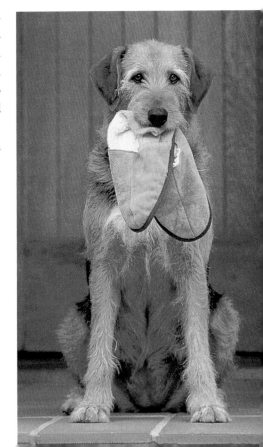

Teaching Your Dog to Retrieve

Some dogs just naturally go after items and bring them to their owners, but others need to be taught. Once you teach your dog how to retrieve you can use this as a way to exercise her.

1 Attract your dog's attention by waving a toy in front of her face. When you have her attention, throw the toy away from her and tell her, "Fetch!"

2 When she goes after it, encourage her to pick it up and bring it to you by telling her to "Come!" Open your arms out wide to welcome her. When she comes to you, reward her with plenty of praise.

3 To get your dog to release the object, put your right hand below her mouth and say "Drop it." If she doesn't release it, continue saying the command and use your left hand to gently force the object out of her mouth. The minute she lets go of it, praise her and pet her. Repeat the exercise several times.

Teaching Your Dog to Roll Over

Watching a dog roll over on command looks like magic but it's actually one of the easiest tricks to teach your dog. All dogs can do it, but the smaller in size they are, the easier it is for them to roll. Very large dogs, such as Irish Wolfhounds and Great Danes, may take more time to train. When your dog can do this really well, you can use hand signals to indicate which side you want her to roll to.

1 Give your dog the "Down" command. Kneel beside her and place one of your hands on her outer thigh and the other on her inner shoulder.

2 As you gently roll her away from you, say "Over," in a confident tone of voice.

3 When she completes the turn and jumps to her feet, make a big fuss over her. Repeat this exercise a few times a day until she can roll over without your help.

Teaching Your Dog to Jump Through a Hoop

This is an easy game that all dogs love, especially when you make a huge fuss over them once they're through the other side. It's also a good way to train your dog to use a doggy door.

Wedge the hoop into a doorway, making sure the bottom of the hoop is touching the floor. Use your most encouraging voice to coax your dog through it.

Teaching Your Dog to Wave

This is a great party trick and children especially will love seeing their dog perform this command. The appearance of a large dog can sometimes frighten people, but if you teach a large dog to wave, strangers will see your dog for the friendly, funny thing that she is and will be encouraged to come up and meet her.

Sit on the floor in front of your dog and command her to sit. Gently touch one of her paws.

2 As soon as she goes through reward her with food, praise or a toy.

3 Once your dog can go through the hoop, raise it off the floor an inch at a time.

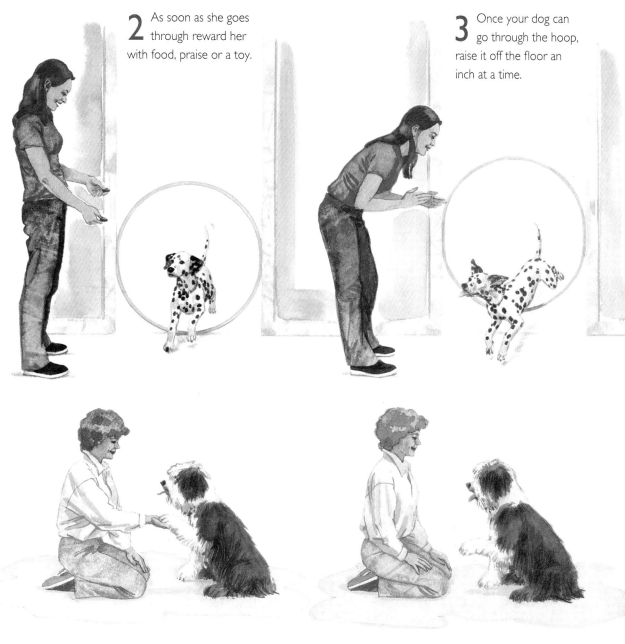

2 The minute she lifts her paw up, pick it up and put it in your hand. Hold it level with her chest for a brief second or two.

3 Say "Wave" and release her paw. Your dog will associate the motion of her paw falling to the ground with the command word "Wave." Quickly praise her with a food tidbit and repeat the exercise.

9 CORRECTING UNWANTED BEHAVIOR

*If your dog has a tendency toward bad behavior,
don't despair. With a bit of firm and consistent training you
can correct his naughty habits. Better yet, you can curb
unwanted habits before they become established by training
your dog as soon as you bring him home.*

Prevention is Better Than Cure

Most of the time your dog will have you laughing at his antics, but once in a while his tricks won't be so funny. Every dog does a naughty thing now and then, like jumping up on guests or chewing your brand new shoes—it's only natural. But when your dog keeps on misbehaving, it's not so easy to grin and bear it.

Appropriate Reactions

There are many easy ways to convince your dog that it's better to be a good citizen in your home than it is to be a mischief maker. One simple solution for most dogs' common behavioral problems is for you to be aware of your own body language.

Because your dog wants to please you, he looks at your reaction to his antics. If you like what he's doing and laugh at him, he'll do it again. If you let him know in no uncertain terms that you disapprove, he'll think twice about an encore. With some dogs, all it takes to stop them in their devilish ways is seeing you frown or hearing you say "No" in an even tone of voice.

Nipping Bad Behavior Early

The best way to stop bad behavior is to prevent it from getting started in the first place. Although you can't be a mind reader, you can anticipate what your dog might do next. For example, when it comes to chewing, imagine what your dog would love to get into if he could. Those expensive new leather shoes you just bought smell so yummy even you notice it. Your dog will be even more interested in them

and he'll check them out the minute you leave them lying around within paw's reach. To stop your dog from chewing them, put them away.

If your puppy likes to bark a lot when you're home, he'll bark even more when you're not there. "With a barker, don't leave him alone in the backyard for 12 hours a day unless the behavior is under control first," says Jill Yorey, a training consultant at the Society for the Prevention of Cruelty to Animals in Los Angeles. If you have to leave him alone for long periods of time, hire someone to come over for an hour or so to play with him. Dogs need stimulation, just like people.

What's His Motivation?

Knowing the motivation for bad behavior is the key to changing it. If your dog doesn't have enough things to keep him busy, then he'll find his own entertainment, however unappealing an activity it may seem to you.

Dogs are companion animals so they naturally prefer being around their owners than off by themselves all the time. Some dogs need more attention from their owners than others, and misbehaving might be your dog's way of expressing this wish. When your dog grabs your wallet and starts gleefully running around the house, your immediate reaction is to chase him. Your dog has succeeded in getting you to play with him. It wasn't the wallet he wanted, it was you.

Once you understand the level of attention your dog wants, and you give him some uninterrupted time, he won't be so disruptive.

Aggressive Behavior

A friendly pet is a joy, but a dog that growls, snaps and has an aggressive personality is a danger to everyone with whom he comes in contact. There are many reasons why your dog might show a rough exterior, but there is no reason to excuse a family pet who growls, snarls or bites someone.

The Importance of Early Socialization

One of the best ways to prevent aggressive behavior is to make sure your dog has been well-socialized. When a puppy goes out into the world for the first time, the experience can be lots of fun or very scary. It all depends on how secure he feels. If he was handled often and exposed to many different sights, sounds and people from infancy onward, he'll take the outdoor life in his stride. If he wasn't, everything new will alarm him. A sheltered existence does not prepare a dog for street noise, other dogs or different people.

When dogs are afraid, they sometimes try to protect themselves by coming on strong and frightening everyone else away first. Underneath an aggressive snarl and stance is usually a dog that didn't feel safe enough when he was very young. As an adult, he is confused and doesn't know how to interact appropriately.

To build your new dog's confidence, snap on his collar and leash and start obedience training right away. Generally, a puppy younger than three months old should not be taken to public areas because he has not had enough time to build up his immunity to contagious diseases. So,

This Golden Retriever puppy is being rolled on his back to see how readily he submits to handling. A very submissive response may indicate an overly timid, and potentially aggressive, temperament.

if your new dog is a puppy, only take him out to public places after he has been vaccinated.

Everyone likes a puppy and wants to pet him. A confident puppy will be very happy to greet strangers and will begin licking and jumping right away, while a pup less sure of himself may back up or hide between your legs.

To encourage your pup's confidence, give strangers a biscuit to hand to him. Remember, your dog will pick up signals from your attitude, so relax and tell him he's a good boy when he accepts the treat and doesn't shy away. If you're nervous and worry about your dog's response, he'll be nervous, too.

If your dog becomes frightened when you're out for a stroll, don't pick him up or coddle him in a baby-talk voice. The worst thing to tell your dog when he's afraid is, "It's okay, don't worry." This will only reinforce his timid behavior. Just stay relaxed and your dog will follow your cue.

Curbing Aggression

To prevent aggressive behavior from developing, teach your dog right away what behavior is acceptable and what isn't. "The first time he growls, don't be afraid to tell your dog 'No!'" says Wayne Hunthausen, D.V.M., an animal behaviorist in Westwood, Kansas, and co-author of *Practitioner's Guide to Pet Behavior Problems.*

"When you do this your dog will recognize that you're serious with the correction and stop immediately." Act as soon as you hear a rumble in your dog's throat. He'll get the message quicker if he knows that the outburst he's about to make is not tolerated.

Removing your dog from the situation is another way to prevent aggression. If you suspect your male dog has a low tolerance of other male dogs, don't let him go nose to nose with one while out for a walk. Or if small children make him nervous, build up his confidence by making him sit and stay in a public playground where there are lots of children running about. Until you feel he's confident and his

Beware the Warning Signs

Dogs are the kinds of animals that wear their hearts on their paws. They use their bodies to communicate what they're feeling, which can be everything from excitement and playfulness to fear, pain or disappointment. It's a universal dog language.

To determine a dog's personality, look at his tail, eyes, ears, mouth and body posture. A dominant dog who may display aggressive behavior if challenged will have a stiff-legged stance and be leaning slightly forward. His lips will be curled, his teeth exposed, and his nose will be wrinkled. His ears will be erect, his

tail raised and bristled, and the hair along the back of his neck and spine will be standing up.

But you should also keep an eye out for less obvious signs. A potentially aggressive dog also crouches down and has a look of fear in his eyes. "He has a 'don't hurt me' look on his face," says Susan Anderson, D.V.M., a clinical instructor of outpatient medicine in the department of small animal clinical sciences at the University of Florida College of Veterinary Medicine in Gainesville. He may also look stiff, walk in a strained, hesitant way or be keeping very still.

Handling an Aggressive Dog

Just because his tail is wagging doesn't mean a dog is friendly. When you meet a strange dog you should always look out for signs of aggression. With a little prevention, you'll save a lot of heartache. If you think a dog has aggressive tendencies, don't approach him. "The last thing you want to do is confront him," says Susan Anderson, D.V.M., a clinical instructor of outpatient medicine in the department of small animal clinical sciences at the University of Florida College of Veterinary Medicine in Gainesville. You should also avoid making eye contact, especially if the dog seems fearful. In canine communication that's interpreted as being confrontational. It's best to just look away.

If an aggressive-looking dog approaches you, drop your head and shoulders and slowly back away. "Be like a tree and wait patiently for the dog to go away," says Dr. Anderson. If you see a snarling dog up ahead on the sidewalk, it's wise to move to the other side of the road.

"You should always correct a dog from trying to become dominant," says Dr. Anderson. "When a dog consistently bumps into you or knocks you over, it isn't by accident."

Mounting you is another sign of dominance. If a dog starts displaying behaviors such as these, ask his owner to regain authority by commanding the dog to "Sit " or "Down," or do it yourself.

actions are reliable, don't leave him around toddlers unsupervised.

Discouraging Aggressive Play

Between the ages of three and six months, puppies begin teething—their baby teeth are being replaced by permanent adult teeth. This physical development also comes at a time when they become more playful with people, and nothing feels more soothing on a puppy's gums than a soft, fleshy hand.

While a little playful gnawing isn't aggressive behavior, it can increase to hard bites and this can lead to aggression. So can other games, such as wrestling and tug-of-war. To prevent your puppy from developing aggressive tendencies,

To prevent your dog from becoming aggressive, don't encourage games where a win–lose situation can arise, such as the tug-of-war game being played by these two Bulldog puppies. As with children, young dogs can become upset if they feel they are coming off second best and the game can easily get out of hand.

avoid playing games that encourage winning, says Debra L. Forthman, Ph.D., an animal behaviorist and director of Field Conservation at Atlanta Zoo in Georgia.

Keep your dog on a leash when you take him for a walk or at any other time he is likely to meet another dog. If you stay relaxed, your dog will follow your cue. If he does get aggressive, correct him by jerking the leash.

Supervising Doggy Introductions

When a dog meets another dog for the first time, they'll immediately want to establish the pecking order. If one dog asserts his authority and the other dog responds submissively, order will reign. The trouble starts when both dogs want to be the leader.

When you take your dog out on a walk, keep him on a loose leash. This way, when he sees another dog and runs toward him, you can pull the leash taut to make the correction more effective. If your dog gets aggressive when a strange dog approaches, try to distract him from noticing the other dog by changing your pace or turning to the right or left frequently. If you see him spot another dog up ahead, don't tense up or tighten your hold on his leash. Your dog will sense that something is wrong from your behavior, and he'll prepare himself for potential danger. If you

remain calm, your dog will also feel more relaxed. Sometimes, however, it may be better to avoid the situation.

If you bring another dog home, put both your dogs on their leashes so they can safely sniff one another and get used to each other's presence under your control. Command both dogs to lie down so that they recognize you as the leader of both. Let them remain that way for a few minutes until they have relaxed, then you can release one at a time.

Fighting

It's always fun to watch two dogs play together. Their romping, rolling and noisy games of hide-and-seek and tag can keep them busy for hours. Most of the time, two dogs who live together will quickly work out their own set of ground rules, and as long as each one takes a turn at being in charge, playtime will remain a fun and energetic experience.

But if a new dog comes on the scene or one dog becomes too excited and escalates the level of play, be on the alert. The play growling and chasing can get out of hand very rapidly.

How do you know if they are fighting or just playing? If one dog continually grabs the other one by the neck and rolls him to the ground, or nips him hard enough that he lets out a yelp, that isn't acceptable. If one dog is smaller or younger, he may become frightened by rough play and turn on the larger dog.

To avoid fights breaking out, be on the lookout if both dogs are sparring—that is, standing on their back legs and biting one another around the ears or head. Dogs that are very dominant, fearful or that have been attacked before are more likely to get into dog fights.

How to Break Up a Dog Fight

If you see your dog fighting with another dog, don't reach in to grab his collar, even though it may seem to be the natural thing to do in that situation. Thinking it's just another part of the other dog, your dog will aim for your hand and you'll more than likely get bitten as a result. Because loud sounds frighten dogs, try clanging two metal items together and shout loudly at them to stop. You can also grab one or both of your dog's back legs (depending on his size) and pull him away from the fight.

When large, strong dogs such as this German Shepherd and German Shorthaired Pointer meet, they immediately set about establishing who's dominant. As long as one dog displays a submissive response, it's unlikely that any fighting will break out.

Another effective way to break up a dog fight is to use the garden hose to spray water on the combatants. If the garden hose is not within reach, a bucket or even a glass of water will do the trick. The water will startle the dogs and stop the fight just long enough for you to grab a collar and separate them.

If you have a male dog, the best way to prevent him from getting into fights regularly is to have him neutered. Not only does this decrease his natural tendency toward aggression generally, it also means that other dogs won't see him as competition in the perpetual quest for dominance.

It's My Space

Some dogs become so attached to their home and yard that they will physically threaten anyone they think is invading their territory. If they sense that someone is coming too close they may hold the "intruder" at bay with an aggressive stance or ferocious barking and growling.

If you take a territorial dog out for a walk and use the same route each day, he'll come to think of the path as his, and won't be too happy to share it with others.

Being obsessively territorial is a trait many dogs are just born with, particularly working breeds. These dogs need little training to become excellent guard dogs, but they sometimes need direction to behave properly the rest of the time.

Barking

Make no mistake—if it's a dog, it barks. Barking is the canine method of communicating and it's hard for humans to miss that distinct sound. When you come home after a long absence and your dog barks to welcome you, it can be a wonderful sound. It's his way of saying, "You're a special person and I'm glad you're home with me now!" But if your dog barks excessively, others won't think it's so wonderful.

Why Do Dogs Bark?

There are many reasons a dog barks. Barking can mean your dog is having fun, is feeling frightened or lonely, wants attention or hears a noise. It's also his way of warning you of danger or that a stranger is approaching.

"The tone of barking changes with the dog's motivation," says David S. Spiegel, V.M.D., a veterinarian in private practice in Wilmington, Delaware, who specializes in treating canine behavior problems. "A panicked or anxious dog barks in a tone and pattern we recognize as distress. This draws us near to help him."

While most dogs bark to say something, others do it just for fun or out of habit. This kind of barking can go on all day and your dog will soon become the neighborhood nuisance.

How to Stop Your Dog's Barking

When you can decipher the barking code and understand what it is that's making your dog bark, you'll soon be able to control the excessive commotion. It just takes good listening skills and very close observation. If he just looks at you

A dog that barks constantly when left in the yard can become a source of annoyance to the neighbors. The most likely cause is boredom, so make sure your dog has plenty to keep him occupied when he's outside.

and barks without any other stimulus, he probably wants your attention. He might be hungry or want to play.

To help your dog expend the energy he might otherwise use for barking, give him lots of physical outlets for expression. Long daily walks will both satisfy and tire him out, as will taking him to a large fenced-in dog park where he can run, play and bark in a controlled environment. If your dog starts barking for you to notice him, slip on his training collar and leash and give him a few obedience drills. He'll have your attention but you'll have his, too. After a few commands to "Sit" and "Down," he'll forget all about barking.

If your dog is left alone for long hours, barking may be his (very loud) way of expressing himself. Dogs are companion animals so they should never be left alone for long periods of time. But if you can't avoid leaving your dog at home by himself, try turning on the radio or television when you leave. Some dogs associate the sound with the presence of their owners and will be comforted and quiet.

You can also give him "puzzle" treats like a ball filled with peanut butter or cheese to play with while you're gone. These will keep him busy for hours as he tries to extract the food. This mental stimulation will also tire him out, so he'll probably spend the rest of the time snoozing.

If your dog barks every time he sees a stranger, keep your window shades drawn or make sure your backyard fence is solid to prevent him from seeing what's going on outside. Don't pet him or reassure him that everything is okay. If you do, he'll think that you are praising him for his bravery and that barking is a good thing to do. Yelling at him to stop barking will just convince him that you're joining his call to alarm.

If your dog barks because he's frightened of something, such as the vacuum cleaner, the lawn mower or a large trash can,

Why Do Dogs Bark at the Mailman?

It's not unreasonable to expect that your dog would recognize the mailman when he comes to your house every day at the same time. Instead, your dog greets him like a stranger with a barrage of furious barks, and you can't figure out why.

To understand this common behavior, put yourself in your dog's position. The first time he sees the mailman coming to the door, he wants to protect his home from this stranger. After a few sharp barks, the mailman leaves and your dog feels proud and confident that he was responsible for driving him away. After that, whenever the mailman approaches, your dog woofs out his noisy alarm. It worked the first time, so he thinks it will work again. And it does. The mailman leaves!

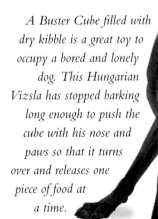

A Buster Cube filled with dry kibble is a great toy to occupy a bored and lonely dog. This Hungarian Vizsla has stopped barking long enough to push the cube with his nose and paws so that it turns over and releases one piece of food at a time.

try desensitizing him to those objects. If you feed him next to these common items or while the motors are running, he'll eventually associate those big scary things with the positive act of being fed. Densensitizing him to objects he is frightened of will not only reduce his barking but will also give him confidence.

Another way to stop him barking is to make a sharp sound that's at least twice as loud as his barking. He'll think twice about barking the next time. Clang two cooking pots together or use an air horn, the kind that is commonly used on boats, suggests Dr. Spiegel.

Begging

Few owners can resist their dog's pleading eyes gazing up at them during dinnertime. "Dogs lust after what we're eating because they see us enjoying it so much," says Dr. Spiegel. "And they just want to join in the fun."

But if you give in just once and feed your dog even the smallest morsel from the dinner table, you'll never be left alone during mealtime again. Your dog will soon act as if he's starving all the time and the begging will progress to drooling, whining, jumping up on your lap and frantic scrambling every time a part of the meal flies off the table by accident.

Why Begging is Bad

When you start sharing your calorie count, not only will you never have another moment's peace, your dog will also start to gain weight. Think about it: On top of his regular portion of dog food, he's eating the occasional buttered roll, piece of meat, leftover pasta, piece of sponge birthday cake, and anything else he can manage to mooch from you.

A canine's digestive system isn't the same as a human's, so your dog can get sick from eating too much people food. You may think you are being loving to your dog by feeding him fried foods or sweets, but love is keeping your dog healthy and feeding him properly.

If you do feed him mealtime leftovers, choose either raw or cooked vegetables, rice, low-fat cottage cheese or small pieces of fruit. A small piece of chicken broiled without the skin can be given as a treat. Put the leftovers in his dish with his regular food the next day or after you've finished cleaning up in the kitchen.

All your dog wants is a tiny piece of what's on your plate. What possible harm can that do? The trouble is, it will be the start of a lifelong habit that can become a nuisance.

Tips to Stop Mooching

1 Never feed your dog from the table and make sure that even small children keep this rule.

2 Ask company not to feed your dog. If that isn't possible, put your dog outside or in his crate when guests come to dine.

3 Ignore your dog's begging. Whenever he is quiet and doesn't beg, praise him and offer him a dog treat after you have finished eating.

4 If your dog jumps up on you, barks or drools on your lap during mealtime, command him to "Down" and "Stay" in a special spot for the duration of the meal.

5 Give your dog a bone to chew on or a ball filled with cheese or peanut butter to play with while you are dining.

6 Feed your dog before you sit down to eat. If he's full, he's more likely to leave you alone.

7 Give your dog some vigorous exercise before you sit down to meals. If he's tired, he'll sleep.

8 If you must feed him leftovers, place them in his dish with his regular food the next day.

Car Chasing

If it moves, your dog will chase it. Balls, bubbles, sticks or falling leaves floating through the air are just a few of the fun things dogs love to pursue. Young dogs in particular love the challenge of moving objects. They make perfect toys and it's delightful to watch a young pup entertaining himself by trying to catch a fly on the window or investigating a tuft of cotton blowing around the yard. Once things come to a standstill they're not nearly as interesting.

As they mature, some dogs become territorial. They feel it's their job to protect their home from intruders, and the chase game that was once so cute soon develops into barking and running back and forth as they attempt to scare away anything that moves or breathes. To a territorial dog, cats and squirrels are just as menacing as kids on noisy skateboards and bicycles.

The first time your dog succeeds in chasing something or someone away, he swells up with confidence and this makes him want to demonstrate his chasing ability again. But when a dog gets enough confidence to start racing after cars, he has become dangerously aggressive and is risking his own life.

Before you allow your dog to run free without a leash, he should be absolutely reliable in responding to your "Come" or "Stop" command. Never chase him if he runs away—he'll just think you want to play a game of catch-me-if-you-can.

Halt!

To prevent your dog from developing into a car chaser, don't encourage chasing behavior. If your dog steals something of yours or he doesn't come to you when you call him, don't chase after him. Instead, call him to "Come," and reward him when he does. Obedience training will be very helpful in making sure the "Come" command is well instilled.

If your dog has already taken to chasing cars, make sure you keep him in a fenced yard or on his leash when he is outdoors. Giving your dog plenty of exercise is another way to curb the chasing instinct. Teach him to retrieve, then spend lots of time throwing balls, sticks or other items for him to chase after and return to you. Hopefully, this will wear him out. Never encourage him to run after anything without bringing it back to you.

To stop your dog chasing things while you are out walking, keep him on a leash and develop

Paws for thought

Do Some Breeds Chase More Than Others?

Almost all dogs enjoy chasing something. Usually, it's what they were originally bred to do, says Jill Yorey, a training consultant at the Society for the Prevention of Cruelty to Animals in Los Angeles. Terriers were trained to hunt and kill weasels and rats, and hound breeds, such as Afghans, Salukis and Greyhounds, were prized for their hunting speed and uncanny ability to see large predators at great distances.

Some working dogs, such as Doberman Pinschers, were bred and trained to trail criminals, while Newfoundlands chased after and rescued people who were thrashing around in icy waters.

Sporting dogs, such as Spaniels, Pointers and Retrievers, have been huntsmen's companions for centuries and are capable of chasing and retrieving many different sizes and types of fowl and other small animals. And to a dog, a car isn't much different from a very big rabbit.

house. When your dog begins to run after it have your friend throw water balloons or something noisy (but harmless) from the slow-moving vehicle. It should startle him enough to make him change his mind.

Try also attaching a 15-foot leash to his choke collar. Again, ask a friend to drive by the front of your house very slowly. As soon as your dog begins to chase after the car, let him run a few feet before you tighten, then quickly release your grip on the leash. Be sure to command "No!" when you do this and take care not to choke him. Keep repeating this exercise until he catches onto the idea.

If the thrill of the chase is what your dog likes most, challenge him with bat-and-ball games in the park or another safe area. This Australian Kelpie mix is having a great time playing tennis with his owner.

his attention span by making him follow your commands and getting him to watch you. If he begins to run after a moving object while walking on his leash, turn abruptly in the opposite direction. When he follows you instead of going after the squirrel or cyclist, reward him with a food treat.

If a moving car still fascinates your dog, ask a friend to slowly drive a car by the front of your

Chewing

Whether you call it gnawing, chomping or teething, it all boils down to the same thing—dogs love to chew. When busy dog teeth meet soft objects you can be sure there'll be a mess. Objects with interesting smells and textures are always alluring, and the more valuable they are to you, the more attractive they seem to your dog, especially if you're not around. After a few sniffs and test bites, your dog will aim to shred your favorite possession into as many pieces as possible, then scatter the evidence.

Reasons for Chewing

Some puppies chew only while their permanent teeth are coming in. Others don't stop chewing until a few years later. Chewing is natural and dogs get a lot of fun and satisfaction from it. Watch your dog rip a pillow apart and you'll see what a good time he's having. Toys, shoes, furniture, a corner of the carpet and even plastered walls can provide hours of entertainment for him.

At times it seems that chewing is premeditated, but it's really a spur-of-the-moment activity. Dogs sink their teeth into things because they feel anxious, are bored or have too much energy. Don't try to stop it. Chewing relieves tension and keeps them busy. Just direct this behavior to objects you find acceptable.

Control What He Chews

Start by giving your dog as many chew toys as possible. Balls, rope toys and Nylabones are just a few suitable objects you can offer him. See which one he likes best and name it. This way when you ask him, "Where's your ball?" he'll be able to respond. When he finds it and starts chewing it, praise him.

Whatever you do, don't give your dog old shoes or socks to chew. He doesn't understand the difference between old and new and he'll just get the message that all your belongings are okay to chew. If your dog starts gnawing away at something you don't want him to, say "No!" and offer him one of his favorite chew toys instead. Rubbing your hands all over the toy before you give it to him will put your smell on the item and make it even more attractive to him.

A puppy explores the tastes and textures of his world through his mouth. Your job is to teach him what he's not allowed to chew—or to keep such items out of reach.

Why are Shoes Such a Favorite?

You would think the strong odor of shoes would deter dogs from chewing them, but the opposite is true. Most dogs are attracted because our footwear carries our scent and reminds them of us, especially when they are home alone and feeling stressed.

Some dogs are also attracted to what we wear on our feet because it feels good in the mouth. Most shoes are made of pliable materials, such as rubber, leather and cowhide, and these materials offer just enough resistance to give your dog a challenge.

But the most common reason is because shoes are within easy reach. "Since shoes are usually what's left lying on the floor, they are common prey," says Suzanne B. Johnson, Ph.D., an animal behaviorist in private practice in Washington, D.C.

If your dog is chewing your possessions out of boredom, be creative and offer him as many different munchables as often as you can. Young puppies love cardboard boxes, milk cartons, the cores from paper towel rolls and just about anything else you can think of that you don't mind cleaning up later. These alternative chew toys are cheap and provide a healthy outlet for your dog's excess energy and tension. Offer your dog a different one each time so he thinks he's getting something new.

The other way to save your possessions from destruction is to make sure you don't leave them lying around. With your dog, it's definitely a question of out of sight, out of mouth. If your dog has taken a fancy to the leg of the kitchen table, make sure you supervise him when he is indoors. If you can't supervise your little chomper, crate him or put him in a safe outside enclosure. And if you have to leave him at home alone, be sure to give him something acceptable to gnaw on in your absence.

You can also sprinkle a hot pepper sauce, bitter apple or pet repellent onto objects your dog begins mouthing. Since dogs don't like the smell of after-shave lotion or perfume, apply some of these to your dog's targets. Or take a soda can and put some pebbles into it. Tie a long string around the can and attach it to the object you don't want your dog to chew. When he starts gnawing away, the can will rattle and scare him.

Oral Fixes

Rubber rings, ropes, pig ears, stuffed toy animals that squeak and toys made from lamb's wool, rubber or canvas are just some of the many chew toys that you can buy for your dog.

You can also make your own chew toys at home. Take an old soccer ball and let out some of the air, just enough to enable your dog to grip it with his mouth. Or fill a rubber Kong toy with cheese or peanut butter. This will keep your dog licking and chewing for hours. Milk, juice and all different shapes and sizes of cardboard containers also make good and inexpensive chew toys. Just be sure to remove any staples before he gets them, as these could be harmful.

Teaching Your Dog to "Drop It"

When your dog starts chewing on your credit card or a detailed project you've left on the desk, you don't want to start a chase game to get them back. Even if you manage to catch up with your dog, you'll be hard pressed to rescue the precious items by prying his mouth open. Once he lowers his head and decides to clamp his jaws down, you're in for a battle. Instead, teach him to "Release" or "Drop it." This command is also useful for when your dog gets hold of dangerous objects or spoiled food.

1 Command your dog to sit in front of you. Give him something he can hold in his mouth. It should be large enough for you to be able to grasp part of it while he has it in his mouth.

2 While your dog is holding the object in his mouth, say "Hold" and praise him for a few brief moments.

3 Hold the leash two feet from his collar and jerk it downward, telling him either to "Release" or "Drop it." At the same time, use your other hand to grasp the object firmly, but don't pull it out of his mouth. The idea is to guide it out of his mouth, not yank it.

4 Praise him lavishly when he drops it. It may take a few tries before he follows this command easily. Keep repeating the exercise until your dog drops it quickly, then test him with other objects. Be sure to praise him so he knows he's done well.

Climbing on Furniture

At some point, every dog will attempt to stake a claim to the furniture. And why not? A couch is not only comfy, it's warm and gives him a view of the house he can't get from down on the floor. If it's located next to a window overlooking the street, this spot will be even more alluring.

If you call your dog even once to jump up there beside you, he'll believe that's where you want him to be all the time. If you ignore him the first time he tries the davenport, or laugh and tell him how cute he looks, he'll think you approve of the new seating arrangement.

This isn't a problem if you don't mind your dog lying on the love seat next to you. But if you decide later you don't want him there, you'll have to convince him that the furniture is very uncomfortable to be on. To do that takes some effort and consistency so it's better to make a firm decision in the first place and stick to it.

Not So Comfy

To discourage your dog from jumping up and sitting on the furniture, lay plastic bubble wrap on top of your sofa. The next time he jumps up he will be startled by the new sound and feel, and jump right back off. For some dogs, that's enough to make them think twice about ever trying to get up again, but others will recognize the bubble wrap and just jump on the sofa when it's not there. If your dog is one of the smarter ones, tuck a bed sheet on top of the wrap and leave it on all the time—or at least until he decides to stay off for good.

You can also place plastic mouse traps under the sheet. These will make a loud snap the minute your dog jumps on the couch and will also scare him into jumping back down. Lightweight plastic mouse traps are not dangerous to your dog because there are no metal pieces, but if you're not comfortable using them, try blowing up some balloons and taping them to the seat cushions. They'll accomplish the same thing.

There are also special mats designed to be placed on top of furniture to deter your dog from jumping up. As soon as your dog jumps up, the mats give a very mild electric shock.

Why Your Favorite Chair is His Favorite Chair

For the same reasons you love it, your dog will also love to sit in your favorite armchair. Besides having your smell, it's probably the most comfortable piece of furniture in the house. It's softened up in all the right places and there may even be cushions or a blanket for extra padding. You've positioned it in a spot where there isn't a draft, and if it's a window seat, there'll be a great outdoor view. Or it may be located in a quiet corner of the room where your dog can just relax. If you keep the candy dish well-stocked on the table beside it, that's also enticing. But most of all, sitting in your favorite chair makes your dog feel close to you, especially when you're not around and he's feeling just a little lonely.

Digging

Turning up the earth is a great canine sport. As the dirt flies every which way, you can see how much fun your dog is having. He's intent on getting to the bottom of it all and doesn't care how long it takes or how dirty he gets. Some breeds dig only when they're young, while others tunnel all their lives.

Why Dig?

Digging gives a dog that might not have much else to do a sense of being busy. And if there's an odor in the earth, he'll want to find out more about it. A rodent could have tunneled far underneath and your dog will want to go after it, especially if he likes to guard his territory or he's a terrier whose ancestors have been digging out small creatures for generations.

If he sees you gardening, he may think it's okay to do the same thing and copy your behavior. To your dog, new plants smell good enough to investigate up close and personal. If it's a hot day, a good dig can give your dog a cool place to lie. Earth provides warmth on a cold day, too. And female dogs who are about to give birth or who are going through a false pregnancy like to dig a cozy hiding place for their puppies.

How to Control Digging

Let him know digging isn't acceptable. If you see him working away, tell him "No!" Then give him a toy to distract him. You'll probably have to repeat the correction a few times before he understands that digging is a no-no. A busy dog is less likely to dig, so take him running with you. This will burn off energy he would otherwise use to journey to the center of the earth.

To deter your dog from digging in certain places, put heavy bricks over that area. Place chicken wire mesh around plants or shrubs you want to protect. If this won't stop him, give him his own digging area full of buried treasures, says Suzanne Hetts, Ph.D., an applied animal behaviorist in private practice in Littleton, Colorado.

If it's hot outside, leave a small wading pool for him to cool off in. And when the weather turns cold, make sure he has shelter or bring him inside to warm up.

Provide a persistent digger with his very own "dig zone" where he can probe to his paws' content. To let him know this is his special digging place, this Boxer's owner has buried some of his favorite toys there.

Eating and Rolling in Dung

Most owners take a lot of pride in the food they serve their dog. So when your dog shows a liking for dung, it can come as a shock. Once he develops a taste for the unspeakable, it becomes a habit that's difficult to break. He gobbles it up as fast as he can, then thinks nothing of trotting over to give you a kiss and cuddle.

The odor is enough to knock you over. And if you think eating his own or another animal's stools is one of the most distasteful things your dog can do, you're right. Until, that is, you see him rolling around in it as well.

Dogs love to roll on the grass for a good back massage anytime, but if there's a nice smelly mess there, so much the better. He loves the smell even if you can't think of anything worse.

Why They Do It

There are a couple of reasons why your dog may consider dung to be a delicacy. It may fill a nutritional need that isn't being met by his conventional everyday dog food. Or he may have seen another dog do it and copied the behavior. If your dog is a Labrador Retriever or Golden Retriever, then he has been genetically programmed to pick up things in his mouth.

As for rolling around in it, this behavior is a leftover from the time when dogs roamed wild. In order to put predators off the trail, wild dogs covered themselves with foul-smelling messes to mask their own scent. Rolling and twisting in dung also probably feels like a good back massage to your dog—nothing else seems to get to those hard-to-reach places along his spine.

How to Stop It

If your dog picks up dung in his mouth while you are out walking, command him to "Leave it." Back in your own yard, supervise your dog's toilet time and clean up immediately afterward. "If it's not there, he won't eat it," says Dorothy Laflamme, D.V.M., a veterinary nutritionist in the St. Louis area and vice-president of the American College of Veterinary Nutrition.

If your dog still persists in dining on dung, try spraying it with a pet repellent, such as bitter apple. You can also sprinkle Adolph's Meat Tenderizer, Accent or a product called Forbid on your dog's food before he eats it. These three products will give his dung a taste even he won't be able to stand.

To stop your dog rocking and rolling in muck, keep your yard free from messy substances you wouldn't want to see in your living room. If your dog is prone to doing this while you're out on walks, keep him on a leash.

If you're exercising your dog outdoors and you see a problem area up ahead, call your dog to "Come" immediately and distract him with a game or a few obedience drills.

Teaching Your Dog to "Leave It"

When you tell your dog to "Leave it" you're really saying "Ignore it immediately." Teaching him not to go near dung or anything else that takes his fancy is a big challenge, so begin teaching this command indoors where it's quiet. Ideally, you want your dog to ignore the item that draws his attention the minute you tell him to.

I With his training collar and leash on, command your dog to sit in front of you. Show him a piece of food and tell him to "Leave it."

2 Shorten the leash, then throw the food a short distance away, all the while telling your dog to "Leave it."

3 When he rushes to get it, jerk the leash. When he stays by your side praise him and reward him with a tidbit. Repeat the process until he understands the command. Test him with more aromatic food before taking the act on the road.

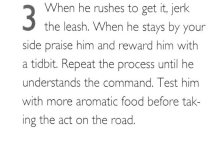

Fear

When a dog doesn't understand something or finds himself in an unusual situation, he may become fearful. A well-adjusted dog who has been handled by lots of different people and constantly exposed to new things will take unusual situations in his stride, says Susan Anderson, D.V.M., a clinical instructor of outpatient medicine in the department of small animal clinical sciences at the University of Florida College of Veterinary Medicine in Gainesville.

A dog who was not so fortunate and was left alone too much when he was young will be confused and may have a difficult time making sense of the world around him.

The Fearful Dog

A dog who gets nervous about many things—people approaching him, going for a ride in the car, loud noises such as thunder or the whir of the vacuum cleaner—is a fearful dog. This kind of dog assumes everything will come crashing down on him at any moment, so he tries to protect himself in anticipation. When people see a dog cower as someone friendly approaches him, they think the dog has been abused. While he may not have been physically abused, his self-esteem has been damaged all the same.

The sight of a dog who is so afraid that nothing can calm him down is disturbing. He may growl, shake or try to run away and hide. And if you don't solve the problem, his fearfulness can turn into aggression and fear biting.

How to Curb Fear

Changing a fearful dog into a stable one is not easy and may take a long time, but it's worth the effort. Don't reassure your frightened dog by hugging him or telling him everything is okay. It's not and he knows it's not. He may be so panicky that he may try to bite you.

Instead, act calm and your dog will most likely follow your example. If you can laugh while your dog is struggling to escape the veterinarian's exam, the upbeat mood will probably rub off on him. It's okay to give your dog a gentle touch when he's nervous but don't make too big a deal out of what's bothering him.

Timidity is not always the result of bad treatment. Your dog can be this way naturally and it may take a long time and lots of patience to build up his confidence. But when you succeed, it will be worth all the effort. Start the process by giving him basic obedience drills.

Obedience classes not only build confidence with every success, they also provide expert guidance and an excellent opportunity for both you and your dog to make friends with others who live in your neighborhood.

To help your fearful dog, socialize him more by taking him everywhere you go. Bring along some dog biscuits and when people approach, ask them if they wouldn't mind giving one to your dog. While he may not take it at first, he will eventually. If you do this often he will soon come to enjoy meeting strangers.

It also helps to handle your dog a lot. Rub your hands all over him as an examining vet might. This will relax him and accustom him to being touched.

You can also enroll your dog in obedience classes where he will learn the basic commands of sit, stay, down, heel and come. Not only does this build his confidence, it also gives you a technique to use with him the next time he gets spooked. He'll regard you as the one in charge and the next time he gets worried, he'll look to you for reassurance.

Fear of Loud Noises

When dogs are afraid of loud noises they have good reason to be. "Their sense of hearing is one hundred times greater than ours is, so everything sounds much louder to them than it does to us," says Dr. Anderson. So don't be surprised the next time you drop a tray of dishes or the alarm goes off and your dog rushes off and cowers in the corner.

To make your dog feel comfortable before the next big boom, play lots of noise games. While he's eating, laugh out loud and rattle some pots and pans. Or pump up the volume on the radio and dance around the room while giving him treats. He'll soon realize that noise is no cause for alarm.

Fear of Objects

You can never predict what objects will frighten your young pup. It could be a large vase placed on the floor, an outdoor garbage can or that tire you put in the yard for him to climb on. Until he becomes familiar with them, your puppy will consider most objects as unknown "monsters." He may stare at a strange object for a while before barking and running backward. If he's feeling brave he might even creep forward slowly

Why are Dogs So Scared of Thunder?

Imagine the sky rattling so loudly it sounds as if it's about to fall down on top of you. That's what dogs hear when it thunders. Because the canine auditory system is far more sensitive than ours, many dogs shiver and shake and are scared to death during noisy storms.

To desensitize your dog to thunder, record the sound of it. Play it back at a low volume when you give your dog a treat or feed him. Gradually increase the volume and repeat the exercise many times until he's used to it. The next time a real storm comes along he'll be waiting for food in his dish instead of hiding under the couch.

You can also try distracting your dog during a thunderstorm. Play games with him or do other things he enjoys to take his mind off being afraid.

and quietly so as not to disturb it. To familiarize your dog with new things, go over to the object and sit beside it. Talk to your dog and reassure him in a very upbeat tone of voice that this is a very nice object. Run your hand over it. When your dog sees that it doesn't attack you, he will gradually become less afraid.

Fear of Strangers

Some people look scary without meaning to. The way they walk might seem menacing or that big hat they're wearing can intimidate a young puppy that hasn't seen much of the world yet. Some dogs are nervous just seeing people other than their family.

If your dog is frightened of people, take him with you when you visit a friend. Ask your friend to stoop down at your dog's side and offer him a small treat. Stand nearby and be calm. Don't yank your dog's collar or leash to prevent him from backing up. If he doesn't want to take the treat, your friend can toss it to him. It can take some time for dogs to be comfortable around other people, so be patient. Don't try to rush his progress.

"Once your dog improves, start asking other people to hold his leash while you stand there," suggests Kathy Marmack, an animal training supervisor at the San Diego Zoo. "This way your dog learns that others can be leaders too."

With enough practice, your dog will soon be confident enough to go sniffing strangers' hands for treats the minute someone new approaches.

If your dog is nervous of strangers, enlist the help of a friend. Ask your friend to stoop down low and hand your dog a food treat or throw one toward him. Over a period of time these friendly gestures will help to build up your dog's confidence.

Hates Being Handled

Your dog likes to be petted, but touch his feet to clip his toenails and he immediately slips and wiggles away. He may also be fussy about having his rear examined or his teeth inspected. It will be difficult to keep a dog who hates being handled well-groomed or have him examined by a vet.

The more a puppy is handled by people of all ages and sizes, the more relaxed he will be in later life.

When puppies are not handled much from birth, tactile sensations are new and strange to them. They're unsure what will happen, so they flip their heads from side to side to see what's going on with your hand. Sometimes female dogs are uncomfortable about their rears being touched, especially if they're in season or soon will be. Young male dogs going through puberty can also be touchy about that area of their anatomy. Other dogs might have had a lot of early stroking but are very strong-willed and want to control their own bodies. "It can be a dominance problem," says Peter L. Borchelt, Ph.D., an animal behaviorist in private practice in Brooklyn, New York.

Feel It, Don't Fight It

Trying to get a grip on a dog who is struggling to free himself is not easy. Besides scratching you, he might also try to bite your hands. If this happens, tell him sternly, "No bite!" Continue holding him and praise him when he stops.

Accustom your puppy to your touch by giving him gentle massages from the moment you bring him home. Talk softly to him as you soothingly stroke all over his body. Apply very little pressure at first. When your dog begins to enjoy it, he'll respond by leaning his body into your fingertips.

With an older dog, put his collar and leash on. While holding the leash, talk softly to him as you pet him where he feels comfortable. Confidently move your hand to other areas of his body, while telling him what a good dog he is. If he doesn't like his paws to be handled, offer him a treat while softly touching one of them. When he allows you to do this, say, "Good dog." If he still resists, tell him in a low, strong voice to "Quit it" and give him a little leash correction. Touch the remaining paws one at a time. Repeat this process until you can lift each foot slightly and are able to rub his toes very gently without him protesting. Practice this several times a day.

Try making a game out of giving him rough pats and tickles after running your hands over his back and tail. Be sure to laugh so he knows it's supposed to be fun. The goal is to make him feel secure enough to accept your authority.

Hyperactivity

Young dogs are naturally excitable—there'd be something wrong with them if they weren't—but adult dogs who have so much energy that they can't sit still are considered hyperactive. If you think your dog is hyperactive, blame his ancestors. Years ago he was probably bred to run all day herding sheep or hunting game. If you take this same dog and leave him at home alone for eight hours in a small backyard with nothing to do, it's not surprising that he will have oodles of energy to burn off when you get home. Running from room to room without being able to settle down is a sign that your dog needs a job to do.

Keep Him Busy

To deal with a hyperactive dog, you'll need to channel his energies into behavior you can live with. Getting upset and yelling doesn't help. Your dog will sense your mood right away, and this will agitate him even more. Instead, give him lots of physical exercise. Take him for long walks or go running or cycling with him. If you have to leave him alone while you work, hire someone to come during the day and take him out jogging or play a vigorous game of fetch with him for an hour or so. With some physical activity during the day, your dog won't be all over you the moment you walk in the door. Try to get up an hour earlier in the morning to allow yourself more time with him, too.

Mental exercise is just as important as physical exercise for a hyperactive dog. Giving him an activity to focus and concentrate on will slow him down, so take him to agility or obedience classes regularly. You can even make a small obstacle course in your backyard. Hyperactive dogs need constant work to keep their energy levels on an even keel, so make these activities a permanent part of your dog's life.

Dogs and Their Diet

Some people believe that with so many dog treats being high in calories and sugar, diet might play a part in raising a dog's energy levels. "But there is no evidence to suggest that hyperactivity in dogs is related to diet," says Katherine Houpt, V.M.D., Ph.D., a professor of physiology and director of the Behavior Clinic at Cornell University College of Veterinary Medicine in Ithaca, New York, and author of *Domestic Animal Behavior.*

Some dogs, especially those that were bred to do the serious job of herding, such as this Collie mix, require a high level of activity to keep them from becoming bored.

Jumping Up

Your dog loves you and to prove it, he wants to greet you by looking you right in the eye. And you love him too. But when you're all dressed up or holding a drink in your hand, you'd probably prefer that he didn't show his love by jumping up in this way. Or maybe your dog's a friendly fellow with strangers, but they may not always be happy to see him up so close, especially young children or the elderly.

When he was a puppy, your dog seemed so cute jumping up on your legs to get attention. At the time he barely reached your knees and weighed only a few pounds. Who could resist petting and picking up such a tiny thing? But when he jumps up now, he may be able to put his paws on your shoulders. He could easily knock you over and cause injury.

How to Stop It

To train your dog not to jump up, you have to reprimand him each and every time. If you allow him to jump up on you when you're playing ball with him on the weekend, then yell the words "Down!" at other times, he won't understand why it's okay one day and not the next. "When you say 'Off' your dog should know you mean it," says Sandy Myers, a behavior consultant and trainer in Naperville, Illinois. Make

A dog's exuberance, as displayed by this Golden Retriever, can be dangerous, so don't let your dog jump up.

sure everyone in the family follows the same rule of not allowing him to jump up. Even if they say it's okay, correct him anyway. It's confusing and not fair to make him follow the rule with some people and not others.

If your dog jumps up on you, don't pet him. He should receive a pat and hug only when all four of his feet are on the ground. This should also be the case when you're sitting on the couch and he tries to climb into your lap.

If you know there are certain times when he is sure to jump up, such as when someone walks through the front door, put his leash on before you even open the door. Plan a training session by asking a friend to come over. When your dog goes to leap, step on the leash close to where he's standing and say "Off." Be sure to give him a substitute command, such as "Sit" soon after you have said "Off." When he sits, praise him with a few pats. He'll soon realize he gets the attention he wants only when he's sitting and waiting for it.

If your dog starts jumping up on someone and you're too far away to step on his leash, say "Off" and toss a soda can filled with pennies near him. The noise should surprise him enough to stop his hop. When he obeys your command, give him lots of praise.

Licking

Some people just giggle and say it tickles, while others say the feeling of their dog's wet and rough tongue on their skin is very unpleasant. Whatever the human reaction, when your dog gives you a lick on your hand or your face, it's a sign of affection.

"When a dog licks your face it's a greeting," says Bonnie V. Beaver, D.V.M., a professor and chief of medicine at the Texas Veterinary Medical Center at the College of Veterinary Medicine at Texas A&M University in College Station. "It's also the way young dogs show submissiveness to older dogs."

And while some people like it when their dogs give them kisses, others do not. Some folks can tolerate the occasional wet peck on the cheek, but when it becomes a continuous stream of licking and more licking, that's unacceptable. If you don't correct him, what starts as affection can become a subtle form of dominance. The more you resist by moving away and saying "Yuck," the more pushy he gets.

To avoid turning into a human lollipop, reassert your authority by correcting your dog when he licks you. Put his collar and leash on and give him a strong verbal command of "No lick!" If he persists give a short jerk on the leash.

"Alter the licking urge by substituting another activity your dog likes better," says Linda Goodloe, Ph.D., an animal behaviorist in private practice in Chester County, Pennsylvannia. Spend more quality time with your dog or give him a new chew toy to occupy his mouth.

An Early Experience

The first lick a dog experiences is right after he is born. A mother licks her newborn pups to clean them and stimulate them to urinate and defecate. Licking is also her way of letting them know that she is their mother. They will always be able to recognize her by the smell of her saliva. A mother also licks her own nipples, which lays down a saliva trail for her pups to follow to find their food supply.

These Golden Retriever pups are showing affection by licking each other.

Overprotectiveness

It's comforting to have a dog who stays by your side, even sleeping on your bed. A protective dog makes you feel safe and loved. But when your dog starts to think of you as his personal property, becoming more and more possessive of you and guarding you against every little thing, it's not so great. An overprotective dog can soon turn into an aggressive one.

When he starts growling because someone new has come to your house and is sitting next to you, or he starts bullying the rest of the household with menacing barks and dominant behavior, your feeling of trust will soon turn to fear. Dogs that don't understand that you are the boss become a problem. And once he senses someone else is afraid of him, he'll protect you even more closely. If your dog is a herding breed, he may even try to nudge you into a corner away from the stranger, or nudge the other person away from you.

Preventing Overprotectiveness

It isn't just big or dominant dogs that become overprotective of their owner—any size or breed of dog can develop this trait. To prevent overprotectiveness, avoid telling him "It's okay" when he growls at someone else. This just reinforces the behavior—he'll think you are giving him the message that growling is acceptable. Instead, begin obedience training as soon as possible. "Asking your dog to 'Sit' will give him something to do and lower his arousal when someone approaches," says Dr. Goodloe.

To let your dog know that you're in charge, don't allow him to sleep on your bed or furniture. When he learns to behave more submissively, you can invite him back on, if you wish.

There are a number of reasons why your dog may become overprotective but it's up to you to regain control over this potentially dangerous situation.

To accustom your dog to other people being close to you, ask a friend to offer him a treat while he's on his leash. Stand close by and act in a relaxed manner.

Possessiveness of Toys

When your dog receives a new toy, especially one he's crazy about, his first reaction is to guard it carefully so no one steals it. He'll take his treasure to a far corner of the house or yard, hold on to it tight with his front paws and lick or chew it. And when someone approaches, his immediate instinct is to protect his find by growling, a trait passed on from his pack-living wolf ancestors.

Teach Him to Share

Some dogs can become so possessive that they will bare their teeth or snap if someone approaches them while they are playing with their toys. This aggressive behavior is not acceptable and can be very dangerous, especially if small children or other pets are part of your household.

Not being possessive with toys is an important lesson to teach your dog. To train him to share with others, put his leash and collar on. Give your dog a new toy, then immediately ask him to give it to you by saying "Drop it." The minute he releases it, even slightly, praise him.

If your dog refuses, ignore the toy and give him a few "Sit" and "Down" commands. These

Make a game of giving your dog a toy and then telling him to "Drop it" in exchange for something else. He'll soon get the idea that it's a win–win situation for him.

obedience drills will remind him that you are the leader of the pack and you are the one who decides whether he may have the toy or not. Repeat the obedience drills several times, then end the session by taking away his toy. "If he still fusses about giving you the toy, then take it away after he's finished playing with it and get rid of it," says Dr. Beaver.

Another way to prevent possessiveness is to offer your dog another toy or a food treat in exchange for the item he is playing with. Tell your dog to "Drop it," and as soon as he releases the item, give him the new toy. A few minutes later give your dog back the original toy, then repeat the exercise a few more times. By making a game of handing toys back and forth, you'll encourage your dog to trust you. Soon he'll be dropping what he has in his mouth as soon as he sees you approaching with something else in your hand.

If your dog gets hold of a real meat bone, it may be the one thing he will not be willing to give up, no matter what you offer him. In this case, it's best just to give in and let him have it, but don't offer the same item to him ever again.

Separation Anxiety

Dogs are companion animals and like to be around their owners. So when you leave the house without your dog, one look in his eyes will tell you he's not happy.

Most dogs accept your comings and goings with a sigh, but others might have a hard time understanding why you're there one moment and gone the next. Your dog may feel insecure and worry that you won't come back. And while you're gone, he may bark, whine or howl in fear. Your worried dog may also become destructive, make messes inside the house, refuse to eat or attempt to escape the yard or house.

Missing You

There are several theories why a dog may be afraid of being away from his owner, says Dr. Anderson. Dogs that have been abandoned once before are the most likely sufferers of separation anxiety—they'll assume they will be left again by their new owners.

Dramatic lifestyle changes, such as moving to a new house or sudden stress in the home, can bring on separation anxiety. And dogs who have had constant contact with their owners (because their owners are retired or work from home) will also find it difficult when their owner has to spend time away from them for some reason.

Ways to Overcome It

"There are many things you can do to make your dog feel more secure when you go away," says Myers. Start by crating him when you are away. Just like some small children who would rather be in their bedroom than wandering around a huge house, many anxious dogs prefer being in a small, confined space. Putting your dog in his crate will help to relax him and will prevent him from pacing about anxiously or trying to escape. He can't destroy the house, either, from inside his crate.

Myers also suggests giving your dog more exercise. "Even if you have to get up earlier in the morning, add a vigorous 20- to 30-minute running session every day prior to leaving him alone. Not only does this tire your dog out, but it reassures him that you are in charge." And when he trusts you as the leader, he won't worry about what you are up to.

Desensitizing your dog to your comings and goings also helps. Get him accustomed to seeing your routine of locking the door, lowering the drapes or putting on your sweater every time you leave the house. Try leaving the house for just short periods of time. In the beginning, leave for a few seconds and come right back. Don't rush to congratulate him the instant you come back in the door—you don't want to make out your absences are a big deal, just an everyday occurrence. If he's been quiet, praise him calmly a few minutes after you return.

Once he seems comfortable with this, gradually add another minute to your absences, then five, and practice going out several times a day. It might take a week or even a month or two before your dog feels calm about being apart from you, but once he's secure, he'll be less nervous about being alone.

Stealing

Thefts can happen all the time in your home. The turkey, warm from the oven, one of your new leather shoes, your wallet or the bones from the trash were all there a minute ago, but now they're not. A clever canine thief waits until you're not looking, then jumps for the counter or dives into the trash to nab the treasure, running off with it as fast as he can.

If you catch your dog in the act, your instant reaction might be to yell at him to stop his antics. But the louder you yell, the faster he runs, and stealing quickly turns into a game he plays to get your attention.

When it comes to food, many dogs can't resist an unattended dinner plate. But when he gobbles the whole thing down in one go, it isn't to attract your attention—he just wants a free meal.

Thwarting the Thief

The best time to correct your dog stealing food or objects is right at the moment he tries to take them, says training consultant Jill Yorey. And the

You can't blame this Doberman for being tempted by the delights on the table. Food is the hardest thing for a dog to resist—it's in his genes to wolf down whatever's on offer.

most effective way to do this is to booby-trap objects so they make a loud, frightening noise as he tries to steal them. Use a long piece of dental floss and tie or tape one end of it to a small piece of meat. Attach the other end to a soda can with a few pebbles inside. Place the meat on the edge of your kitchen counter and leave the room. When your dog goes in for the grab, he'll get the shake can as an unexpected surprise, and it won't take long for him to come running out of the kitchen without his treat. (If your dog wises up to the sight of the shake can, you can cover it with a kitchen cloth).

This same method can be used on anything your dog loves to swipe. You can swap the shake can with a noisy batch of keys and tie them to important papers left on the desk, shoes in the closet or anything else that takes your dog's fancy. Sprinkling Tabasco sauce, pepper flakes or bitter apple on objects of your dog's desire is another way to deter him from stealing. But be warned—many dogs don't mind the extra flavor, says Myers.

If you have a particular area in the house you want to protect from your dog's pilfering paws, such as the den or kitchen, check out the foolproof gates made for toddlers, or ask your vet or other pet owners for advice. They may be able to give you some amusing suggestions. With your persistence and patience, your thieving dog will eventually come to the conclusion that crime doesn't pay.

Unwanted Sniffing

When two dogs meet, they will inevitably spend the first few minutes sniffing each other's private parts. "Sniffing is your dog's way of learning information about a new animal," says Dr. Spiegel. Because dogs have such a strong and powerful sense of smell they can often detect whether the other dog is a male or a female, and whether they have been around other animals or not.

So when your dog meets new people, it's only natural that he greets them by sniffing. Your dog might even think there is nothing wrong in lifting a woman's skirt or nudging a man's crotch, but this behavior makes many people rather uncomfortable—especially if the sniffing gets out of hand—so it's up to you to teach your dog to greet your human friends in a manner that is more socially acceptable.

Stop That Sniffing

To prevent your dog from getting too pushy in other people's private places, put your dog's collar and leash on when you are expecting guests. Be ready to correct him with a "Leave it" command and a slight jerk on the leash if he tries to nosey around where you don't want him to. Follow the "Leave it" command with a "Sit" or "Down" command so that you can praise your dog when he complies with your wishes.

If your dog sniffs you in such a way, don't step backward or move out of his reach. Your dog will interpret this as submissive behavior and he'll begin to think that he's in charge. Instead, make him back away from you by moving forward into him and saying "No!" in a strong, clear voice. You can also offer him a substitute item to become interested in and reward him for leaving you alone.

A dog's desire to sniff can increase tenfold when you take him outdoors for his daily exercise sessions. If your dog is the kind who sniffs constantly while you're out walking, use the same "Leave it" command and a little leash correction. This way he'll know he doesn't have to investigate every odor he encounters.

With his powerful sense of smell, your dog can collect all kinds of fascinating information from his passing doggy friends and acquaintances, but he must be taught that his nosiness is not acceptable to humans.

Whining

A whining dog, especially one who does it constantly, is bound to get on everyone's nerves. If your dog whines loudly and persistently, it may be a sign that he is stressed or overexcited. This may be because he wants something he can't do himself: to be let out of his crate, to be fed, to be given free rein to chase a cat or to go for a walk. Whining can also mean that your dog is so excited that he doesn't know how to calm himself down.

Steps to Stop Whining

If you don't correct this behavior, a strong-willed dog will soon learn he can get what he wants if he whines long enough. To stop the whining, don't coddle your dog with baby talk or pet him reassuringly. Try to ignore it. Only when he stops whining should you give him some attention. That way he learns that he gets rewarded when he doesn't whine, not the other way round.

Giving your dog something to do will also take his mind off whining. If he starts whining, ignore it and command him to "Sit" or "Lie down." After a few obedience drills most dogs will forget what they were whining about.

You can also correct your dog's whining by telling him in a strong, low voice, "No whine!" Make sure your voice is not too harsh because an angry correction will just make some dogs more nervous or anxious. When he responds by being quiet, pet him and praise him. Once he understands "No whine!" try giving him the command to whine, says Mary Kay Snyder, a professional animal trainer, formerly with Birds and Animals Unlimited in Lake Forest, California. "Being able to respond to commands, and receiving praise for it, will help boost the confidence of an anxious dog."

Why Do Dogs Howl at Sirens?

Just like her wolf ancestors, a mother will howl to inform other dogs of her location soon after giving birth to her pups. A dogs' howl is a way of saying, "I hear you out there," "I'm over here" and "This is my territory," says Stanley Coren, Ph.D., a professor of psychology at the University of British Columbia in Vancouver and the author of *The Intelligence of Dogs.*

Unfortunately, the high pitch of a siren is very similar to the pitch of an animal's howl. So when an ambulance or fire engine rushes by with its siren on and your dog starts to howl, there is little you can do. He is just naturally returning the call of the wild.

This Basset Hound is just doing what comes naturally when he answers the call of a siren. Praise him strongly when he learns to stop when you tell him to.

PART THREE

Essential Care

One of the great pleasures of owning a dog is taking care of his simple needs, by giving him plenty of exercise and attention— along with a few choice accessories.

10   FUN AND FITNESS

pages 170–183
No matter his shape, age or size, your dog is going to love exercise. It's the doggy way of getting healthy while having a great time.

11   THE BEST ACCESSORIES

pages 184–191
All those extra-special things your well-dressed and much-loved dog shouldn't have to do without.

12   CARING FOR LATCHKEY PETS

pages 192–197
How to keep your stay-at-home dog happy and entertained when you're out at work for most of the day.

13   TRAVELING IN COMFORT

pages 198–209
From a quick trip to the park to the vacation adventure, on wheels or by air, how to put your dog at ease when you're on the move.

10 FUN AND FITNESS

*Big or small, every dog needs her daily workout. It could be a two-mile jog,
a swim or a steady walk—or simply playing chase and fetch for
15 minutes around the apartment. Not only is exercise
good for her, but she's also having fun. And that makes
for a happy and healthy dog.*

Why Exercise is so Important
pages 171–172
Regular exercise increases
stamina and strength, and dogs
love to get their paws moving

Exercise Guidelines
pages 177–179
Match her activities to her age
and natural abilities

Too Much of a Good Thing
page 182
How much is enough and what
are the warning signs that she
may be overdoing it?

Fitness Fundamentals
pages 173–176
Even if your dog is a born
athlete, there are certain basics
that belong in every fitness plan

Sports Dogs Love
pages 180–181
Watch her eyes sparkle when
you discover the games that
really turn her on

Organized Activities
page 183
If she's bored by the usual, fire
her up with an organized
canine activity

Why Exercise is so Important

Dog owners know how much their canine companions adore sharing an afternoon jaunt or dashing after a ball in the park. But exercise is much more than just huge fun—it's also doing your dog a whole lot of good.

"A good exercise program will help keep your dog from becoming overweight, which has been linked to health problems such as heart disease, respiratory difficulties and arthritis in dogs," says M. Christine Zink, D.V.M., Ph.D., a lecturer in pathology at Johns Hopkins University School of Medicine in Baltimore, Maryland, and author of *Peak Performance: Coaching the Canine Athlete*. Regular exercise will also expand your dog's lung and heart capacity, and will help give her good stamina and lots of all-round energy.

The well-exercised dog is less likely to get bored or restless and develop troublesome traits, such as digging, barking and chewing.

"Exercise causes the release of endorphins in the brain," explains Dr. Zink. These are chemicals that give your dog a great feeling of well-being. And what better way to keep her content than with a natural high?

Keeping Fit

Exercise is for fun and for fitness. But throwing a leash on your dog and strolling down the street at a snail's pace for five minutes isn't going to do the trick. She needs more of a muscular and cardiovascular workout than that to get her legs, heart and lungs going more than usual. She needs a proper exercise and conditioning program, and if you're going to take the time and energy to exercise your dog, you might as well make it satisfying and worthwhile for her. It will help her develop strength and endurance, and her timing, balance and coordination will improve. You might even find that you start to see and feel some benefits, too.

"A good conditioning program combines cardiovascular work, flexibility, strength work, speed work and weight control," explains Mike Bond, agility judge, owner-instructor of Agility Ability School in Naperville, Illinois, and a regular columnist for *Front and Finish*, a newspaper devoted to dog obedience training.

A dog needs muscular strength so she can move her body in whatever way she wants to go. She also needs this strength to accelerate fast and get

Your dog can be included in many kids' activities, because games are great exercise. This Golden Retriever won't have any trouble sleeping after an afternoon of rollerblading.

For dogs that tend to put on weight, such as this Beagle, regular exercise will keep them in great shape.

up to speed when she's running, jumping and playing. And it will help her avoid injury, as well as improve her joint stability.

Endurance training helps your dog keep going over the long term. If she jogs long distances or competes in field trials or other types of sustained activity, then she will really appreciate this. Conditioning and exercise will also strengthen the muscle fibers, and you will have a thoroughly toned dog, says Dr. Zink.

Exercise is also one of the best ways to keep your dog's weight under control. Feeding smaller portions will probably make her thinner, but burning off excess calories with an exercise program will not only make her thin, it will also make her fit. Letting a dog spend an extra hour or two outside in the backyard won't do either, says Dr. Bond, because most dogs don't get much of a workout just puttering around. Conditioning is the key.

Keeping your dog fit is an everyday thing, and conditioning an out-of-shape dog takes time. But that's time the two of you get to hang out together having fun, getting rid of her excess energy and keeping her healthy and happy.

Safe Beginnings

If all these benefits make you want to put on your running shoes and take your dog along on a five-mile run, that's great, as long as she likes

Why Do Some Dogs Run Around in Circles?

All is peaceful in the sitting room when, suddenly, your pooch gets up from her favorite spot on the rug and starts charging around and around the room like a mini tornado. Then, spent and happy, she returns to the rug and curls up again.

She's just letting off steam, the same way that children do when they run and wrestle. If she charges around like this more than twice an evening, it may be that she needs to be given more exercise. Take her for longer walks, roll a ball for her to chase or try an energetic sport.

Although most dogs outgrow their fun-running by the time they're about three years old, some, in particular terriers, may continue to do this until they are past middle age.

five-mile runs and you work up to it gradually. Before starting her on an exercise program, ask your vet to give her a complete physical, advises Dr. Zink. You'll get a good idea of her general health, and you'll also know if she has any conditions, such as a heart murmur, diabetes or hip dysplasia, which could mean that certain types of exercise are a problem for her.

Even if your dog has a health problem, she still needs to exercise and be fit. Your vet will put together an exercise regimen for her that she will enjoy and that gets her in good shape without causing her any discomfort.

Fitness Fundamentals

You want to create an exercise program for your dog that is safe. So start off slowly, be consistent and patient, and you can gradually increase the level of activity when she shows that she's ready for more. Take it real easy if your dog is still a youngster. Puppies aren't as coordinated as adults. Their muscles aren't fully developed and their bones are softer, says Dr. Zink. They are also more susceptible to the heat and cold.

"Puppies do need some moderate exercise, but serious fitness training shouldn't start until after they are 14 months old," advises Dr. Zink. That's when the last of the growth plates on their bones close. Increase your young dog's fitness program gradually, over a period of several months, she suggests. And give an adolescent dog time to develop her coordination and get used to her maturing body.

Warming Up

Aerobics, jogging, gym—if you've ever exercised, you'll know that you should always start with some gentle stretches. Doing a warm-up is the best way to protect yourself from muscle strains and other pains. And this may come as a surprise, but it's no different for your dog. Begin all her exercise sessions with a gentle warm-up, between five and ten minutes long, advises Dr. Zink. This helps prevent

injury by stretching the tendons and ligaments, and getting the blood to the muscles and nerves. Start with several minutes of unhurried walking, then do some stretching exercises, says Dr. Bond.

To keep his award-winning agility dogs limber, Dr. Bond gently warms them up by bending and straightening each of their legs a few times. Next he has them walk slowly around and between his legs to increase their flexibility.

You've probably seen your pet play bowing or arching her back, and it's doing her good. Dr. Bond praises his dogs whenever they do these motions, from the time they are puppies. They relate the words "Stretch, gooood," with the actions, and eagerly stretch their spines on cue.

This Fox Terrier is being given a few gentle limb bends and stretches by his owner before embarking on an exercise routine. A few minutes' warm-up like this will help prevent your dog from pulling muscles and tendons or from putting too much strain on his body. And don't forget to include some similar cooling down stretches at the end of the session.

Brisk walking speeds the whole system up a notch, but remember to start slowly and work up the pace gradually.

Cardiovascular Training

With the warm-up over, the real action can begin. "The best exercise to get the heart, blood and lungs working is walking," says Dr. Bond. But start off slowly and increase your speed and distance over time. When both of you are walking faster and farther without puffing and panting, you can try trotting and jogging. Mix it up with a short sprint now and again. The change of pace will get her using different parts of the same muscles, says Dr. Bond. And it will also help keep things interesting. Why not make a game of it by calling out "Come on, chase me!" as you take off. Your dog will think it's great sport.

Strength Training

Hills are good for your dog; stairs too. Choose the route with the big hill when you go for a walk. Dash up the stairs at home. It will build up her strength, says Dr. Bond. Have someone hide a treat at the top. Walk her up to the treat the first few times and she'll soon be eager to race to it on her own. Play tag on the slope rather than on the flat. If your dog likes retrieving, throw a toy or a ball up the hill for her to fetch.

Start doing a variety of these games just a few times and gradually build up to doing them several times over—but never enough to bore her.

Speed Conditioning

It's easy to condition your dog to run at speed, and she'll have a great time doing it, says Dr. Bond. Send eager fetchers after toys, balls or Frisbees thrown on level ground. She will be able to stretch right out and really extend her body and her muscles, with the wind in her fur.

If she doesn't know about the joys of chasing a ball and you think she'd like it, why not teach her. Make sure she smells the ball first and sees it leave your hand, advises Gee Weaver, foster care coordinator for the Animal Relief Center in Whitefish, Montana. Roll it only a few feet from her at first. If she's interested, praise her and roll it again. Only do it a few times, never enough to tire or bore her. When she learns to love it, let her attitude be your guide. Always quit while she's still raring to go, so that it remains a great game, a treat that she always looks forward to.

This Border Collie pup is discovering the delights of the fetching game, never dreaming that she's exercising. Always quit while it's still fun and take care not to overtire her.

If a rolling or bouncing ball isn't her idea of a good time, then get her to run at speed to you by calling her from some distance away. Have someone hold her at one end of the yard while you go to the other end. Face her and call her with open arms. Just be ready to dodge out of the way as she hurtles toward you, and pile on the praise for her when she arrives.

Chasing games, complete with lots of sprints and changes of direction, are another way to get fit with speed. Make sure you're in good enough shape to play them safely yourself, and don't let her overdo it.

For a dog that loves water, such as this Terrier mix, swimming is great exercise—gentle on the joints while building all-over stamina.

Cooling Down

A leisurely saunter, followed by a few stretches, is the perfect way to bring another session of fun to an end and give your dog's body time to slow down again. "Vigorous exercise should never stop suddenly," says Dr. Zink. "Cooling down is just as important as warming up."

Non-Weight-Bearing Aerobic Exercise

Some dogs think water is strictly for drinking, but for those that like to get everything wet, swimming is a great way to get a non-weight-bearing aerobic workout. "This benefits the muscles, heart and lungs without putting stress on the bones and joints," says Dr. Zink. That means it's especially good for dogs with hip dysplasia and other joint problems.

Swimming is also the best way to condition your dog during the hot summer months, says Ken Marden, a field trial and hunting test judge, and a breeder of German Shorthaired Pointers in Titusville, New Jersey. A swim will get her using all her muscles. It will increase her heart rate and build up her stamina. And no matter how hot it is, your dog will always keep her cool—there's no risk of heatstroke when she's splashing about.

Running in Comfort

"Natural is always nicer," says Bob McKowen, a dog show and field trial judge in Leola, Pennsylvania. After all, there was no such thing as concrete when dogs were created. People can wear protective running shoes when pounding the pavement, but your dog runs around on only the pads she was born with. For your dog, nothing beats nicely mowed grass as a running surface. It has a natural elasticity, is kinder to her pads and is gentler on her joints, ligaments and tendons. If you're just walking or going for a light trot, however, concrete is fine, as long as the sun hasn't made it too hot.

"If you want your dog to love the water, start her when she's young," advises Marden. "Carry her out about ten feet from shore, turn and face land, gently place her in the water and praise her all the way as she swims to shore. If you toss her into deep water, you'll frighten her and she'll grow up with an aversion to swimming."

Some dogs are natural swimmers and others are not. (There are some retrieving breeds, such as Labrador Retrievers and Golden Retrievers, that even have webbed feet.) "It may take a while before your dog learns to use her hind legs as well as her front ones," says Marden. But you can help her out here. Support your puppy's rear by placing one hand, palm up, under her tail and between her back legs until she realizes that she makes better progress using four legs rather than two. Above all, make it so much fun that she can't wait to do it again.

"Once your dog is a super swimmer, be careful that she doesn't tire herself out," says Marden. If she's retrieving from water and she's getting slower and slower, or if her front feet start splashing when she's swimming, it's time to quit for the day.

Make exercise a game for your dog, as with this Boston Terrier retrieving her ball, and it will never seem like a chore.

Working Together

Exercising by herself is no way for your dog to get the workout she wants. "Tying a dog up outside inhibits her from stretching out and achieving a full range of

Why Do Dogs Love to Chase Balls?

Greyhounds race around the track chasing a mechanical lure that looks vaguely like a rabbit. Other dogs instinctively chase anything that runs away from them—a cat, a squirrel, a rabbit...even a bouncing ball.

The dog's wild ancestors needed a strong chase instinct to catch game. Without it, they wouldn't have survived. Nowadays, that instinct for a good chase isn't a question of survival, so it tends to get focused on the rubber ball that you throw for her down in the local park—it moves, and she can tear after it and catch it. It's just something that some dogs love to do.

motion and it gives her a nasty jolt each time she reaches the end of the chain at a trot or a gallop," explains Weaver. If you must tie or chain your dog, Weaver recommends using an overhead trolley cable. It will get rid of some of the problems and give her more room to run.

Unless you live far from the dangers of modern life, it's simply not safe for dogs to wander on their own. "No matter where you live, this is asking for trouble," says Weaver.

There are all kinds of risks waiting for the unwary dog that roams free, including being hit by a car. It's important that you always keep her company as she explores, and keep her safely on a leash whenever she's out.

Exercise Guidelines

Every healthy dog needs 30 to 45 minutes of exercise a day, says Bob McKowen, a dog show and field trial judge in Leola, Pennsylvania. Exercise can mean all sorts of active dog-fun things. For a tiny dog, a proper workout could be accomplished without having to leave a studio apartment. Medium to large dogs might need a brisk two-mile walk or a vigorous play session inside a spacious fenced park or yard. It all depends on your dog's breed or body type and her age.

What's Right for Your Dog

When working out how much and what kind of exercise your dog needs, consider her breed or, if she's a mixed breed, look at her body to get some clues about what you think she'd like to get up to. Your dog is probably no longer doing what her ancestors were bred to do, but if you can match her exercise needs to her breed needs, she'll get the maximum out of her daily routine and enjoy it all so much more. And whatever you settle on, just make sure you always include a warm-up of simple stretches and a cool-down afterward.

Spaniels of all kinds were bred to take water in their stride. They had to retrieve game, no matter where it fell, for their owners.

The All-American Mix

With a mixed breed dog, let her size and the activities that she most enjoys guide you when setting up an exercise regimen just for her. If she's medium to large, start with a 20-minute walk or jog twice a day, followed by 10 minutes of her favorite game, be it chasing a Frisbee or ball, playing tag or swimming. If she's pint-size, exercise her in the same way as any toy breed.

Sporting Types

These breeds, which include spaniels, pointers, setters and retrievers, as well as the Vizsla and Weimaraner, thrive on vigorous outdoor activity. They also enjoy activities with a mental challenge. A brisk 20-minute walk or jog, followed by at least 10 minutes of strenuous play, gets a sporting dog off to a good start. This should be repeated later in the day, or let her have a good swim instead if she likes water.

Hound Dogs

Sighthounds were originally bred to run down speedy prey. So their ideal exercise program could include 20 minutes of brisk walking and jogging, followed by an opportunity to stretch out and run (in a safely fenced area) for 5 or 10 minutes. If there's no place to let your hound run, set aside 30 minutes for the two of you to have a morning jog. She will also relish a game of chase after a long, brisk walk.

Scenthounds, which worked at a slower pace with their noses to the ground, tend to be a little more laid-back. Give your scenthound a walk and jog for 20 to 25 minutes, unless you can persuade her to play ball or tag with you for part of the time. Any dog with a breed name that includes "retriever" will enjoy a game of fetch or catch, and she'll also love swimming. Most spaniels like to fetch and are also partial to a swim. While small enough to get a certain amount of exercise from playing indoor games, Dachshunds still need a 15-minute walk every morning. Whichever workout fits your hound, do it again in the evening.

The Workers

Working dogs traditionally kept going for as long as their services were needed, herding livestock in all weathers. Give your working dog a workout for 20 to 30 minutes every morning by walking and jogging with her, or combine walking with some strenuous game playing in the yard. Repeat this later in the day or take her for a good long swimming session instead.

Terriers

Terriers always led very active lives—they were constantly busy hunting and sniffing out prey. Large terriers need a brisk walk lasting for 20 to 30 minutes in the morning, or a slightly shorter walk and 10 minutes of rowdy play in the yard. Some of them also enjoy a swim. Do it again in the evening. Smaller or less active

If you let her, this lively little Jack Russell Terrier would chase sticks until your arm gave out. Be sure to take a break before she wears herself out.

terriers will stay in shape with a 15-minute walk morning and evening, provided you play some indoor games together each day. Terriers love the chase; some will fetch too, while others prefer to "play-kill" a toy. Most can also be easily taught games such as hide-and-seek and tag.

Toys

Dedicated lap-sitters, toys are probably the least active of all dogs. A 15-minute walk morning and evening is enough for most tiny dogs, provided they are also encouraged to play indoor games. If you can't manage long walks, teach your dog to retrieve a ball—then you can exercise her from your recliner. Many toy breeds have a strong instinct to chase and retrieve, so a bouncy ball the right size for her mouth or a small Frisbee will make the ideal basis for a game.

Non-Sporty Types

Non-sporting dogs are a varied lot, and certainly not the couch potatoes that their group name suggests. So look at your dog's size and body style before establishing an exercise program. For example, the smaller ones, such as the Boston Terrier, Schipperke and Bichon Frise, need the same amount of exercise as the smaller members of the terrier group. However, the Keeshond, Standard Poodle, Finnish Spitz and Dalmatian should be exercised in the same way as any sporting or working dog.

The Herders

These dogs are noted for their stamina. A brisk walk or jog for 20 to 30 minutes, along with some time to chase balls or flying Frisbees, will start your herding dog's day off right. You could either repeat this in the evening or take her for a swim. And with her energy and her intelligence, she will find games with a purpose, such as hide-and-seek, especially appealing.

The Custom-Made Constitutional

You know your dog better than anyone, so that makes you her ideal personal trainer. When you are developing an exercise program especially tailored to her needs, there are a few things, in addition to the type of dog she is, that you should keep in mind.

A dog that seems exhausted after her workout may want less of a good thing. And if there is an abrupt change in your dog's attitude toward exercise and she suddenly tires easily, she could be ill, so take her to your vet. A noisy or destructive dog probably isn't getting a long enough workout. Try giving her more exercise.

The breeds with a super-short nose, such as the Bulldog or Pug, often have difficulty with their breathing. If your dog is in this category, go easy with her exercise program. Be especially cautious when the weather is humid because of the risk of heatstroke, and always exercise her during the coolest part of the day.

A dog that is overweight or just plain out of shape should never start out with a full-fledged workout. Instead, give her a quarter of the recommended amount of exercise for two weeks, increase this to half the recommended amount for a couple of weeks, and then increase it again to three-quarters for another two weeks. By the end of six weeks, she should be ready to go the distance.

For the dog that is starting to show her age, make her workout sessions lighter, but don't stop altogether. Exercise keeps older dogs stimulated and supple, and helps their bodies to stay fit.

Sports Dogs Love

Romping with their litter-mates—that's how dogs in the wild learned what they needed to know and had fun. So practically every puppy you'll meet will enjoy wrestling with another playful puppy or pouncing on a squeaky toy and play-killing it with violent shakes of her head.

"All dogs are inquisitive and like to watch what's going on around them," says McKowen. So your dog will love a walk or jog to explore the neighborhood. Not only is it good exercise, but it will keep her mind alert and she can catch up on the local dog gossip, too.

Then there are activities for the more specialized tastes. "Just as people enjoy doing the things that they have a natural affinity for, whether they be ball games, music, water sports or art, dogs also enjoy the activities they were designed to do," explains McKowen.

Giving Chase

If full-speed dashes are your dog's cup of tea (or bowl of water), create a chasing toy by using a fishing rod with several feet of fishing line attached to a white plastic garbage bag. To give your speedster a good workout, all you have to do is twitch the bag to make it go in circles and change its direction as she gives chase. Let her catch the bounding "bunny" and rip into it at times, so she knows she has a chance of winning.

Retrieving Games

Many dogs relish games of fetch or catch and will happily chase balls, Frisbees, sticks or the field dummies made especially for retriever training and drop them back at your feet. If retrieving is your dog's favorite hobby, you could try her with swimming after sticks or floating toys.

For this Australian Shepherd, leaping to catch a Frisbee in full flight is the greatest game going.

Flying After Frisbees

Some dogs find Frisbees the last word in fun, preferring them to balls and sticks, and they will perform amazing contortions to snatch them out of the air. Start low and slow, rolling the disk on the ground, gradually working up to aerial acrobatics.

Hide-and-Seek

Teach your dog to play hide-and-seek by getting one of her favorite kids in on the game. Get the child to hide in the closet with a treat in his hand and the door slightly opened, then tell your dog to go find him. When she does, it's time to reward her with the treat and lots of praise. If she has

Why Won't Some Dogs Fetch?

You throw the ball as far as you can and your dog tears gleefully off into the distance after it. But instead of bringing it back, she crouches playfully in the grass with the ball between her paws. She wants you to throw it again, but she won't bring it back. Clearly, she hasn't mastered the concept of the fetching game yet.

Many dogs, especially the hunting breeds, have a genetic tendency to retrieve, says Bob McKowen, a dog show and field trial judge in Leola, Pennsylvania. But dogs that were born with different sets of inherited skills, such as following scents or herding sheep, may be less inclined to bring back a ball or stick.

Every dog can be taught to retrieve, however. If you want it to be her getting the exercise instead of you, you may want to sign her up for advanced training. Once she knows what's expected, you'll have a hard time getting her to stop.

This dog is right at home with water, diving into the lake alongside her owner, who has checked first that it's safe.

getting a wet dog back aboard can be a real challenge, unless she's wearing a lifejacket with a handle on top, which you can use to lift her out. If you don't plan on sticking to the shallows, a life jacket is a good idea so she can float if she gets tired. And when you finally coax her out, keep your distance while she gives a good shake.

Play-Killing Squeaky

Play-killing might sound like an odd kind of sport, but for puppies it's the last word in fun, and older dogs enjoy it too. It's like hunting small prey, the closest city dogs get to the thrill of the chase and kill. Some canines can get hours of entertainment this way.

Hold a toy with a built-in squeaker in your hand and squeeze it a couple of times to tease your dog. Then throw it. If your dog responds by pouncing on the toy and shaking it hard enough to scramble her brains, you've just discovered one of her favorite games. Don't leave her alone with her toy, though. She could tear it apart and swallow the metal squeaker.

trouble at first, get the child to call her softly. When she understands the game, she'll be ready to sniff out more challenging hiding places.

Swimming

A delight on a warm day, swimming is loved by some dogs and hated by others. If your dog is a waterbaby, then she'll like this exercise option. It's easiest to enter from land than from a boat—

Too Much of a Good Thing

During most activities, your dog will run faster, work harder and cover more ground than you do. "She may have so much heart that she keeps going past the point of exhaustion, just because she thinks you want her to," cautions Dr. Bond. It's up to you to use common sense, practice moderation, and watch her for signs of fatigue or for difficulty in breathing.

Heatstroke

Dogs don't have a very efficient way of keeping cool, and can succumb all too easily to heatstroke during hot weather. Avoid exercising your dog too vigorously in the heat of the day, and in particularly hot weather be sure to keep her routine pretty relaxed. If she appears distressed and you suspect heatstroke—for example, her sides are heaving or she can hardly stand—follow the steps in "Heatstroke" on page 380.

Pad Problems

While her paws are strong and sturdy, they are also unprotected from things that you, in your socks and shoes, don't even notice. Exercise your dog during the coolest time of the day throughout summer, and check the temperature of the pavement before you step out. Place your hand on it for several seconds to make sure it's okay. If it is still hot from the sun, it will burn her pads.

Winter brings different pad problems. Road salt, unlike ordinary salt, can burn your dog's feet. (It can also burn her mouth if she bites at her feet, and her belly if she kicks salt on herself while trotting along.) Road sand isn't any better. The chemicals it contains to melt ice can also burn her feet. To prevent pad problems, towel off her chest, underbelly and feet when you finish your walk. This will get rid of any snow and chemical residues between her toes.

When your dog plays in clean snow, take the normal precautions against frostbite, such as not letting her stay outside for too long on ice-encrusted snow or when there is a big wind-chill factor. Check for cracked pads or tiny cuts on her pads afterwards. Pads sometimes become dry in the winter, just as our hands do, and a daily dab of medicated Vaseline can be very soothing.

The Best Time for Exercise

Exercise is fun time for the two of you, and it can be any time that suits your schedule and the climate where you live. "In summer, take her out early in the morning or at dusk to avoid the heat and humidity," says Mike Bond, agility judge and owner-instructor of Agility Ability School in Naperville, Illinois.

Your dog won't thank you for making her exercise on a full stomach. So be careful not to feed her immediately before or after a strenuous workout. And don't let her gulp lots of water just before or after exercise, either. Instead, give her a short drink before and during the activity, and a moderate amount of water once she cools down.

Organized Activities

If you and your dog are bored with the same old walk around the neighborhood or if throwing a ball has lost its spark, organized dog activities may be exactly the inspiration the two of you need, advises Marden. Here are some things you might want to try.

Agility

Agility trials are one of the most enjoyable ways to exercise your dog, says Marden. These timed events involve directing your dog through a course complete with a colorful variety of planks, jumps, tunnels and other obstacles. "The training required practically guarantees that your dog will be in tip-top condition," he adds. Mixed breeds and purebreds can compete at events organized by the United States Dog Agility Association, United Kennel Club (UKC), North American Dog Agility Council and American Mixed Breed Obedience Registry (AMBOR). The American Kennel Club (AKC) has events for dogs of all breeds registered with it.

Obedience

In novice obedience, dogs are judged on their ability to "Heel" at all speeds, "Come" when they're called, "Sit-stay," "Down-stay" and stand for a judge's examination. Advanced

obedience trials include retrieving over hurdles, obeying hand signals, scent discrimination and more. The AKC trials are purebred-only affairs, while all kinds of dogs can compete at UKC and AMBOR events. But, says Marden, even if you never compete, attending obedience classes and practicing what you have learned exercises your dog's mind and body and often turns problem pets into great companions.

Lure Coursing

If your canine companion is a sighthound, she's welcome in the physically demanding sport of lure coursing. When slipped (released) by their owners at the hunter's "Tally-ho," three hounds will race off to chase the lure. The lure changes direction several times over the 800-yard course and the dogs are judged on speed, agility, stamina, enthusiasm and ability to follow. "To keep them in peak condition, most lure-coursing enthusiasts run their dogs nearly every day," says Marden.

Agility events are open to all types of dogs; the height of the obstacles in the course is adjusted to suit the dog.

Herding Trials

The AKC herding trials are open to purebred dogs from traditional herding breeds. They are evaluated on their ability to round up sheep, ducks or cattle and bring them through gates to a pen. "This requires quickness, stamina and obedience, a combination to keep your dog in lean and hard condition," says Marden.

11 THE BEST ACCESSORIES

There are a few things that will make life easier and more comfortable for you and your dog. These aren't optional extras; they're the belongings that will keep him happy and healthy. And by providing them, you'll be letting him know how important he is to you.

What Your Dog Needs
pages 185–186

Life's little essentials—for eating, sleeping, playing and looking good

The Identifiable Dog
pages 187–188

Don't take a chance on losing him when it's so easy to improve the odds on getting him back

Stepping Out in Style
pages 189–191

What every well-dressed dog wouldn't be caught on the street without

What Your Dog Needs

Your dog doesn't need a wardrobe full of designer togs and toys. But there are some accessories that he really should have, for his good health, good behavior, and all-around good feeling about life. In addition to his crate or bed, the other little essentials include dishes, toys, grooming equipment, a form of identification, and at least one collar and leash. Depending on his breed and the climate where you live, he may also need a warm jacket or coat, a rain slicker and even boots. And as a good dog owner, you shouldn't forget a pooper-scooper or some other means of cleaning up after him.

Designer Dishes

Your dog will need at least two bowls, one for food and one for water. Separate dishes are more convenient than partitioned bowls, advises Susan Stronberg, owner of Noah's Bark pet store in Kalispell, Montana. It's much easier to change the water if you don't have to cope with food in the other half of the bowl. "And if your dog tends to tip his bowls, weighted dishes will keep his dinner and water where they belong," she adds. These dishes are wider at the bottom than the top and come in plastic or stainless steel.

If your dog has long, floppy ears, they may dangle in his food and water. "A dish with an inner rim that allows his mouth to get into the bowl but keeps his ears out will solve the problem," says Stronberg.

If your dog prefers to sleep in a basket, it will need to be big enough for him to stretch out in. This Labrador is sharing her well-padded bed with her litter of puppies.

A Comfy Bed

Your dog is going to need somewhere to lay his weary head at the end of a long day. You might decide on a crate, especially if he's only a pup and you want some help with house-training. Cover the bottom of the crate with newspaper for easy cleaning while he's still learning the rules. He can graduate to a crate pad or a piece of carpet in the bottom when his bladder control gets more reliable. Make sure that you put a chew toy and

Weighted, nonslip bowls

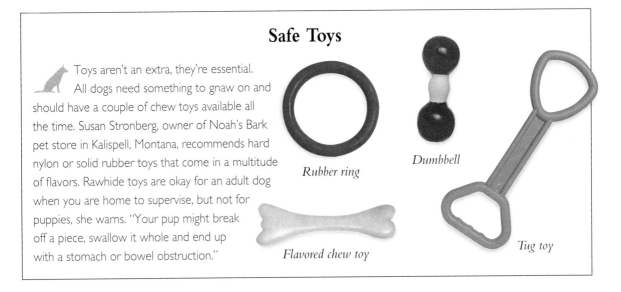

Safe Toys

Toys aren't an extra, they're essential. All dogs need something to gnaw on and should have a couple of chew toys available all the time. Susan Stronberg, owner of Noah's Bark pet store in Kalispell, Montana, recommends hard nylon or solid rubber toys that come in a multitude of flavors. Rawhide toys are okay for an adult dog when you are home to supervise, but not for puppies, she warns. "Your pup might break off a piece, swallow it whole and end up with a stomach or bowel obstruction."

Rubber ring

Dumbbell

Tug toy

Flavored chew toy

a blanket or towel in the crate, to make it a cozy place for sleeping, where he'll also be happy to take a nap sometimes during the day.

A basket with a cushion or blanket might be more his sleeping style, or a comfy dog bed that you can buy at your local pet supply store. When it comes to bedding, it really depends on what works for your dog and you.

Grooming Gear

Every dog needs some sort of a brush, a toenail trimmer, shampoo and a soft tooth-brush, although the type of grooming implements will depend on your dog's coat. Ask the people at the pet supply store what type of grooming implements your dog needs, advises Penny Zorn, profession-al groomer and co-owner of the Poodle Parlor in Kalispell, Montana.

Brush

Comb

Thinning scissors

The same combs and brushes simply won't work on every type of coat. You should also match the size of the brush to the size of your dog.

Don't hesitate to wash your dog if he needs a bath, says Zorn. Use a quality shampoo that is pH balanced for dogs. Do not use a shampoo formulated for humans, because it will remove too much oil from his coat. A conditioning, detangling rinse is helpful for most long-coated dogs, but Zorn advises against a rinse if your dog has extremely oily hair.

Toothbrushes made especially for dogs come in a range of sizes. There are some with large ends for big dogs or little ends for small dogs. Some fit on your finger like a thimble to make brushing easier. Dog toothpaste comes in both chicken and beefy flavors that dogs like—he won't appreciate the human variety.

The Identifiable Dog

You want your dog to be able to show his ID, so that everyone who meets him knows who he is and who he belongs to, especially as there might be an occasion when you're not around to speak up for him. He needs a collar and a couple of ID tags, although they can be removed if your dog is stolen, or lost if your dog is lost. You might consider using a more permanent form of identification, such as a tattoo or a microchip, and registering him in a national database.

Collars

Flat leather or nylon collars with buckles are good everyday collars for most dogs. However, rolled (round) leather collars with buckles work better for dogs with long hair or thick ruffs, according to Stronberg, because they don't mat the hair beneath the collar the way flat collars tend to. Buckle collars are either single or double ply, and come in a variety of lengths, not to

Rolled collar

Leather collar with studs

Leather collars

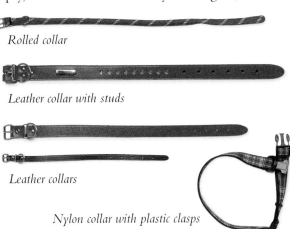

Nylon collar with plastic clasps

mention a veritable rainbow of colors. There are even collars decorated with rhinestones or bows, for those more formal canine occasions.

Adjustable nylon collars with plastic clasps are fine for small or well-behaved dogs, but they aren't always strong enough for large dogs or dogs that pull hard on the leash. And if you have a puppy, check his collar each week to make sure that it has not become too tight—you will be surprised at how fast he grows. Tight collars are uncomfortable and dangerous.

Some collars are specially designed to be worn during training. If your dog attends training school, get him the type of collar recommended by his instructor, advises Amy Ammen, director of Amiable Dog Training, host of "Amiable Dog Training with Amy Ammen" on MATA Television in Milwaukee, and author of *Training in No Time* and *Dual Ring Dog.* Many instructors use chain training collars, also known as choke chains. Others use rounded nylon choke collars or even flat buckle collars. "To avoid accidents, remove the choke collar when you aren't training," Stronberg advises.

Rabies tag

ID Tags

At least two tags should be attached to your dog's everyday collar. One should be his numbered rabies vaccination tag. The other should show your name, address and phone number. If he is tattooed for permanent identification, he should also wear a tag or special collar imprinted with the 800 number of the database on which he is enrolled.

Tattoos

Unlike a collar tag, which can be lost or stolen, a tattoo remains with your dog for life. If you opt for a tattoo, wait until your dog is fully grown before having the procedure done, so the numbers won't become distorted. Vets, veterinary technicians, humane society personnel, kennel operators, breeders and groomers may do the tattooing procedure in your area. Ask your vet for a recommendation.

Your dog will have his tattoo on the inner thigh. It can be a computer-generated number from the dog registry of your choice or you can use your social security number. The procedure isn't painful, and most dogs accept their tattoo graciously, although the buzz of the clipper and the vibration of the tattoo needle disturb some. "The whole process takes only about a minute and a half when done by a skillful tattooer," says Mitch Rapoport, executive director of the National Dog Registry.

For a small one-time fee, you then register your dog with one of the national databases, such as the National Dog Registry, American Kennel Club (AKC) Companion Animal Recovery, InfoPET, Identi-pet, and Tattoo A Pet. Ninety-five percent of lost dogs that are tattooed and registered have been recovered. "The key word is 'registered'," says Rapoport. "A

Your dog should wear his rabies and ID tags at all times, like this Chesapeake Bay Retriever. You might also have him tattooed.

tattoo or a microchip number is no different from a license plate. Unless it's in a database somewhere, it has no value."

Microchips

A microchip with a number code is another method of permanent identification. The chip is the size of an uncooked grain of rice, and it is encased in a capsule that causes no adverse effects. Your vet will inject it under the skin between your dog's shoulder blades, explains Keith Wall, D.V.M., technical services veterinarian with Schering-Plough Animal Health, manufacturer of the Home Again microchip. No anesthetic or tranquilizer is required, and your dog will react to it the same way he reacts to getting a vaccination. Puppies as young as six weeks can receive microchips, and then be enrolled in a national database for life.

When a lost pet is found and taken to a shelter or humane society, a scanner is passed over his shoulders to check for a microchip, and he is also checked for a tattoo. If a number comes up, the shelter informs one of the national databases and they then locate the owner.

Although scanners could previously read only microchips of the same make, a universal scanner can now recognize all formats, explains Bryan Simpson, manager of AKC Companion Animal Recovery. Your vet may carry the AKC's Home Again chip, the InfoPET chip or the AVID chip. The newest scanners can handle them all, and the national databases cooperate to reunite lost dogs with their owners as quickly as possible. "Just remember though, we can find you only if we have your correct address and phone number. If you move, update your information with the database immediately," says Simpson.

Stepping Out in Style

Your dog is going to be out and about, whether it's for his daily constitutional, taking in a dog obedience class, or accompanying you on a visit to friends. Whenever he puts in a public appearance, he'll need a leash and you'll want a way of cleaning up after him. Depending on the kind of dog he is, you may also want to consider a coat, slicker or shoes for bad weather.

Leashes

Leashes, also called leads, come in several lengths and widths to accommodate dogs of all sizes and to feel comfortable in your hands. The most popular lengths are four feet or six feet, but retractable leashes are great for walks in the open. They extend up to 15 or 20 feet and retract to whatever length you wish at the push of a button. These give your dog plenty of room to explore while he is still well under your control. "When choosing a leash, consider what activities you share with your dog, his size, and how obedient he is," says Stronberg.

Leashes are made from leather or nylon and are available in single ply, double ply, or braided, for added strength. Don't weigh a small dog down with a heavy leash. Your obedience instructor may recommend a specific style, but if not, choose one that you find attractive and that suits your pocketbook.

Muzzles

Most dogs go through life without ever wearing a muzzle. However, if your dog needs one, get a nylon muzzle that allows him to pant and drink water but not to bark or bite, advises Stronberg. Some muzzles are meant for grooming purposes only, so make sure that what you buy fully covers your needs.

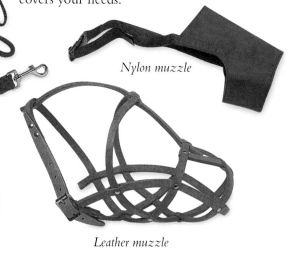

Nylon leashes

Nylon muzzle

Retractable leash

Leather muzzle

The red hat on this Airedale crossbreed has no real purpose, but it amuses the dog's owner and the dog doesn't seem to mind. Such whimsical touches can make passersby respond in a friendly way toward an animal and get him used to receiving attention from strangers of both sexes.

Canine Couture

If your dog is going to be out in the cold, the rain, or the snow, he may need more than his fur coat to keep him cozy. There are many jacket and coat styles to choose from to suit your dog's special needs. For example, if your dog is so short-coated that he's practically bald on the chest and belly, go for a style that protects him below as well as above. Rain slickers are handy for keeping your dog dry when he has to be walked in bad weather. "Polar fleece is popular for dog jackets and coats because it provides insulation, keeping the dog warm and drawing away mois-ture," says Stronberg. "Beware of thin, knitted sweaters. They don't ward off snow, rain or extreme

cold and are generally chosen mainly for the sake of their appearance."

Good-quality polar fleece boots with cordura nylon soles are good for protecting his feet against snow and rain, or when hiking in rugged

This dog's colorful jacket covers his back and belly, keeping him from getting cold. Alaskan weather calls for more padding and for protective boots at far right.

The owners of this Rottweiler didn't want their friends to be put off by the breed's image. They know he's a cool dude and want him to look the part. The sunglasses also protect his eyes from ultraviolet rays.

terrain. "Take your dog along to your local pet store to be properly fitted," advises Stronberg.

If socializing your dog is difficult because he looks so big and tough that strangers are scared of him, try tying a bright bandanna around his neck or attaching a big fake flower to his collar. Imagine the effect of a Rottweiler wearing a silk poinsettia in December or a daffodil to celebrate spring. Instead of looking formidable, he'll look more friendly, and most people are likely to greet him with a smile. He'll soon be getting his share of socialization from those he meets.

Also fun, although not every dog thinks so, are the colorful hats with visors made especially for dogs.

Pooper-Scoopers

Pooper-scoopers come in many varieties, and are available at pet supply stores. The most popular styles are made of aluminum and have either a rake-like base for cleaning up grassy yards or a smooth

Hand-held pooper-scooper

Pavement pooper-scooper

Paws for thought

Do Dogs Like Wearing Clothes?

With such a nice fur coat all his own, how do you think your dog will feel about being seen on the street done up in a fleecy jacket? His attitude toward his wardrobe is inevitably going to be affected by how well it fits and how smoothly you introduce him to it.

Whatever you get for him, make sure it's the right size. It shouldn't rub him around the leg holes or irritate his neck. Get him to feel good about being dressed by putting the item of clothing on him gently. Make a big fuss over him for looking so handsome, then take it off after just a few minutes. Next time you dress him, make a fuss again, and let him wear the item longer. Soon, he'll be used to it, and happy to step out with it between him and the winter winds.

Coats and jackets are easy enough to get used to, but what about boots? "It's pretty funny to see a dog take his first steps with boots on," says Susan Stronberg, owner of Noah's Bark pet store in Kalispell, Montana. "But most dogs adjust readily—especially if they're sometimes bothered by ice clumps forming between their pads."

base for cleaning up pavement and concrete. Some dog owners prefer to carry a plastic bag. This fits in a pocket or purse and is turned inside out for the pickup, then closed and tossed in the nearest trash can.

12 CARING FOR LATCHKEY PETS

You want to make your pet's life happy and carefree, but the sad reality is that dog biscuits don't fall out of the sky. You can't be with her all day, every day, but you can help her to be more content during the times that you're away.

Home Alone
pages 193–194

Strategies to help your pet pass the time while she's on her own

Inside or Out?
pages 195–196

Consider her need for security and stimulation when deciding where she'll spend her days

Pet-Care Services
page 197

Don't let your dog get distressed—hire a pet sitter or enroll her in doggy day care

Home Alone

Wouldn't it be wonderful if you could spend all day, every day, with your dog, playing ball together, going for long walks and napping in the noonday sun? Unfortunately, few of us are lucky enough to live such a life of leisure. After all, somebody's got to go out and earn enough to put food in the bowl, blankets in the basket, and chew toys under the Christmas tree.

Dog are very social creatures and they crave companionship and stimulation. While you're at work, your dog will be stuck at home, trying to find ways to while away the hours until your return. Each dog handles this separation differently, says Larry Lachman, an animal behaviorist in Laguna Hills, California.

Some dogs cope quite easily, while others have trouble dealing with the fact that they are often left alone. The good news is that there is much you can do to help your dog deal with the temporary separation.

Keeping Her Entertained

Being alone from time to time is something most people look forward to—it gives us a chance to catch up on some of the things we want to do. We can amuse ourselves with a good book, a favorite TV show, or even indulge in a hobby such as painting, model building or sewing.

Obviously, dogs don't have hobbies. And they don't like being alone, either. "Dogs are pack animals, and when they are isolated, they feel lonely, bored, stressed, anxious and frustrated,"

says Robin Kovary, a professional dog trainer and behavioral consultant in New York City, and president of the American Dog Trainers Network. That's just the nature of dogs, she explains. It's this deep attachment to her family that makes your dog such a wonderful pet.

Unfortunately, this same attachment can be hard on your dog when her family is not around. So how can you help her to feel okay when she has to be left on her own?

If your dog has used up all her excess energy, she is more likely to sleep contentedly while you are gone. And when she's asleep, she can't be getting into mischief.

Care when you're there. Pay lots of attention to her when you are home, says Lachman. A few hours a week of occasional interaction just isn't enough for a dog that stays home by herself. "When dogs spend a lot of time alone, they also need to spend a lot of time with their owners, getting both exercise and attention," he says.

Get her moving. Liz Palika, a dog trainer in Oceanside, California, and author of *All Dogs Need Some Training*, recommends a regular exercise schedule for dogs left alone during the day. "I suggest to my training students that their dogs be given two good aerobic workouts each and every day, one in the morning and one in the evening," she says.

Keep her busy. Another way to help your dog cope is to give her something to do. Kovary suggests providing her with toys that can be filled with kibble, cheese or other foods. She will be occupied for hours working on one of these toys as she tries to get the food out.

Consider the Breed

Every dog has her own unique temperament and personality, but your dog's breed plays a large part in the way she looks at the world. Some breeds are generally more capable of being alone all day because of the temperament they have inherited as part of their breed characteristics,

What Do Dogs Do All Day?

No, she's not checking the pantry or catching up on Oprah. *"If the owner works eight hours a day, most dogs will sleep for those eight hours," says Larry Lachman, an animal behaviorist in Laguna Hills, California. But not all dogs are so laid-back—some get upset at being left alone. They may destroy furniture, dig up the yard or bark and howl all day. If your dog is not the stay-alone kind, you may want to hire a pet sitter to spend time with her, or book her into doggy day care.*

says Lachman. Dogs that were bred to work alone, for example, terriers and hounds, cope better with isolation because they are more independent and less reliant on their owners' attentions. Breeds such as German Shepherds and Golden Retrievers were meant to work closely with humans, and are not good candidates for keeping themselves company. You'll need to consider your dog's personality before you decide how well she can handle being left alone.

Dozing in the sun after a morning of activity, this dog is the picture of contentment. If your dog must stay alone while you work, extra attention when you can be with her is crucial. She needs lots of regular exercise, and the reassurance and stimulation that your company provides.

Inside or Out?

A dog that stays home when her owner is at work can while away the day indoors or out. Both have their advantages and disadvantages. You'll have to decide which option offers the most stimulation and the best security for your dog.

The Outdoor Life

Your first instinct may be to leave your dog outside. After all, if she's outdoors, she can go to the bathroom whenever she needs to. She can look through the slats of the fence at people passing by. She will also get lots of fresh air, and can chase birds and squirrels that venture into her yard.

This may sound ideal, but there are some hidden problems. "There are many risks to leaving a dog outside all day while you're away," says Kovary. "To relieve her boredom, your dog may find a way to escape from your yard; or she could be stolen, teased or harassed by passersby."

Behavioral problems may also develop. "Some dogs have a tendency to become overly aggressive when left outside all day," explains Kovary. "They can get very frustrated with people passing by." Another emotional hazard is fear, which can be brought on by larger dogs, car noises and thunderstorms. "Thunder can be very scary to your dog, and if she is trapped outside while it is going on, she may become so panicked that she will literally claw her way out of the yard," says Kovary. Be especially careful when fireworks are likely to be let off. Many pets run off in panic and are lost at such times.

The Best Pet Doors

If keeping your dog exclusively indoors or outdoors doesn't appeal, you need a doggy door. This is a panel that allows your pet to exit when she needs to relieve herself or get a breath of fresh air, then re-enter when the weather threatens or things get scary outside, says Larry Lachman, an animal behaviorist in Laguna Hills, California.

Pet doors come in a number of different styles. If you are concerned about the risk of theft to your home, Robin Kovary, a professional dog trainer and behavioral consultant in New York City, suggests you purchase one with a magnetic or electronic locking device that responds to something on your dog's collar. Only your dog can gain entry.

Don't expect her to know automatically how to use a doggy door, says Kovary. "Some dogs are afraid. You may have to teach her how to use it with treats, a leash, and lots of encouragement and praise."

This Pomeranian doesn't have to scratch or bark to be let in. Her entrances and exits are made in a dignified manner through her own private doorway. Well-designed doggy doors can also be locked for those times you need to keep her in or out.

The Indoor Life

You dog is safer indoors where she can escape from loud noises and other scary things. She will be less likely to develop aggressive behavior, and neighbors won't be bothered by nuisance barking.

The downside of being indoors is that she won't be able to relieve herself when her bladder is full. Adult dogs can physically cope with this, but it may not be too comfortable. Also, if she is lonely and there's not a lot stimulating her, it will be the furniture that is likely to bear the brunt of her boredom and frustration.

Preparations and Provisions

If you choose to chance the great outdoors, there are provisions you will need to make for your dog, says Connie Cleveland, a dog trainer in Fountain Inn, South Carolina. "It's important to provide a securely fenced yard to keep her at home, safe from other wandering dogs," she says. "A dog should also be able to get out of the wind or rain. Fresh drinking water is a must, too, and make sure it can't be spilled in your absence." One way to do this is to attach a bucket to a fence or place an eye bolt on the side of her doghouse to hold the water container. Or use a heavy ceramic water dish. The indoor dog will need water too, and toys to keep her occupied.

Whether indoors or out, dogs should never wear a choke collar while unsupervised because of the risk of it catching on something. Use a flat-buckle collar instead, advises Cleveland.

In the Doghouse

If your dog will be spending her days outdoors, you must provide her with a safe and cozy doghouse where she can sleep and escape the elements. Commercially made doghouses are available at pet supply stores and through mail-order catalogs.

A doghouse must be big enough to accommodate your dog, but not so big that there will be heat loss. "If the doghouse is too big, the warmth from the dog's body won't be enough to keep her cozy because there is too much space to warm," says Robin Kovary, a professional dog trainer and behavioral consultant in New York City. "A doghouse also needs to be well-insulated to keep out the cold or the heat." Kovary also advises that it is important to keep the doghouse up off the ground by placing it on some kind of platform. "Water and moisture will seep in if it rests directly on the ground," she explains.

Pet-Care Services

Until recent years, dogs with owners who worked all day had little choice but to stay home and bide their time. Now, there are other options: pet sitters and doggy day-care centers. Doggy day care and pet-walking services are excellent ways of helping lonesome dogs through the day, says Lachman. "Dogs love to be with a group." The company of people and other dogs in these environments can make all the difference in the world to the dog that is blue without you.

Services at Her Service

Pet sitters are professionals who will come to your house while you are away. They will walk your pet, feed her, give her fresh water and spend time petting her and talking to her.

An even newer service, which is growing rapidly in popularity, is the doggy day-care center, a place where you can drop your dog off in the morning and pick her up again at night. Here, your pet will be walked and provided with the company of humans and other dogs while you are absent. Regular play sessions are part of the deal at most centers, and you can rest assured that your dog is having a grand old time.

Making a Choice

When choosing any of these services, be sure to check out the reputation of the individual or company with whom you will be leaving your dog, suggests Kovary. You can do this by asking for references and following up on them. With doggy day-care centers, make sure walks are included. "Walks are important for a dog," says Kovary. She also warns that dogs may start to forget their housebreaking if they are expected to eliminate indoors at a day-care center.

Choose a day-care center that requires proof of immunization, screens dogs for good temperament, and puts only compatible dogs together, recommends Kovary. "Check to be sure that the facility, play area and enclosures are secure so that dogs can't escape or be stolen," she says. After all, having fun and being safe is what staying at a doggy day-care center is all about.

Dog walkers specialize in taking dogs out while owners are at work. They always take more than one, so not only does your dog get her exercise, she gets some company, too.

13 TRAVELING IN COMFORT

It's vacation time, and everyone is busy packing their bags and getting ready for the annual holiday—your dog included. If you plan ahead, traveling with your dog can be the greatest fun.

Taking a Car Trip
pages 199–203

Prepare your pooch so he can enjoy life on four wheels

Up, Up and Away
pages 206–207

Strategies for traveling by air with your dog

Travel Accessories
pages 204–205

The things the well-traveled dog should always pack in his suitcase

Home Away from Home
pages 208–209

How to find dog-friendly campsites and hotels, or a good boarding kennel if he can't go with you

Taking a Car Trip

When you're traveling by car with your dog, half the fun is getting there. He will enjoy roadside scenery almost as much as you do, and he may even spot a few other traveling dogs as they cruise down the same highways. To ensure that your canine companion, and the rest of the family, have a comfortable trip, get him ready well in advance for his time in the car and for the new sights and sounds he'll encounter.

Preparing Your Pooch

Several weeks before you're due to set off, start acquainting your dog with the sorts of things he's going to come across on vacation. "To reduce the stress of his first trip, your dog should be introduced to a wide array of situations," says Wendy Ballard, publisher of *DogGone*, a newsletter about traveling with dogs.

New Sights

Focus first on people, advises Ballard. "Have your dog meet a variety of people: young and old, thin and heavy, mustached and clean-shaven, folk with eyeglasses, with canes or in wheelchairs," she says. If your dog is familiar with different kinds of people before he goes away, he'll be more comfortable when he meets them in new surroundings. It's also important for your dog to be comfortable around animals. "Dogs should have opportunities to meet other dogs," says Ballard. "Introducing your dog to horses, cats and other animals isn't a bad idea either."

Strange Surfaces and Sounds

Your dog could find some new situations strange. "Be sure your pet is comfortable stepping on all types of surfaces," says Ballard. He may find floor grates, elevators and moving walkways very scary.

It's important that the traveling dog has a tolerance for traffic noises, even if you don't plan on walking him down Hollywood Boulevard to see Lassie's pawprint outside Mann's Chinese Theater. "Desensitize your dog by taking car rides on a highly trafficked thoroughfare," she advises. "Open the windows to let the noise in. Work up to a walk along that busy street."

Exotic Food and Drink

Your dog might have a hankering to try the local canine cuisine, but a sudden change of diet could give him diarrhea. So when on the road, avoid the chili with beefy bits or Cajun-style meaty chunks. Play it safe and give him his usual food.

If it's just a short trip, take along his regular food, says Priscilla K. Stockner, D.V.M., executive director of the Center for Humane Education in Escondido, California. "On longer trips, take enough of the dog's usual food to mix gradually with whatever he will be eating," she advises. This also goes for water. "Take a supply of your dog's usual drinking water. After 24 to 36 hours, start mixing it gradually with the new water he'll be drinking."

Feeling Queasy

People are not the only ones who get carsick. Dogs can suffer from motion sickness, too, with

You and your doggy friends will be safest if they can't scramble all over you while you're driving. It's also more secure for them if you have to make a sudden stop. One solution is to install a barrier and make a pooch-only area at the back of the car, as the owner of these two dogs has done. This is particularly effective if you have a station wagon.

disastrous consequences. You can help your dog avoid getting sick, or at least help him to feel better if he does succumb.

Dog-Proofing the Car

If you know your dog doesn't have a happy traveling tummy, make sure you dog-proof the car before you set out. Also do this if it's his first long-distance adventure and you don't know how he'll react—just in case. A plastic tablecloth placed on the backseat will protect the interior, says Elizabeth Altieri, D.V.M., a veterinarian in private practice in New Jersey. "The cloth underside of the tablecloth will stick to the seat, while the plastic part will be easy to clean should your dog get sick on it," she explains.

The most effective way to dog-proof the car is to keep your dog in a pet crate when traveling, says Dr. Stockner. If he doesn't already have his

own crate, you'll need to get him used to it for a month before you travel. Do this by feeding him in it, she says. "A crate is the safest way to ride in a car, for both the dog and you." If you have to make a sudden stop or there's an accident, your dog will be safe in his carrier. A barrier at the back of the car is also a good security measure.

Anxiety Overcome

Many dogs vomit in the car simply because they are anxious, explains Joanne Howl, D.V.M., a veterinarian in private practice in Rochester, New York. It's got nothing to do with your driving skills. It's just that things are whizzing past him in an alarming way. So get him used to riding in the car.

"Spend a little quality time motionless in the car," says Dr. Howl. "Let him check out the car while you read a chapter of your book. Give him a dog treat, give him a pat, then take him out of the car." Once he's decided the car's the place to be, take him on a quick cruise around the neighborhood. "Soon you can ride to the store, then across town, then anywhere you want without your dog throwing up," she says.

Easing the Queasies

Withholding food is one way to deal with the problem of carsickness, says Dr. Howl. "Don't feed your dog for at least eight hours before the trip," she explains. "Empty stomachs might get sick anyway, but at least there's nothing to expel."

Your dog shouldn't have anything to drink for the two hours before you set off. "Once on the road, small, frequent sips of water or ice cubes can be given," says Dr. Howl. "Don't let your dog get dry or dehydrated, but on the other hand, a belly full of water can quickly become a backseat full of water."

If these tactics don't work, you can always try medication. Your vet can prescribe drugs that will stop your dog getting carsick, or he can recommend over-the-counter products designed for humans that can be given in dog-sized doses.

Helping Him Feel Better

If your dog is sick when you're on the road despite all your efforts, Dr. Howl suggests a number of things to make him feel better. "Pull over and take him for a walk. Or try opening the windows if it's cool out, making sure not to let your dog hang his head out the window. If it's

Always keep your dog on a leash when you are in unfamiliar territory. If he becomes separated from you, he won't know where to turn and may panic. His collar tag should have contact information written on it, too.

Safety First

When you're on the road, you might be tempted to stop for the local specialty at a roadside diner, or to take a tour of the local museum in a small town you're passing through. But if your dog's along for the ride, you're going to have to forget it.

"Leaving your dog in the car while you stop for lunch or go sightseeing is probably the most dangerous thing you can do while traveling with your pet," says Elizabeth Altieri, D.V.M., a veterinarian in private practice in New Jersey. "On a hot day, the temperature can quite quickly get very high inside a car," she explains. "Your dog can die from heatstroke in a very short time, even if the windows are rolled down part way and he has access to drinking water."

"There are other reasons why leaving your dog in the car unsupervised is not a good idea," she says. "Dogs often get territorial when they are inside a car, and your dog could bite someone who comes by. Or he could be stolen, which is something that happens all the time."

hot in the car, turn on the air conditioner and point it at the dog." She also says that some dogs like an ice cube to chew on.

Another option is to give your dog some of his favorite toys to play with on the trip. "You can try squeaking a favorite toy at him to get his mind off his sick belly," says Dr. Howl.

Time for a Break

When you're on the road, the number of times you stop to give your dog a chance to stretch his legs will depend on the dog. "If your dog is quiet in the car, you can take him out

Vacation Checklist

Food & water bowl

Collar & leashes

Collar identification tags with your permanent and temporary addresses and phone numbers

A supply of your dog's medication, if any (be sure to write down the name and dosage so it can be replaced if lost)

Plastic bags or newspaper to clean up after him

A supply of your dog's regular food and water

Can opener for dog food

A few favorite toys and treats

Your dog's bed or favorite blanket

Dog brush

Pet crate, if your dog is trained to use one

Flea and tick repellent

Tweezers for removing ticks

Why Do Dogs Stick Their Heads Out of Car Windows?

We've all seen cars drive by with a dog hanging his head out the window, the breeze in his whiskers and a blissful look on his face. No one knows for sure why dogs do this, but we can guess. Larry Lachman, an animal behaviorist in Laguna Hills, California, suggests it's because dogs have such an amazing sense of smell. Some dogs find the scent-filled wind blowing in their face simply irresistible. The sensation is obviously one of life's pleasures.

Delicious it may be, but it's not so good for his eyes, says Priscilla K. Stockner, D.V.M., executive director of the Center for Humane Education in Escondido, California. The wind can carry flying particles, and make eyes dry and irritated. It's best if you're a party pooper and keep the window up.

as often as you wish for breaks," says Dr. Altieri. "If he's hyper, hold off on taking him out of the car, since this may only aggravate his problem."

Regardless of how he's taking to life with wheels, make sure you stop every four to six hours to give him a toilet break, says Dr. Altieri. Most roadside rest stops have a special area for dogs to relieve themselves, and places where your dog can run about. Keep your dog on a long leash while he romps, and maybe even play a game of ball. "It's important never to take him off his leash when you stop along the road or you could risk losing him," warns Dr. Stockner.

Travel Health Tips

Whenever your dog is away from his familiar territory, he can be at risk from parasites and infections. It's a good idea to contact the State Veterinarian in the state you plan to visit to find out about the local nasties.

Ticks are a problem whether your dog is visiting Arizona or the Adirondacks. But if you are going to be outdoors a lot, especially in New York, Connecticut, New Jersey, Pennsylvania, Maryland, Rhode Island, Wisconsin or Minnesota, ticks can pose a special danger: they can spread Lyme disease. "The best protection is to keep ticks at bay by using a quality tick repellent," says Joanne Howl, D.V.M., a veterinarian in Rochester, New York. "Examine him daily for ticks, and remove them."

And while you're on the case, keep an eye out for any burrs, thorns and other plant parts he may have picked up. They can cause a lot of discomfort if they get lodged in between his toe pads or in the ear canal.

Wherever you go on holiday, your dog can be affected by heartworm, carried by mosquitoes, says Dr. Howl. It is found in every state, but is more prevalent east of the Rockies. If you are traveling to an area known for heartworm and your dog doesn't take preventive medicine, take him to your vet for a checkup and prescription well before your departure date.

Spending time in the wild and drinking from rivers and streams, your dog may develop severe diarrhea caused by giardia, a common waterborne parasite. Carry fresh water if you're not going too far or for too long, or purify it as you would for yourself.

Your dog may come in contact with organisms that cause fungal infections, says Dr. Howl. Blastomycosis, which is found mostly in the Mississippi, Missouri, Tennessee and Ohio Valley areas, can affect any part of a dog's body. Histoplasmosis is also in this region; it affects the lungs and gastrointestinal tract. Coccidiomycosis, found in the desert regions of California, Nevada, Utah, Arizona, New Mexico and Texas, often affects the lungs and bones. You can't prevent contact but the infections are treatable, so if you notice your pet is under the weather weeks or even months after your trip, see your vet, advises Dr. Howl.

Make time for a ritual daily tick hunt. These ubiquitous pests carry disease and can cause your dog problems if not removed promptly.

Travel Accessories

There are all kinds of nifty items available to make your vacation with your dog convenient and enjoyable. There are collapsible water dishes for long car rides or hikes through the woods. If your dog is going sailing with you, he'll need his own life jacket. The canine companion hitting the trail

with the family can have his own dog backpack and carry his share of the load. A tie-out to restrain your dog at campsites and other outdoor areas always comes in handy.

Tie-out with leash

For safe and comfortable car travel, you might find that a barrier, to create a pooch-only area at the back of your station wagon, is just the thing. Or you may want to put him in a car seat harness to restrain and protect him on short trips. You will find these accessories at your local pet supply store, or through dog-oriented mail-order catalogs. Camping and outdoor stores also sometimes carry doggy travel items.

The dog sauntering down the track, at the far left, is helping to carry some of the camping supplies. With a properly designed backpack, he can at least take responsibility for his own food and water. If you're going to go out on a boat together, make sure he's wearing his life jacket—the dog on the left has sure gotten used to the idea. And for driving your dog about town, get him a car seat harness. This dog on the right is being kept safe in his place.

Up, Up and Away

Orville and Wilbur Wright they're not. The closest most dogs want to get to the speed of sound is the low-level flying they do as they tear across the park, leaping small creeks in a single bound. For some dogs, even that's a bit too racy.

Dogs are happiest with four feet planted firmly on the ground. Air travel is stressful, and if your dog is traveling in the cargo hold, which is where most dogs are placed, you won't have access to him. So you won't be able to comfort him if he starts to feel a little queasy. At least make sure he has a familiar blanket for both comfort and warmth.

As a rule, experts try to dissuade owners from taking their pets on airplanes. If it's not possible to avoid flying, it is important that you prepare him for the air up there with all possible care.

Crate First

An airline-approved pet crate is a must for taking your dog on the plane. Start preparing your dog at least a month before your trip, suggests John Hamil, D.V.M., a veterinarian in Laguna Beach, California. If he's not already crate-trained, get him used to the crate he'll be riding in by feeding him in it and encouraging him to sleep in it.

Health Check

You will need to take your dog to the vet for a checkup and health certificate, says Dr. Hamil. Health certificates are required for all pets that are transported by air, and are usually valid for 30 days for domestic travel, and 10 days for international flights. If you are flying to an international destination, contact the consulate of that country to find out what inoculations he'll need, and whether he must be quarantined before or after entering the country.

You can also discuss the possibility of giving your pet tranquilizers, although these are not recommended in most situations because they

Gradually get him used to an airline-approved pet crate well before your planned trip. Over as long a period as possible, increase the time he spends in it until it causes him no distress to be confined.

can interfere with your dog's ability to cope with changes of temperature.

Ticket to Ride

Be sure to make your reservations well ahead of time. A possible bonus of booking early is that your dog may be able to fly in the cabin with you, provided his carrier is small enough to fit under the seat in front of you. Since only one or two pets are usually allowed in the cabin on a flight, the earlier you make your reservations, the more likely you'll be to secure one of these spots.

Book a nonstop flight, if possible, and fly at a time of year and time of day when there is less likelihood of outdoor temperatures being hot. "For dogs in the cargo hold of a plane stuck on a runway, heat can be a killer," says Dr. Hamil. By booking a direct flight, there is less likelihood that your dog will end up in this situation. Night and predawn flights are the safest for pets traveling in summer.

Finally, make sure you book yourself on the same flight as your pet. Don't send him on ahead of you, or on a later flight.

Flying Time

Your dog should have nothing to eat for eight hours before the flight, and nothing to drink for two hours before. Get to the airport early. "Dogs are usually shipped as freight, which means you should check in two hours before you fly," says Dr. Hamil. Make sure that he has a familiar cushion in his airline crate. Your name, address and phone number should be written clearly on

This Belgian Tervuren checks in with his owner. Dogs are often loaded well before departure time, and usually travel in the airplane's cargo hold. It's up to you to watch over his welfare if delays occur.

the crate, including your destination address in case there's a mix-up.

Once you're on the plane, Dr. Hamil suggests that you advise the crew that there is a dog in the cargo hold and insist that they tell the pilot. Then, if something happens that could endanger your pet's well-being, such as the plane being held for some time on a hot runway, the pilot can arrange for your dog to be cared for.

If such a situation arises and you are worried about your friend below, don't be afraid to speak up, says Dr. Hamil. Let the crew know that your dog's safety is of the utmost importance to you.

Home Away from Home

Just like the rest of the family, your dog needs somewhere to rest his head at the end of the day. With a little research before you leave, you'll find just the place—a campsite, a hotel or, if he can't be with you, a boarding kennel, for a happy stay.

Under Canvas

Canines love camping out, but not all campsites love dogs. National Forests allow dogs at campsites, but some National Parks and State Parks do not. If you plan to visit one, call ahead to check if dogs are allowed. Dogs should always be kept tethered in a campsite for the comfort of others, the preservation of wildlife and your dog's safety.

Dog-Friendly Hotels

If your dog's the Jacuzzi and spa type, you may well opt for one of the many hotels around the country that put out the welcome mat for pets. Check hotels in the area you're visiting before you leave home, and book in advance. Don't just drive somewhere and hope to find a hotel that takes dogs. You may end up sleeping in the car.

Tracking Down Dog-Doting Digs

"There are many available guidebooks on where to stay with your pet," says Maria Goodavage, author of *California Dog Lovers' Companion* and *The Bay Area Dog Lovers' Companion*. "If you are an Automobile Association of America member, you can use the organization's free guides. You can also call the local humane society in the area where you will be staying and ask for a reference to a good dogs-allowed hotel." Many bed-and-breakfast hotels are also happy to have dogs.

"Start by picking a place that sounds good to you, then do a little research," says Goodavage. Call and talk to the owners to get a sense of how welcome your dog will be. "If dog treats are provided or other special canine services, chances are your dog will be very welcome."

The Well-Behaved Guest

He's on holiday, but his good manners shouldn't be—it's up to you to make sure he's showing his best behavior. "Dogs make incredible guests if their owners know how to handle them," says Goodavage. This means taking some precautions to ensure that your dog does not disturb other guests or ruin the room.

"Whatever you do, don't leave your dog alone in a hotel room," says Goodavage. "An anxious dog can tear a hotel room apart in no time." If you must leave your dog alone for a short time, keep him confined to his crate. Be sure to inform the hotel manager so cleaning staff don't get a nasty surprise when they enter the room.

If your dog tends to bark at strange noises, ask for a room where there's little foot traffic, says Goodavage. She also recommends bringing a sheet from home to put on the bed if your dog likes to cuddle up with you at night. No one wants him leaving his hair on the bedclothes.

If your dog isn't housebroken, he isn't hotel-broken. If you have any doubts about his toilet habits, go camping instead.

Make sure hotel proprietors are really happy to see your dog—that he's not just allowed, but truly welcomed.

Boarding Kennels

It's not always possible, or sensible, to take your dog with you, especially if you're flying. He shouldn't be left at home either, unless you can get a friend or family member to move into your house to dog-sit while you're gone. If that's not possible, a boarding kennel may be the best choice.

There are about 6,500 boarding kennels to choose from in the United States and Canada. This is going to be your dog's temporary home in your absence, so don't just drop your dog off at the first one you drive past on your way out of town. Reassure yourself that the kennel you choose will be providing him with the kind of care that he's used to from you.

Choosing the Right Kennel

Ask dog-owning friends for recommendations or check the Yellow Pages, says Jim Krack, executive director of the American Boarding Kennels Association. Then call your local Better Business Bureau and ask if any complaints have been lodged against the kennel you've decided on. Telephone the kennel to make sure it can take your pet while you will be away. "Also make an appointment to visit, to see it for yourself," advises Krack. "A personal visit is essential to determine whether it will be satisfactory."

When you arrive at the kennel, take a good look around. Is it neat and clean? Are enclosures high enough so a dog can't climb out? Are they made from sturdy, well-maintained materials? Are there solid dividers between them so neighboring dogs can't make contact with your pet?

Quality Care

It's also important to determine what level of care and supervision your pet will receive. "Proper supervision is the key to good boarding," says Krack. "Pets should be checked frequently during the day by someone who is trained to recognize signs of illness and distress." Some experts recommend using only kennels that provide such supervision around the clock.

Find out how water is provided. "Individual containers full of clean drinking water should be available to each animal," says Krack. Ask, too, if you can bring a supply of your dog's regular food. If his diet doesn't have to be changed, he shouldn't develop diarrhea while you are gone.

Finally, be sure that the kennel requires all dogs to be immunized against distemper, parvovirus, rabies and tracheobronchitis, and that veterinary services are available should they be needed.

PART FOUR

Food, Glorious Food

It's a dog's favorite topic, a real conversation starter: "What am I having for dinner today?" This is a question that will occupy your dog's every thought from the time she wakes up in the morning until the food bowl goes down on the floor. The good news is, there's plenty of tasty, nutritious food to choose from.

14 | NUTRITION FOR LIFE

A dog needs a diet that both tastes good and is good for her. If you aim for quality and balance, with a touch of variety to cover all nutritional needs, you will see it in your dog's health, vitality and sleek condition.

15 | CANINE CUISINE

You've got so many possibilities for making your dog's stomach and tastebuds happy. Canned food or dry, a snack or a meal, store-bought or homemade—how to find the food that's right for her.

14 NUTRITION FOR LIFE

*When it comes to feeding time, you are truly your dog's sole provider.
Racing to the kitchen when she hears the can opener or the telltale
rattle of kibble hitting her bowl is about as close as she comes to fending
for herself. So be sure she gets food she will thrive on—carefully
balanced to suit her needs.*

Your Dog's Nutritional Needs
pages 213–216
To choose the right food,
find out what nutrients your
dog really needs

Special Requirements
pages 217–222
Puppies, pregnant or nursing
moms, older dogs—just some of
the canines with special needs

Getting Enough Water
page 223
One of the most important
things you do for your dog is to
give her plenty of fresh water

How Much Food is Enough?
pages 224–225
An easy guide to evaluating
your dog's ever-changing
food requirements

Canine Eating Problems
pages 226–227
Don't despair—both greedy
pooches and fussy eaters can be
brought back into line

Your Dog's Nutritional Needs

Your dog needs a supply of certain nutrients. They help her to grow and they keep her immune system in good working order so she can generally get along in the healthy, energetic way she likes. The six basic nutrients that all living things need—and that includes dogs—are clean water, proteins, carbohydrates, minerals, fats and vitamins.

A dog's individual nutritional requirements will determine how much of these nutrients she should have, and that will vary depending on her lifestyle. Is your dog active or sedentary? Young or old? A working dog that hunts, herds or races? Is she suffering from a chronic or temporary health condition? Is she pregnant or nursing a litter of puppies?

"Foods containing the right amounts of the six nutrients must be eaten by the dog to balance her particular body needs," says Edmund Dorosz, D.V.M., a veterinarian and nutrition specialist in Fort McCloud, Alberta, and author of *Let's Cook for Our Dogs*. "Once eaten, the food will be broken down and processed into usable forms for the many cells of the dog's body. This, very simply, is dog nutrition."

Water

This building block of all life is one of your dog's most vital requirements. She can go for a while without food, but without water she would soon become dehydrated or suffer heatstroke and other serious conditions. An adult dog's body

This German Shepherd may lap up more than two quarts of fresh water a day, so fill her bowl frequently so that she always has plenty to drink.

weight is 50 to 60 percent water; a puppy's is more than 80 percent. Since dogs can't always tell you when they are thirsty, and even Lassie might have trouble pouring herself a glass of water from the tap, have a bowl of fresh water available for your dog at all times. A dog of medium size that eats a diet primarily of dry food could require upward of two quarts of water each day.

Proteins

Dogs don't actually require proteins as such; what they really need are the amino acids that make up proteins. Dogs manufacture some

explains Dr. Dorosz. "They need to get this protein from animal sources."

Carbohydrates

There are simple carbohydrates, such as sugar, and complex carbohydrates, such as starches and fiber. They help provide your dog with energy and also keep the intestines functioning smoothly so that food waste passes through the system efficiently.

Fiber is often included in diets designed to help a dog lose or maintain weight, because it may make a dog feel full without sending the calorie count through the roof. High-fiber diets are traditionally prescribed for dogs that have weight problems.

The preferred source of carbohydrates in many commercially prepared dog foods is corn, followed by soybeans and wheat. Recently, rice has become a popular ingredient, particularly in special formulations for dogs that have developed an intolerance to other grains. Carbohydrates are an important part of your dog's nutritional needs, although they should make up no more than about 50 percent of a balanced canine diet.

Fats

We humans are certainly preoccupied with fat in our food, but there's no need to transfer that anxiety onto our pets. Any diet too high in fatty foods will make for an overweight dog, but that doesn't mean you should throw out the fat completely. Fats should be properly balanced with

amino acids, known as the nonessential amino acids, within their bodies. They must get the rest—ten essential amino acids—from their food, specifically from animal or plant products that contain protein.

Proteins from animal sources, such as eggs, meat and fish, are high-quality, or complete, proteins. Incomplete proteins come from grains and vegetables, and they contain only some of the essential amino acids. You might suppose that the more "high-quality" proteins your dog gets, the better, but it's not as simple as that. Your dog needs both forms of protein, because they work together to ensure her cell-building, blood-clotting, infection-fighting and myriad other bodily processes are all working okay.

If your dog is a normally active and healthy dog, just a small amount of protein will get her by. The only exceptions are puppies, pregnant or nursing females, and dogs that work hard. These dogs might need a greater ratio of protein in their food. "Young and active dogs need more protein in their diets—young dogs for growth and active dogs because they are constantly breaking down more tissue, such as muscle tissue and red blood cells, which needs to be replaced,"

other nutrients, and are essential to her good nutrition and health, as well as being an important source of energy.

Feeding your dog the proper amount of a complete and balanced dog food should ensure that she gets the right level of fat, but beware those extras that can literally tip the scales out of favor for your dog. Too many calories are often the result of too much fat—too many biscuit treats, too many table scraps.

Very active, hard-working dogs may benefit from a diet that is higher in fat, and protein, than would be healthy for their less active canine counterparts. Sled dogs, for instance, can eat up to 40 percent of the dry matter of their diet as fat, says Dr. Dorosz. That would be enough to make most dogs as wide as they are long!

Minerals

If you've ever read a pet food label and wondered why there was a measure of the food's "ash content," wonder no more. They aren't really adding ash to your dog's chow. The term actually refers to a laboratory testing method that is used to measure the total mineral content of a food.

Minerals either trigger chemical reactions within the body or serve as building blocks for specific bodily systems, such as nerve tissue (magnesium), skin and enzymes (zinc), or heart and kidneys (potassium).

Generally, your dog doesn't need a lot of minerals. For instance, the amount of iron her body needs to affect her red blood cells is measured in parts per million. Other minerals, such as calcium and phosphorus, are needed in relatively larger amounts to ensure she has healthy bones. "If a dog is fed a complete and balanced diet,

there is no need to supplement her diet with minerals," says Francis Kallfelz, D.V.M., a professor of nutrition at Cornell University's College of Veterinary Medicine in Ithaca, New York. "At best, it has no value whatsoever. At worst, it could be harmful." Most commercial dog foods will provide your dog with the minerals that she needs.

Vitamins

Just as your dog's body needs minerals, it also needs vitamins for vital chemical reactions and normal metabolic functions. She requires the same vitamins from her food as you need from yours, except for vitamin C, which dogs are actually able to manufacture in their own bodies.

Vitamins are divided into two groups: those that are soluble in water and those that dissolve only in fat. The B vitamins, which help convert food into energy, are water soluble, as is vitamin C. This means that they need to be replenished every day, and any excess is simply passed out again in the dog's urine.

Dogs appreciate a regular routine, so feed your pet her meal at the same time each day, either morning or night, whichever fits in best with the rest of the family.

Fat-soluble vitamins, such as vitamins A, E, K and D, have a bit more staying power in the body, which is fortunate, because deficiencies can cause serious problems. By the same token, excess amounts of these vitamins, especially vitamin A, can lead to trouble.

Achieving the right balance shouldn't be a problem. "There's really no reason to supplement with vitamins as long as you are feeding a complete and balanced diet," says Rebecca Remillard, D.V.M., an animal nutrition specialist at Angell Memorial Animal Hospital in Boston. "I'd only suggest supplements if you are feeding your dog a homemade diet. Then you need to make sure the food is nutritionally balanced." If you choose to prepare your dog's food at home,

Dr. Remillard suggests you review her diet with your vet to check if any supplementation is needed—your vet will advise you on this.

When to Feed

Most adult dogs can sustain their energy and nutrient levels on one meal a day. "Feeding a dog once a day is fine," says Dr. Kallfelz. "You just need to be sure that you give that meal at the right time to suit your household." For a family that's away at work and school most of the day, it makes sense to feed your dog at night, since someone will be home to let her out after she eats. On the other hand, if there's always someone at home during the day, a morning feeding might suit you and your dog better.

High Protein, High Cost—Should You Spend the Money?

It's not hard to spend as much on your dog's meals as you do on your own. Premium foods abound and are available in pet supply stores, through your veterinarian and sometimes in grocery stores. "Premium" usually translates into high-protein. The question is, are you getting what you pay for and does your dog really need it?

"You need to look at the quality of the ingredients," advises Edmund Dorosz, D.V.M., a veterinarian and nutrition specialist in Fort McCloud, Alberta. "Protein is expensive if it is of high quality, and high quality means meat." Vegetable- or grain-based proteins, primarily from corn or soybeans, may bring down the price of the food but they are harder for your dog to digest, making the protein harder to absorb. You may need to feed your dog more if the food has a high fiber content to make sure she gets adequate protein. She, in

turn, will produce more waste, and depending on her size, this could be a real inconvenience for you.

This is not to say that vegetable- or grain-based protein is bad. By combining the right kinds of protein, such as rice and soy, your dog will get complete protein that contains all the essential amino acids. This sort of high-fiber diet might work well if you are trying to keep your dog lean. The fiber could make her feel full even though she's getting fewer calories.

When buying commercial dog food, go for one that addresses your dog's individual needs and is a good-quality food. But make sure you're not just paying for fancy packaging. Look at the labels and assess how many nutrients your dog will be getting in each bowl of food. "A lot of money is spent on marketing," says Dr. Dorosz. "Read the ingredient list to be sure you're getting high-quality, meat-based protein."

Special Requirements

While all dogs need the important nutrients in their diet, how much they need depends on their age, health and level of activity. Adhering to a special diet may be as easy as picking pet food designed for puppies off the grocery shelf or carefully regulating when and how much you feed your diabetic dog. If you ever have a question as to whether your dog should be on a special diet, talk it over with your vet.

Puppies

Anyone who has watched a puppy grow into adulthood knows how quickly those pudgy little faces mature into decidedly grown-up looking mugs. And how quickly that ball of waddling fur becomes a gangly, all-legs adolescent tearing through your home.

It's not surprising then that, pound-for-pound, puppies need more calories than adult dogs. After all, it's during that first year that a dog will experience the greatest amount of growth of her whole life.

"Young puppies need energy and balanced nutrients at levels up to three times what they will need as adults," explains Dorothy Laflamme, D.V.M., a veterinary nutritionist in the St. Louis area, and vice-president of the American College of Veterinary Nutrition. "This decreases after about four months, but remains greater than adult needs until the puppy is fully grown at ten months to two years, depending on when the breed reaches maturity."

Puppies like these Jack Russell Terriers need plenty of calories to sustain a steady level of growth during their first year. Feed small meals several times a day at first.

Puppies also require more high-quality protein, which they can get from eggs, milk or cottage cheese. These are both tasty and easily digested. Or you can opt for commercially prepared puppy food, which is formulated with the special requirements of puppies in mind.

Don't Overdo It

Most pups are weaned between six to eight weeks, so your pup will already be eating solid food by the time you bring her home. Even though it seems as if she wants to eat you out of house and home, don't let her. She will have growth spurts, but you should feed her only the amount she needs to maintain a steady, average rate of growth. "There's this general American picture of the perfect healthy puppy being roly-poly, which is absolutely wrong," says Julie

Hold the Onions

When it comes to food, dogs will taste-test just about anything. So it is a rare pooch that won't gobble down whatever falls—accidentally or by design—to the floor. Most of the time, your dog is in danger only of gaining a little weight. But if onions happen to be what she finds at her feet, she could be in for real trouble.

"Onions can cause hemolytic anemia, a condition in which red blood cells are destroyed," says Kathy Michel, D.V.M., a clinical assistant professor of nutrition at the University of Pennsylvania School of Veterinary Medicine in Philadelphia.

The impact of onion seems to be closely linked to size, with smaller dogs being affected more severely than larger ones. "We had a Westie in our care that had eaten onion soup mix made into a dip. The amount of onion in the final product was pretty small, but it was still enough to make the dog very ill," recalls Dr. Michel.

Besides watching what falls to the floor when you are chopping onions, make sure your trash can is secure and never give your dog onion-flavored anything. And if you choose to cook your dog's food at home, hold the onions.

Churchill, D.V.M., an assistant clinical specialist in small animal nutrition at the University of Minnesota's College of Veterinary Medicine in St. Paul. "Erring on the side of lean is better than overfeeding, especially with large breeds."

If your dog eats too much, she'll grow too fast, which could spell trouble later. Rapid, disproportionate growth of bones and muscles could lead to hip dysplasia and other joint problems.

Puppies that will eventually grow up into big dogs are especially susceptible to musculoskeletal problems if they grow too fast. "Any puppy that is going to grow to an adult size of more than 75 pounds is on a different, rapid growth curve that extends over a longer period of time and must be fed accordingly," explains Dr. Churchill. "We've seen a significant impact in the reduction of orthopedic problems in dogs that have been kept lean from puppyhood."

It is also important to keep down the calcium levels in food your large puppy eats. Too much calcium can actually interfere with her normal bone and cartilage development. "For large breeds, calcium should make up no more than 1.1 percent of the dry matter," says Dr. Churchill. While you won't find this information on any pet food labels, you can call the manufacturer's toll-free line for a more detailed nutritional analysis. The call will be well worth your while, given that you could help prevent your dog from developing a painful condition.

Puppies from small breeds, on the other hand, are not as prone to these types of orthopedic problems. They are, however, particularly susceptible to low blood sugar levels and other problems, explains Dr. Laflamme.

"These very small puppies should be fed small amounts at least four times a day when they are very young to make sure they receive adequate nutrition," she says. "Once they are 10 to 12 weeks old, three times a day is adequate, and then twice a day after about four months."

Puppy Food Until When?

Growing puppies require proportionately more calories and nutrients than their adult counterparts. But when a pup's rate of growth slows noticeably, that's a good time to switch her to an adult maintenance diet. "As a general rule, when a dog has reached 75 to 80 percent of her adult size, it is a good time to switch from puppy food to an adult diet," says Dr. Remillard.

"When that actually occurs for each dog is quite variable. We're talking about the most diverse species on the planet, with some adult dogs weighing 2 pounds and others 200 pounds." Generally, the smaller the dog, the earlier she will reach what is considered maturity.

Hard-and-fast rules are difficult when you're dealing with this level of diversity. Your vet will be able to advise you. Watch for changes in her eating patterns and be aware of the average adult weight for her breed. With puppies of mixed breed, use the four-month rule of thumb: at four months, a puppy is roughly half her adult size. While hardly scientific, it's still a fairly useful benchmark if you're uncertain just what exotic mix of breeds you're working with.

Frequent Feeding

Puppy tummies are small so they can't hold enough food at one time to see them through an entire day. Until your puppy is about four or five months of age, feed her three meals a day. Be sure to moisten her chow with warm water if you feed her dry puppy food. Not only does this make it tastier, but it's also easier for her to eat with her puppy teeth until they fall out and are replaced by permanent teeth.

From four or five months until about nine months of age, feed your puppy twice a day. If she still enjoys her food moistened, indulge her for a while. But remember that crunching on dry food will be better for her teeth in the long run, since the chewing action cleans them.

By 10 or 11 months, you can probably start feeding your puppy an adult diet once a day. When you switch your puppy to a maintenance diet, reduce the number of feeds. If you choose to feed her a different food, make the changeover gradually. This will be easier on her digestive system and her taste buds. Over seven to ten days, substitute ever-increasing amounts of the new food for her customary fare.

Pregnant or Lactating Dogs

Pregnancy is a good time to pamper your dog—just be sure not to confuse pampering with pigging out. There's no need to increase her daily rations until around about the third trimester, when she's seven weeks pregnant, and

This Collie should have all the food and water she wants while she is nursing her puppies, but as she weans them, gradually reduce her rations to normal.

then only by about 10 to 20 percent. The real eating starts after the pups are born. "Don't overfeed your dog during pregnancy and underfeed during lactation," says Dr. Remillard. "If she gains too much weight during gestation, she can have trouble whelping the puppies."

After a dog delivers her puppies, you should increase her daily ration by another 10 percent for the first day after she gives birth. Then let her eat to her heart's content (no boxes of chocolates, of course). Feed by "free choice" rather than on a schedule during the first five weeks of lactation, recommends Dr. Remillard.

The puppies' demand for milk will increase daily for the first 20 to 30 days, so the mother must be allowed to eat what she needs to keep up with her family's demands. There's another plus to having food readily available during this time. "At about three weeks, the puppies start nosing around in their mother's food and very shortly will be getting a good part of their nutritional requirements this way," says Dr. Remillard.

"Lactating dogs have very high nutrient needs, as much as three to four times what's normal," says Dr. Laflamme. "They should be fed diets intended either for growth and reproduction or 'all life stages.' Adult foods may be too low in calories or nutrients. Yet it's important to return her to pre-pregnancy levels of intake after the puppies are weaned so that she avoids any weight gain." And make all dietary changes gradually.

Older Dogs

Feeding an older dog is often similar to feeding a less active dog. It's not your dog's age that matters so much as her retired way of life. But while she may need only three-quarters of the calories of her former diet—because she prefers daily

This 13-year-old mixed breed dog still enjoys a game of fetch. Although she may be slower, it's important to keep up the activity and feed her good-quality protein.

strolls to daily jogs now—her need for the essential nutrients may be proportionately higher.

"Older dogs require very good quality protein," explains Dr. Dorosz. "By-products, such as hair and hooves, are protein, but of low quality. By comparison, eggs provide the highest quality protein." Buy a premium food or ask your vet to recommend a food for your aging pet.

Be careful not to overfeed an older dog. Too much food combined with a low activity level could easily cause her to pack on the pounds, and that could lead to health problems. "Obesity is the number-one nutritional disease among all dogs," says Dr. Churchill. "And some older dogs may become prone to it if their appetite continues and their exercise decreases, which is why reducing the calories in the diet can be helpful."

Some foods formulated for older dogs restrict protein to prevent kidney problems. However, such a cutback may not be necessary, says Dr. Churchill, since renal disease is not common in older dogs. And if your dog doesn't actually have a problem, there is really no need to restrict the amount of protein she eats. "If she's getting regular veterinary care and has a diet tailored to meet her individual condition, that should be fine," Dr. Churchill advises.

Working Dogs

While you might consider a hard game of fetch in the backyard with your dog a real workout, it's probably more taxing for you than your dog. True working dogs are the breeds that herd sheep or cattle, that run arduous sled races or spend hours in a cold, wet marsh with their duck-hunting owners. And they need a diet rich in high-quality protein and fat to maintain peak stamina and good body condition.

"Dogs differ from us in several respects," says Dr. Dorosz. "They have more heart and muscle in comparison to their total body weight, and their cardio-respiratory system is superior to ours." Also, dogs do not sweat in the same way people do. Depending on the breed, the dog has greater stamina and oxygen capacity than us, too.

Back to Nature

Traditionally, dogs maintained a well-balanced diet as meat eaters. From their prey's flesh, bones and organs, they got high-quality protein and minerals; from its stomach contents, carbohydrates, vitamins and vegetable- or grain-based protein; and, finally, from the indigestible feathers or hair, fiber.

But unless you live on the African savanna and your dog regularly takes down a wildebeest, you've got to do your best to replicate her traditional diet. You can do this with commercially prepared foods, some of which contain a very high ratio of meat-based proteins, as well as a balanced amount of the other essential nutrients. Go for one that addresses your dog's nutritional needs and buy a high-quality food. Look at the labels and assess how many nutrients your dog will be getting in each serving of food.

Alternatively, you can get back to nature in your own kitchen. Some dog owners are choosing to return their dogs to what they consider a more natural diet, namely, bones, raw meat and partly cooked vegetables (they simulate the partially digested stomach contents of a dog's prey). Proponents of this approach say their dogs are healthier and happier. But many veterinarians caution against going too natural.

"There's nothing wrong with raw or partly cooked vegetables, but I could never recommend feeding bones, or raw meat or eggs," says Rebecca Remillard, D.V.M., a nutrition specialist at Angell Memorial Animal Hospital in Boston. "This is purely from a safety standpoint, not a nutritional one. I often end up surgically removing bones from dogs' intestines, and there are virulent bacteria in meat and eggs, *E. coli* for example, that can affect dogs the same way they affect humans."

If you have the time and the desire, a compromise on a diet that is closer to her ancestral days is to cook her dog food at home. This way, you know exactly what form of protein is included—animal-based or a nutritionally sound balance of vegetable- or grain-based protein—as well as what's not included, preservatives or additives. Go over your proposed recipe with your vet to ensure that it has the nutrients your dog needs in the correct ratio for her, says Dr. Remillard.

These hard-working sled dogs need a diet rich in high-quality protein and fat to remain strong and fit for their tasks. And because they must often be out of doors in freezing temperatures, they burn off even more calories.

These differences become important when you come to feeding the working dog in order to keep her at peak performance.

Working dogs thrive and work best when fed on animal proteins and animal fats, explains Dr. Dorosz. "Cereals, vegetables and carbohydrates play less of an energy role." Make sure you buy a food with high-quality, animal-derived protein, not one that is high in corn or soy.

A hard-working dog might benefit from twice-a-day feeding, but be careful not to feed her immediately before or after a strenuous workout. Feeding too close to vigorous physical activity can result in vomiting or diarrhea, and she won't feel like giving her all. It's the same with water, says Dr. Churchill. "Don't let your dog resume strenuous activity until at least 30 minutes after she has had a drink."

Another factor to consider when feeding your working dog is how much time she spends out of doors in cold weather. Generally, dogs need to get 7.5 percent more calories for each 10°F drop in temperature.

Giving your hard-working dog small, light snacks in the field is an okay way to keep her energy up, as long as she'll take them. "Many working dogs get too high strung and refuse to eat when they're working," says Dr. Churchill. "This is why feeding a high-fat, nutrient-dense food is a better option for some very active dogs."

Eating for Long-Term Problems and Convalescing

If your dog has been diagnosed as having a health problem, it's important that you work with your vet to fine-tune a diet specifically designed for her. The type of food she eats can often be a great help in easing the condition. For instance, a diet for a dog suffering from kidney disease would have decreased levels of protein, phosphorus and salt but increased caloric density—more power to the punch, since she may be receiving less food.

A convalescing dog could also benefit from her special eating needs being met. If your dog has lost weight due to an illness or surgery, Dr. Kallfelz suggests that you might increase the caloric density of her food until she reaches her pre-illness weight. If her normal diet is dry food and you want to encourage her to eat, try moistening it with a little warm water or even a little bit of stock or canned food.

There are prescription foods formulated to address the nutritional needs of dogs with a wide range of health conditions. These are available only through your veterinarian, who will work closely with you should your dog ever need to be put on this kind of special diet.

Getting Enough Water

Dogs just love water. And while they need all the essential nutrients to survive, they need water most of all. Fresh, clean water. Dogs can go for an amazing length of time without food, but without water they'd perish in a few days.

Make sure she has fresh water, says Kathy Michel, D.V.M., a clinical assistant professor of nutrition at the University of Pennsylvania School of Veterinary Medicine in Philadelphia. "If the water's not fresh, some dogs will drink only when very thirsty." Clean the bowl and change the water every morning, then check it during the day. This is especially important in hot weather or if your dog spends time outside.

For an expectant or lactating mom, continual access to clean, fresh water is most important. Water carries nutrients to the developing fetuses and also helps flush wastes out of the mother's system. During lactation, she needs lots to keep up her milk supply for her new family.

Your dog can drink however much she likes, whenever she likes, except around serious exercise time. (Her water bowl should be off-limits for at least 30 minutes before and after exercise.) Generally, you need never be concerned about giving her "too much" water. Talk to your vet if you notice a marked increase in your dog's water consumption, though. "Diabetes, kidney failure, Cushing's disease and other things are all characterized by increased thirst," says Dr. Michel.

Perrier for Pooches

Bottled water for the dog who happily drinks from mud puddles or toilet bowls? Is premium H_2O a case of marketing over mind? Not necessarily. "If you won't drink what comes out of your tap, why should your dog?" asks Edmund Dorosz, D.V.M., a veterinarian and nutrition specialist in Fort McCloud, Alberta. "She may turn her nose up at your fresh tap water and go instead to a mud puddle because she's turned off by the chemicals she smells in her bowl."

This question of water quality and palatability is closely tied to your particular locality and preferences. "Water quality is so variable," says Kathy Michel, D.V.M., a clinical assistant professor of nutrition at

the University of Pennsylvania School of Veterinary Medicine in Philadelphia. "Some is of very high quality and tastes great. In other places, it might be of equal quality, but taste terrible. If your dog absolutely must drink adequate amounts of water and the only thing she likes is bottled water, then give it to her."

Some bottled water may contain flavors that a dog finds distasteful. So if you're going to try her on bottled, make sure there's fresh tap water available, too, suggests Julie Churchill, D.V.M., an assistant clinical specialist in small animal nutrition at the University of Minnesota's College of Veterinary Medicine in St. Paul. Your dog will decide which flavor she prefers.

How Much Food is Enough?

Eating is an all-time favorite canine activity and most dogs will lick the bowl clean and then ask for seconds with a winning tilt of the head. Your dog is not the best judge of when enough is enough, so it's up to you to decide how much she can eat.

Catering for the Individual Dog

The right amount of food varies with the individual dog. Every can or package of food has guidelines printed on it. The trouble is, these are written with the "average" dog in mind, but nobody knows quite what the average dog looks like, let alone how much she needs to eat.

Even if they happen to weigh the same, all dogs are unique. Their activity levels differ, their ages differ and their metabolisms differ, so their nutritional requirements differ as well. The feeding guidelines provided on dog food containers are good starting points. Then focus on the needs of your very own not-at-all-average dog.

Helpful Guidelines

You can work out how much your dog needs to eat by learning to evaluate her overall body condition, then adjusting her food accordingly. Many vets are now recommending that you use a five-point scale to determine her body condition and work out how much food she should be receiving each day.

To assess your dog's body condition, take a good look at her from the back and from above to see if she looks lean or heavy. Then put your hands over her ribcage to see if the ribs are prominent or heavily padded over with fat. Armed with this information—how your dog looks and how her ribs feel—you can use the chart opposite and accompanying illustrations as guidelines to evaluate your dog's body, so you know to give more, less or the same amount of food as usual.

Your aim is to feed your dog the right amount of food so that her body is "ideal." But if your check shows that she is on the overweight side, she's getting more food than she can use and you should cut it back. And if she's underweight, she's not eating enough, so feed her more.

Four Simple Steps

Feeding your dog the correct amount is a very simple process. Dr. Churchill suggests owners follow these four steps:

1. Choose the most complete and balanced dog food you can find.
2. Follow the feeding guidelines on the package.
3. Evaluate your dog every two weeks.
4. Adjust your dog's rations—always do this gradually—until she matches the ideal "score" on the chart opposite.

Whether your dog is a puppy, middle-aged or geriatric, active or relatively sedentary, by following these guidelines you will help ensure that she remains at a healthy weight. With this method, you can monitor your dog continually and adjust how much you feed her in response to the changes in her body and her lifestyle.

How Does Your Dog Rate?

This chart and illustrations will help you to determine whether your dog is very thin, underweight, ideal in size, overweight or obese. Then adjust how much you feed her until she is "ideal."

Score 1 Very Thin	Ribs	Easy to feel, with no fat cover.	
	Tail base	Prominent raised bony structure with no fat under the skin.	
	Abdomen	Severe abdominal tuck; accentuated hourglass shape.	
Score 2 Underweight	Ribs	Easy to feel, with minimal fat cover.	
	Tail base	Raised bony structure with little fat under the skin.	
	Abdomen	Abdominal tuck; marked hourglass shape.	
Score 3 Ideal	Ribs	Possible to feel, with slight fat cover.	
	Tail base	Either a smooth contour or some thickening; possible to feel bony structures under a thin layer of fat.	
	Abdomen	Abdominal tuck; well-proportioned lumbar "waist."	
Score 4 Overweight	Ribs	Difficult to feel, with moderate fat cover.	
	Tail base	Smooth contour or some thickening; still possible to feel the bony structures.	
	Abdomen	Little or no abdominal tuck or "waist;" back slightly broadened.	
Score 5 Obese	Ribs	Very difficult to feel, with thick fat cover.	
	Tail base	Appears thickened; difficult to feel the bony structures.	
	Abdomen	Pendulous, bulging belly, with no "waist;" back markedly broadened; trough may form when muscled areas on either side of the spine bulge at the sides.	

Canine Eating Problems

It's easy not to worry about a dog being a few pounds over her optimum weight—until you realize that a 25-pound Dachshund is like a 160-pound man ballooning to 220 pounds. And while some dogs don't know when to stop, others turn up their noses at all your offerings. There are solutions for both problems.

Overweight Dogs

"Obesity is the number-one disease problem in our pets today," says Dr. Dorosz. "There are more fat dogs than ever before. The primary problem is too many calories and not enough activity." Overweight dogs can develop all sorts of health problems and they will likely have a shorter-than-expected life span. "There is no question that a lean dog is far healthier and will live longer," says Dr. Dorosz. She will also be able to enjoy and get a whole lot more from life.

Obesity generally has three causes: genetic, dietary or hormonal. By far the most common cause, and the one discussed here, is dietary overindulgence. But before you rush to put your obese dog on a diet, have her checked by your vet to make sure there is no underlying medical condition. Once you've determined it's her appetite and not something else, you're ready to tackle this weighty matter.

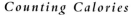
Counting Calories

"The first thing you need to do is discover why your dog is overweight," says Dr. Michel. Do this, she suggests, by taking a careful inventory of her diet for a few days. This way you'll have a good idea where the calories are coming from. Is she getting into the cat's food? Are your kids tossing her the stuff on their plates they don't want? Do your neighbors slip her treats? Is your garbage can secure and out of reach?

"Once her food sources are under control and you know where the calories are coming from, this audit will be easier," says Dr. Michel. "The next step is to take away unrestricted food." This may mean feeding the cat behind a closed door and keeping the dog away from the table at mealtimes until everything is cleared away. "And clean up your own act if you often toss her tidbits when you're preparing food," she adds. "Or at least count this in her total food intake."

Once you've eliminated all "supplemental" snacks, if your dog is still overweight, you need to set about reducing her calories. "The objective is for her to lose body fat while conserving lean muscle tissue," explains Dr. Dorosz. "There are commercially prepared reducing diets on the market that are primarily

Treats from the table can quickly add up to one overweight dog. If you like slipping her snacks, at least feed her less of her own food to compensate.

low in calories and high in fiber." Indigestible fiber makes up 15 to 25 percent of the food. The dog feels satisfied because she has something in her stomach but the food doesn't have too many nutrients. "The fat content is lower also, but protein, vitamins and minerals are kept at the regular amounts so that muscle and bone tissue are not affected," says Dr. Dorosz.

There are some other important steps you can take to help slim down your overweight pooch:

- Avoid high-calorie treats.
- Have only one person in charge of feeding. That way, you have complete control over when she eats, and what and how much.
- Combine an exercise program with reducing the number of calories she eats.
- Feed your dog on a regular schedule and on time, so she doesn't get too hungry and decide to self-supplement from garbage cans.
- Give love, attention, affection and play as rewards, instead of snacks.

Each dog is different. Some will lose weight faster than others. Keep an accurate record of your dog's diet and weight loss, or lack thereof. And keep your vet informed of her progress, as you may need to discuss other strategies. For more tips, see "Weight Problems" on page 350.

Fussy Eaters

Nothing can be more frustrating than a finicky eater. When you've paid good money for a nutritious, supposedly delicious, bag or can of premium chow and your dog turns her nose up at it, the one growling will most likely be you.

What turns a dog into a picky eater anyway? Most likely it's you, her owner. If you change foods frequently, you're teaching your dog to hold back to see what "better" stuff is yet to

If you indulge your dog's every food whim, you'll quickly teach her that if she turns her nose up at your offerings, something better might appear.

come. By feeding table scraps, whether intentionally or on the sly via an equally picky five-year-old, your dog learns there's a tastier world out there if she just holds out. "Table food has to be more palatable to dogs than dog food," says Dr. Michel. And smaller dogs, which are more likely to be pampered, can become very picky.

"Try mixing her kibble with a little canned food and increasing the ratio of dry food as she becomes accustomed to it," says Dr. Michel. Moistening food with water or stock is another way to whet an appetite. "Or try warming canned food to above room temperature but below body temperature," she says. And if you've got the time, you could see how your pampered pet responds to your homemade dog food.

There's also the dog that develops a "brand preference," where she will eat only one type and brand of food, and of course it's going to be the most expensive brand in the supermarket. To combat this, Dr. Michel feeds her own dogs the same three different dog foods every day in combination.

(15) CANINE CUISINE

Apart from the attention he gets from you, eating is probably your dog's greatest pleasure in life. Not only that, it's the very foundation of his health and well-being. Don't just grab the first dog food you spot in the supermarket; weigh up the alternatives and get the food that's going to work best for him.

Different Types of Dog Food
pages 229–233
How to decide on the dog food for him, when there are so many packages and names and flavors to choose from

Feeding Equipment
pages 236–237
Sometimes there are special needs, sometimes it's simply a question of convenience when considering the right bowl for him

Snacks
pages 234–235
From quick treats for tricks to the rewards he can really savor for being a great dog

Special Diets for Special Pets
pages 238–239
When there's a health problem, the first step is to see that his diet is in order

Different Types of Dog Food

A walk down the pet food aisle of the local pet supply or grocery store can put your head in a spin. There's canned food, dry food and food that looks like soft, moist chunks of meat. There's gourmet food, natural food and food that's made with everything from basic ingredients, such as beef and chicken, to exotic meats, such as lamb, turkey, venison and catfish. It's an amazing array, and of course you want to get what's best for your food-loving friend.

If you stick to well-known brands that offer complete, balanced nutrition and that have been tested by feeding trials, it's hard to go wrong. Whether you buy canned, semi-moist or dry dog food is a matter of preference—yours and your dog's. Each has advantages and disadvantages.

Canned Food

Paws down, canned food is probably the favorite of most dogs. Although a human nose may wrinkle at the first whiff from an open can, a dog is generally delighted by the smell and taste of what's inside. The palatability of canned food makes it a wise choice for small dogs that are sometimes finicky, for dogs that have trouble keeping weight on and for dogs that are aging and whose teeth are no longer in the best condition.

Canned food is expensive, however, when you consider that it contains as much as 70 percent water by weight. It also spoils quickly once it's opened, so you can't leave it out for him all day.

To help keep canned food appetizing, here's a tip from Christine Wilford, D.V.M., a veterinarian in private practice in Seattle and a regular columnist for the *American Kennel Club Gazette*. "If you haven't used a full can, always take the remaining food out of the can and wrap it tightly in plastic, pressing out all the air. This will keep it as fresh as possible and prevent oxidation, which is what makes it unpalatable," she says. Refrigerated in this way, the food will last for two or three days.

If your dog likes it and you don't mind having to refrigerate it or the way it smells, a high-quality canned food is a good choice.

Semi-Moist Food

Another canine favorite is semi-moist or soft-moist food. Like canned food, it tastes good, but it's not as messy and doesn't spoil as quickly. There's no need for refrigeration after opening, and packets often come in single-serving sizes, making them handy for owners in a hurry.

Semi-moist foods have such a long shelf life because they are high in sugar and preservatives, and that's their only potential drawback.

Canned food   *Semi-moist food*

"For healthy dogs, semi-moist foods are fine," says Lisa Freeman, D.V.M., Ph.D., clinical nutritionist and assistant professor at Tufts University School of Veterinary Medicine in North Grafton, Massachusetts. "But dogs with certain diseases, such as diabetes, might do better on canned or dry food."

Dry Food

If you want to provide your dog with good nutrition while making less of a dent in your wallet, dry food is the way to go. Dry food is crunchy, so it's less likely to accumulate on teeth and contribute to dental tartar and plaque. And it is every bit as nourishing as canned food. "Canned dog food that looks like meat is no more nutritious than dry dog food that's made with meat meal or other sources of animal protein," says John Hamil, D.V.M., a veterinarian in private practice in Laguna Beach, California. And dry food can be left out all day without spoiling, so your dog can nibble when he pleases.

For the best of both worlds, you can add some punch to your pooch's dry chow by mixing in a little canned food for flavor. The cost won't be as high as feeding him canned food only, and your dog will definitely lick his chops at dinnertime.

Premium, Name-Brand or Generic?

Whatever you feed your dog, always be sure it's a high-quality food. But what does that mean when it comes to choosing the brand of food? Should you be stocking up on a high-priced premium brand from a pet store, or can your dog's nutritional needs be met just as well by a name-brand food from the grocery store or even by a no-name generic food? Vets differ in their answers, but what really matters is your dog's individual nutritional needs. There is no single wonder food to meet the needs of every canine.

The Virtues of Premium Foods

Premium foods are the five-star meals of canine cuisine. These are the foods that often have the exotic ingredients, that include more meat protein to grain protein and use different kinds of dyes and preservatives. But the main difference between premium foods and their more humble cousins on the dog food shelf is the density per volume, says Dr. Wilford. A tablespoon of a premium food is likely to contain more digestible, absorbable nutrients than a tablespoon of nonpremium food. Your pooch can eat a smaller amount of premium food to be well-nourished; with nonpremium food, he'll need to eat more.

"Premium foods, being more digestible, make it easier for the dog to extract the nutrients, to get what he needs out of the food," says Margaret Duxbury, D.V.M., a veterinarian in private practice in Amery, Wisconsin, and a contributor for *Dog Fancy* and *DOGS USA* magazines. If your dog needs to put on a few pounds because he's recovering from an illness or because he's a picky eater, a premium food is a wise choice.

The higher cost of a premium food is made up in savings on the amount served, and on the amount later eliminated by the dog, explains Dr. Wilford. "If you've got a big dog and you're feeding him a premium canned food, you'll be buying less, and there'll be a whole lot less coming out the other end," she says. "There's

Dry food

Why Do Dogs Like Cat Food?

Dogs are attracted to cat food for the same reason they're attracted to dog food, garbage cans and the barbecue five doors down: they can't resist that wonderful smell. And cat food sure does smell.

Cats are a lot more picky than dogs about what they'll eat, and if the food they're presented with doesn't announce itself loud and clear to their nostrils, they won't touch it. So manufacturers make sure that cat food has plenty of aroma to tempt finicky felines. For dogs, this aroma is the last word in temptation.

much less odor, and the stools are usually firmer, so they're easier to scoop up." For the average healthy dog, the biggest difference between premium and nonpremium foods is stool volume.

Name-Brand Quality

Name-brand grocery store foods are just as nutritious as premium brands, according to some vets. Like most premium brands, they are produced by well-known companies that spend huge sums on product testing, research and customer service. So what's the difference?

Sometimes it's just a matter of the amount of animal protein versus grain protein, or that the more expensive products contain more exotic ingredients, such as organic grains or unusual meats. Or they may have differing types or amounts of dye and preservatives.

"In my experience, premium foods are really not a whole lot better than moderately priced foods," says Dr. Hamil. "Premium products, I think, sell because of their snob appeal: 'We cost more; therefore, we must be better.' On the other hand, you should certainly make sure that whatever food you decide on does contain high-quality ingredients."

Animal protein, eggs or cheese are all high-quality ingredients that should appear first or second on the ingredients list, says Dr. Duxbury. She recommends that you pick a food and stick with it for as long as your dog is doing well on it. "A food is doing its job when your dog has a shiny coat, he doesn't have trouble maintaining his weight and he has plenty of energy to do the things he likes to do," she explains.

Are Generic Foods Okay?

With premium and name-brand foods you can be sure of the nutritional quality, but is it really necessary to pay those steep prices? Wouldn't a generic food do just as well? Often, the answer is no. While the labels on some generic foods say the contents are complete and balanced, the food's nutritional benefits have not necessarily

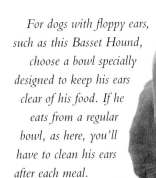

For dogs with floppy ears, such as this Basset Hound, choose a bowl specially designed to keep his ears clear of his food. If he eats from a regular bowl, as here, you'll have to clean his ears after each meal.

been tested on dogs. That means you don't really know what the food is doing for your dog.

"A dog food can claim to be complete and balanced in a couple of ways," explains Dr. Freeman. "One way is to do feeding trials on dogs, where you measure certain things according to specified parameters. The other way is just to calculate how much of a particular nutrient—vitamin A, for instance—you need for a dog and put that much in the mixture." If the latter method has been used, it's impossible to know whether nutrients in the food are actually being digested and absorbed by the dog, says Dr. Wilford. A label might claim that a food contains 20 percent protein, but maybe only 10 percent of that is in a form that a dog can readily use.

In addition, generic foods have fewer calories than more expensive ones, so your dog must eat more of a generic food to get the same amount of energy as he would from a name-brand or premium food. "You're not really saving money when you buy a generic food," says Dr. Wilford. "It looks like 12 ounces, but if you boiled it down to the nutrients, there would be less in the can. It pays to buy better food."

The other factor is that ingredients in generic foods may change, according to what's cheapest. This can result in your dog having an upset stomach when his food is suddenly different, even though you think it is the same.

When you have a dog in a special life stage, such as pregnancy or puppyhood, or your dog has a particular illness or is an athlete, it's probably better to spend the money for a higher quality food, says Dr. Freeman. If you do buy a generic food, Dr. Hamil advises that you find one that meets the standards set by the American Association of Feed Control Officials (AAFCO),

Why Do Dogs Hunt Through the Garbage?

Have you ever fed your dog only to find him half an hour later, rooting through the garbage can, happily chomping down leftover meat scraps and licking out old ice cream cartons? What makes a well-fed dog want to eat that old stuff, anyway? Surely he can't be hungry already.

It's got nothing to do with his appetite. It's because of his keen sense of smell and a survival instinct left over from the days when dogs were wild. A dog will seek out and eat food whenever he can, because before dogs were domesticated, they never knew where their next meal was coming from. Although we've been feeding them for a long time now, the age-old hunting instinct still kicks in when a dog smells something wafting on the wind. It's dinnertime, and from his nostrils' point of view, the ripe scent of garbage holds as much promise as a bowl full of doggy delicacies.

which governs the manufacture of pet food. "Unless a bag has the AAFCO label, you have no way of knowing whether what it says on the label really *is* in the bag, and whether it's proportioned properly," he explains. "And if it is proportioned properly, you don't know about the digestibility of the products that are included."

Dr. Wilford agrees, saying, "Without an AAFCO label, you don't know what's in a generic food. And that's why it's cheaper."

This English Bulldog doesn't need to be hungry to be intrigued by aromas coming from the garbage can. He will always have a nostril out for the main chance.

Cheesy Carrot Muffins

Cheese and carrots are two favorite canine tastes. Here is a recipe that combines them in a healthy, hearty muffin that your dog will love.

1 cup all-purpose flour
1 cup whole-wheat flour
1 tablespoon baking powder
1 cup grated Cheddar cheese
1 cup grated carrot
2 large eggs
1 cup milk
$1/4$ cup vegetable oil

Preheat the oven to 350°F. Grease a muffin tin or line it with paper baking cups.

Combine the flours and baking powder and mix well. Add the cheese and carrots, and use your fingers to mix them into the flour until they are well distributed.

In another bowl, beat the eggs. Then whisk in the milk and vegetable oil. Pour this over the flour mixture, and stir gently until just combined.

Fill the muffin cups three-quarters full with the mixture. Bake for 20 to 25 minutes, or until the muffins feel springy. Be sure to let the muffins cool before letting your dog do any taste testing. If he's a medium to large dog, one muffin will be a great snack. Make it half a muffin for a toy or small dog.

Homemade Food

For the dog with medical problems or special nutritional requirements, or with allergies to certain foods, colorings or preservatives, a homemade diet can be a good idea. For instance, if he has kidney disease or a skin problem and turns up his nose at commercially made therapeutic diets, he may find a homemade diet much more to his liking. "I often tell people that the best food in the world is not worth anything if your dog won't eat it," says Dr. Hamil. Homemade diets such as boiled rice and chicken or hamburger, can also be used for short-term problems such as upset tummies that cause vomiting or diarrhea. The bland diet will soothe your dog's stomach.

To prepare your dog's food at home, you'll need lots of time and a recipe that is nutritionally balanced for your dog's needs. The main advantage of commercially prepared dog food is convenience, points out Dr. Hamil. Do-it-yourself food can also work out to be more expensive than buying dog food at the store—pet food manufacturers save by bulk purchasing.

Don't go in for experiments. "Get a recipe that's tried and true, preferably from a vet or a reliable source, such as a veterinary technician," advises Dr Wilford. "The ingredients in a homemade diet should be comparable to what you eat yourself—and everything must be fully cooked."

Snacks

Treats are a great way to teach your dog tricks or just to reward him for being your best friend. But too many treats can quickly cause his waistline to expand. Like all good things, they should be given in moderation, especially if he's overweight or has a health problem.

There are all kinds of dog treats, even low-calorie treats for dogs that need to shed a few pounds. "If your dog has to follow a specific diet for medical reasons, ask your vet to recommend something as an appropriate treat," advises Dr. Hamil. The treats you choose depend on why you're giving the treat and what he likes to eat.

Biscuits are satisfyingly crunchy and have the added benefit of helping to scrape tartar off teeth. Tiny biscuits are good rewards during training sessions. Soft-moist treats are also good training rewards because they are gulped down quickly. But don't forget that they are high in sugar and preservatives, so give them sparingly.

Something chewy, such as a jerky treat, is a "just-for-being-a-great-dog" reward. Another treat that will have him enjoying himself for hours is an artificial bone or toy with a hollow that you can stuff with peanut butter, cream cheese or small, soft-moist food.

Then there are cookies. They come in lots of fun flavors, such as pumpkin, peanut butter and liver-chip, and are often made with healthful ingredients such as whole-wheat flour. But that doesn't mean you can give them to him by the handful. Calories are calories, after all.

Even people food can be a treat, as long as you make the right choices, advises Dr. Wilford. "Treats are not your leftovers from the table; they're not bones, or the skin off the chicken, the carcass from the turkey, the fat trimmed off the steak. Treats should be healthful. So I get the potato chips, the chocolate and the popcorn with butter and salt. My dogs get the green beans, the carrot sticks and bits of

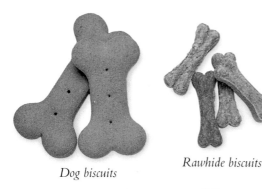

Dog biscuits

Rawhide biscuits

Rawhide sticks

Rawhide balls

Small dog biscuits

Rawhide doughnuts

Rolled knot bone

lean, cooked meat. They also like popcorn, but they skip the butter and salt."

Dogs have also been known to enjoy the odd stalk of broccoli (beware, though: it can cause gas) and fresh tomatoes. And bits of apple, banana and avocado, grapes, strawberries and other berries, as well as peeled, sectioned oranges all make good, healthy treats for your dog. Before you give him his vegetable or fruit snacks, be sure you wash them. And keep it to a few pieces at a time—you don't want to give him diarrhea.

Remember that treats should be special. If you give them to him all the time, they won't be.

Jerky

Puppy biscuits   *Dog cookies*

This Weimaraner knows he's done well. He's got a biscuit to prove it—an ideal treat if given in moderation, because a biscuit will give him good, crunchy chewing and also help keep tartar from collecting on his teeth.

Is It Okay to Give Your Dog a Bone?

Knick-knack, paddywhack, give a dog a bone
This old man came rolling home.

That old man probably wasn't doing his dog any favors by giving him a bone, says Christine Wilford, D.V.M., a veterinarian in private practice in Seattle and a regular columnist for the *American Kennel Club Gazette*. Bones might seem like the natural thing to reward a dog with when he's been a good boy, but they can break a dog's teeth. Sometimes, they may become lodged in his throat or cause constipation. There's even a chance of them splintering and puncturing the intestinal tract—an injury that usually requires surgery and is sometimes fatal. Sterilized bones aren't recommended either, as they can get wedged in a dog's mouth or throat, and they cause problems if swallowed.

"There are other items that provide everything a dog gets from a bone—the chewing, the playing and the satisfaction—and they are much less likely to harm him," says Dr. Wilford. Alternatives to bones that will give him the same satisfaction and the same hours of enjoyment are rawhides, Nylabones, pig ears and rope bones.

Feeding Equipment

Your dog doesn't need a fork and spoon when he has his dinner, but well-designed food and water bowls will make his meals more enjoyable, not to mention less messy for you. A good bowl is sturdy, easy to clean, won't tip over easily, and has plenty of room for his muzzle. Be sure you keep his dishes clean, washing them out or running them through the dishwasher regularly so that encrusted food doesn't build up and attract bacteria and bugs.

The Best Bowls

Dog bowls can be metal, plastic or ceramic, and he'll need one for food and one for water. Metal and plastic bowls have the advantage of being inexpensive, lightweight, easy to clean and unbreakable, but ceramic ones are often more attractive, with decorative designs. They are also heavier, so it's not as easy for your dog to shove them around the floor or knock them over. However, ceramic dishes may require hand-washing as they aren't always dishwasher-safe. If you choose a ceramic bowl, make sure it was made in North America. Some foreign-made ceramics contain high levels of lead, which can leach into food or water and harm your dog.

If your dog is tall or deep-chested, or you've got a puppy that will grow to be that way, consider buying raised feeding bowls. They are more comfortable for him to eat from, and are recommended for dogs that are prone to bloat, because a dog swallows less air as he eats if he isn't bent over. An older dog with arthritis can find it painful if he has to bend too far for his food, so he will also appreciate raised bowls.

Other special bowls you can buy include those with moats around them that will keep out ants and other crawling insects. And there are also bowls shaped to keep floppy ears from dragging through the food and water.

Nonslip bowl for a dog
with a narrow muzzle

Plastic bowl with moat
for keeping out ants

Metal bowl for a dog
with a wide muzzle

Ceramic bowl

If feeding time is a free-for-all, it's impossible to monitor whether each dog is getting his fair share. It's much better if each dog has his own bowl and is fed the right amount for his size and needs. This also prevents fights breaking out.

Automatic Watering and Feeding Systems

Dogs are creatures of habit and they like to eat at the same time every day. But with busy schedules and traffic jams in the average dog owner's day, it's not always possible to get home right when your pooch is expecting to get his evening meal. If this is a common problem for you, an automatic feeding and watering system might be the answer. You can buy dishes that work on a timer and that pop open at whatever time you set them to. They can be filled with either dry food or, if you buy a deluxe model that keeps canned food refrigerated, with moist food that won't spoil during the day.

To ensure that your pooch always has fresh, clean water, you can buy a dish that can be attached to a reservoir, such as a two-quart plastic bottle, or to a garden hose. Just keep the reservoir filled, making sure you change the water daily, or leave the hose slightly turned on. The bowl will refill automatically as your dog empties it.

The automatic timer on the feeder above can be set to open the lid of each compartment at the time you specify—very handy if you sometimes can't be home for when your pooch likes his evening meal. This Afghan Hound at right gets five-star service. His owner has solved the problem of messy ears with a woolen collar that holds them clear of the food, and the raised bowl saves his back.

Special Diets for Special Pets

The benefits of nourishing food and of diets designed for special needs, are not just for us humans. Dogs, too, can benefit from what we now know about healthy eating, and from the wide variety of high-quality foods available. Pet food manufacturers have developed all sorts of products, from vegetarian foods to therapeutic diets for dogs suffering from allergies, kidney disease, obesity and other health problems. Some veterinary researchers are even investigating ways that diet can affect cancer in dogs.

If you're wondering whether your dog should be on a special diet, discuss it with your vet. In the case of obesity, for instance, weight gain might be caused by a medical problem rather than by too much food and too little exercise. It's always a good idea to bring your vet into the picture before you change what your dog eats.

In any case, many therapeutic diets are available only by prescription.

Is a Vegetarian Diet a Good Idea?

Give your dog a bowl of beans, carrots, brown rice and a veggieburger and chances are he'll wolf it down, not because he's a conscientious vegetarian but because it's food and it's in front of him, so of course he's going to eat it. But is such a meal good for his health?

"Dogs are natural carnivores, and their lives are short enough that the properties of meat that can sometimes be a problem for people really don't become a problem for dogs," says Dr. Hamil. "Unlike cats, dogs can exist on a vegetarian diet if you're careful about the ingredients, but from a health standpoint, I see no reason why you would want to prevent your dog from eating meat. If you have a philosophical objection to feeding meat to your dog, then I guess you could justify a vegetarian diet—although I doubt the dog is going to buy into the philosophy." Dr. Freeman agrees that dogs are not suited to a vegetarian lifestyle. "Your dog may well become

When it comes to food, "no" doesn't figure largely in a dog's vocabulary. Obesity is probably the most common reason for pets to be put on a special high-fiber, low-calorie diet. Obesity may not seem too serious, but it can lead to heart problems, among other things, or put too much strain on his joints. So if he seems a little rotund, lighten his load.

Do Dogs Like Garlic?

Garlic is rumored to ward off bloodsuckers such as vampires and fleas. Perhaps that's why it's so common in dog treats and even in some dog foods— the perfect comeback to the next flea looking for a free lunch and a free ride at your dog's expense. Although it most likely has more to do with the fact that dogs love garlic, invariably snarfing up anything that contains the faintest whiff, without much encouragement.

Too much garlic will, of course, give your dog bad breath, and you're the one who has to live with that. In high doses, it can also be bad for his health, causing problems with the red blood cells. "It's okay to use a small amount of garlic as a flavoring, but don't overdo it," says Lisa Freeman, D.V.M., Ph.D., assistant professor at Tufts University School of Veterinary Medicine in North Grafton, Massachusetts.

deficient in various substances, which can have a poor effect on his general health, if meat is excluded from his meals," she says.

Medical Diets

As a dog owner, it's good to know that these days there is high-quality veterinary care and nutrition available for your pet, with special diets that will contribute greatly to his well-being. "Medical diets have been one of the real breakthroughs in veterinary medicine," says

Dr. Hamil. There are foods specially formulated and manufactured for young dogs, adult dogs, working dogs, old dogs and dogs with specific health problems. Each diet has its place, and with your vet's help, you can find the one that is just right for your dog if he has special health needs.

The most common special diets are those for weight control, says Dr. Wilford. These involve specially designed dog foods with reduced calorie levels or high levels of fiber to bulk the food up without adding extra calories. A high-fiber diet can also be helpful for dogs with diabetes.

Hypoallergenic diets can benefit dogs that have skin problems. These diets usually contain protein and carbohydrate sources that a dog is unlikely to have been exposed to, such as fish and potatoes.

A dog recovering from a severe illness may be prescribed a bland, soothing diet that will be easy for him to digest and help to calm his stomach. And if your dog is diagnosed as having kidney disease, your veterinarian may prescribe a low-protein diet to help keep the condition under control. Note, however, that a low-protein diet will not prevent kidney disease.

Then there are the dietary considerations of the dog that's getting up in years. "Many foods marketed for older dogs have restricted protein, but there's no medical reason to change an older dog's food without a diagnosis of some kind for a pre-existing disease," says Dr. Wilford. "Just because your dog has turned seven does not mean that he needs to change to a food designed for older dogs."

Keep feeding him the food he's used to for as long as it suits him. You will only need to alter his diet if your vet diagnoses a problem and recommends that you make a change.

16 PREVENTION

You can provide all the care your dog needs to live a long and healthy life. Learn how to spot the signs that mean something isn't quite right, make sure she has a vaccination program tailored for her, and never hesitate to seek your vet's help when you need it.

Choosing a Vet
pages 253–256
Both you and your dog should feel comfortable with the vet you choose

Care Begins at Home
page 243
Keep an eye on your dog and know the warning signs that you need to watch for

Nothing to Worry About
pages 248–250
Setting your mind to rest about some doggy characteristics that might seem strange

Powerful Prevention
pages 257–259
A suitable vaccination program is the best way to prevent serious illness

The Home Checkup
pages 244–247
Familiarity breeds confidence: you'll soon learn to notice when something's amiss

Common Problems
pages 251–252
Many of your pet's minor ailments are easy to deal with at home

Medicinal Relief
pages 260–263
From popping pills to squirting drops—tips on how to make sure she takes her medicine

Care Begins at Home

You will be calling on the advice and care of the experts from time to time, but the good health of your dog starts with you. In fact, your home health care—everything from popping a heartworm pill into her mouth once a month to giving her a regular checkup—is crucial to her well-being. There's no need to worry about putting your vet out of a job, because you'll definitely still be needing him, but you don't have to be rushing off to the clinic every time your dog scratches, sniffs or sneezes.

Watching for Problems

Your dog will probably spend about 2 hours a year seeing your vet and about 8,700 hours a year with you. That's seven days a week, 52 weeks of the year. You are the person who knows her favorite food, the amount of exercise that is just right for her, where she hides her rawhide bone and how she greets you when you get in at night. You're the person who knows how she looks and feels and behaves when everything is A-okay with her. That makes you the person with the perfect qualifications to recognize when she's not feeling her usual self. And being able to spot changes in your dog's behavior or appear-

ance is the most important thing you can do to maintain her good health.

Suppose, for example, you notice a slight limp after she's been playing in the yard. Or you feel a lump in her skin that wasn't there a week ago. By noticing changes early, you will be able to take action before anything serious develops. That's why vets usually recommend that you give your pet a thorough checkup about once a week.

Warning Signs

There are some obvious telltale signs that will let you know when your dog isn't feeling well. "Notice if either her appetite or her activity level has changed," says Katherine Houpt, V.M.D., Ph.D., professor of physiology and director of the Behavior Clinic at the College of Veterinary Medicine at Cornell University in Ithaca, New York, and author of *Domestic Animal Behavior*. When dogs aren't feeling well, they often don't feel like eating a full meal, and they certainly don't feel like exercising as much as usual. And because eating and exercise are two of her all-time favorite things, if she does not feel like doing them, you'll know there must be something wrong.

Checking your dog over once a week can be an opportunity to have a cuddle while also making sure that she's feeling okay.

The Home Checkup

The best way to keep your dog healthy is to notice any sign of a problem before it becomes a problem. And the best way to do that is to give your dog a complete once-over every week. That way you will pick up subtle changes that may indicate all is not as it should be.

Do a physical check all over her body. You should also find out how her heart and lungs are functioning. This doesn't mean that you need to hang out with a stethoscope around your neck. You don't need fancy accessories to take your dog's pulse, check her breathing and circulation, and make sure she's getting enough fluids. If you do it regularly, you will know what is normal and what is not quite right.

Taking Her Pulse

Your dog's pulse tells you how her heart is doing, and if it's normal, then she's doing just fine. If it's unusually fast or slow, that's a sign that she isn't feeling so good.

To take her pulse, you'll need to get a little friendly. The idea is to find the femoral artery, because that's where the pulse is strongest. It's on the inside of the upper thigh (on the rear legs), and you'll be able to feel it either when your pet is standing or when she's lying spread-eagled on her back. The artery is usually fairly prominent. Put one or two fingers on it and count the number of beats in 15 seconds. Multiply that number by four to get the beats per minute. The rate depends on the size and age of a dog.

To take her pulse, locate the femoral artery on the inside of her upper thigh with your fingers. Count the number of beats in 15 seconds and multiply by four to get the number of beats per minute.

A dog's normal pulse can vary a lot, depending on the kind of breed she is. Generally, larger dogs tend to have slower heart rates than smaller dogs, but the normal heartbeat for average-size dogs ranges from between 60 to 150 beats per minute. Ask your vet to tell you what heartbeat you should expect for your dog, and remember that the beats should always be strong and regular and never feel weak or erratic.

Another way to check your pet's heart rate is simply to put your hand on her chest just behind her left elbow—effective if you're having trouble finding the artery. The heart gives a double beat, so what you're feeling for is a lub-dub rhythm.

Breathing

Checking your dog's breathing is another great way to find out how she's doing. To check her breathing, count the number of breaths she takes each minute. Watch the rise and fall of her chest to get your count. Depending on her breed, she will probably breathe between 10 and 30 times a minute. If she seems breathless or the breath is rapid when she's at rest, take her to the vet.

This is a seemingly simple task, but it can get a bit tricky if your dog is a panter, huffer or wheezer. Distracting her with a toy will sometimes quiet the panting. If it doesn't, don't feel bad. Many vets have faced the same problem.

Circulation

Your dog's heart may be beating but it's only doing the whole job when the blood is getting around to all the tissues in her body. You can actually make sure the blood's going where it should by checking what vets call the capillary refill time. Lift the lip from the side of her mouth and press firmly (but gently) with your finger on the gum above the canine tooth. When you release the pressure, there should be a pale spot that becomes pink again within two seconds as blood quickly refills the capillaries. If it's pale for longer than two seconds, there is a problem with your dog's circulation and you should see your vet right away.

Fluid Levels

A critical part of your home checkup is making sure your dog has enough fluids in her body.

Dogs that get dehydrated—it could be from overheating, for example, or from an internal problem such as kidney disease—can go into shock, and that's an emergency. To check for dehydration, gently grab some skin over your dog's shoulder, then carefully pull and twist it before releasing. If she has enough fluids, her skin will be very elastic and will snap back into position in a second or two. If she is dehydrated, the twist will persist, creating a "tent" in her skin that takes longer to slip back into place.

Taking Your Dog's Temperature

Whenever you think your dog is looking or feeling a little low, taking her temperature will give you some answers. But you can forget about under her armpit or her tongue. The way to take your dog's temperature is by using a rectal thermometer—which is why she'll need one all her own.

Taking your dog's temperature is easy. Lubricate the tip of the thermometer with some petroleum jelly, then stand or kneel alongside your dog, facing her rear. Lift the tail and gently twirl the thermometer into the rectum, going in about an inch or two. Praise your dog and keep her distracted for the two minutes it will take to get an accurate reading. If you've bought a high-tech digital thermometer, you won't have to wait even that long. The normal temperature for a dog is 99.5° to 102.5°F. If it goes above 103°F, it is considered a fever.

Incidentally, if you'd rather not get this intimate with your dog, you could spend the extra money on an aural thermometer and get the temperature from inside her ear almost instantly.

The All-Over Exam

Check over your dog's body on a regular basis. You will become familiar with what's normal for her, and soon learn to pick up on any signs of physical changes before they are obvious to anyone else. Here's what to look for.

When you feel along the spine, there should be no sign of pain. If the ribs are too prominent, your pet may be underweight. If you can't feel her ribs at all, she is probably overweight.

Check around the anus for matted hair as well as tapeworms, which will look like grains of rice. Check to make sure the anal sacs, two pouches on either side of the opening, are not swollen.

Check her hind end for evidence of fleas—you may see them scurrying through her fur or you could see some "flea dirt," which looks like comma-shaped brown or black specks. When you apply gentle pressure over the hips, there should be no signs of pain.

Feel the abdomen gently for any painful areas. Check for rashes in her armpits or the groin area.

Pick up her legs one at a time to make sure there isn't any pain or stiffness.

The ear canals should look clean, with no sign of inflammation and no unpleasant odors. The ear flaps should not look red. Check carefully for ticks.

The eyes should be clear, bright and alert, with no discharge or redness.

The nose should be moist, never dry or cracked, and free of any discharge. There should be no loss of dark pigmentation.

Check her mouth for any broken or missing teeth, and to see if there is a buildup of tartar on her teeth. Her breath should smell fresh and her gums should be firm and pink, never red or bleeding. Press the gum firmly and then release: the color should return completely within two seconds.

There should be no sign of swelling when you look at her throat area. Gently press her throat just above the collar, around the windpipe area, to make sure she doesn't cough.

The fur should be free of mats and in good condition. Separate the fur to check that her skin is smooth, clean and uniform in color.

Watch the rise and fall of her chest to see if her breathing looks regular, comfortable and normal.

Look at her feet. Check between the toes for lumps, sores, matted hair, burrs and ticks. Examine the pads for cracks or cuts, and check if her nails need trimming.

Nothing to Worry About

Dogs are very different from people. They have some special features that you will notice as you're checking over your dog, and although they might look like a symptom of something quite alarming the first time you see them, they are perfectly normal. There's no need to panic, and don't go rushing off to your vet. You'll soon be so used to these canine peculiarities that you'd think something was odd if they were missing—and you'd be right.

The Third Eyelid

This is not the canine equivalent of being able to see into the future. All dogs have an upper and a lower eyelid as well as one extra, known as the third eyelid, or nictitating membrane. The third eyelid sweeps across the eye on a diagonal from the inside bottom to the outside top.

"It works like a windshield wiper in a car, clearing debris from the surface of the eye," says Dan Lorimer, D.V.M., a veterinary ophthalmologist in private practice in Southfield, Michigan. Your dog's third eyelid not only helps protect the eye, it also produces some of the tears that keep her eyes moist and lubricated.

You can catch a glimpse of the third eyelid in the inner corner of the eye. If your dog is ill, and especially if she's dehydrated, it may protrude a little bit more than usual.

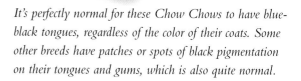

It's perfectly normal for these Chow Chows to have blue-black tongues, regardless of the color of their coats. Some other breeds have patches or spots of black pigmentation on their tongues and gums, which is also quite normal.

Extra Teeth

Just like people, pups have two lots of teeth—the puppy teeth, which they lose, and the ones that replace them, the permanent teeth. However, puppy teeth don't always fall out before the permanent teeth arrive. So you may see two teeth pressed very close together, especially the pointy canine teeth three along from the front teeth. If you lift your pup's lips, you may see a curved puppy canine tooth wedged next to a straight permanent canine tooth.

"Don't worry," says Kenneth Lyon, D.V.M., a veterinary dentist in private practice in Mesa and Tucson, Arizona, and the co-author of *Dog*

Owner's Guide to Proper Dental Care. "Most of the time, the puppy tooth will fall out on its own." When you take your pup for her first dental visit at six months of age, the vet will make sure that all of her permanent teeth are coming in properly. He will also advise you on what to do about any puppy teeth that want to hang in there.

Black Tongue

A black tongue sounds like the first sign of something nasty, and it looks kind of unusual if you're not used to it. But it is simply a natural skin pigmentation that you will see in some breeds, especially the Chow Chow. Other breeds may have at least a few dark spots. This is normal and nothing to be worried about.

Bellybutton

Your dog has a bellybutton, just like you do. It's the place where the umbilical cord was attached when she was born. You will find it right in the center of her body at the bottom of the rib cage. It may show up as a scar or a slight bulging area.

If you have a puppy and she has a little outie, it may mean she has a hernia, where the stomach protrudes slightly through an internal layer in the bellybutton region. It's no big deal, and your vet will explain what needs to be done to correct it during one of your early visits.

"In most cases, an umbilical hernia can be easily repaired during the operation to neuter your dog," says Lynn M. Harpold, D.V.M., a veterinarian in private practice in Mesa, Arizona.

Calluses

Calluses are hairless patches of thickened skin. If your dog is big and heavy and likes to "drop" to the ground to take a rest, then you might find them on her elbows. If she's a small dog, such as a Dachshund, and likes scooting along on her belly, then she might develop calluses on her breastbone. It's the constant action wearing away at the skin and toughening it that causes a callus, just as your elbows get rough when you lean on them too often. This is just ordinary wear and tear and not a medical problem, unless the callus becomes infected.

If your big dog is prone to roughened elbows and you think she'd look better without them, put pads on the offending areas for protection. If breastbone calluses are her problem, you're going to have to encourage her to use her feet rather than her stomach to get around.

Dewclaws

Dewclaws are those "extra" digits, or toes, on the inside of each of your dog's ankles, that just flop along doing nothing. If we wait around a few thousand years, dogs will probably lose them entirely through evolution, but for now, most dogs have them. They're not usually a problem, but because they don't get down to ground level, the nails never get worn down.

You'll need to trim your dog's dewclaws regularly so they don't become overgrown or loop around and grow into the skin. And like any of her nails, they can sometimes catch on the carpet and bleed when they tear.

Dewclaws are the vestigial fifth digits on the inside of a dog's legs, left over from when dogs climbed trees. In some breeds, these are removed soon after birth.

For some breeds, it's de rigueur to have the dewclaws removed—that's what the standard for the breed calls for. In these instances, a dog's dewclaws are surgically removed by a vet within a few days of her birth.

Nipples

Your dog will have sets of nipples running down each side of her body from the chest to the belly. Dogs evolved so many nipples to make sure all the pups in their litters—and they can have from one to more than twelve—get fed. In male dogs and neutered females, the nipples remain quite small. They develop into breast tissue only during pregnancy and milk production.

Penis

The genitals of male dogs are a bit unusual. They always have a semi-erect penis and for good reason; there's a bone in there, the os penis. So he's not that way just because spring is in the air, he's like that all the time.

When a male dog is erect, you might be able to see the pink penis extended past the foreskin and then a large lump at the base of the penis. It is this bulbous penis that creates a "lock" when a male dog is mating so that he and the female dog will remain joined together for about half an hour, to increase the likelihood of the female getting pregnant. This bulbous penis may look a little odd, but don't worry, it is exactly the way he's supposed to be.

Stud Tail

You might notice a bald spot above your dog's backside. Some dogs, mostly males that haven't been neutered, develop a thick, oval, hairless patch on the top of their tail base, known as stud tail. Sometimes, the skin becomes scaly or oily. It could be a kind of acne, because hormones seem to exacerbate the problem. And although it might look a little alarming, it's usually harmless. Only if it becomes irritated or infected will your dog need to see the vet.

What Does a Cold Nose Really Mean?

Folklore has it that a dog with a cold nose is a healthy dog. According to vets, however, a cold nose is not an accurate barometer of how a dog is feeling. "It may or may not be an indicator of health or disease," says Lester Mandelker, D.V.M., a veterinarian in private practice in Largo, Florida. "Any dog can have a cold nose and still be sick," he explains. "Or a dog can have a dry, warm nose and be feeling completely fine." Humidity, body temperature and the flow of tears through the ducts into the nose all play a role in determining whether your dog's nose is dry or moist, warm or cold. So there's no need to feel your dog's nose, because whatever the temperature, it's not going to tell you anything about the state of her health.

Common Problems

Dogs usually don't have very exotic problems. Distemper, mange and hip dysplasia are all common enough, but they aren't even close to the top of the list of common canine problems. It's the mundane health hassles that will take up most of your attention—things like gum disease, vomiting or diarrhea, worms and fleas, as well as a variety of behavior problems. As with most things, a little prevention will go a long way toward keeping your dog healthy.

Gum Disease

It's true that dogs in the wild don't brush their teeth, but that's not much of an argument against dental care. Our ancestors didn't brush their teeth either, and we can only guess how many teeth they had left in their later years. The fact is that more than 85 percent of dogs have inflamed gums by the time they're four years old, all because of poor teeth care. This can lead to a variety of dental problems, including losing teeth. Consider teeth cleaning as an important part of your pet's grooming and hygiene routine. For more information on how it's done, see "Clean Teeth" on page 408.

Upset Tummies

Possibly the first you will know about her eating something that didn't agree with her is when you find the vomit or diarrhea. You'd think prevention would be easy, but someone might slip her a slice of pizza or a bite of burrito, and she's bound to nose out an open and unattended garbage container at some stage. No dog can resist temptation when it smells that good, so you're going to have to get used to dealing with the occasional tummy upset. For more information on coping with the aftermath, see "Diarrhea" on page 312.

Worms and Fleas

Worms are another common, yet completely preventable, condition in dogs. If every pup were routinely wormed, it would be only a matter of time before worms were eliminated entirely from our pets. Worming is most effective when your dog is young—generally from 2 to 20 weeks. If you wait until your pup is several months old to do anything about these visitors, they'll have already unpacked their bags and

Fleas are as common as dogs. Make sure they are under control when you check your pet once a week—they particularly love the area on her back near the tail.

taken up residence for life. Worms remain hidden in a dog's tissues even after successful treatment, only to put in an appearance when she's stressed or has a litter of pups, say. And so the cycle continues.

If you have a pup, you should assume that she has worms—studies have shown that some 75 percent actually do, even when routine tests don't detect them. For more information on waving goodbye to unwanted guests, see "Worms" on page 353.

As for fleas, they've been around for millions of years and there probably isn't any chance they will become extinct soon. However, there have been some recent developments that will give you more than enough ammunition to stand a fighting chance of winning this battle on the home front. For more information, see "Fleas" on page 325.

Keeping Out of Trouble

Believe it or not, behavior problems are the number one reason people take their pets to the vet. The truth is, most behavioral problems are entirely preventable and can be managed with

This young Rottweiler must be gently but firmly trained to respect and not destroy her owner's belongings. Seek help with her training before her behavior becomes a big problem.

When to Call the Vet

There's a lot you can do at home to care for your dog's health. But when there's something the matter with her, your vet is there, specially trained to interpret her symptoms and to make her well again. So don't hesitate to keep in close contact. This is especially important if you notice one of the following:

- Your dog has an adverse reaction to a vaccination or medication.
- She may have eaten poison or a poisonous plant.
- She has been hit by a car or otherwise suffered some kind of trauma (even if she seems okay).
- She has a high fever of 104°F or more.
- She is experiencing pain, especially around the abdominal area.
- She has had vomiting or diarrhea for more than 24 hours.
- She demonstrates aggression toward a family member or guest.
- She appears disoriented.
- She has a seizure or convulsion.

---

the right sort of home care, and without the need for costly drugs or visits to the vet.

"Train your pet, and start when she's a puppy," advises Gary Landsberg, D.V.M., an animal behaviorist in private practice in Thornhill, Ontario, and co-editor of *Dog Behavior and Training.* "You want to prevent the problem from happening in the first place, not deal with treating it after the fact." Good training is one of the most crucial aspects of preventive therapy, and easily as important as any of the vaccines or medications your dog will ever receive.

Choosing a Vet

One of the most important things you can do for your dog's health care is to find a vet who suits both you and your dog, so take the time to make an informed decision. This isn't always easy. One vet may appear to know all the facts but leave you in a cloud of confusion, while another seems hopelessly out-of-date but has a great bedside manner. How do you decide which vet is best for you?

Feeling Comfortable

The thing to look for when choosing a vet isn't the number of credentials on the wall or the number of dogs in the waiting room. What really matters is how comfortable you feel once you're in the examining room—and, of course, how comfortable your pet feels.

You should feel okay about asking your vet all the questions you have on your dog's health. The vet who is well-suited to you is one who will discuss all the issues on a level you fully understand. "It's important that you and your pet are comfortable with the veterinarian you choose," says Mike Paul, D.V.M., vice-president of the American Animal Hospital Association. "The veterinarian should be able to communicate with you and make you feel comfortable about asking questions."

The Quest for a Vet

One of the best ways to find a vet is to ask your friends who they use. Even though their expectations may be very different from yours, at least you'll get a sense of which vets they like, and why. When it's time for you to make an appointment, you will already have an A-list of names to try.

The next step is to call the clinic and speak to the receptionist to get some general information. You'll want to find out what hours the clinic operates and how many days a week. Is it open late, and what about on Saturdays? Are visits by appointment only, or can you just drop in? And what if there's an emergency and you want to be able to come in right away?

If you're satisfied after this first round of 20 questions, go ahead and make an appointment. Chances are, you'll be happy with your choice.

What to Ask Your Vet

There are no foolproof ways of selecting your vet, but be as objective as you can when making the decision. And remember, you can always change to another. When you first visit a vet, you will also get a chance to see the facilities and meet some of the staff. Think about whether you like what you see, and whether the staff seems friendly and helpful. In addition, you may want to ask a few questions to help you decide if this is the right choice for you.

Q **What services are available at this particular clinic?**

A A clinic may be a general veterinary practice. Or it could offer a smorgasbord of services, including emergency services, specialty medicine, boarding facilities, grooming, even behavior counseling and training. One-stop shopping or a good basic service, you want a facility that is organized in a way that will work for you and your dog.

Q **Whom should I contact in case of after-hours emergencies?**

A Most clinics are open from eight or nine in the morning until six or seven at night. Emergency clinics open as the clinics are closing down and stay open until seven or eight in the morning. It's unusual for a vet to handle his own emergencies—he needs his sleep, after all. Usually, your vet will refer you to an emergency clinic for problems that occur after-hours, and you will have to transfer your pet to your regular clinic the next day. But it's important you know how your vet will handle emergency services, so you know who you are likely to be dealing with if any late-night pet problems occur.

Q **What veterinary specialists are there in the area and how do referrals to them work?**

A What you're really trying to find out here is if the vet is comfortable about calling in the experts on a particular veterinary problem. You want a vet who can be objective about his strengths and weaknesses and not think that he can fix everything himself. There may come a point in your pet's life when she needs to see someone with a specific expertise—a cardiologist, for example, or a dermatologist. You wouldn't expect your family doctor to be an expert in brain surgery, behavioral counseling, root canals and eye exams, and there's no reason why your vet should be any different.

Q **What are your special medical interests and those of the other vets in the practice?**

A It's helpful to know if your vet has special interests, such as managing behavior problems. In addition, the skills and interests of his colleagues can also be important, because vets share information about their cases and help each other find the best solutions. If your pet develops a certain problem—hip dysplasia, for example—it will be very comforting to know that someone on the staff has an interest, say, in orthopedic surgery and is up-to-date on the latest treatments.

Q **What are the credentials of the vet and the affiliations of the clinic?**

A You want to know that the vet has graduated from an approved veterinary school. And the year he graduated will tell you how many years' experience he has. Also, knowing that the clinic has affiliations with the American Animal Hospital Association or another organization that monitors practices will give you a certain amount of reassurance.

Q **Do you accept pet health insurance policies in this clinic?**

A Not all clinics recommend or honor pet health insurance, so if you have a policy, it's important to find a vet who will honor it.

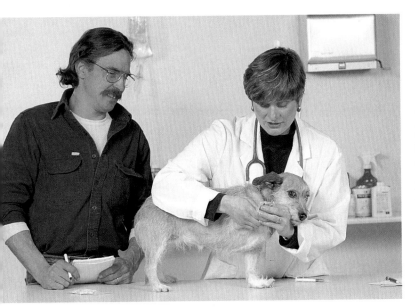

This little dog looks quite relaxed with her owner's choice of vet. It's important that you feel at ease asking your vet to explain anything you are concerned about and that she does so in terms you can understand.

Q **Which vaccinations do you consider essential, and what vaccination schedule do you recommend?**

A Some people have strong feelings about the extent to which their dogs should be vaccinated. If you feel this way, you'll want to find a vet whose views are compatible with yours. A cautious vet who vaccinates for everything might be just what you're looking for because you don't like taking any risks when it comes to your dog's health.

Alternatively, the vet may carefully select and vaccinate against only those diseases that your dog is at risk of contracting in your particular area. If you're worried about the potential side-effects from too much vaccination, the second vet will suit you better.

Q **To which conditions is an animal of my dog's breed genetically predisposed?**

A Certain breeds of dogs have a higher-than-usual risk from particular health problems. It's important to make sure that your vet has the latest information on the possibilities and knows what to look for in the future.

Q **What do you recommend that I keep in my home first-aid kit?**

A The answer can range from "I don't like an owner to have a first-aid kit" to "Here, I already have a prepared list of the things you'll need." If your tummy wobbles at the first sight of blood, you need a vet with the first answer. If you feel confident about administering some basic first-aid, then the vet with the second answer is going to be the one for you.

Q **What medications do you feel I can give my dog at home?**

A Most vets don't want you to give your dog medicine without coming into the clinic first—that way, they can be absolutely sure what the problem is and what your dog needs. If you want to be able to get advice over the phone (along with the appropriate dosage of medicine to give) when your dog has a mild touch of the runs or some other simple problem, be sure to find a vet who won't insist on a consultation.

When to Visit the Vet

Once you've found yourself a good vet, don't be a stranger. If you have a puppy, you'll be visiting the clinic fairly often. Most vaccination programs start at about six to eight weeks of age and continue every few weeks until your pup is three or four months old. After that, she should have a dental checkup at six months to make sure her permanent teeth are coming in properly and then another visit for an examination and her vaccines when she is one year old. From then on, an annual visit is usually enough, unless your pet has special needs. Even after your dog becomes a senior citizen, annual visits will be okay, except when you're worried about something or a problem needs monitoring.

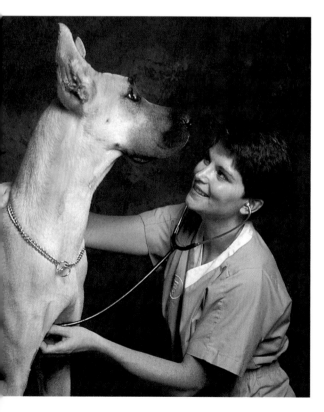

Does Your Dog Need Insurance?

Veterinary care can cost a lot of money, which is why more and more people are signing up for pet insurance. Is it a good investment?

"It can be," says Lynn M. Harpold, D.V.M., a veterinarian in private practice in Mesa, Arizona. "Some plans are excellent and include preventive care as well as coverage for a sick pet, while others provide only a few benefits."

Like its human counterpart, pet insurance works best to cover unexpected and expensive situations. For example, if your dog is hospitalized with a serious illness, the insurance coverage will seem like a godsend when you're faced with medical bills that could total hundreds or thousands of dollars.

Insurance isn't for everyone, however. For one thing, not all veterinarians accept health insurance. One survey found that only about 43 percent of vets do accept it, and 64 percent of those don't recommend it to their clients.

There are many reasons for the lukewarm reception. Some people simply aren't receptive to the idea. Many policies aren't all that good, and vets don't enjoy the extra paperwork.

Before signing up for pet insurance, make sure you understand what the plan covers and whether it meets your needs, says Dr. Harpold. In addition, check with your vet to make sure he accepts the insurance and will honor the plan.

Most vets have a knack for establishing a good rapport with their canine clients. This Great Dane is having her heart checked by her vet. The normal rate varies quite widely according to the breed and size, but if the beat is weak or unsteady, your vet will investigate further.

Powerful Prevention

There are some common canine diseases out there to which all dogs are susceptible. But vaccines will protect your dog from quite a few of these illnesses, from parvovirus, rabies and distemper to Lyme disease. As well as oral medications to prevent heartworm, dogs get a series of initial vaccines as pups and are then revaccinated annually. You'd think your dog would be feeling like a four-legged pin cushion, but many of the vaccines are combined in one shot.

Basic Vaccinations

Even though vaccines can protect your dog from many common conditions—as well as some that aren't so common—some vets believe that giving more vaccines than are absolutely necessary can stress a dog's immune system and make him more rather than less likely to get sick.

While some vaccines, like the one for rabies, are absolutely essential, others are optional, depending on where you live and whether or not your dog is often in contact with other dogs. Your vet will help you plan a vaccination schedule that is tailored to your dog's individual lifestyle. Here are the vaccines that are usually offered.

Rabies

Your dog must be vaccinated against rabies. It's the law—and for very good reason. Rabies is a viral disease that's deadly for people and pets.

Parvovirus

This viral disease is very common among dogs and can be extremely serious. It damages a dog's intestinal lining, and treatment is intensive and expensive. Your dog really should be vaccinated against this disease. In fact, if you want to board your dog at a kennel, the kennel will insist that she has been vaccinated.

Distemper

This is a viral disease that affects the respiratory, gastrointestinal and nervous systems. It's also contagious and easily passed from dog to dog. Even though distemper is rare, it can be deadly, so most vets recommend vaccinating against it.

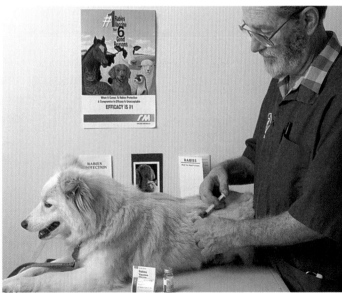

Your dog must be vaccinated against rabies and from time to time you will be asked to show proof that she has been. This is for your protection, hers and that of the whole community.

Canine Hepatitis

This viral disease of the liver rarely occurs these days because the vaccination program against it has been so successful. However, while that means your dog doesn't necessarily need it, the vaccine is often difficult to avoid because it is included in most commercial multivaccine preparations. It would be quite expensive to exclude the hepatitis vaccine.

Coronavirus

Like parvovirus, coronavirus causes diarrhea. Even though it's not as dangerous, the coronavirus infection can still be mighty hard on a young puppy. It's spread by social contact, so if your dog spends considerable time with other dogs or if she is boarded or shown, she should have this vaccine.

Parainfluenza

This viral infection is the most common cause of canine coughing. A vaccination is usually required by kennels and veterinary hospitals before your animal can be boarded. It is given annually as a standard inclusion in your dog's vaccine schedule.

Leptospirosis

This bacterial disease affects the liver and the kidneys. It is only prevalent in some parts of North America, notably where there are deer and rodent populations that spread the bacteria. If you live in one of the affected areas, then your dog needs to be vaccinated.

Canine Cough

This is the dog world's equivalent of our common cold. Affected dogs develop a hacking cough that lasts for weeks. The coughing can spread the infection to other dogs. Although the name "kennel cough" has been around for decades, there's a move to lose that moniker because it suggests that kennels are at the heart of the problem. Dogs do get canine cough at kennels, but they also get it at dog shows, groomers' facilities, pet shops and even at veterinary offices. It's not caused by just one germ.

Dogs become susceptible when they develop any of a number of viral infections (including parainfluenza), which are then followed by a bacterial infection called *Bordatella bronchiseptica*. The bordatellosis vaccine is squirted up your dog's nose to protect against the bacterial infection. Kennels usually require this vaccination.

Lyme Disease

Transmitted by deer ticks, Lyme disease can cause intense joint pain and other symptoms. Your dog needs a Lyme disease vaccination only if you live in areas where the deer ticks are present, or when you're visiting such areas.

Preventing Heartworm

No one had heard of heartworm about a decade or so ago, but now it's everywhere and every dog is at risk. And that's unfortunate, because this potentially fatal infection, caused by a parasite spread by mosquitoes, is so easy to prevent. "Despite improved diagnostic tests and preventive drugs, many pets still do not receive this protection," says Dr. Harpold.

Before starting your dog on a heartworm protection plan, your vet will run a blood test to make sure she is not already infected. Assuming that she's in good health, she's ready to start taking her pills.

There are two types of heartworm medication. The first is diethylcarbamazine citrate (Filaribits), a tasty treat given on a daily basis. More convenient are the medications given once a month, such as ivermectin (Heartgard) or milbemycin oxime (Sentinel). These have the added benefit of giving you a little leeway. Even if you're a day or two late with the pill, your dog will still be protected. Some dogs are sensitive to ivermectin, Dr. Harpold adds. If your dog isn't able to take it, your vet will find a substitute that works.

And regardless of whether she's taking a daily or monthly pill, she'll need to be tested from time to time. Dogs taking the daily pill need to be tested annually. Those on a monthly pill for six months will also need to be tested annually. Those on a monthly dose who have to take it for eight months a year (because that's how long the mosquito season lasts in their area) need to be retested every two to three years.

Mosquitoes spread heartworm, and these days no area is free from this potentially fatal infection. So come mosquito season, your dog needs to receive a daily or monthly tablet to keep her protected and safe.

When Should Prevention Start?
Years ago, vets used to recommend starting preventive therapy one month before mosquito season and continuing for one month beyond its end. However, this was when dogs took daily preventives and you couldn't afford to miss a few days. With the new monthly preventives, computers are on the job to predict when dogs

should receive their first and last doses for anywhere in North America. Call your local vet to find out the best time to start your dog's treatment. And if all else fails, the old standby can't be beaten— start one month before the mosquito season and continue it for one month afterward. It's not high-tech, but it is simple, and it works.

Side Benefits
You don't want your dog getting heartworm, and that's the best reason to make sure you give her those tablets. But there are other perks to good heartworm control, because some of the once-a-month products also help control intestinal parasites.

For example, medications that contain oxibendazole (like Filaribits Plus) also protect against roundworms, hookworms and whipworms. Medications that contain pyrantel pamoate (such as Heartgard-30 Plus) control roundworms and hookworms. Drugs containing milbemycin oxime can prevent hookworms and treat roundworms and whipworms. And when lufenuron is included (in a drug like Sentinel), it also helps treat fleas. That's a lot of parasite control for one tablet a month.

Medicinal Relief

From time to time, your dog may need some medication to treat a health problem. Although some drugs are administered as injections by your vet, most will need to be given at home, and your dog will be calling on you to perform the honors. If she is going to get better, it's important that she takes the medications exactly as your vet has prescribed and that the entire prescription is used, even when it's obvious she's feeling a whole lot better after just a few doses. The medications won't do their job if you don't give them exactly as prescribed.

Giving Medications

There's no point in telling your dog to swallow a pill because it's going to be good for her. She's heard that line before. Besides, she's already sniffed the thing and she knows it's going to make her tastebuds feel a whole lot worse.

You're definitely going to have to work on your bedside manner if you want to do better than that. If your dog is very well-trained and used to being handled, then of course giving her medications will be easier than if she's never had a lesson in her life. But even the best-behaved dogs can find medicine a tough pill to swallow. Here are a few tips on how to make that medicine go down.

Popping Pills

Some oral medications taste great and your dog will beg you for more. But in most cases, you'll be delivering a capsule or a pill that does not taste or look like a treat and yet you need to

One trick you must learn is getting your dog to swallow a pill. Point her nose upward and pull her lower jaw open. Place the pill well back in her throat and close the jaw. Hold her mouth closed and massage the throat until you're sure she has swallowed the pill.

administer it several times a day, without fail. Whenever possible, take the easy way out. If you can disguise the medicine inside something that is a treat, such as a piece of cheese, some peanut butter or even a cocktail weenie, and your dog takes it without a fuss, you've won the battle.

If she is not so easily fooled or if she's caught on to your little game, you may decide simply to take the shortest distance between two points—in this instance, between your hand and her stomach. It's not difficult to pop a pill down her throat, but it does take a little practice.

The method most often recommended by vets is to point your dog's nose toward the ceiling with your hand over it to steady the snout. Keeping the nose pointed upward, use your other hand to pull open her lower jaw and then pop that baby right at the back of her throat. Most vets follow the pill with two of their fingers to initiate a gag response and a swallow from the dog, but you might feel more comfortable just closing her mouth.

After the pill goes in, keep your dog's nose pointed upward and massage her throat until you see her neck move in a swallowing motion. Don't be lulled into a false sense of security, though. Many a dog will fake the swallow, then regurgitate the medicine behind the sofa when you're not looking. So watch her closely until you're sure it's gone down.

Pouring Liquids

When giving your dog liquid medicines, avoid spills by putting the medicine in a dropper or syringe—most dogs won't want to use a spoon. Tip her nose up toward the ceiling, with your hand steadying the snout. Insert the syringe or

With liquid medicines, use a dropper or syringe to draw up the correct dose of medicine. Insert the end of the dropper or syringe in the side of her mouth and gently squeeze in the liquid. Work slowly, giving her plenty of time to swallow the medicine.

dropper into the lip fold at the side of her mouth and slowly squeeze in the liquid, giving your dog plenty of opportunity to swallow. This isn't the same "pitch it in" approach you'd use for capsules or tablets. You don't want to give the liquid too fast or too much at a time, because she may breathe it into her lungs.

Giving Eye Drops

You can be sure your dog isn't going to like eye drops, but when they're needed, they often have to be given throughout the day, sometimes every three to four hours. This is a good job for two people, if you can get someone to help. One person can sit your dog down and gently keep her head still, pointing her nose toward the ceiling. The second person can be in charge of rolling back your dog's upper eyelid and getting the drops into her eye.

If you need to do this procedure alone, and you probably will at times, you will need gentle

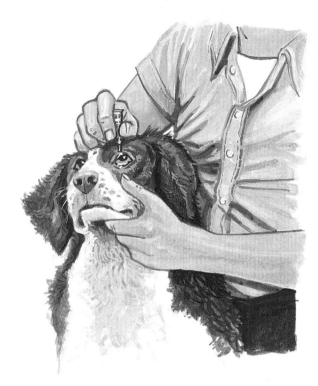

To administer eye drops, particularly if your dog is a little resistant, put her in the "Sit" position and kneel beside her. Cup her chin in one hand and tilt her head back. Squeeze in the required number of drops with the other.

but firm control. Put your dog in a "Sit" position and, approaching from the front, use one hand to roll back the upper eyelid gently with your thumb and apply the drops to her eyes with your other hand.

If your pet is a tad more skittish, put her in a "Sit" position and kneel down beside her. Extend your arm gently around her neck as if you're going to apply a headlock. Cup her chin in the palm of your hand and tilt her head back until her nose is pointing to the ceiling. Use your other hand to apply the number of drops, as recommended, to each eye.

Giving Ear Drops

If you have no problems with tablets, liquids and eye drops, administering ear drops will be a piece of cake. But be very careful what you're putting into those ears. Ear drops are not always safe—especially for dogs that may have other, undiagnosed problems, such as a perforated eardrum. Ingredients found in some over-the-counter medications can cause deafness if they trickle down into the inner ear.

To be safe, it's a good idea to check with your vet before putting anything stronger than a mild saltwater solution into your pet's ears. Then, to

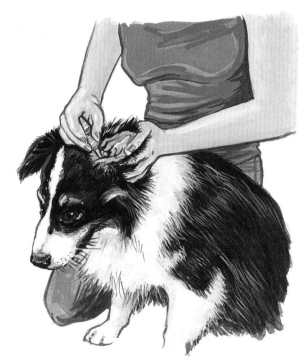

To apply ear drops, put your dog in the "Sit" position and kneel beside her. Pull her ear flap up gently and drop the required amount of medication directly into the ear canal. Fold the flap over the ear canal and rub gently to work the fluid into the ear.

put the drops in, gently grasp an ear flap and introduce the correct number of drops into the vertical canal. Fold the flap over and massage the ear gently. Now repeat on her other ear.

If there is a lot of debris in the canal, don't bother. Instead, check with your vet about how to proceed, because no ear medication will get to where it will do the most good if the vertical ear canal isn't completely clear.

Also, be aware that some ear medicines contain alcohol. If your dog has any sores in her ears, these products could launch her into orbit. That not only won't fix the problem, but your dog will become "head shy" and be unlikely to trust you with her ears again. So be extra careful with this very delicate part of her anatomy.

Feeding for Relief

A sick dog will often need a change in diet until she's feeling better. After all, if she's been vomiting or having diarrhea, her digestive tract will need some quiet time to recover. In most cases, that means a rest from food for 6 to 12 hours. It's also important to make sure she keeps up her water intake, unless she's vomiting. After that, stick to a bland diet, such as boiled chicken or beef with rice, until her intestines recover and signs of the stomach upset have disappeared.

It's not only digestive complaints that may require changes in her diet. Dogs with heart disease may be put on a low-salt diet. Dogs with kidney disease are typically given a diet with small amounts of high-quality protein.

Your vet will be able to recommend a diet from more than a dozen prescription diets for such varied problems as obesity, gum disease, and more serious health concerns, such as urinary tract "stones" and even cancer.

Your Dog Care Diary

Keeping a notebook of your dog's health isn't the most exciting thing you could be doing, but it can pay off when she gets sick. Your dog's health diary can help you to remember when she started having symptoms, what she was doing at the time, along with many other details that may help speed her recovery.

Many vets will give you a record book to keep track of her vaccinations. This information is important—you will need it if you want to board your dog at a kennel or enter her in a dog show. But don't stop there. Get yourself a notebook for each of your pets. It doesn't have to be fancy and it doesn't need to be big, since you'll probably use no more than a dozen pages.

Write your dog's name on the cover of the notebook. On page one, titled "Problem Master List," note every medical problem your pet develops, followed by the date you noticed it and the date she started getting better. This is your pet's medical history in a capsule. It contains the important information that you must remember to pass on if, for example, you change vets, see a specialist or have to visit an emergency clinic, or your dog goes to live with another owner.

The remaining pages in your notebook will just be a log of veterinary visits and health comments. Don't underestimate the value of this apparently trivial information. For example, if your dog is scratching and you see in your logbook that she was also itchy last year at the same time, there's an excellent chance that you have just helped confirm a pollen allergy. It really is a very good idea to keep your own personal records.

17 NEUTERING

You love your dog. But how do you feel about the patter and piddle of lots of pups, and finding them good homes? Dogs that don't need to be bred are happier and healthier being romantically unattached.

Sure, there are some stories around about how neutered dogs get fat and lazy, or are emotionally unfulfilled. And there's the cost and concerns about surgery. It's very easy to project our fears onto our pets, but neutering actually does make lots of good sense. Here, we separate the facts from the myth and rumor and present the benefits, to show why this simple and straightforward procedure is best—for you and your dog.

Family Planning
pages 265–266
Neutering explained—the why, when, how and how much...and whether there's an ouch factor involved

The Benefits of Neutering
pages 267–269
For the health and welfare of your dog, for your own ease of mind

Family Planning

There comes a time in the life of every dog owner when they have to decide whether their pet is going to be a parent or not. Left to their own devices, dogs will make up their own minds, usually before you have even noticed the small hole in the fence.

Dogs will spend most of their time and energy out on the town, looking for love. And given half a chance, they'll mate at every opportunity. If a litter of 1 to 12 pups arrives almost every six months, that's a lot of extra mouths to feed.

For the welfare of your dog and for your peace of mind, you'll need to give careful thought to the question of neutering. Your doggy Don Juan won't be slow in the search for love, so don't put off thinking about it for too long.

What is Neutering?

The neutering operation itself is an extremely safe procedure, done under general anesthetic, to remove the dog's reproductive organs. These organs produce the sex hormones: testosterone in males, estrogen in females. The dog's instinct to mate is driven by these chemicals, which also make it possible to breed. In the neutering procedure, males have their testicles surgically removed from the scrotum. With females, the uterus, fallopian tubes and ovaries are taken out.

After the operation, your dog's dating days will be over. And in four to six weeks, he'll have lost all desire to mate. There'll be no more yard breakouts to find a friend. Your female dog will

Whether your pet is of mixed parentage or the purest of bluebloods, he is part of your family. He will be more integrated and loving toward you if he's not being distracted by desire. He'll also be less likely to get into trouble, because he won't be out wandering.

never again turn into a whining, pacing she-dog in heat. Imagine it. After six weeks, broken fences, nights of broken sleep, not to mention broken dog hearts, will all be a thing of the past.

When to Get It Done

Dogs are usually neutered when about six months old. Female dogs are best spayed before their first heat, or estrus, cycle, which happens at around six months. Doing the operation before she goes into heat for the first time prevents estrogen from stimulating her mammary tissues, says Jay Geasling, D.V.M., a veterinarian in private practice in Buffalo, and president of the American Animal Hospital Association. This reduces the likelihood of her getting mammary tumors when she gets older.

Male dogs are neutered between six months and one year of age. "Neutering at this age is a tradition in veterinary medicine that began some time ago," says Dr. Geasling. "Ultimately, a dog owner should have a dog neutered at the age that their individual vet recommends. And that is usually around six months."

It's never too late for your dog to be neutered. If your more mature dog hasn't had the operation yet, there's no reason why he can't now. However, the younger the dog, the better his chances of avoiding complications.

The Cost

The cost of neutering varies, depending on where you live. It also varies according to the size of the dog—basically, larger dogs cost more. Neutering a male dog can cost between $65 and $125. Vets will charge slightly more to spay a female, usually about $85 to $160, since the surgery is more involved than for a male. Altering elderly dogs or dogs with health problems may also cost a little more, as they tend to need a few diagnostic tests. These will ensure that the surgery goes smoothly, and provide your dog with the best surgical care for his condition.

Neutering is a lifelong investment. It will help your dog stay happy and healthy...and it's hard to put a price on that.

Does It Hurt?

Neutering involves an operation—needles, an anesthetic and an overnight stay at the dog hospital. It's not going to be one of his favorite experiences, but your vet will be taking all the care in the world, and your pet will be quite okay.

Fat and Lazy

Many people worry that if they neuter their dog, he'll put on weight and lose his desire to run and play. But it's not neutering that causes obesity and inactivity. Certainly, after neutering, a very small drop in your dog's metabolism may occur, but this would have happened anyway, because of age, says Allan Paul, D.V.M., small animal extension veterinarian at the University of Illinois College of Veterinary Medicine in Urbana.

"At about one year of age, as pups are becoming adults, their metabolism will begin to slow down." The weight gain that many people notice a few months after neutering is actually the result of what usually happens when a dog grows out of the puppy stage—the dog gets more food and less exercise. If you're worried about your dog's weight, Dr. Paul says to watch his diet and make sure he gets regular exercise. Neutering isn't the issue.

He will experience very little discomfort with the surgery, says Mary Beth Leininger, D.V.M., president of the American Veterinary Medical Association. He'll be under anesthesia, so the operation itself will be painless. There are few risks, adds Allan Paul, D.V.M., small animal extension veterinarian at the University of Illinois College of Veterinary Medicine in Urbana. Many recent improvements in surgery on animals and anesthesia mean that neutering is routine and extremely safe, he explains.

Your dog may feel a little tender until the wound heals. This is a normal part of the recovery process and it won't last long. Your vet can give him something to help him with any pain.

The Benefits of Neutering

A dog that has not been neutered is obsessed with the urge to mate. He'll either be constantly frustrated or constantly looking for satisfaction—that can get him into risky situations. It also means that he isn't focused on you.

If your unneutered dog is a female, the chances are that despite your vigilance, she'll suddenly, somehow, be pregnant. And, of course, the puppies are adorable, and having a litter in the house keeps everyone entertained. But they need vaccines and special food, and that can start to add up financially.

Most important, each pup needs a good, permanent home. And they're not always so easy to find. Especially when there are already so many dogs out there with nowhere to go.

The cost of neutering may not be cheap. But neither are her baskets full of pups, or the really big fence you have to build to foil his show-jumping routines. Unneutered dogs are also susceptible to a number of diseases that are not a problem in neutered dogs, and the medical bills can really begin to pile up.

Dogs that are neutered live longer, healthier lives, and make better, more enjoyable companions, says Leslie Sinclair, D.V.M., director of companion animal care for the Humane Society of the United States.

"Unless you have a purebred show dog that you plan to breed as part of a well-thought-out, ongoing breeding program, you really should have your dog neutered," Dr. Sinclair explains.

Good Health Reasons

If your dog hasn't had the operation, all he'll want to do is mate and breed. You might think you've got all exits covered, but a dog with love on his mind will do whatever it takes to find a date. He'll make escape attempts and roam far from home in the quest for Ms. Right. There might be the chance of romance; there'll also be lots of dangers out there on the road.

Dogs that roam are more likely to meet up with other dogs, which increases their chances of catching diseases. They also get into garbage cans, eat antifreeze and gobble down any of the other assorted goodies that their tastebuds love but their stomachs can't take. They might be struck by a car or attacked by other animals.

If your dog is running free and bites a person or harasses other pets and livestock, he could be in serious trouble, and you will be legally liable. And in rural areas, dogs that chase or kill livestock are often shot by farmers protecting their animals. A lot of cruising canines just don't make it to retirement age.

Superman has nothing on this Boxer, leaping a fence at a single bound when his nose tells him it's time to check out the girl next door.

Breeding for Profit

Breeding your purebred dog might seem like a good way to help out a little when it comes to paying the dog-food and vet bills. In reality, however, there's very little money to be made from breeding. "If you're doing it the right way, there is no way you will make money," says Wayne Cavanaugh, vice-president of communications for the American Kennel Club.

The cost of prenatal care, tests, dietary supplements and food for the mother alone will cost a bundle, explains Cavanaugh. Then there's the money you'll spend on food and veterinary care for the pups before you sell them. "And it can be hard to sell puppies of the less popular breeds," he says.

Responsible breeders breed their dogs because it is their hobby, and because they want to improve the breed in terms of its health, personality and physical characteristics. They usually find good, caring homes for the litter of puppies before they will breed their dog. And they tend not to make money because they put every cent they earn back into their dogs, to give them proper care.

Raging hormones also cause a few health problems that neutered dogs will avoid. Males that have been neutered won't get testicular cancer, says Lori Tehgtmeyer, D.V.M., a veterinarian in private practice in Oak Park, Illinois, and a veterinary staff member of American Online Pet Care Forum. They will also have fewer problems with prostate disease.

Female dogs have even more to gain, explains Dr. Tehgtmeyer, since neutering reduces the likelihood of mammary cancer and cancer of the ovaries and uterus. "Nor do they get uterine infections." And it shouldn't be forgotten that when they give birth, female dogs can sometimes get into difficulty.

Neutering your dog will help him avoid the hormonal health worries. And it will keep him close to home, where you can keep your eye on him and make sure all's right with his world.

Better Behavior

If your dog hasn't been neutered, there will be some days you'll be tempted to give him an X for attitude and a Z for behavior. After the operation, he'll almost always get straight As.

It's not because he'll have a personality change. Nor will he suddenly go all wimpy, boring and lazy. It's just that he'll tend to be less aggressive with other dogs, and other dogs won't be as likely to get aggressive with him. No urge to battle over territory. No reason to argue about girls. That means fewer fights around your neighborhood. He'll stop turning up on the doorstep licking his wounds and feeling sorry for himself.

He won't be obsessed with the great escape, either. No more digging holes under the fence, or trying to run out the front door at every opportunity. You might even notice a decrease in that very unattractive quality of his, urine marking. Unneutered males feel compelled to lift their legs as much as possible to send a message to other males about their territory, Dr. Paul says. Your neutered dog has other, more important things on his mind. Like you.

It's the same for girls as for boys. There'll be no more living with a victim of her hormones. And that entourage of eager males that she used to attract won't be hanging around your front yard every six months, with an eye to the main

An unneutered male, such as this English Bulldog, will be lifting his leg continuously to mark what he considers to be his territory. A neutered male will still mark, but he doesn't need to tell everyone that this is his patch.

chance. You can stop worrying about keeping her in and keeping them out. With none of that going on, you'll both be more relaxed. And she will be more bonded with you.

Neutered dogs are generally easier to be around, says Dr. Sinclair. "When a dog is not neutered, nature is telling him to put most of his energy into reproducing. When you take away that need to mate, you get a better companion."

You also get a dog that's easier to care for, adds Dr. Sinclair. "One study has shown that most people relinquish their dogs to animal shelters because the animals are too much work," she says. "Further research reveals that, in most cases, these dogs were not neutered." The reason is simple. "Neutered dogs are a lot less trouble, and so are more likely to be kept by their owners."

The Sad Problem of Dog Overpopulation

You've probably seen stray or homeless dogs wandering the streets, or children standing out

in front of your local supermarket giving away puppies. In most cases, you're witnessing the problem of dog overpopulation.

What you don't see, fortunately, are the huge numbers of dogs that are humanely killed each year in animal shelters because they have no home to go to.

"Across the country, two to four million unwanted pets are euthanized every year," says Dr. Sinclair. That's a lot of unwanted dogs, with no homes. Neutering is one of the best ways of reducing the number of homeless dogs.

For the dog population as a whole, for you, and, most important, for your dog and his well-being, Dr. Sinclair believes that neutering your dog is one of the most important and responsible things you can do as a dog owner.

The Need to Breed

The idea that it's not fair to take away a dog's ability to breed has no real foundation, because a dog doesn't need to mate and have a litter of pups to be truly happy. There could be a little bit of projection going on here. But just because you might think that having children is one of life's great fulfillments doesn't mean your dog feels the same way. Dogs actually don't need to experience parenthood to be happy, loving pets.

In fact, dogs that are neutered tend to be more content since they are not feeling the frustration that comes with being unable to mate whenever they want to, says Leslie Sinclair, D.V.M., director of companion animal care for the Humane Society of the United States. "The dog is happier without these frustrated urges."

18 BIRTHING

The birth of a litter of pups is a natural and wonder-filled process. Your dog will appreciate your helping hand as she goes through the eight to nine weeks of expanding waistline, then the actual birth of her pups and the care of her new family. Be there for her, reassure her and help her out when she needs you.

Caring for the Expectant Mom
pages 271–273
There are many things you can do for your mom-to-be, as well as preparations to be made for the birth

The Big Day
pages 274–276
What to expect during the birth and how to be a help to your dog, as well as some advice on when to call the vet

Mom and the Newborns
pages 277–279
The new mother will do much of the caring, but she and her babies will enjoy the support that you can give, too

Caring for the Expectant Mom

Maybe it was planned, or maybe she got out or her mystery man got in—at just the wrong time. But from the swelling of her belly, it's clear that your dog is expecting. Dogs have been having litters of pups without any help from us for a very long time now, so you can cancel the Lamaze classes. It is a good idea, however, to take your mom-to-be to the vet for a checkup, says Christine Dresser, D.V.M., a veterinarian in private practice in Medina, Ohio, and a Pug breeder. Your vet can help to determine how many weeks along she is. And by talking to your vet, you will understand and feel at ease about the pregnancy, the process of birth and what to do if there's an emergency. There are also things you can do for the expectant mother, and preparations to be made for the big day.

The Telltale Signs

The pregnancy will last 57 to 63 days, or eight to nine weeks, although it's hard to tell a dog is pregnant until at least the fifth week. Ideally, your dog will be at least two years old, in good health, with her vaccinations up-to-date. A bigger belly doesn't always occur in first-timers, but the nipples do tend to enlarge, notes Bonnie

Her sagging tummy and enlarged nipples indicate that this Bull Terrier is in a late stage of pregnancy. She needs to keep up a reasonable level of activity, and she may ask a little more of you than usual. Make sure her diet provides all that she and her unborn puppies need.

Wilcox, D.V.M., a veterinarian in private practice in Preemption, Illinois, and co-author of *The Atlas of Dog Breeds* and *Successful Dog Breeding*. Your dog might also put on some weight and be a little more cranky and demanding than usual.

An ultrasound is expensive, but you may want to take your dog along for one if you can't stand not knowing if she's pregnant or not. It will give you confirmation at about 24 days. It might also be worth considering if you need to plan time off from work around the time she's due, or if she has any health problems. There are certain medications, such as corticosteroids, that should be avoided because they can affect the litter, explains Glenn Craft, D.V.M., a veterinarian in private practice in San Clemente, California.

As the pregnancy proceeds, your dog's breasts and nipples will become more prominent. In the final seven to ten days, she'll start to display nesting behavior and look for a safe, comfy spot to have her pups. This is the time to introduce her to the whelping box that you've prepared and lined with newspaper. She'll probably circle inside it and shred the newspaper until she's satisfied with her nest.

"If she's a young dog, she's going to seem very concerned, yet not really know why she's doing it," says Dr. Craft. To ease her mind, place the box in a quiet area away from the household hustle and bustle. She'll appreciate your support, but keep it calm and low-key.

Food for Two, Five or Ten

There'll be no cravings for ice cream in the middle of the night. And as long as you feed her good, high-quality food, you don't need to change her diet during the first three to six weeks. Toward the end of the pregnancy, gradually change her over to a high-performance lactation formula or puppy food—this will give her more of the nutrients she's putting into the pups. Ask your vet to recommend a brand, and keep her on this food while she's nursing.

For the last two weeks, feed your dog three or four small meals a day, recommends Camille Mcardle, D.V.M., a veterinarian in private practice in New Hope, Minnesota. "She doesn't

---

The Whelping Box

About two weeks before the birth, prepare a box so your dog will have a safe and comfortable place to have her babies. A child's plastic wading pool is perfect. Your dog can get in and out without any trouble, the sides will keep the puppies in, and it's easy to clean. A crate is good if she's a small dog—you can cover it with a towel or a blanket to give her privacy.

Or you can build her a wooden whelping box. You'll need to scale it to suit the size of the mother-to-be. She should be able to stretch out at full length, with there still being plenty of room for newborns to grow into lively puppies. Make sure the box has no sharp edges, and use lead-free paint so that gnawing pups won't be harmed.

To make the box especially safe for pups, add a shelf about four inches wide around the inside. Position it about four inches from the bottom of the box—this will prevent mom from accidentally trapping a pup against the wall. Keep one side of the box low, so she can get in and out easily.

Put the box in a clean, quiet area where your dog will be comfortable giving birth, says Glenn Craft, D.V.M., a veterinarian in private practice in San Clemente, California. Line it with newspapers for quick cleanup, as well as a favorite blanket for your dog's comfort. Show her the box at least a week before the puppies are due to arrive, and encourage her to start nesting in it, so she'll know she's meant to use it when the time comes.

Do Dogs Have Bellybuttons?

Unless you look closely, you'll never see your dog's bellybutton, but it is there, somewhere below the spot where you rub her soft belly.

As with humans, a dog's bellybutton marks the place where the umbilical cord was attached before she was born, explains Bonnie Wilcox, D.V.M., a veterinarian in private practice in Preemption, Illinois. "Some dogs have little outies instead of little innies," she adds.

have the capacity in her abdomen for the stomach to fill very much. Let her have as much as she'll eat in 15 minutes."

Supplements aren't a good idea, especially calcium or other minerals, says Dr. Wilcox. "They can cause abnormalities in the developing puppies, or a severe depletion of calcium in the blood when your dog tries to nurse," she explains.

Red raspberry leaves given as a tea during the last few days of the pregnancy can help reduce stress and settle the mother-to-be, says Dr. Craft. "Raspberry can also strengthen contractions and lubrication during birth," he explains. You can use dried raspberry leaves or raspberry tea bags, which you'll find at health food stores. Pour two cups of boiling water over two teaspoons of leaves or one bag, then leave it to steep for 10 to 15 minutes. When it's cool, your dog can drink the tea. If she doesn't like it, mix it in her food.

Staying Active

Exercise is especially important for a pregnant dog. It keeps her muscles toned, and that helps during labor. Do what you usually do. Take her on her regular walks and let her continue her other activities until she gets too big and ungainly to enjoy them.

"If she's used to jumping in field trials, it's okay until she's uncomfortable," says Dr. Wilcox. "She shouldn't just laze around." Even at the end of the pregnancy, be sure your dog has a turn or two around the yard each day.

Grooming, Please

So she's a bit on the wide side. That's no reason for her not to look and feel her usual gorgeous self. And all dogs like to feel clean. So groom her as usual, and give her baths when necessary. Make sure you keep her out of drafts until she's totally dry, though. And if she needs a bath in the last two or three weeks, be extra gentle so the unborn pups aren't harmed or disturbed.

Like this Bearded Collie, your pregnant pet will still enjoy sessions of play, her usual exercise and lots of attention from you. Don't neglect her grooming, but always handle her gently, especially her sensitive areas.

The Big Day

If your dog could talk, you know she'd probably be saying that the sooner those pups are out of there, the better. You've had the puppy shower and she's become quite used to the new whelping box. In fact, over the past few days, she's been nesting and tearing up the newspaper in there every time you check. It looks as if her big day can't be too far away.

What to Watch For

Two or three days before delivery, your dog may lose her appetite and have a slight discharge of thick, clear mucus from her vagina. During the last week of pregnancy, you may want to take her temperature twice a day. You'll know that the birth is imminent when her temperature drops below 99°F—the pups will probably start putting in an appearance within 24 hours or so.

Make sure you have arranged for someone to be with you for the delivery, just in case there is a problem and you need to play midwife. No matter how much your dog loves you, if she's in pain she may bite, so another pair of caring hands can help to hold her. "Whelping should never be done alone," says Dr. Wilcox.

Stage One

Signs that the mother-to-be has entered the first stage of labor are panting, shivering and restlessness. She may also vomit. As the pups move into position for delivery, her belly will begin to sag, explains Dr. Wilcox. She may walk around, unable to get comfortable, and she may come to you often, so give her lots of reassurance. This stage can last from 6 to 24 hours—it's different for each dog.

Stage Two

As labor continues, she'll finally settle down to the serious business of pushing. She may lie on her side as the contractions increase, sometimes panting, whining and groaning. Stay calm, speak softly and lovingly, and stroke her slowly to help her feel better.

"It's best not to have the whole family watching," says Dr. Mcardle. She doesn't want to be distracted or disturbed. You'll know she's about to give birth when you see a sac emerging.

The Samoyed below is just about to give birth. She is panting as the contractions increase, and obviously prefers to lie down to deliver the first of her puppies.

Hello Puppies!

Your dog may give birth lying down or standing up. If she prefers to stand, you'll need to be there to catch the pups. As a pup is delivered, the mother tears the placental membranes in which the puppy is wrapped and eats them. The puppy then takes his first breath. Mom bites off the umbilical cord and may eat the afterbirth, which usually appears a few minutes after the pup. She'll then lick the puppy dry, which will keep him warm and stimulate his breathing.

Keep a tally of the afterbirths: if there isn't one for each puppy, it means that a placenta has remained in the uterus, and your veterinarian will need to remove it to make sure that your dog doesn't develop an infection.

If your dog doesn't remove the placental membranes from a pup within five minutes of birth, or doesn't bite through the pup's umbilical cord, you'll need to get into the act. "Keep his head down and use a little bulb syringe to suction out any mucus in the mouth," Dr. Craft says. "Clamp off the umbilical cord with your fingers, then cut it with blunt-nosed scissors. Tie the cord off with unwaxed dental floss or thread,

When to Call the Vet

Giving birth is a natural process. Everything usually goes quite smoothly, and your dog can manage all by herself. But from time to time, she may get into difficulties. If you notice any of the following, don't delay in calling your veterinarian.

- If the normal discharge that occurs a few days before the birth is greenish rather than clear. This indicates fetal feces and probably means that at least one of the placentas has detached.
- If the birth hasn't begun within 24 hours of her temperature dropping.
- If a puppy hasn't appeared after about 20 minutes of strong contractions. Your dog's inability to get the pups out can be life-threatening not only to the puppies but also to your dog, explains Glenn Craft, D.V.M., a veterinarian in private practice in San Clemente, California.
- If your dog pants and acts as if she's going into labor but doesn't, or she goes into labor and then stops for more than three hours. These are signs that contractions are not taking place and your dog may need a cesarean section.

Unless you've done it before, watching a dog give birth can be a mysterious, unsettling process, adds Camille Mcardle, D.V.M., a veterinarian in private practice in New Hope, Minnesota. "If you're worried or frightened about your dog's progress at any stage, don't hesitate to call in veterinary help."

One pup has made his way down the birth canal and out into the world. His mother licks him dry to keep him warm and stimulate his breathing. If for some reason your dog doesn't do this, you will need to step in and assist in getting the newborn off on the right track.

and dab the area with iodine to disinfect it. Rub the puppy vigorously with a clean hand towel. You want to hear him cry."

The pups may appear every few minutes, or your dog may rest for an hour or two between each delivery. After all the pups are born, you will probably see a green, dark red or brown discharge. This odorless fluid is a natural part of her body's cleansing process and may last several weeks. There's no need to worry about this unless an odor develops, which could mean there's an infection and you should see the vet.

When to Help

As the birth proceeds, keep your eye on the clock and jot down when things start and stop. If your dog seems to be having hard contractions, is panting and pushing, and seems stressed, one of the puppies may have become lodged across the birth canal instead of heading downward. If a puppy doesn't appear within 20 minutes of continual strong contractions, call your vet for advice. He may talk you through turning the pup or recommend that you bring your dog in.

Regular weighing shows that this three-week-old puppy is making good progress. This is the easiest way to make sure that puppies are getting enough nourishment and are not needing special supplementary feeding.

This is probably the most common problem during delivery, says Dr. Wilcox. "The first puppy dilates the cervix, but not enough. As there may not be time to get to a vet, you will have to help with the delivery."

To be the midwife, reach up to the cervix with your fingers (make sure your hands are clean and your nails trimmed) to see how the puppy is positioned. Most pups come out nose first, stomach down, but it's also fine if they're born rear-first. Hold the pup's body—not his legs or head—firmly but gently, and let the contractions push the pup out. Remember that your dog is probably frightened and in pain, so have somebody hold her head to prevent her biting you.

After-Birth Care

Check that the puppies are all nursing strongly and that everyone has found a nipple. It's vital for them to get milk from their mother during the first three days of life. That first milk has a substance called colostrum, which provides antibodies that protect the puppies from disease until they can be vaccinated.

Weigh each puppy and jot down the weight in a notebook. You'll need to weigh them on a gram or ounce scale every 12 hours for at least the first week, to make sure they are gaining weight. It's the easiest way to make sure they're thriving. And if they're not, you may need to supplement their feeding with formula. "The puppies should remain vigorous," says Dr. Craft.

It's also a good idea to have mother and pups checked by your vet in the first 24 hours. He can make sure there aren't any other puppies still inside the uterus, or any retained placentas, and he can examine the pups for umbilical hernias, cleft palates or any other problems.

Mom and the Newborns

Once the pups are safely delivered and nursing, what they need is warmth and quiet. If necessary, secure a heat lamp about four feet above the center of the box to keep everyone comfortable. Just don't have the heat source too close to the pups—you don't want them to get too hot or to become dehydrated.

Care for New Mothers

You'll want to ensure that mom is in fine fettle after the birth. If she doesn't feel like eating solid food for a day or so afterward, Dr. Mcardle advises giving her puppy milk replacer formula. Feed it to her three times a day until her appetite returns—this keeps her nutrients and fluids up.

Keep a close eye on your dog in the days after the birth. If she seems shaky or weak, or suddenly collapses, go to the vet immediately. She may need a calcium injection if she's milking heavily and not getting enough nutrients. Check her temperature daily, and if it climbs to 103°F, she needs a checkup. (A dog's normal temperature is between 100.5° and 102°F.) She may have a uterine infection, explains Dr. Mcardle, and it needs to be treated quickly. Also examine her mammary glands to make sure they feel full and warm. If they seem hot or hard, again, you need to visit your vet.

Peace and Quiet

For mom's comfort and the pups' safety, keep noisy kids and curious neighbors away. "You have to check on the family, but you really shouldn't have people in there looking at them," Dr. Wilcox says. After the first few days, start picking the puppies up and handling them a few times a day so they become used to the presence and scent of people. Clip their toenails so they don't scratch each other or injure their mother's sensitive nipples.

For the first two weeks, the puppies—born blind and deaf—will live in a silent, sightless world, spending their time sleeping, eating and growing. Even in sleep, however, they should be vigorous, their tiny paws paddling as they dream

These one-week-old Brittany pups can't see what's going on—their eyes won't open for at least another few days. But they can feel their owner picking them up and handling them. Do this three to four times a day, and your pups will be at ease with people.

of their lives to come. Their eyes and ears will not start to open until they are from ten days to two weeks old.

As the Weeks Go By

Spend a few minutes a day keeping the whelping box and living area clean. At about three and a half weeks, it's time to start the puppies on solid food. When they stop nursing, the mother will

probably feel pretty uncomfortable. Your vet may advise giving her a mild diuretic for a day or two to help to relieve the pressure, says Dr. Mcardle. And once the puppies are weaned, cut back on the amount of food you give her.

By this time, of course, the pups' eyes and ears will have opened. (If you see some discharge coming from the pups' eyes, Dr. Craft advises that you ask your vet to treat what is likely to be a bacterial infection.) The pups will also be moving around much more, roughhousing and learning to get along with one another. Your family should spend time handling the puppies and playing with them, but Dr. Craft advises against allowing much outside traffic around the litter during the first four to six weeks. "Be very selective about who comes in the house, and make sure everyone who handles the pups has clean hands," he says.

When they're about four weeks old, take the puppies to your vet for their first deworming. Use a crate or a large laundry basket or a box with high sides for the trip. Worming should be repeated at eight weeks and twelve weeks. Vaccinations start at six to eight weeks.

Leaving Home

Pretty soon it's time for the pups to go to their new homes. At between seven and eight weeks of age, they are ready to leave their mother, says Dr. Craft. However, with some breeds, especially those that are small, it's best to wait until ten weeks or so as the pups may have problems with

How to Bottle Feed a Puppy

Sometimes puppies are unable to nurse, either because they are weak, their mother has refused them, or they have been orphaned. You'll then have to take over with bottle feeding. Cow's milk doesn't provide the nutrients a puppy needs, so be sure you use a commercial formula from your vet or the pet store. Read the directions for mixing the formula and for the frequency of feeding, and make sure the nipple on the bottle you use has a hole big enough for the puppy to take in the milk.

"Don't turn the puppy on its back to bottle feed," says Glenn Craft, D.V.M., a veterinarian in private practice in San Clemente, California. Hold him upright at a 30-degree angle, in the position he would be in if he were nursing on his mother, with your hand beneath him. Then gently tilt his head a little upward as you put the nipple in his mouth. If the puppy still has trouble taking in milk, you may need to seek help from your vet.

Paws for thought

Is Mom Sad When Her Pups Leave?

Dogs have emotions. They know happiness, fear and sadness. It's not surprising, then, that mother dogs mourn when their pups have to leave them.

"The mother searches for the missing pup if she hasn't seen him leave home," says Glenn Craft, D.V.M., a veterinarian in private practice in San Clemente, California. To make the transition easier, don't put her in another room, then let her come out and find that one of her young ones has gone. Every time one of her pups leaves home, let her see the new owner take the pup away. "She'll still fret and whine, but at least what's happened won't be a mystery to her," explains Dr. Craft.

What is Dad's Role?

If the puppies' father is part of the household, he has an important part to play in their young lives. He serves as a role model, teaching them how to behave, to interact with other dogs and understand the intricacies of pack hierarchy. He shows them how to play, and may even help mom with cleanup. "You can see the way the pups mimic their dad," says Glenn Craft, D.V.M., a veterinarian in private practice in San Clemente, California. "The male can definitely be around them."

You'll find, however, that mom probably won't want him around for the first four weeks. "It's as if she senses that he doesn't know how to be gentle," Dr. Craft explains. "Let mom call the shots, but don't make it a point of jealousy or he could harm the pups. You might start by taking the pups and showing them to the male, or restrain the female when he visits." Once the puppies are weaned, you can allow dad to play with the pups so long as you're around to watch what's going on, advises Bonnie Wilcox, D.V.M., a veterinarian in private practice in Preemption, Illinois.

---

low blood sugar, triggered by stress, if they leave home too young.

"People often let their puppies go too soon," says Dr. Craft. At this age, the puppies are learning from their parents how to be dogs. This and the interactions with their siblings are crucial. "With my own Mastiffs, I've seen that pups that went early to their new homes had some behavior problems when socializing with other dogs. The ones we kept longer were more mellow, more confident, more mature and socialized."

Resist the urge to show them off. While the puppies are growing at a staggering rate and mom is rebuilding her strength, they need plenty of rest, undisturbed by visitors.

19 CARING FOR THE OLDER DOG

Your dog is lucky: he has you, a loving and compassionate owner who cares about his well-being. With the support of your vet, you can make his golden years as happy and comfortable as he wants them to be.

As Time Goes By
pages 281–284

He's getting older, so keep an eye out for those telltale changes

Making His Life a Little Easier
pages 285–286

How to provide the extra tender loving care that will help your older dog through the day

When to Let Go
page 287

Think of what's best for your dog when making this very difficult decision

As Time Goes By

It starts with you noticing little changes in your pet. It's subtle, but you know him so well, you're sure something's going on. When he gets up from his nap, his joints seem a little bit stiffer. You go for your daily walk in the park and it's clear he's not going to win any races with the squirrels. And you don't remember him ever asking to be let out this much before.

The changes you're seeing are the result of old age. And in dogs, much the same as in humans, changes caused by aging can affect what they get out of life. Certain conditions your dog will be prone to can be treated by your vet. Then there are the things that you can do. By making some simple adjustments to his environment and daily routine, you can provide him with a lifestyle that is low on stress and big on ease and enjoyment.

The Signs of Age

That distinguished touch of gray around his muzzle is a real giveaway. Your dog is entering his senior years. According to Wendy Brooks, D.V.M., a veterinarian in private practice in Los Angeles, there are a few other obvious signs to look out for. "As well as graying around the muzzle, slowing down and gaining weight are pretty common," she says. "It's not so different from the way humans age."

There's one sign dogs don't share with us, says Dr. Brooks. Many older dogs get a cloudiness in their eyes. "This is called 'nuclear sclerosis,' and represents a hardening of the lens protein," she explains. This makes the dog's eyes cloudy, a bit like cataracts, though it's quite different. With cataracts, the dog's vision is affected and he'll need medical attention. With nuclear sclerosis, his eyesight is okay. If you notice your dog's eyes are getting cloudy, ask your vet to check him.

Common Complaints

As the years pass, your old friend's body will begin to slow down, and some illnesses become more likely. We tend to think of health problems such as arthritis and bad breath as being what old age is all about. But Dr. Brooks says many of the problems we think of as conventional "signs of aging" are actually illnesses that can be successfully treated. "There is a saying in medicine that 'age is not a disease'," she says. "An owner should not see a dog slowing down and say 'Oh, he's just old.' Often, there is a disease going on, and that disease can be treated."

With recent advances in veterinary medicine, animal doctors can now cure many of the ailments of the more mature dog. Vets see the care of older animals as an important facet of dog health care says Michelle Brownstein, D.V.M., a veterinarian in private practice in Rochester, New York. "As a result, dogs are living longer and healthier lives." It's a good idea to take your older dog to the vet whenever he's not looking or feeling up to par. Talk to the vet about the physical signs and changes in behavior you've noticed since your last visit. "Vets rely on owners for clues to diagnose medical problems in older dogs," explains Dr. Brownstein.

Arthritis

That stiff-legged walk he's developed looks painful, and it is. Arthritis, also called "degenerative joint disease," is one of the more common and potentially crippling effects of old age. It's the result of years of use, of running, walking, sitting, jumping and generally doing all the doggy things he's always done. The affected joint loses its lubrication, or cartilage gets damaged, or there's some other bone problem. "It can happen after a dog has been walking on an imperfectly formed joint for many years," says Dr. Brooks.

But there's no need for him to shuffle with a stiff walk. There are new medications to help the older dog deal with the pain of arthritis, says Dr. Brownstein. "Many of the new drugs introduced in the past few years seem to slow the degeneration down as well as reduce the pain." So, if your dog seems to have developed a few aches, creaks and groans in his bones, take him to the vet for evaluation and treatment right away. Head the problem off before it really sets in.

Canine Dental Disease

Once upon a time, he'd flash you a "grin" and his teeth would be white. Nowadays, they're more like yellow, or is that...brown? And a whiff of his breath is enough to take your breath away. Bad teeth and bad breath. What a combination. You'll know it when you see and smell it, and dogs that are up in years tend to have it. It's not from all that dog food he's eaten over the years—it's the start of canine dental disease.

As well as giving him smelly breath and a gappy grin, dental disease can cause more serious problems for your dog. "Dental disease is a major contributing factor to heart and kidney problems in older dogs because of the harmful bacteria that accumulate in unhealthy gums," explains Dr. Brownstein. The best way to stop problems is to keep the teeth clean. "Dogs, like people, need to have their teeth cleaned on a routine basis," Dr. Brownstein says. "If this is not done, bacteria, plaque and tartar build up, which lead to the loss of teeth."

He Needs to Go and Doesn't Know

The last time you found a puddle in the house, he was ankle-high. Now you're cleaning up after him again. It's frustrating, but incontinence affects many senior dogs. As they get on in years, they can have trouble holding their urine or feces. Sometimes, accidents happen.

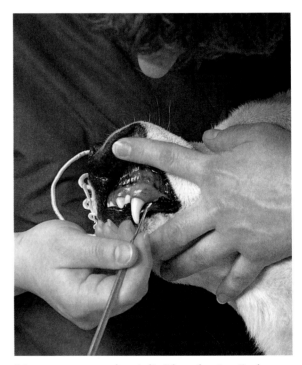

Most vets recommend periodic "deep cleanings," where they get down to the hard-to-reach plaque underneath the gums while the dog is anesthetized.

Do Dogs Get Embarrassed?

There are dog diapers for sale in the local pet store and maybe they will help your dog with his leaks. But will he lie on the floor and cover his eyes with one paw at the very thought of such an indignity?

"Embarrassment and modesty are certainly important in our human social structure, but I doubt anyone can confirm it in the dog's," says Steve Aiken, owner of Animal Behavior Consultants in Wichita, Kansas, and the "Pet Shrink" on America Online Pet Care Forum. But as a dog ages, he gets very fond of his routines. "For this reason, an unexpected elimination problem can be very stressful," says Aiken.

If your dog has a mild case of the leaks, taking him for more toilet trips outside may do the trick. Contact your vet, too. Medication can help if it's a case of lost muscle tone. The vet will first check to make sure there is no underlying cause. "There is usually an answer and a drug that can help, but you must rule out urinary tract infection or another internal disease or metabolic problem first," says Paul Schmitz, D.V.M., a veterinarian practicing in Broken Arrow, Oklahoma.

If medication doesn't do the trick, take special care so that his incontinence doesn't lead to other health difficulties. "Keeping him dry and clean is very important," Dr. Brownstein explains. "Urine can burn the skin, and feces can attract parasites, so bedding must be changed frequently."

Weight Gain

When a dog is getting on in years, his body and metabolism both slow down. So it is far easier for him to put on weight than it used to be. Weight problems are often seen in elderly pooches, says Dr. Brownstein. "Obesity is perhaps one of the most common and easily preventable health problems in older dogs." She explains that they have different

Give your dog a regular weigh-in. This way you can be sure that he's not eating too much or exercising too little.

nutritional requirements from their younger counterparts, so they need a different diet. They also need to keep up their exercise.

Coughing

This can be a real problem, especially for diminutive canines, whose tiny airways are easily blocked. Dr. Brooks says that coughing can happen to all dogs in old age, but is seen most in smaller breeds. "Airways in aged lungs begin producing too much mucus and actual bronchitis develops," she says. "This can be uncomfortable for the pet, as well as annoying for the owner." If your dog develops a cough, take him to the vet right away. The vet can prescribe medications that will stop, or at least soothe, the problem.

Eyes and Ears

Some senior dogs can slowly lose their vision or their hearing. There's no reason to worry, however. If you think that your dog isn't as keen-eyed or sharp-eared as he once was, it's time for a visit to the vet. Your vet may be able to reverse or arrest the condition. Even if that's not possible, your dog can still live a comfortable life. With the love and emotional support of a caring owner, a dog can adapt to many kinds of physical handicaps better than you might expect.

A Few Other Things to Look Out For
There are other problems an old dog may face, including heart disease, diabetes, kidney and liver problems, endocrine disorders and cancer. This may sound like a frightening list of ailments, but between you and your well-prepared vet, you'll be able to keep such problems under control.

How Long is a Long Dog Life?

When you look at a Chihuahua and then at a Saint Bernard, it's hard to believe that they are members of the same species. That's one of the most amazing things about dogs—how different the breeds can be. Many breeds vary not only in appearance, but also in personality and style. And, of course, longevity.

It's a fact. Some dogs live a lot longer than others, and the distinctions seem to be all about size. "The giant breeds live to be between seven and ten years of age, making them the breeds with the shortest life spans," says John Hamil, D.V.M., a veterinarian in private practice in Laguna Beach, California. Age goes up as size goes down, Dr. Hamil explains. Dogs such as the West Highland White Terrier, Beagle and Dachshund can live for more than 15 years.

No one knows for sure exactly why size makes a difference in the life spans of dogs, although there are factors that contribute to the shorter lives of the bigger breeds. For example, bloat and certain heart problems are much more likely in larger dogs.

So where do mixed breeds fit into this? "It's a lot harder to predict the life span of a mixed breed," says Dr. Hamil. "You can get a rough idea based on the dog's size, but in general, you just never know."

Even if your dog is one of the big guys, it doesn't mean much. Dr. Hamil says it's important to realize that the age range for each breed is just a broad indication. "These are generalities," he says. "There are many reasons why an individual dog may live a longer, or indeed a shorter, life than expected."

Saint Bernard
Giant Breeds
Life span: **7–10 years**

Bernese Mountain Dog
Large Breeds
Life span: **8–12 years**

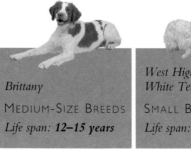

Brittany
Medium-Size Breeds
Life span: **12–15 years**

West Highland White Terrier
Small Breeds
Life span: **up to 15 years**

Making His Life a Little Easier

Along with taking your older dog to the vet when he's feeling his age, there are many things you can do to help him kick back and enjoy his golden years. Don't worry about a pastel-colored doghouse with a chaise longue and a view of Miami Beach. All it takes is a few simple adjustments to his environment and daily routine, and a little consideration, to help him through the day.

Coping with Incontinence

All dogs love to get out in the open air and feel the grass between their toes, but for older dogs with a bladder problem, more frequent trips outdoors are a must. "Make it possible for your pet to have access to the outdoors or to a safe place to urinate or defecate," says Dr. Schmitz.

According to Dr. Schmitz, you can help your pet if he's suffering from incontinence by re-adjusting his lifestyle. "You might consider making it comfortable for your dog to live outside, even if that hasn't been the case in the past." If drug therapy doesn't help your dog's problem, this may be the best solution for all concerned.

Keeping in Shape

Just because your dog is slowing down a bit, it doesn't mean he has to stop altogether. If he does, he'll start to put on weight. To make sure he stays fit and trim, weigh him monthly, suggests Dr. Brownstein, to keep an eye out for any changes. Help keep his weight down by feeding him a "senior" dog food, created to meet the nutritional needs of dogs over seven or eight years of age. "These foods are generally lower in fat and calories and also higher in fiber," says Dr. Brownstein. She warns that dogs with kidney problems or diabetes may require a specific prescription diet from their vet.

Dr. Brownstein also recommends that the more mature dog gets regular exercise to keep in shape. The pace might be a little slower and gentler than it used to be, but it's good to keep him active. (If your dog has turned into a bit of a couch potato, be sure to get him checked out by your vet before you sign him up for that Frisbee-catching competition at the local park.)

Coping with Blindness

If your dog has started bumping the furniture, walking into walls instead of through doors, chances are he's losing his eyesight. For most dogs, this is a gradual process, so they have time to get used to this new state. You can help, too. Dr. Schmitz recommends that you provide your dog with a consistent environment, one that does not change very often or even at all. "Do not move things around in your pet's surroundings," he says. If you have to move a

A graying muzzle and cloudy eyes show that this dog is creeping up in years.

piece of furniture, do it gradually so your dog can get used to the changes a little at a time.

Dr. Schmitz also suggests you talk to your blind dog to help guide him through his domain. Audible cues, such as "Oops!" or "Watch it!" will warn him of impending collisions and encourage him to find his way around.

Help for the Hard of Hearing

For deaf dogs, the advice is similar. Use visual cues to communicate with your dog once his hearing has gone, recommends Dr. Brownstein. She suggests anticipating the problem by training your dog to understand hand gestures when he is young. "Consider teaching your dog hand signals for the basic commands." This way, you can still "talk" to your dog even when he can't hear.

Dr. Schmitz points out that even though a dog may be losing his hearing, it might be less of a problem than you think. "Remember, a dog's hearing is better than ours to begin with in most cases, so a small hearing loss may not have as much effect on them as it might on one of us."

Easing Tired, Old Bones

Your dog is beginning to show the effects of arthritis, you've taken him to the vet and he's taking his tablets. You can also make some minor changes at home that will help him get around. Cover slippery floors with a mat or two so he can keep his feet under him on the slick surface. Raise his food and water bowls off the ground so he doesn't have to bend. Put them on a low table, or in a raised holder designed for dog bowls. Make sure his bed is extra soft, and put a cushion, preferably one made especially for dogs, in a warm, dry spot inside the house for him to lie on. He'll appreciate the relief these changes bring.

Change is Too Strange

The elderly pooch may be quite set in his ways. Even if he's in good physical shape and seems to be handling his retirement with aplomb, it's a good idea to keep changes to a minimum, says Dr. Brownstein. "Older dogs do not adapt to sudden changes easily," she explains. Keep him in mind when you rearrange the furniture, redecorate, or alter your schedule. Even a change in the time you feed him and take him for a walk can cause him distress. And an addition to the family might also upset the older dog.

Caring for Dogs with Diabetes

Sometimes, dogs get age-related diabetes in their later years. Although it can't be cured, it can certainly be treated, so your dog can still get a kick out of life. "A diabetic pet can be a joy and can most times be no different than living with any other non-diabetic pet," says Paul Schmitz, D.V.M., a veterinarian in private practice in Broken Arrow, Oklahoma. A conscientious owner can help a lot.

"Vets can help owners control the effects of the disease on their pets," Dr. Schmitz explains. It's not usually an expensive disease to treat. "But owners must go into the treatment with their eyes open and with the idea that their dog is a member of the family." It requires some commitment, as the diabetic dog will need regular care.

You will have to create a schedule that allows you to give insulin or oral medications properly, to feed him at the same time every day, and to keep his stress levels to a minimum. "This requires a little more time to be spent with your pet," says Dr. Schmitz. "But that can't be all bad, now can it?"

When to Let Go

We love our dogs so much that we want them to live forever. Sadly, this isn't how nature works. So when the time comes, it's important for you to be there for him, to make his passing as easy for him as possible.

Euthanasia is something we don't like to have to think about, but it's best to be prepared before it actually happens. It is a simple and painless procedure that your vet will perform when you've decided it's time. It results in a peaceful and dignified death. Some pet lovers view euthanasia as one of the greatest gifts we can give to a suffering pet. But it's understandable that most people find, when it comes to the time, that letting go is very hard to do.

"Euthanasia is unquestionably the most difficult decision any pet owner will ever have to make," says Dr. Brownstein. "Most of us wish our pets would simply pass away in their sleep, which would allow us not to have to face the issue. Unfortunately, this rarely happens." More often, the dog's quality of life deteriorates, and the owner starts to see that the dog is having more bad days than good. When this happens, it's time to discuss euthanasia with the vet.

"The key question every pet owner has to ask of themselves is whether their beloved pet still has dignity, is free of pain and has a good quality of life," says Dr. Brownstein.

Before you begin trying to make any decisions, talk to your vet. "Have a consultation either by phone or in person to discuss the issues at hand," says Dr. Brooks. She emphasizes that it's important to have this discussion before going through the process of deciding, since you may find that the problem your dog is having isn't so bad after all, and may even be curable.

There is support for people who lose their pets, and also for those who are trying to decide about euthanasia. "Today, pet loss and pet grieving are recognized by the human medical community and there are numerous support groups and specialists who can help you deal with this most difficult time, both before and after losing your pet," explains Dr. Brownstein. Do what feels right to you, and is best for him.

A peaceful and dignified death may be the kindest and most loving way to say goodbye to a faithful companion.

PART SIX

Easing Common Complaints

You don't expect your dog to spend her entire life in perfect health. From allergies and arthritis to weight problems and worms, dogs are vulnerable to a variety of health complaints. Once you know the tricks, you can take care of many problems at home and she'll be wagging her tail again in no time.

AGING

Even though dogs age much more quickly than people, they experience many of the same changes with the passing years. They move a little more slowly than they used to. And they're a little more susceptible to certain conditions, such as arthritis, kidney disease and heart disease.

Your dog might experience some behavioral problems, too, similar to those caused by senility in people, explains Gary Landsberg, D.V.M., an animal behaviorist in private practice in Thornhill, Ontario, and co-editor of *Dog Behavior and Training.* You might notice that your older dog becomes less attentive or playful, for example, or that she's forgotten commands that she used to know by heart. Her quick responses to sights and sounds may not be all they once were, and she

She may have slowed down a bit, but this elderly Golden Retriever still responds to her owner with the love and delight she's always shown.

may even surprise you with puddles inside the house as she loses her good toilet habits.

But with you and your vet around to see that she's comfortable and to take care of any special needs, she'll be more than happy to kick back and relax and share the years of companionship still to come with you.

Caring for Your Senior Dog

It can sometimes be difficult to tell whether changes you notice in your pet are due to a medical problem, a behavioral problem or a combination of the two. But while you can't turn back the clock, there is a lot you can do to help your dog enjoy her senior years.

Anticipate some changes. It's not unusual for older dogs to become less responsive or to forget their training. So don't assume your dog is deliberately ignoring you when she doesn't respond to your call or she just stands there when you tell her "Sit." Those surprise puddles in the house could be because she's lost muscle tone, has an infection or other medical problem. Or maybe she just forgot she had to go outside. Extra toilet training isn't going to help here. Stay calm, clean up the mess, and think about visiting your vet real soon.

Keep in contact with your vet. Most dogs will have a veterinary checkup once a year, but now that she's getting up in years, you might want to make your visits a little more frequent, especially if you notice something different that you're concerned about.

Report any unusual changes to your vet right away, recommends Dr. Landsberg. That includes behavioral as well as physical changes. "One study showed that fewer than 10 percent of pet owners advised their veterinarians of behavior problems in their

Aging

older dog, yet more than 60 percent of dogs were exhibiting problems when the same owners were asked to fill out a questionnaire," says Dr. Landsberg. It's important that you don't take changes in your dog for granted or dismiss them with, "Oh well, it's just old age." There may be things that can be done to help her.

Your vet will give your dog a complete physical examination and run tests to check for any disorders common in elderly dogs. If there is a medical cause for the problem, he will treat her for this. If the problem turns out to be partly or purely behavioral, don't give up hope. There are new drugs that can help to slow some of these changes or even lead to an

As your dog gets up in years, it's a good idea to make her visits to the vet more frequent than before. Your vet and you can work together to ensure that she is doing fine.

improvement in her behavior. Drugs such as L-deprenyl (Anipryl) or nicergoline, combined with a retraining program, can often help improve the quality of life for many dogs and their owners, explains Dr. Landsberg. Your vet will also advise you on what you can do to help your dog at home.

Be sympathetic to aging senses. Your dog may lose some of the sharpness of her senses. Her eyesight may fade, she may not hear as well as she once did, and even her sense of smell may be somewhat impaired. Your dog will accommodate and adjust to this gradual process, so much so that you may not even notice at first. But do try always to be considerate of your older pet and her set routines.

Any sudden changes could be stressful or downright confusing, so they're best avoided. If you have to move the furniture

or do a major remodeling and your dog's eyesight isn't what it used to be, take her on a tour of the new layout rather than spring it as a surprise.

When she's sleeping peacefully, don't startle her with hand contact, even if you think she must have heard your approach. Announce your presence by kneeling close to her and gently calling her name or perhaps clapping your hands softly as you walk up to where she is resting.

Keep her walking. Your dog will benefit from regular exercise and enjoy it as much as she always has, although the pace will probably be slower. After all, while she might be old in years, you want to keep her feeling young in spirit and exercise is a great way to keep her alert and interested in what's going on around her.

If she doesn't have the old stamina, just change her schedule to include more outings of shorter distances. This will also provide her with extra opportunities to go to the toilet, and the dog that has lost some of her toilet training will appreciate this. And if she gets sore after exercising, a nice massage or a warm bath will do

Aging

Keep taking your aging dog for regular walks even if she can't manage to go as far or as fast as she once did.

wonders for aging joints. Exercise will keep your dog's joints mobile and supple, her heart pumping and her body in shape so she doesn't start piling on the pounds. There is nothing like a walk followed by some gentle games to sustain your dog's joy in life.

Feed her right. A healthful, balanced diet will work wonders for your older dog. But be careful not to overfeed her, especially since she may not be as active as she once was. It's important that you watch she doesn't become too weighty, as this can lead to a number of health problems.

There's no need to switch her to a special diet, however, unless your vet specifically says to do so. While some dogs benefit from low-protein, high-fiber diets, others do much better eating food with high-quality protein, low fiber and lots of water-soluble vitamins. In some cases, vets may switch more mature dogs to highly digestible puppy foods.

Most elderly dogs will benefit from supplements rich in antioxidants, such as vitamin C and vitamin E, which help combat some of the deterioration that aging can bring. An older dog also needs more B vitamins to help her kidneys work more efficiently.

Your dog will have her own individual health needs, so if you pay close attention to her and how she's getting along and plan her activities and meals with this in mind, she will enjoy a long, happy and healthy retirement.

ALLERGIES AND HAY FEVER

She scratches. She licks. She bites at herself. In short, she's itchy and she wants it to stop. Before you settle on the obvious culprit and reach for the flea powder, check first that it isn't an allergy.

Allergies are one of the most common conditions in dogs. In fact, in some parts of North America they even rival fleas as the main cause of canine itching and scratching.

Don't expect her to sneeze a lot and blow her nose. The telltale signs that your dog has an allergy are:

- She starts licking and chewing at her paws.
- There is redness around her armpits and groin area.
- She rubs her face.
- She generally scratches and itches all over.

It's unusual for a pup to get an allergy. Most dogs are at least six months and usually more than one year old when they first develop an allergic reaction to a substance, called an allergen. It could be pollens, molds, house dust, a type of grass—all the same things we have allergies to.

Whether she has her very own "allergy season"—when the allergy affects her at a particular time of the year—or she's itchy all year long will

Allergies and Hay Fever

Why Does She Scratch, Not Sneeze?

You can always pick the people with allergies. They're the ones with the streaming eyes and the sneezes that threaten to lift the roof. But for dogs it's very different—they scratch and gnaw and lick and chew. And yet the allergies are caused by the same kind of reaction in the body. So why the different effect?

"Allergic dogs develop the same types of antibodies to substances in the air that they are allergic to as people," says Gene Nesbitt, D.V.M., an animal dermatologist in private practice in Standish, Maine, and a consulting staff dermatologist at Tufts University School of Veterinary Medicine. The difference in the reactions you see is all about where the antibodies are actually located. "The antibodies are found predominantly in the respiratory tract in humans and in the skin of dogs," says Dr. Nesbitt. So that's where all the action happens: Humans sneeze and their eyes weep, while dogs scratch away at their skin.

depend on what the allergen is. For example, if it's ragweed that she's allergic to, the itchiness will be worse in the fall; if the problem is house dust, the itchiness will probably be a year-round thing.

Easing the Symptoms

The good news for your dog is that there is a lot you can do to lessen her need for a good scratch. There are products like antihistamines and marine oils that will relieve her symptoms and make her feel a whole lot more comfortable.

Some of the antihistamines designed for relief of allergies in humans are effective in about one-third of canine cases, and you can purchase most from a pharmacy without a prescription. Diphenhydramine (Benadryl), clemastine (Tavist) and chlorpheniramine (Chlor-

Trimeton) have all been used successfully with dogs. Ask your vet to recommend an antihistamine that will suit your pet and the dosage that you will need to give her.

Marine oils are also very useful for treating allergies. These oils, derived from certain cold-water fresh fish, contain anti-inflammatory agents. Given

Before you can give your dog relief from her itches, you must track down the cause. If it's an allergy, discovering what she is allergic to could involve some real detective work.

Allergies and Hay Fever

daily, they will curb the symptoms in about 20 percent of dogs with allergies. When they are used with antihistamines, the overall success rate jumps to more than 50 percent. So there's a good chance that you will be able to help alleviate her symptoms, but if not, your vet will investigate further.

Avoiding Allergens

As a general rule, trees produce pollens in spring, grasses in summer and weeds in the fall. So if your dog's allergic season is a particular time of year, then this is one clue to tracking down what she's allergic to. House dust and mold allergies are year-round, although molds tend to be worse during damp periods. A dust-mite allergy gets worse when humidity is high. But to be really clear about what your pet is allergic to, you will need to have her allergy-tested by your vet.

Once you've worked out that either dust, mites, molds or pollens are her problem, there are some preventive measures you can make around your house that could really benefit your allergic dog.

Beware of the bedroom. "Don't let your house-dust-allergic pet sleep in your bedroom," says Kevin Byrne, D.V.M., an animal dermatologist and lecturer at the University of Pennsylvania School of Veterinary Medicine in Philadelphia. The bedroom has one of the highest dust mite populations in your home, so closing your door at night could be doing her a mighty mite-free favor.

If that's impossible, Dr. Byrne recommends special covers to control allergies. These encase your mattress, box spring and even pillows to contain the mite population. Contact your local dermatologist—veterinary or human will do—to find out about suppliers near you.

How to Allergy-Test Your Dog

If you suffer from allergies, then you may have had the "prick test" to work out what you're allergic to. The same test can be done on your dog. Your vet will inject small amounts of substances that may be the cause of her problem into the skin on her side, then measure her reactions. In this way, the vet can isolate the allergens, the substances she's allergic to. The entire test is completed in less than an hour and she will experience only a little pain—the hardest thing for most dogs is having to lie still while the testing is done.

The next step may be to treat your dog using immunotherapy, or allergy shots, by giving her injections of small amounts of the allergen. For example, if she is allergic to ragweed, the injections contain ragweed pollen. By gradually increasing the amount of ragweed, the resistance to ragweed is also slowly increased. This doesn't cure the allergy; it just means that if the immunotherapy works, your dog won't overreact (that is, have allergic symptoms) when exposed to the allergen next time because she has become used to it through the injections.

If your dog itches for most or all of the year, it's worth your while to discuss allergy-testing and immunotherapy with your vet. Your vet may give corticosteroids for short-term relief, but these have too many side effects to be used over a long period of time. Testing combined with immunotherapy is not only the most successful long-term control technique, it is also an extremely natural approach.

Allergies and Hay Fever

Wash allergens away.
Washing your sheets, blankets and comforters in hot water every seven to ten days is a good way of removing potentially allergy-causing particles, recommends Dr. Byrne. And washing her bedding will get rid of flea eggs and larvae as well. All this washing and cleaning is certainly going to keep you busy, but it's a simple and potentially effective way of making your dog's life a little less itchy.

A bath is just the thing to give your dog immediate relief when the allergic itches set in. Use cool water to soothe her skin and wash allergens from her coat.

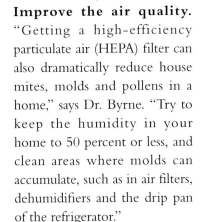

Improve the air quality.
"Getting a high-efficiency particulate air (HEPA) filter can also dramatically reduce house mites, molds and pollens in a home," says Dr. Byrne. "Try to keep the humidity in your home to 50 percent or less, and clean areas where molds can accumulate, such as in air filters, dehumidifiers and the drip pan of the refrigerator."

Watch for outdoor problems. Keep her away from recently mown lawns, as these tend to be rich in pollens and molds, suggests Dr. Byrne. And if you know it's a particular plant or weed that gets her

going, at least weed it out of your yard and try to ensure that she doesn't come into contact with it when out and about.

Keep her covered. Try putting your dog in a T-shirt or sleepers before letting her go outside. This might help to limit allergens coming into direct contact with her skin. Pop her head through the head hole, then put her two front legs through the sleeves. With the clothing pulled down over her body, she's ready to get out among the grasses. For the dog with very sensitive feet, you could also try getting her to wear booties.

Instant Relief

If she's having an attack of the scratches and needs immediate, short-term relief, give your dog a bath. This will help remove pollens, molds and dust from her coat, so at least they won't then be absorbed through the skin. And the water will be soothing on itchy skin.

Run the water cool because warm water will only increase her itchiness. Add something soothing, such as colloidal oatmeal, to the bath water, or rinse her off with medicated rinses containing antihistamines, 1-percent hydrocortisone or topical anesthetics. Your vet can also prescribe a rinse for you to apply after her bath. Don't wash it off—leave it on so that it can keep working.

You can't always be giving your dog baths, of course, so in between times, use one of the sprays that are available that have the same itch-relieving properties as those listed above. She will certainly thank you for the relief that these little attentions bring.

ANAL SAC PROBLEMS

If you notice that your dog is dragging her backside along the ground, chances are she's got an anal sac problem. The anal sacs are one part of your dog that you'd possibly prefer not to get to know too closely. These two pouches on either side of the anus accumulate a foul-smelling liquid—a concoction that seems to work as a wonderful scent-marking apparatus and communicates information about its owner to other interested dogs.

The anal sacs usually empty themselves of this liquid when a dog has a bowel movement. But sometimes they don't fully empty and then they impact, enlarging like tiny balloons and causing a painful sensation.

Your dog will have one of two classic responses to this unpleasant situation. She will either "scoot" her backside across the floor trying to unload the sacs, or she will bite and chew at the area beneath her tail. Both can cause damage.

"You may also notice signs of pain when grooming or petting the dog around the tail area," says Gene Nesbitt, D.V.M., an animal dermatologist in private

Dogs pick up a lot of personal details from sniffing the tail area of passing acquaintances. Their greeting ritual immediately establishes a newcomer's sexual and social status.

practice in Standish, Maine, and a consulting staff dermatologist at Tufts University School of Veterinary Medicine.

The first time you see her doing this, take her to your vet. He will examine the area to determine if the problem is one of simple impaction or whether something else, such as an infection, is going on as well. Then treatment can start.

Draining the Pain

The good news about anal sac problems is that they are usually easy to control. The most direct method of remedying the situation is to squeeze the sacs and force the contents out. This indelicate task is referred to professionally as "expressing" the anal sacs—it isn't a job for the faint of heart.

With a helper holding your dog firmly, raise her tail. Place your gloved thumb and index finger on the anal sacs, which you will be able to see at the five and seven o'clock positions of your dog's anus. Squeeze gently, and have a piece of gauze or a tissue ready to catch the expressed liquid.

Anal Sac Problems

Why Do Dogs Sniff Each Other's Hind Ends When They Greet?

You'd think they were long-lost bosom buddies, the way your dog greets another dog at the park and they both busy themselves putting their noses to each other's hind end. They might have met before or they might be complete strangers, but in the dog world, this is the polite way to behave—the hind-end sniff is the universal canine "How do you do?" "Dogs gain information from each other regarding gender, status and even identity from the smells they find there," says Katherine Houpt, V.M.D., Ph.D., professor of physiology and director of the Behavior Clinic at Cornell University College of Veterinary Medicine in Ithaca, New York.

"Fluid from the anal sacs gives off odors that may play some role as a calling card when dogs exchange introductions," adds Gary Landsberg, D.V.M., an animal behaviorist in private practice in Thornhill, Ontario. As well as sniffing the hind end, dogs also tend to sniff the head and groin areas to get information from other dogs, he explains. "Identifying social and sexual status is important to dogs," says Dr. Landsberg. That's why they have developed such a ritualized greeting, usually involving eye contact, circling the other dog and sniffing the groin, face and hind end. They get the goods on the other dog and then they know how to behave toward each other.

Your dog will not thank you while you are performing this service and the smell of the treasure you collect will be enough to bring tears to your eyes. You can take your dog to the vet whenever she seems to be suffering and get him to do the expressing. But an anal sac problem can recur, because although it is easy, if unpleasant, to remedy, it can be hard to cure. You could be seeing a lot of your vet, so you may

want to ask him to show you how expressing is done. Always try it for the first time at your vet's office, so you can be supervised and helped out if you change your mind—you may find you prefer periodic visits to the clinic after all.

If you decide you're up to the task, you will always need a helper, someone to hold and have firm control of your dog while you are down at the business end. You may also want to muzzle your dog. This is important because even a gentle dog can bite when in pain, and expressing the anal sacs can be painful.

The procedure is accomplished by firmly grasping and raising your dog's tail so that the anus is puckered. You should now be able to see the anal sac openings at the five and seven o'clock positions of the anus. Make sure you are wearing either surgical or latex gloves on the hand that is actually going to do the deed. Then, put your index finger on the side of one sac and the thumb on the side of the other and gently press thumb and forefinger together, forcing the anal sac contents out of the openings. It is important to use

Anal Sac Problems

a touch that is firm enough to force the contents out of the sacs but not so firm as to damage the walls of the sacs and cause them to rupture and become infected. And have a gauze or tissue in your gloved hand to collect the smelly material. You don't want it ending up anywhere but there.

Other Care

Whether you or your vet are doing the expressing, the pressure can usually be relieved immediately. However, your dog may continue to feel pain or itching in the area, in which case you'll need to undertake some additional care at home. This could be as simple as getting your dog to sit in some water to which you have added Epsom salts or an antiseptic. If the area is infected, your vet will prescribe antibiotics for you to administer.

You should also discuss your dog's diet with your vet, as a small food change could actually fix a recurring problem. "Since the anal sacs normally empty at the time of defecation, a soft or poorly formed bowel movement may pass without causing the sacs to empty," says Dr. Nesbitt. He explains that diarrhea is one of the most common causes of anal sac problems. "After considering other medical causes, a change in the diet to one that creates more bulk may be helpful," he advises.

ARTHRITIS

Yes, stiff knees and creaky elbows are as much a part of growing old for dogs as they are for us humans. Veterinary surveys suggest that 20 percent of adult dogs will develop osteoarthritis, also known as degenerative joint disease—a painful inflammation of these vulnerable areas. It's usually a part of the normal aging process and is the most common form of arthritis. Occasionally, rheumatoid arthritis affects dogs, too.

Whatever the cause, because dogs tend to run around a lot more than we do, arthritis can be a real check to their good times. But while it can't be cured, it's possible to give your dog a lot of relief.

What to Look For

In most cases, you can't predict when arthritis will start or, indeed, if your dog will develop it, but there are some circumstances that make it more likely. If your dog has a history of hip dysplasia, elbow dysplasia or osteochondrosis (a condition in which bone and cartilage in the joints break down), then there's a very good chance that she will get osteoarthritis.

Apart from these instances, arthritic changes tend to appear when a dog has reached about 75 percent of her estimated life span—around 7 years old for a large dog and up to 11 or 12 years for a small dog. However, there's nothing inevitable about arthritis and many dogs never get it.

You'll know that your dog is one of the unlucky ones when you notice that her joints seem stiff and sore or she shows signs of lameness. She may also have difficulty getting up, especially after she's been resting or sleeping for a while. And you may hear her whimpering while she tries to get about.

If you think your dog has arthritis, it's important that she is checked by your vet. He'll not only provide medical help, but will also recommend a number of simple home remedies that can bring big benefits.

Arthritis

Massage around your dog's aching joints before or after exercise. This increases the blood supply to the area and will relieve the pain.

sedentary, simply because their owners are nervous about causing additional pain. But exercise is very important because it keeps the joints working, which improves mobility. Plus, exercise makes the muscles stronger, which will help keep her joints stable. "Naturally, you won't exercise your dog when she is lame or hurting," says Dr. Keller.

The key is regular, gentle exercise, rather than getting your dog to be a competitive athlete. A

Giving Relief

There isn't a cure for arthritis, but there's a lot you can do at home to relieve the pain and improve joint mobility. And chances are your dog will be happy, healthy and moving right along for years to come.

Keep her weight down. "Don't let your arthritic dog get overweight," says G. G. Keller, D.V.M., a veterinary radiologist and the executive director of the Orthopedic Foundation for Animals. Extra pounds just put stress on joints that are already overloaded.

There's no need to put her on a crash diet, though. Take the weight off gradually, over the course of about 12 weeks, by going easy on the treats and table tidbits you give her. A food with less fat and more fiber might also make her load a little lighter. Keeping your dog trim is especially important if she has osteochondrosis or hip dysplasia. Reducing the burden on her joints can sometimes postpone the onset of arthritis by many years.

Get her moving. Dogs with arthritis are often quite

Use your hands and fingertips when massaging. Work in small circular movements around the problem spot, kneading gently.

Arthritis

leisurely 20-minute walk twice a day will be just fine. And remember that swimming is also an excellent form of exercise for a dog, especially one with arthritis, because her legs get a rest from supporting her weight. The water does it instead, and that reduces pressure on those aching joints.

Give some hands-on care. You know how good a massage feels to tired muscles and joints. Well, your dog will enjoy a brisk massage to her achy bits almost as much as you do, especially after her walk.

Massage doesn't have to be fancy. Just use your hands and fingertips to rub the sore areas in small, circular movements. Then gradually knead gently around the affected area and back again. This will increase the blood flow to the muscles and provide her with temporary, soothing relief—and she won't mind all the extra attention at all.

Keep out the cold. "Dogs with arthritis can be affected by adverse weather conditions," says Dr. Keller. So on those cold, wet days, you may want to offer her some additional comfort, such as an extra blanket or a layer of bedding. A

Do Dogs Fake Being Hurt?

Everyone is a sucker for a limping dog with mournful eyes. But you've probably wondered if she's really in pain or if she might be exaggerating, just a bit, to get some extra attention.

Although most dogs don't start out faking illness or injury, it is certainly possible that they learn to over time, says Gary Landsberg, D.V.M., an animal behaviorist in private practice in Thornhill, Ontario. "This happens when the owner accidentally rewards the behavior and the dog learns that it 'pays off,'" he explains.

If you pamper your pet when she's hurting—by giving her extra treats, for example, or letting her sleep on your bed—she'll soon learn that acting hurt has its benefits. So she may put on a bit of an act even when she's feeling better, simply to reap the rewards.

It's fine to take extra-special care of your dog when she's feeling sore. Just don't overdo it or you may find that you've created a full-time, four-legged thespian in the family.

massage will warm things up a bit, and even though she won't thank you for it at the time, a warm bath can help joints stay loose and limber, resulting in fewer creaks and groans later on.

Easing the Pain

Even though there isn't a cure for arthritis, there are a number of medications that can ease the pain and keep her comfortable. There are dozens of drugs to choose from, but one of the most effective is also the oldest and least expensive: aspirin. It not only relieves pain, but also reduces the joint inflammation that often goes with arthritis.

When the arthritic aches are flaring, vets usually recommend that you give about a quarter of a 325-milligram tablet for every ten pounds of pooch. To be safe, it's always best to check with your vet before giving aspirin (or any medication, for that matter) to your dog.

Another medication that your vet may prescribe is carprofen (Rimadyl). "It's a new veterinary drug, similar to aspirin, but causes even less stomach irritation," says Lester Mandelker, D.V.M., a veterinarian in private practice in Largo, Florida, and co-author of *Burns Pharmaceutical Index.*

"Nutritional supplements such as Cosequin and Glycoflex are purported to help dogs with arthritis," adds Dr. Keller. They contain nutrients that help form and repair cartilage. "But, to date, there has been no scientific proof that these supplements work." Your vet will recommend the product that best suits your dog's needs.

BAD BREATH

Whether you call it "doggy breath" or halitosis, bad breath makes getting up close and personal with your dog the last thing you want to do. And, unfortunately, it's all too common.

In dogs, as in people, bad breath often occurs when bacteria-laden plaque collects on the teeth. Unlike humans, dogs don't brush their teeth.

Those unexpected kisses take on another dimension if her breath is knocking you over. Keep your dog nice to be near with good oral care. Another important benefit is that her teeth and gums will be clean and stay healthier.

This means the plaque, along with the smell, won't go away. Worse, the bacteria can lead to gum disease, which gives off additional pungent odors.

How to Quell the Smell

There's really no reason to put up with your dog's bad breath. By making a few changes in her diet and practicing basic oral hygiene, you'll soon have her smelling sweet again—and you'll be protecting her teeth and gums at the same time.

Keep her teeth clean. The easiest way to take the edge off

doggy breath is to brush your dog's teeth every day or so. Pet supply stores sell special brushes and tasty, meat-flavored toothpastes designed with canine tastebuds in mind. At the very least, you can wrap a piece of gauze around your finger and quickly rub the surface of each tooth to remove food particles and plaque. For more information on getting her pearly whites really clean, see "Clean Teeth" on page 408.

If your dog's breath is truly overpowering or the teeth are distinctly discolored, you will

Bad Breath

want to take her to your vet or veterinary dentist to have her teeth professionally cleaned and polished before you start with her home care. Not only will you notice a big improvement in her breath, but once her teeth are clean they'll be easier to maintain in the future.

Avoid frequent feeding. Changing your dog's eating habits may also improve her breath. When dogs have food available all the time, their constant noshing makes it easier for plaque to accumulate. What's more, the steady supply of food particles on the teeth allows bacteria to thrive. So feed your dog just once or twice a day.

Is Doggy Breath Normal?

Almost every dog owner will occasionally complain about her pet's breath. Dog's usually get bad breath for the same reason that people tend to have it—their teeth are not brushed regularly. And that makes bad breath as normal in dogs as it is in people.

In fact, a dog's breath could easily be fresher than a human's, says Gregg DuPont, D.V.M., a veterinary dentist in private practice in Seattle. After all, dogs don't make a habit of eating garlic or onions or pizza, which are a common cause of many cases of bad breath in people, says Dr. DuPont. "Dog breath would be fresher than human breath if only they brushed their teeth thoroughly twice a day." Quite simply, if we brushed our teeth as infrequently as most dogs get their teeth brushed, the only ones that would be kissing us would be our dogs, not our spouses.

Brushing your dog's teeth regularly will go a long way toward keeping her breath sweet and pleasant. You can use a brush and toothpaste specially designed for dogs to take care of her oral hygiene needs.

Give her breath-friendly treats. If you give your dog the occasional table scrap or too many biscuit treats, don't be surprised when her breath gets worse instead of better. Carrots, rawhide chews or nylon bones—especially the kind with raised "dental tips"—are better treats because they'll remove plaque without adding calories.

And before you know it, her "doggy breath" will become a breath of fresh air.

Suspicious Smells

While bad breath usually means your dog needs her teeth cleaned, it can sometimes be a sign that something else is wrong. Diabetes can change the smell of your pet's breath, as can kidney disease. With both these illnesses, she will also likely drink and urinate more than usual and may lose weight. So if you notice her breath is a little different than the usual doggy breath smell, it's best to get your vet's advice.

BLOAT

Dogs aren't exactly known for being delicate eaters. They'll often gobble a bowl of food and slurp down a dish of water as though it's the last meal they'll ever have. This can be a serious problem—and not simply because of their display of bad table manners.

Vets aren't sure why, but dogs that swallow a lot of air while eating—or during vigorous exercise or when they're under stress—can develop a dangerous digestive condition known as bloat. Bloat causes the stomach to expand like a balloon, which can be very uncomfortable. But that's not the worst of it. In some cases, the stomach will actually become twisted, cutting off the flow of blood to the stomach and possibly to other organs, as well.

A dog with bloat will often seem restless and uncomfortable. You may notice that the abdomen is swollen and puffing out behind the rib cage. If you lightly flick the area with your finger, it may make a sound like a taut drum.

Bloat is always an emergency. It also comes on very quickly, so if you even suspect there's a problem, you have to get your pet to the vet immediately.

Preventing Bloat

Once bloating occurs, the only thing you can do is rush your dog to the vet. But there's a lot you can do to prevent it. Here's what vets recommend.

Watch what and when she eats. Since bloat often occurs when dogs have gobbled large amounts of food, it's best to feed your dog several small meals a day rather than give her one or two large meals or have food available all day long.

If your pet normally eats dry kibble, moisten it with some water before giving it to her. This will let the food do a lot of its expanding on the counter instead of in her stomach. Also, when gulping down dry food, your dog will tend to swallow more air; with moist food, she'll swallow less—which is why canned food is less likely to cause bloat than the dry kind. And make sure that while her water bowl is full throughout the day, you don't give her anything to drink during mealtimes.

Stop the gulping and gobbling. You can help to reduce the amount of air your dog swallows along with her food by making a few simple alterations to the way she eats. Raise her food bowl off the ground so that she

Find some way to raise your dog's food and water bowls as a measure to prevent bloat. If you take this simple precaution, she won't gulp in so much air as she eats and drinks.

Bloat

The Breeds Most Susceptible to Bloat

Any dog can get bloat, but large dogs with deep chests are the ones most at risk. In addition, purebreds are three times more likely to get bloat than mixed breed dogs. The dog breeds that are most susceptible to bloat are:

- Boxers
- Gordon Setters
- Great Danes
- Irish Setters
- Saint Bernards
- Standard Poodles
- Weimaraners

Weimaraner

Irish Setter

Standard Poodle

doesn't have to stretch her neck to reach the food. This will help reduce the amount of air she takes in. Pet supply stores sell elevated food stands. Or you can simply put her bowl up on a chair or step stool at about head height. You can also try putting a large object like a rubber ball in the bowl of food. Your dog will have to pick around the object to get to her food, and that should slow down her eating.

Don't exercise her close to mealtimes. Be sure that the hour before and after meals is an exercise-free zone. When dogs exercise, they breathe more heavily and get more air.

Give her digestive system a chance to settle down before adding something extra to the mix—whether it be food on top of too much air, or too much air on top of food.

Watch out for stress. It's no easier to prevent stress in your dog's life than it is in your own. But it's worth making the effort when there are lots of changes going on at home because dogs that are stressed can swallow large amounts of air, which can lead to bloat.

This is especially likely to be a problem if your dog is going to be spending time in a kennel. Not only is this naturally stressful, but she'll be getting less supervision than when she's at home with you. Let folks at the kennel know that you're worried about bloat, and they will be sure to keep an extra close eye on her.

CONSTIPATION

You don't see dogs browsing in the laxative aisle at the pharmacy, but they get constipated just like people—and when things aren't moving the way they should be down below, it can get very uncomfortable.

Constipation usually occurs when a dog has had to wait longer than usual to relieve herself—for example, if she has had to spend a long day indoors while her human family is away at work and school. This allows the stool to get dry and hard. In addition, not getting enough water and fiber in her diet and not getting

enough exercise can also lead to constipation.

Curing Constipation

It's not difficult to relieve (or to prevent) constipation. In fact, many of the same things that work for people will help keep your dog regular, too.

Up the exercise. One of the simplest remedies for constipation is to take your dog out for regular walks. Not only will this give her plenty of opportunities to relieve herself, but the exercise will help to stimulate the intestines to move things along a little faster, naturally.

Make some dietary changes. For dogs that are frequently constipated, vets often recommend increasing the amount of fiber in their diets. Dietary fiber absorbs water in the intestine, making the stools larger, softer and easier to pass. A sprinkle of bran cereal on her food will add a healthy amount of dietary fiber. Canned pumpkin is also good. Or you could add cooked vegetables, fresh fruits or milk to her food—this may cause a little mild diarrhea and remedy the problem.

Keep the water bowl full. One cause of constipation is not getting enough water.

Fluids are essential for keeping the stool moist and the digestive tract working well. And with all that extra fiber she'll be eating, she'll need even more water. So make sure to keep her water bowl full so she always has enough to drink.

Don't bother with laxatives. While we humans might resort to laxatives when we've given up on the prunes, for dogs that's not such a great idea, says veterinarian Dr. Lester Mandelker. "Over-the-counter laxatives may well do more harm than good," he explains.

Long-Term Problems

In most cases, constipation won't last more than a day or two. If it goes on for longer than that, however, there could be a more serious underlying problem, such as an intestinal obstruction, and you should contact your vet.

Incidentally, don't assume that straining is always caused by constipation. Dogs will also strain when they have diarrhea or even when they're trying to pass a bladder stone. If your dog is straining for a long time or seems to be very uncomfortable, you should play it safe and call your vet.

COUGHING

Coughing is a natural reflex in humans—we do it almost every day—but in dogs it usually means they have a viral infection. They're especially prone to a condition called canine cough, also known as kennel cough. It occurs when viruses invade the upper airways, making them ticklish and sore, and the dog develops a hacking cough that can hang around for weeks.

Canine cough isn't particularly serious and will usually go away on its own. In some cases, however, it can make your dog more susceptible to other—and more serious—infections. And it is very contagious and readily passed from dog to dog. That's why vets usually recommend protecting dogs against canine cough conditions such as parainfluenza and bordatellosis. "Nothing has done more to eliminate kennel cough than the use of these vaccines," says Dr. Mandelker.

It's not common, but coughing can also be a sign of more serious illnesses, such as bronchitis, pneumonia and asthma, or even heart disease. That's why it's important to call your vet if the cough persists for more than a day or two, or if your dog is coughing constantly.

Soothing Suggestions

Your vet can treat some of the underlying causes of coughs,

but it's up to you to relieve her discomfort in the meantime. Here are a few tips you may want to try.

Moisten the air. Dry air makes the mucus in the throat and airways dry and sticky, and that makes your dog want to cough. To provide quick relief, plug in a vaporizer near where your dog sleeps. (Just be sure that the cord is out of reach.) Another strategy is to take your dog into the bathroom with you when you're bathing or taking a shower. The warm, moist air will lubricate her

While your dog has a cough, you may prefer to use the type of harness this German Shepherd mix is wearing. Her usual collar or choke collar may be uncomfortable and irritate her throat, and that could make her want to cough more.

throat and airways—it will work wonders with her cough, even if it does make bathtime a little crowded.

Try an over-the-counter medicine. "In mild cases, cough suppressants such as Robitussin DM can be given to dogs if they are in a lot of discomfort," says Dr. Mandelker. "DM" stands for dextromethorphan—the active ingredient in many cough suppressants. Your vet will tell you what dose is right for your dog. For more severe coughs, he may give you a prescription for a stronger cough suppressant to use instead.

Exercise her with care. You won't want to cut out her exercise completely, but you will want to take it easy—the usual race around the park might have her hacking the whole way home. If she starts coughing from all the exertion, back off on the exercise.

Be especially gentle when using a collar, especially a choke collar, as these can be very uncomfortable for sensitive throats. Until the cough is better, you may want to put her usual collar aside and walk her using a harness that goes around her chest.

Adjust her diet. Dogs with coughs usually have sore throats, too, and dry kibble can be painful going down. If your dog eats dried food, you may want to moisten her kibble with a little water until she's feeling better. It's also a good idea to supplement her water supply with a little beef broth. Giving her extra flavor to savor will help ensure that she drinks plenty of fluids, which will help keep her throat moist and speed the cough on its way.

DANDRUFF

Dogs may not worry about flakes on their coats, but they get dandruff just as often as people do—and for some of the same reasons.

Most dandruff is nothing more than dead skin cells that are being shed. Dandruff tends to get worse in the winter months when the air is drier. In some cases it may be caused by skin mites or mild infections, as well.

It's not a health problem, just a question of how she looks—unless your dog's snowflakes won't go away despite your best efforts or you notice scabs, crusting or itching. In such

cases you will want to get your vet's opinion on the problem.

Dandruff Control

All dogs get dandruff, but it tends to be most visible in short-coated dogs, such as Doberman Pinschers and Vizslas. You may not prevent it entirely, but there are ways to control the problem and make it a little less obvious.

Wash it away. What your dog needs is bathing, more frequent bathing. In fact, twice a week should do the trick. This will help wash away the dandruff before it gets a chance to really build up.

Before you start in with the water, make sure that you are armed with the right dandruff-defeating equipment. Since dandruff is really the accumulation of dried, dead skin cells, it is important to use a shampoo with good cleansing ingredients, such as sulfur, salicylic acid or selenium disulfide.

If your dog has a dandruff problem that is caused by yeast—and your vet will be able to tell you if it is—you may need a shampoo that includes antifungal ingredients, too, advises Tufts University animal dermatologist Dr. Gene

Dandruff

Nesbitt. Lather her up well and massage it into her coat. You might even want to leave it on for a few minutes, so the active ingredients can really do some good. Use cool water because it will be more soothing and less itch-inducing to her skin, and rinse her off thoroughly.

It might take a month or two of this regimen to bring the dandruff under control, but once it is, you can ease off a little. Bathing her every two to four weeks will keep her coat looking and feeling good.

Make much of moisturizers. All this water and bathing could actually dry out her skin, so it's important that you follow up with a good moisturizing rinse, which might include ingredients like lanolin, lactic acid, glycerin and propylene glycol. This will help keep her skin well-lubricated and increase its moisture content.

Pet supply stores also stock a range of moisturizing sprays to protect her skin between baths. Follow the manufacturer's directions as to how often you spray her with one of these.

Brush her often. On the days when you don't bathe her, give her a good brushing. This is another excellent way to get rid of those dead skin cells, as well as any loose hair that's hanging around.

Diet away dandruff. A little dietary intervention might be in order, too, because dandruff can occasionally be caused by a

More frequent baths will help in the battle against doggy dandruff, as long as you are armed with the appropriate shampoo or rinse. Your vet can check what is causing the problem and advise you of the best measures to take.

fatty acid deficiency. If you feed her a balanced commercial diet, this is unlikely. But it might be best to upgrade your dog's diet if she is normally fed a generic type of dog food—it might not be giving her all the nutrients her skin needs. A dog food of better quality could be all the extra help she needs to get her skin back in shape.

Add some fatty acids. Your vet will probably recommend supplementing her diet with fatty acids anyway. The ingredient she needs is linoleic acid, found in safflower and sunflower seed oils and, in smaller amounts, in corn oil. "In a typical case, your vet will recommend that you add a half teaspoon to one tablespoon of vegetable oil to each meal, depending on the size of the dog," says Dr. Nesbitt. However, if you're adding an appreciable amount of vegetable oil to her diet, she'll also need some extra vitamin E to keep the balance right between her intake of fatty acids and vitamin E. Check with your vet about the correct amounts for your dog.

DENTAL PROBLEMS

Cavities aren't common in dogs, so they don't have to worry too much about needles and fillings and bad teeth being pulled. Their dental problems are different. The most common reason for dogs to be sitting around in dentists' waiting rooms is periodontal disease. This causes damage around the teeth and can develop into gingivitis, which damages the gums. And these canine dental problems sure are common—85 percent of dogs older than four years of age suffer from periodontal disease.

If your dog is more than a few years old, she probably has a coating of hard, brown material on her teeth. It's known as tartar, or calculus, and although it does make her smile look less than attractive, it's not the cause of all the tooth trouble. The main culprit is the stuff you don't see, called plaque. Plaque is a thin, sticky, bacteria-laden substance that forms on the teeth.

"Although calculus looks terrible while plaque is almost invisible, it is the plaque that causes periodontal disease and leads to gingivitis," explains

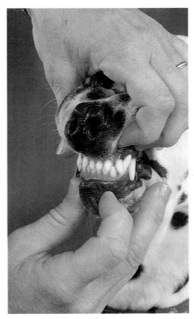

This Dalmatian gets an A-plus for her dental care. She has no tartar buildup on her pearly whites and her gums look firm and a good color.

Gregg DuPont, D.V.M., a veterinary dentist in private practice in Seattle.

If your dog has developed one of these conditions, your vet will have to treat her with professional teeth cleanings.

The best way to avoid that happening is to keep your dog's teeth, gums and mouth—and her breath—in mint condition. And you can do that by getting into the habit of taking care of her teeth with a regular dental hygiene routine.

Preventing Dental Problems

Dental problems are definitely something you can stop before they even get started by putting a simple prevention program into practice at home.

Do a daily plaque patrol. "Brushing your dog's teeth every day is vital to maintain ongoing dental and periodontal health," says Dr. DuPont. You might find having to do this once a day a bit daunting, but plaque accumulates quickly and you have to brush often to keep it under control. And because tartar develops from plaque, if you stop the plaque from settling, the tartar doesn't stand a chance. This is a good thing because once tartar accumulates, it takes more than a toothbrush to get rid of it.

Use dog products. Her teeth-cleaning accessories should include a toothbrush and a toothpaste made specially for dogs. Human toothpaste has a higher level of fluoride and it can contain sodium or detergents, says Dr. DuPont. It's also designed to be spat out, not swallowed. But your dog is unlikely to go for the spit-and-rinse option, and swallowing the human variety could upset

Dental Problems

her stomach. So stick with a product designed for dogs. Dog toothpastes come in poultry, beef and other flavors, so she'll like the taste of them, too.

Start off slowly. Your oral hygiene program will have most success if you start slowly and patiently, says Dr. DuPont. You want your pet to think of teeth-brushing sessions as enjoyable and positive time spent with you, not a punishment, he explains. Start by getting her comfortable about having her mouth touched.

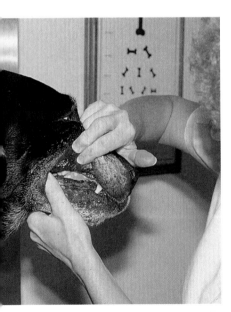

Your vet's annual examinations will ensure that problems are caught early. He may clean her teeth himself using a light anesthetic so she's comfortable.

Do Dogs Ever Need Braces?

Braces tend to be a bad memory from many a human's teenage years. Dogs, too, have been known to endure a mouth full of metal, although strictly for medical reasons—most dogs are content with their toothy grins, even if they are a bit crooked.

Dogs only have to get braces if their teeth are aligned in such a way that it seriously affects their ability to eat. They don't wear braces merely to make their teeth straighter or more appealing. Even breeds such as Boxers and Bulldogs, which naturally have crooked teeth, are unlikely to wear braces unless their teeth are so crooked they're not working the way they should.

"In fact, orthodontic treatment could be considered a cause for disqualification by the American Kennel Club," says Gregg DuPont, D.V.M., a veterinary dentist in private practice in Seattle.

For about a minute each day, lift her lips and rub around her teeth with your fingers. Try a little garlic powder or some other good-tasting substance on your fingers if she resists, and always pile on the praise. After about a week, she should feel okay about this and you can move on to a toothbrush and a little bit of paste—just let her lick the brush.

When she's comfortable with this development, start wiping the brush downward on the front teeth. Use gentle, circular motions and slowly increase the area you cover until all her teeth are being cleaned. Brushing doesn't need to last more than a minute, and always let her know what a good dog she's been. For a detailed guide to how it's done, see "Clean Teeth" on page 408.

Try other alternatives. "There's no doubt that brushing your dog's teeth is the most important part of dental home care," says Ken Lyon, D.V.M., a

Dental Problems

veterinary dentist in private practice in Mesa, Arizona, and co-author of *Dog Owner's Guide to Proper Dental Care.* "But there are also gels, rinse solutions and other anti-plaque products that are available, as well as a prescription dog food designed to reduce tartar buildup." Your vet will pre-scribe one of these products if he thinks your teeth-brushing efforts need a little extra help. Most rinses are squirted on the gum line, while gels are rubbed on the teeth.

Give her some crunch to munch. Giving your dog hard, crunchy snacks and kibble will help keep her teeth clean *if* she takes the time to chew them rather than swal-lowing them whole. They're not enough by themselves, but their abrasive action will cer-tainly scrape off some of the plaque, says Dr. Lyon.

If she's a biscuit gulper rather than a biscuit chewer though, there's not a whole lot of teeth cleaning going on, so you might want to give her a com-pressed biscuit coated with anti-plaque and anti-tartar ingredients. "This could truly be considered a tartar-control treat," says Dr. Lyon.

Put her jaws to work. A hard rubber chew toy, especial-ly one with grooves, is a great way for your dog to have some fun and do her teeth some good, too. The rubber will scrape under the gum tissue and dislodge the material that can accumulate there.

Steer clear of soft rubber chews because they can some-times damage teeth, advises Dr. Lyon. Instead, go for the prod-ucts specially designed with dental ridges, which you will find in a pet supply store.

The hard rubber bone this Dalmatian is working on is doing her teeth more good than she realizes. As well as being good exercise for her jaws, it's also dislodging debris from under her gums.

This lucky Irish Setter is enjoying a special nylon chew toy with ridges, designed to give gums and teeth a good scraping while she munches.

But ban the bones. Dogs love gnawing and chomping on big bones, but those bones aren't doing her teeth any favors. Chewing a hard bone can damage your dog's teeth, and a bone shard could get lodged in her mouth or even cause choking or vomiting. Baked rawhide can be hard and brittle, and that can spell trouble, so do best by her teeth and avoid it, too.

Take her for regular check-ups. Give your vet the oppor-tunity to do the occasional oral once-over on your dog—it's a

Dental Problems

great way to make sure that everything is okay and that problems are caught early before they develop. "Pups should have their first dental checkup at 8 to 16 weeks of age and again when they are six months old, so that any problems can be identified and treated," says Dr. DuPont. (Just for the record, dogs have 30 puppy teeth, then 42 adult teeth, divided into 4 canines, 12 incisors, 16 premolars and 10 molars.)

After that, most veterinary dentists recommend that your dog's teeth be checked once a year. You can have it done at the same time as her annual vaccinations. Your vet may recommend giving her teeth a professional cleaning, known as a prophy, to clean out the plaque underneath the gums. Then her pearly whites will be a clean slate for your home health care.

DIARRHEA

Okay, so this isn't a topic for dinnertime, but you're sure to have a question or two about diarrhea when you discover a surprise on the living room carpet and your dog looking

It will be almost impossible to stop your dog from tracking down a trash can occasionally, and her forays may result in a bout of diarrhea.

sheepish, sitting in the corner. There's nothing unusual about her having the occasional bout of diarrhea. After all, no matter how vigilant you are, she will still manage to sneak the odd dawn raid on the garbage or pick up an intestinal virus from one of her canine buddies down at the park.

There are many different types of diarrhea, explains Dr. Mandelker. There's the basic, improperly formed soft stuff, but diarrhea can also contain mucus or fresh blood. And while most cases get better with no help in a day or two, diarrhea from parvovirus, for example, can cause profound dehydration and intestinal damage in that time.

Most likely, she's got a straight case of the runs and she's going to have to lay off the food for a while. Occasionally, the diarrhea could be a symptom of something more serious and your vet will tell you to bring her in. Check your dog carefully to see if she has fever, vomiting, abdominal pain or if she seems depressed. If you notice any of these symptoms or if the diarrhea contains mucus or blood, call your vet. Just be prepared to describe the problem before you telephone for advice.

Dealing with Diarrhea
Diarrhea is one way your dog has of getting bad bugs out of her body—and fast. In a weird kind of way, it's actually doing her good. But that doesn't mean that she or you want it around for too long. So here are some tactics your vet may suggest to slow the flow.

Fast her first. Vets recommend that dogs with diarrhea skip a meal or two so their upset tummies have a chance to rest. When there's nothing going in, there won't be anything there to come out again. But if things don't slow down, you should talk to your vet.

Go bland. After she's missed a couple of meals, you can start her back on food again, but her tender stomach will appreciate a change from the usual. Make her a bowl of something bland, like boiled hamburger or skinless white chicken meat mixed with rice or farina—one part meat to two parts rice or farina typically does the trick.

Feed her this for one to four days, depending on your vet's advice. Once the diarrhea has finished, you can slowly reintroduce her regular food by gradually substituting it for the bland food over the next three to four days.

Keep the liquids up. Your dog's body can lose its essential fluids very quickly through diarrhea, so it's important that you ensure she doesn't become dehydrated. Always keep her water bowl full and check that she is actually still continuing to drink.

Even when she is fasting, she should still be drinking. If she doesn't seem interested in her bowl of water, then giving her ice cubes to lick or chew will keep her liquid levels high.

Try an over-the-counter medicine. "In simple cases of diarrhea, home remedies such as Pepto Bismol or Imodium can be given once or twice," says Dr. Mandelker. A quarter to a half of the dose recommended for a child could help firm things up again. Sometimes it's best to let nature run its course, so use medications only if your vet advises you to.

When It Won't Go Away

Even if your dog seems to be fine, diarrhea that continues for more than two days could be a problem and you should call your vet. Conditions that can result in chronic diarrhea, such as a food allergy, colitis or pancreatic problems, will get better only with your vet's help.

DROOLING

There's nothing quite like having a beloved pet rest her head in your lap...only to find a puddle of spittle there moments later when she wanders away. Not even Pavlov's dogs drooled all day long, so what is the problem here?

Your dog is probably drooling because she is one of those breeds whose lips are designed in a way that allows saliva to pool, collect and then overflow out of her mouth. It's not that she produces more saliva than other dogs—though you might find that hard to believe. It's just that she doesn't swallow it all.

Breeds that Drool

When it comes to too much saliva in all the wrong places, the worst offenders are these three breeds:

- Newfoundlands
- Saint Bernards
- Basset Hounds

Saint Bernard

Drooling

This is what you'd have to call the chronic drooler.

Of course, all dogs are going to let out a little saliva when there's food around or they get really excited. It's completely natural and nothing to worry about. But if your dog isn't a regular drooler and she suddenly starts producing excess amounts for no apparent reason, it could mean anything from a broken tooth to insecticide poisoning. You want to get her to your vet right away.

Dealing with Drooling

There really aren't any magic potions or solutions to make your dog drool less—and not even a Southern California canine wants to contemplate cosmetic surgery in the hope of improving the situation. But you can limit the effects of the big wet.

Dry her down. Drool veterans know to carry a towel with them whenever they go out with their dogs. It's easy to wipe down around her mouth whenever things start looking a little too moist. If you want to cut back on time spent on slobber patrol, try getting her to wear a bandanna around her neck. Fold a bandanna made of

The smart-looking bandanna this Australian Shepherd is sporting is not just for looking good. It will also help protect her coat from drooling.

an absorbent fabric in half, then tie it so the triangle part hangs down over your dog's chest. This solution can be stylish as well as functional.

Set her place. Dinnertime can be drooling time for any dog, no matter how dry around the mouth she normally is. A place mat under her dish will help keep the surrounding floor dry and make cleaning up afterward as simple as whisking the mat away when she's done. If she's a die-hard drooler, a place mat should be de rigueur, unless you don't mind the

puddles that are bound to form in her dining area.

Avoiding Infection

While we're on the subject of lip conformation and saliva, certain dogs have a lip design that can increase the likelihood of infection. "Some dogs, although they do not actually drool, have extra lip skin that creates a fold in the lip," says veterinary dentist Dr. Gregg DuPont. This fold is in the lower lip, just behind the canine teeth.

"This is particularly prominent in most Spaniel breeds, including Cocker Spaniels, Springer Spaniels and Brittany Spaniels, and can lead to infection from the moist and bacteria-rich environment," he explains. The lip folds can be altered surgically so bacteria don't build up, but most owners prefer to simply clean the area once a day.

Use a cotton-tipped swab to get down into the fold and get rid of any accumulated gunk. Then dip another cotton-tipped swab in peroxide, chlorhexidine or alcohol—only use alcohol if there are no cuts around your dog's mouth—and gently cleanse the area.

Ear Problems

Dogs may have only two ears, but they seem to have more than their share of problems that can erupt there.

A dog sitting on her tailbone with her rear leg up, thumping away like crazy at her ear, is a common enough sight. Chances are she's trying to get a little relief from some kind of problem that's bothering her there. It could be a colony of ear mites that has taken up residence, or her itchy ears could signify some other type of irritating ailment.

Ear Mites

Ear mites are one of the most common causes of canine ear troubles. The tiny, crablike mites are passed from dog to dog, or cat, or any other furry pet you might have. They munch on ear wax and other debris and secretions in the ear canal, and although they will rarely bite, sting or otherwise hurt, they can lead to intensely itchy allergic reactions, causing dogs to scratch their ears raw. But they're easy for your vet to diagnose and easy for you to treat at home, even if they can be a little persistent at times.

You'll have to be persistent too, and one step ahead of them.

If you suspect your dog has ear mites, lift up the ear flap and take a look inside. Even though ear mites are difficult to see, the debris they leave behind—a brownish-black discharge that resembles used coffee grounds—is quite visible. Get your vet to confirm that this is indeed the cause of all her ear scratching, and he will advise you on what type of ear drops you should use. It will typically take four to six weeks of treating your dog with the drops to get rid of the mites.

Go after traveling mites. Ear mite products go directly into your dog's ear canal and they work fine there. However, ear mites have eight legs and they do what any parasites do when you squirt insecticide into their home: They move to a new neighborhood, usually at the base of the tail. When the medication in the ear canal wears off, they head home as if nothing had happened.

The way to avoid this trap is to not only treat her ears but to also use a flea powder or spray over your dog's whole body. Most common flea treatments, including pyrethrins, perme-thrin, rotenone, carbaryl and organophosphates, will kill ear mites on the body surface.

Treat all your pets. Don't stop at the dog with the obvious problem. Ear mites are passed readily from pet to pet. If you have more than one pet, remember to treat every animal on the premises (dogs, cats, ferrets and rabbits included). Otherwise, you might find your pets are just playing "pass the mites."

Be persistent. You will have to treat your dog (and all the other four-legged creatures at your place) for up to a month —that will cover the entire life cycle of the mites from egg to full-grown critter. If you stop too soon, you won't get rid of every last one of them. And make no mistake: Mites can be very difficult to eradicate.

As a last resort, your vet may recommend stronger medications, possibly even injections, that will kill the mites on board. However, if your dog is still in contact with the mite carrier, she will still be susceptible to new infestations.

Ear Infections

Dogs can often get bacterial or yeast infections in the ear canal.

Ear Problems

"Dogs with recurrent ear infections don't 'catch' them from other dogs," says Stephen Waisglass, D.V.M., a veterinarian in private practice in Thornhill, Ontario. Rather, there is an underlying reason why they are susceptible to infections, he explains.

It could be:

- Your dog's ear shape; floppy ears or small ear canals, in particular.
- Humid conditions or a fondness for swimming.
- Overdoing the ear care; excessive hair plucking or cleaning efforts, or irritating cleansers or drops.
- Health problems such as allergies, food intolerance or a hormonal imbalance.

If you notice debris in your dog's ear canal or on her ear flaps, or if her ears are red, hot or tender, she could have an infection and you should take her to the vet for treatment. If she constantly tilts her head, she could have inner ear problems. Your vet will be able to diagnose the underlying cause of her trouble and set about fixing the problem.

Regular checks for foreign objects such as grass seeds should also be routine.

Ears that allow air to circulate freely, such as those of this German Shepherd, are easy to check and clean.

Preventive Ear Care

The best way to keep your dog's ears healthy is to follow a regular ear care program. Here's what vets recommend.

Check her ears weekly. Good ear care begins by regularly inspecting the insides of the ears. "Owners should check their dog's ears weekly as part of their regular grooming regimen," says Dr. Waisglass. You're looking for clean ear canals, with no signs of

Before cleaning your dog's ears, be sure that the ear canals are free of debris. If there is debris, use a cotton ball to remove it, but take care not to pack it down further.

inflammation, no nasty odors and no redness around the ear flaps. While you're at it, check carefully for ticks, and don't forget those ear mites.

There's no need to explore the ear canal too deeply; just check the external area, then lift the flap to find out what you can smell and see.

Do a regular cleaning. You can keep your dog's ear canals clear and free of parasites by cleaning them out. Make this a part of your regular bathing or grooming routine. But before you put any solutions in your dog's ear canals, make sure you discuss it with your vet first. After all, the ears are a very sensitive part of your dog. "Many antiseptics and antibiotics can cause deafness if they get down to the middle ear,

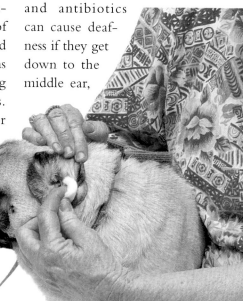

which they may do if the ear drum happens to be ruptured," says Dr. Waisglass.

After making sure the ear is clear of debris, dip a cotton-tipped swab into ear-cleaning solution. Then gently clean around and between the ridges of the ear flap—but be careful not to push the swab too far into the ear canal. You can use a swab safely in the ear canal as long as you can always see the cotton end, says animal dermatologist Dr. Kevin Byrne. "The swab should be pointed down and not in toward the head," he advises.

You must be careful not to pack debris farther down into the canal when using the swab, however, adds Dr. Waisglass. So if there is any excess fluid and debris in the ear opening, use a cotton ball to carefully remove it. And if the cleaning solution doesn't contain drying agents, apply a very small dab of a commercial agent so her ears will dry out. For more information on how to clean your dog's ears, see "Clean Ears" on page 405.

Ignore the hairs. Just because your dog's ears are sprouting hairs thicker and faster than granddad, don't automatically reach for the tweezers. "I don't recommend routinely plucking the hair from the ear canals of dogs who otherwise have healthy ears," says Dr. Byrne. The exceptions are where the hair is stopping the medication from getting into the problem area or the infected material is blocked from draining out of the ear, he advises. Then a little judicious ear-hair-plucking is called for.

EATING DUNG

To dog owners everywhere, this doggy activity seems kind of inexplicable and pretty downright objectionable, especially if the dog in question is the snuggling type. But for dogs that like to indulge, disgust doesn't enter into it and they will often be surprised by their owners' reactions when they behave in this very unattractive way.

Eating dung—which vets refer to as coprophagia—can be normal in certain situations. For example, a mother nursing her pups will clean up after them until they are about eight weeks old. But for the most part, vets really don't know why some dogs will eat the stuff and others won't. There could be a number of reasons, says animal behaviorist Dr. Gary Landsberg, especially when you take into account that dogs' keen sense of smell attracts them to unusual odors. Some dogs may have a digestive problem or they could have a nutrient deficiency.

Fortunately, dung eating rarely results in health problems, but you will definitely want to ban this bad habit—for your sake if not for your dog's.

How to Help Her Stop

The fact is, a lot of dogs eat dung, even if only occasionally. But you can help stop your dog from developing any illicit tastes. Here's how.

Add some enyzmes. Vets suspect that some dogs eat stools because they have a digestive problem that means they can't completely digest the food they eat. Perhaps they realize the stool contains undigested nutrients, which can be used to supplement their diets.

If you have a dog that thinks feces is a gourmet treat, try adding digestive enzymes to her food to make it more completely digested. This helps dogs give up the habit in about

Eating Dung

30 to 40 percent of cases. Pancreatic enzymes are available by prescription, and there are many over-the-counter, plant-based products you can use, too. Look for preparations that contain ingredients such as chymotrypsin, papain, bromelain or cellulase at pet supply stores, health food stores or pharmacies.

Give her quality foods. Some dogs with a nutritional deficiency will consume the stools of horses and cats, for example, to get a nutrient boost. So be sure to feed your dog a high-quality, balanced diet to ensure that she gets all the vitamins and nutrients she needs.

Give her plenty to chew on. "In some cases, dogs will eat feces simply because they are hungry," says Katherine Houpt, V.M.D., Ph.D., professor of physiology and director of the Behavior Clinic at Cornell University College of Veterinary Medicine in Ithaca, New York, and author of *Domestic Animal Behavior.*

"They may also do it when they lack other things to chew on," says Dr. Houpt. If you suspect that she might be on light rations, try giving her a little more food. And make sure she has a couple of chew toys to play with—a flavored rawhide bone could keep her occupied for hours.

Beat her to it. Make sure you remove temptation wherever you can. If you have a cat, put the litter tray in a place where your cat can get to it but your dog can't. "Clean up the yard regularly and not within sight of your stool-eating dog," says Dr. Landsberg. You don't want her to associate you with the situation in any way.

"And keep her on a halter or leash while you're out and about," he adds. This way, you will be able to steer her clear of other animals' leavings and correct her if she goes for something she shouldn't.

Keep her busy. "Don't forget the behavioral component," says Dr. Landsberg. Your dog could be doing this out of boredom or because it has become a compulsion with her. Give the dog that can't keep away from dung more exercise, training, play activities and better all-round general supervision when she's outdoors, advises Dr. Landsberg. And, hopefully, feces will gradually lose its fascination.

ELBOW DYSPLASIA

We don't usually think of dogs as having elbows, but that's exactly what the joints on the front legs really are. Your dog's elbows are designed to be strong, yet mobile. The elbow joint holds the bones tightly together, yet allows enough flexibility so she can run and jump with astonishing grace and agility.

In some dogs, however, the elbow joints don't fit together as tightly as they should. They have a certain amount of "wobble" in the joint, which can lead to pain and stiffness, especially when they've been playing hard.

This condition, called elbow dysplasia, is thought to be hereditary, and it tends to set in even before a dog reaches her first birthday.

If you suspect your dog either has elbow dysplasia or is at risk of getting it because her parents had it, your vet will probably recommend taking x-rays. Diagnosing the problem early on will allow you to take some preventive measures to protect the elbows from further damage. And if the joints haven't already deteriorated,

Elbow Dysplasia

your vet will probably suggest surgical intervention to correct the problem.

Easing the Aches

One of the most powerful remedies for controlling the discomfort of elbow dysplasia is simply to watch your dog's weight. By keeping her on the light and lean side, you will ensure that she has less weight to carry around, which will reduce pressure on all the vulnerable joints.

Because of the reputation calcium has for healing weak bones, people are sometimes tempted to give supplements to dogs with elbow dysplasia. But don't do it, says Dr. Mandelker. Instead of strengthening your dog's bones, calcium supplements will actually interfere with the normal growth of both the bones and the cartilage, and that can make elbow dysplasia even worse.

It's also important to make sure your dog gets regular and gentle exercise. Exercise helps strengthen the muscles, ligaments and tendons around the elbow joints, while at the same time increasing lubrication that helps the joints to move more easily. Obviously, you don't want to overdo the exercise, but keeping her moving on a daily basis can be very helpful.

A 20-minute walk twice a day will do her good. Or try a swim, as long as the water isn't cold and she can get warm and dry after it. For more information on help for sore joints, see "Arthritis" on page 298.

When your dog's elbows are acting up, your vet may recommend giving her medications to help control the pain and swelling. Applying heat or cold several times a day can be very soothing. In addition, your vet

Breeds Most Susceptible to Elbow Dysplasia

Some dogs get elbow dysplasia and some don't, and the reasons why aren't fully understood, but genetics clearly plays a role. The breeds that are most susceptible are:

Bloodhound

- Bearded Collies
- Bernese Mountain Dogs
- Bloodhounds
- Bullmastiffs
- Chow Chows
- German Shepherds
- Golden Retrievers
- Labrador Retrievers
- Mastiffs
- Newfoundlands
- Rottweilers

Bearded Collie

Elbow Dysplasia

may advise that you give your dog a cartilage-protecting agent, such as Adequan and Hylartin V, and nutrient combinations that will help repair her cartilage.

Since elbow dysplasia is often an inherited condition, your vet will probably recommend having your dog spayed or neutered. And if you are buying a breed of dog prone to this condition, get a pup only from a breeder who will guarantee the dog's family has been free of elbow dysplasia for at least three generations back.

You don't have to take the breeder's word for it—ask to see the certification from the elbow registry of either the Orthopedic Foundation for Animals or the Institute for Genetic Disease Control in Animals, which will guarantee your prospective pup is "clear" of elbow dysplasia.

EYE PROBLEMS

You may not see too many dogs running around in spectacles, but they have problems with fading eyesight and eye infections, just as we do. One thing's for sure though, they get by much better than us.

> ## Can Your Dog's Eyes Be Tested?
>
> Dogs don't need to read an eye chart, not when there are such fun things as maze tests, obstacle courses and tracking cotton balls to help a veterinary ophthalmologist assess how well they can see. If your dog can find her way out of a maze or over an obstacle course without bumping into anything, then your vet will know that her eyesight is up to scratch. Similarly, he might suspend a cotton ball in front of your dog and move it back and forth to see if she can track it visually.
>
> "There is also a range of instruments to evaluate the eye," says Dan Lorimer, D.V.M., a veterinary ophthalmologist in private practice in Southfield, Michigan. If your vet suspects an eye disease such as glaucoma, where fluid increases pressure in the eye, he will use an instrument to determine the intraocular pressure of your dog's eyes. Staining solutions are used to check for corneal ulcers, and strips of blotting paper measure the amount of tears that the eyes produce.

After all, they don't need dog food cans with large print to tell them whether it's chicken or beef; they've got their highly refined sense of smell (and taste) to work out the finer details of life.

Cloudiness in the eyes is one of those bothersome things that often happens to a dog as she gets older. It's called nuclear lenticular sclerosis and it can look a lot like cataracts but it's nowhere near so serious. "It can reduce close vision, but this is not nearly as important in dogs as it is in people, since dogs are rarely expected to read the fine print," says Dan Lorimer, D.V.M., a veterinary ophthalmologist in private practice in Southfield, Michigan.

You might not realize at first that your dog has a vision problem, because dogs are incredibly adaptable and she will possibly compensate with her other senses. Some of the signs you might notice are that she negotiates obstacles poorly, stumbles on steps or curbs and experiences night blindness, explains Dr. Lorimer. If you notice that her eyesight is failing, take her to the vet for a diagnosis to make sure it's nothing serious.

Eye Problems

Do Dogs See in Color or Black and White?

Have you ever wondered what the world looks like through your dog's eyes? Is it like watching an old black-and-white TV or can she see things in glorious Technicolor? "Dogs are thought to have limited color vision in the green and yellow range," says Dan Lorimer, D.V.M., a veterinary ophthalmologist in private practice in South-field, Michigan. So that park full of green grass really is a sight for doggy eyes, although your dog will have trouble finding a yellow toy in it. But color isn't so important, and neither is focusing close up—dogs use their powerful noses for the fine detail. They have better long-distance vision and peripheral vision, and can see well in dim light.

Another common problem is discharge and debris in the corner of your dog's eyes, sometimes referred to as "eye goo." These are natural secretions that accumulate, and a good wash is often all she needs.

Conjunctivitis, an inflammation usually caused by allergies or infections, is another common ailment that will make her eyes red and itchy.

Helping Failing Eyes

Although impaired vision, even blindness, is a handicap, dogs often cope much better than people do. "They usually adapt very well to their loss of vision," says Dr. Lorimer. Still, while you can't improve her eyesight, there's a lot you can do to make life easier for the pet that isn't seeing 100 percent any more.

Leave things where she'll remember them. With her eyesight not all that it once was, your dog will use her memory of the way things were to negotiate her way around the house. So don't suddenly move the sofa to a new position, because she's bound to walk into it rather than around it. Leave her food and water bowls where they've always been, so she'll be able to find them.

If you must redecorate or relocate the furniture, take your pet on a gentle guided tour so she can work out the new lay of the land. Use lots of verbal encouragement to help her find her way around objects and get where she wants to go.

Protect her from trouble spots. You need to take extra precautions around stairways or other potentially dangerous areas such as the kitchen. Put a child gate in front of any doorway or opening that you don't want your dog to have access to except when she's with you. If you use the same keep-out strategies you would for a new puppy or a toddler, your pet should do just fine.

Stimulate her senses. Just because your dog can't enjoy the scenery doesn't mean that she won't like the fresh air and good smells that a nice walk offers. She still needs to get adequate exercise and stay fit, although you'll need to be keeping your eyes open for the both of you—think of yourself as her seeing-eye-person.

You will now find a harness a much better tool than a choke

Eye Problems

collar, because you will need to have greater control over her to rein her in more often. The harness will give you a much more gentle form of control.

"Encourage your dog to use the other senses," says Dr. Lorimer. Noisy squeaker toys could raise her spirits. Or another dog could make a good companion, engaging her in smell and touch games—the kind of games most dogs play.

Easing Irritable Eyes

Eye discharge isn't a problem, except that it looks a little unsavory, and you can easily keep it under control by washing away the muck once a day. If your dog has conjunctivitis or some other eye infection, get your vet's advice first.

Do Dogs Ever Need Corrective Lenses?

You're not likely to be ordering glasses or contact lenses for your dog anytime soon, because fine print isn't that important to her—she'll sniff out the bottom line with her excellent sense of smell. However, there are times when corrective lenses can make a difference—but not for seeing. Vets sometimes use special lenses called hydrophilic soft contact lenses, which act as a kind of bandage to help dogs with damaged corneas, says Dan Lorimer, D.V.M., a veterinary ophthalmologist in private practice in Southfield, Michigan. "These contact lenses are thought to enhance healing and reduce pain," he explains.

The best step is to wash away any discharge or debris that has collected in your dog's eyelids. This will soothe away the scratchy, itchy feeling and help heal any infection. "The discharge can be cleared away with warm water or an over-the-counter eye wash," says Dr. Lorimer. Use a soft, clean cloth or a cotton ball. Dip it in the water or eye wash, wring it out, then carefully

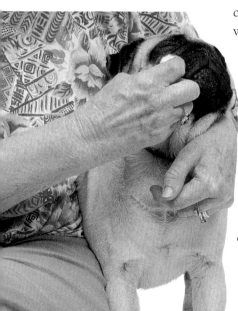

Keep your dog's eyes free of the muck and debris that normally collect in the corners by wiping them from the outside toward the center with a moistened cotton ball.

wipe around your dog's eyes, picking up all the discharge as you go. And there are a variety of cleaning products available from pet supply stores to tackle the stains that may be left on her fur by eye discharge.

Genetic Problems

There are a number of eye diseases caused by genetic problems in certain breeds. For example, most cataracts are seen in particular breeds of dogs, including the American Cocker Spaniel and Doberman Pinscher, and younger dogs rather than the gray set are affected. "If you see what you think are cataracts in an older dog, you're probably seeing nuclear lenticular sclerosis, which is a normal aging change," says Dr. Lorimer. If your dog develops cataracts and her vision is impaired, an operation will almost always resolve the problem.

Progressive retinal atrophy is another inherited disease. It involves a loss of function of the retina in the back of the eye, which typically results in blindness. The vision is slowly but progressively impaired, so you may not be aware that your dog has a problem at first. But while there is no effective treatment, most dogs will adapt to it with your help.

To help control these unfortunate problems in purebred dogs, the Canine Eye Registration Foundation (CERF) was formed, and veterinary ophthalmologists evaluate purebred dogs on an annual basis. If you are buying a purebred dog, always make sure that the parents are CERF-tested and cleared of any hereditary eye diseases, and get a copy of the results. If your dog's parents never had genetic eye problems, there's every chance your dog won't either.

The very best thing for your dog when she has a slight fever is time and lots of attention and comforting from you. Naturally, you'll see your vet if a fever is high or persists for more than a day or so.

FEVER

You can forget about putting your hand to your dog's forehead if she seems a little low. Time to reach for the rectal thermometer instead—see "Taking Your Dog's Temperature" on page 245 for tips on how it's done. A dog's normal temperature is between 99.5° and 102.5°F. If you get a reading of anything above 103°F, your dog has a fever.

The most common causes of fever include a viral or bacterial infection or a reaction to medication, says Dr. Mandelker. Occasionally, a fever indicates something more serious, such as an immune-system problem or even cancer, but in most cases it is just a temporary reminder that your dog isn't

feeling well and needs to take things easy. "If the fever persists for more than a day or if it is higher than 104°F, you should seek veterinary care without delay," advises Dr. Mandelker.

Easing Fever

Once you discover that your pet has a fever, there's absolutely no cause for panic. Just do what you would normally do if it were you that was running the temperature.

Ease off the activity. A dog with a fever isn't going to be in the mood for vigorous exercise or play. Let her mosey around at home, doing what she wants to do, which is likely resting in a quiet spot and sleeping it off.

Give her lots of liquids. Make sure you give her plenty of fluids, either by keeping her

Fever

water bowl full or, if she doesn't seem very interested in the liquid variety, by giving her ice cubes to chew or lick. Beef broth will be tastier to your dog and may tempt her to drink more, and sports drinks such as Gatorade are good because they help to replace lost electrolytes.

Do nice things for her. Spend some comforting quality time with your pet—everyone likes to feel pampered when they're not feeling well and you know your dog is no exception. Settle down with her and watch a favorite movie together or give her a nice massage to help her relax. If she thinks soaking in a bath is nice rather than nasty, then giving her a

bath in cool to lukewarm water is a comforting touch that could also help bring her temperature down.

Try some over-the-counter relief. Aspirin can be very effective for lowering your dog's temperature. Vets usually recommend giving one-quarter of a 325-milligram tablet of buffered aspirin once or twice a day. But to be safe, it's always a good idea to check with your vet before giving human medications to pets.

Monitor her progress. Recheck your dog's temperature every six hours or so, to see how she is doing and if the fever is coming down. If it persists for more than a day, see your vet right away.

FLATULENCE

Once your windy pet starts winding up, one of you will have to go outdoors before you forget what fresh air is. But the smell-driven separation doesn't have to be permanent. "Flatulence is caused when bacteria in the digestive tract break down food items and produce gas," says Dr. Mandelker.

No matter how disturbing flatulence may be to your nose, it is rarely a serious health concern, he adds. What's more, there are tactics you can use in the battle of the bad smells.

Eliminate the soy. Not all foods are created equal when it comes to creating gas. Although there may be a

Your dog can't help offending—flatulence is a normal part of digestion. But it doesn't always make her pleasant to be around. You could try a change of diet; it can be a good way to lessen those unwanted olfactory surprises.

genetic component to some of the fumes, with breeds such as Doberman Pinschers and Boxers being more windy than other breeds, a change in your dog's diet can really make quite a difference.

The culprit could be soybeans, which pack a lot of protein and can produce a lot of gas in dogs that find it hard to digest. So start by eliminating dry foods, which tend to be high in soy content, in favor of canned meat diets, advises Dr. Mandelker. Alternatively, go for low-soy dry foods, because soy really is no friend to the flatulent pet.

Add some enzymes. One option is to add digestive enzymes to her food before she eats. These enzymes will help digest the food before it is consumed, Dr. Mandelker explains. And better digested food means sweeter smelling air. You can get these digestive enzymes at health food stores and pharmacies.

Give her charcoal. You can try adding charcoal to your dog's diet to help detoxify some of the noxious gases while they are still inside the intestine. Activated charcoal is sold over the counter at most pharmacies. But use it only for two to three days at a time and follow your vet's advice on how much you give her, because charcoal can absorb nutrients as well as gas.

Exercise it out. Take your flatulent pet for lots of excursions out of doors. The activity will help move the gas through the intestines, so it may be released instead of building up inside. At the same time, exercise can stimulate your dog to have a bowel movement, which can also help reduce gas later on. And you and she will always appreciate the improvement in air quality outside.

FLEAS

When your dog has fleas you're going to know all about it, because for every flea that she's scratching at, there may be 100 more hanging around. But if you've ever had a problem with fleas (and let's face it, few dog owners haven't), you should be rejoicing at new developments that have allowed superior flea control without any exposure to harmful insecticides.

Fleas are not pushovers. It will take effort and persistence

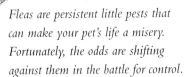

Fleas are persistent little pests that can make your pet's life a misery. Fortunately, the odds are shifting against them in the battle for control.

on your part before the whole gang is going to role over and die. But in the past decade, researchers have been focusing on the flea that actually affects dogs. Before that, all the advice and research was based on the wrong flea—the rat flea—whereas the flea that likes bugging your pooch is the dog flea. But now that we've got a positive ID on the right enemy, our lines of defense have really improved.

Fleas are not just biting pests; they also transmit a number of diseases to dogs, including tapeworm infection, typhus and tularemia. They can be intensely itchy and uncomfortable for your dog. And they're not always easy to see. Don't automatically think that all is well if

Fleas

you part the fur of your scratching dog and don't see fleas. She might only have a few fleas, which are going to be a little difficult for you to find. But her problem could be that she might be allergic to the flea saliva—and it only takes a few bites from a few fleas to send a dog with that kind of allergy into a mad scratching frenzy. If your dog is scratching and you can't find an obvious culprit, do her a favor and get her checked out by your vet.

Sprays are a great way to start your battle against fleas. Some sprays are safe to use even on puppies and pregnant dogs.

Fighting Fleas

There's no way you can get rid of all fleas in one hit. There simply isn't a product like that to be had. But you can achieve complete control in three to four weeks, the duration of the flea life cycle. It's not easy, but if you persist, the reward will be a flea-free pet and a flea-free household.

Spray once a month. Tackle the adult fleas first by treating your dog's coat with a flea spray. There is a wide range of insecticide sprays to choose from. Pyrethrins, made from chrysanthemums, are very safe but don't last very long. Some synthetic pyrethrins, such as permethrin, do slightly better, but seem to be toxic for other species, especially cats.

Now added to the armory of flea control for your pet are two products that offer safety to people and pets, effectiveness against adult fleas and once-a-month convenience.

Products such as Advantage, containing imidacloprid, kill almost all the fleas on your dog within 24 hours. Then there are the products such as Frontline, containing fipronil, which work against both fleas and ticks and are safe to use even on puppies and dogs that are pregnant. With these new products, you only need to spray the fur on your dog's back once a month to have the dog fleas dying in droves.

Collar the flea problem. Insecticides will certainly put adult fleas out of action, but they won't put a dent in the eggs, larvae and pupae in and around your house. So as soon as you let down your guard for a minute, there will be a whole new crop of adult fleas for you to have to do battle with. So your next tactic is to use something that will stop the fleas from reproducing.

One option is to put a special kind of flea collar on your dog,

Can Fleas Fly?

You're giving your dog's coat a going-over and there's a flea within fingernail reach. One minute it's there and the next it's gone. You'd swear it flew off—or at least that it had eaten super-strength jumping beans for breakfast.

Fleas are wingless insects, so they can't really fly. But that doesn't mean they can't cover a lot of territory. Fleas have a powerful elastic protein located above their hind legs, which permits them to jump 150 times their own length in a single bound. A critter less than a quarter-inch long leaping two and a half feet—that's the equivalent of a human jumping the length of three football fields. And if that isn't amazing enough, fleas can accelerate to 140 g's, which is 50 times the acceleration of the Space Shuttle after lift-off.

Maybe NASA could spend some time checking out fleas before they redesign their space program for the new millennium. But in the meantime, you've got to get the jump on those superbugs.

one containing an insect growth regulator (IGR) such as pyriproxyfen, methoprene or fenoxycarb. These are fake flea hormones that trick the flea eggs and larvae into drying out and dying. In fact, an IGR-laced collar is a bit like birth control for fleas.

The collars are very safe and will work well against your dog's flea population for as long as the label indicates.

Choose a collar carefully. There are many other kinds of collars, but they may not be as effective. Traditional flea collars wrap some pretty potent insecticides around your dog's neck, yet they don't seem very helpful, especially when fighting a heavy infestation. They will kill some fleas, but they won't touch any larvae or eggs.

Electronic flea collars have not yet been proved effective

and make a buzzing sound in your dog's ear all day—you can't hear it, but your dog can. So why pay good money to drive your dog crazy?

Give her a pill. Another way to stop flea eggs and larvae before they get started is with a product called Program. It contains a compound called lufenuron, which stops the fleas' hard shell from developing. Without that protective coating, the fleas die.

This product, which you can get from your vet, is given orally just once a month. Lufenuron has also been combined with a heartworm preventive medicine in a product called Sentinel, so if you live in an area that's bad for heartworm, you might want to consider this optional extra.

Go for a good combination. In order to control fleas it's important to go after the adults and the eggs and larvae at the same time. So whichever product you choose for killing the eggs, be sure to also use an adult-only product to hit the grown-ups from all sides.

Keep her combed. Use a flea comb regularly to stop a possible flea infestation in its tracks. This type of comb is

Fleas

not expensive, and if you comb her down carefully for five minutes every day, you'll get those little critters leaping out of their hiding places. Their favorite dens are the middle of the back, the base of the tail, the back of the neck, the armpits and the groin region.

Dip the comb in a little jar of rubbing alcohol and the fleas will drown instantly. (Even if you don't get any fleas, you might see little comma-shaped pieces of dirt on the skin, which are actually flea feces. If your comb is fine enough, you will pick up some of it.) Always do this outside—if you don't catch the fleas as they jump ship, it's better they end up in the grass than on your carpet.

The bath is optional. A bath will have her current crop of fleas jumping overboard real fast, but there will soon be others to take their place. And while flea shampoos do kill fleas, they offer no residual protection. As soon as the shampoo is rinsed away, all that protection slides down the drain. Wash your dog to keep her clean, but you can really only regard bathtime as a very short-term solution in your fight against fleas.

A short coat, such as this Golden Labrador's, is easy to comb with a fine-toothed flea comb like those shown at right. As well as getting rid of fleas, it will help remove dirt.

Suck them in, suck them up. Once you've treated your dog, it's time to turn your attention to the flea population in the house. Go at them with the vacuum once a week, although you might want to do high pet-traffic areas more frequently, especially around her bed. Eggs and larvae will be sucked out of the carpet, the cracks and any other favorite flea spots and into the vacuum bag. You can then take the bag out of your cleaner and pop it—fleas, dirt, eggs and all—into a plastic bag and knot it closed tight, never to be heard from again.

Your vacuuming has an added bonus—aside from your reputation for fine housecleaning. The vibrations stimulate hiding fleas to come out into the open, where they are more susceptible to any sprays that you might want to use.

Spray indoors. Select only safe, nontoxic insecticide sprays, such as pyrethrin, to target adult fleas in the house. Handheld sprayers are the most convenient, because you can concentrate on favorite flea spots as well as getting under couches and beds.

Foggers are easy to use but don't get to all the places fleas hide. And the chemicals also land on surfaces such as tables, kitchen counters and beds, where you definitely don't want them, fleas or no fleas.

Put out some powder.
Polyborate (a cousin of borax) is a powder for your house that gives flea control for up to a year, depending on your floor surface. Get the pest-control professionals in to apply it.

Have weekly wash days. Launder your dog's bedding once a week to wash away any unwanted guests. Use the warmest temperature the fabric can stand—and the fleas can't.

Work on the yard. Banishing fleas from your yard isn't the nightmare you might imagine. For a start, they can't survive out in the middle of the yard because sunlight kills them— fleas like shade, humidity and controlled temperatures.

If you think your yard is a potential haven for fleas, you could spray around the garden edges, doghouse and patio with chemicals such as diazinon, which aren't broken down by sunlight. Or you could water your yard with worms.

Yes, you did read correctly. You can now purchase microscopic worms called nematodes from pet supply and garden stores. They attack flea larvae and cocoons without harming other good-guy insects. Apply them to your lawns, gardens and even sand by putting them in a hose sprayer and "watering" away. All you then need to do is wet the area weekly and reapply the worms every month until the fleas are all gone—at which point the worms will go, too.

FOOD ALLERGIES AND INTOLERANCE

We often think of food allergies and food intolerance as being the same. They both cause your dog to have an adverse reaction, but they're not quite identical. Your dog has a food allergy when her immune system reacts against certain ingredients in her chow, like soy protein.

A food intolerance, on the other hand, doesn't affect the immune system at all. Instead, it occurs when certain ingredients in the food (lactose is a common offender) upset the stomach, intestines or another part of the body.

While the underlying causes are different, food allergies and food intolerances are similar in that they can make your dog feel miserable. Occasionally, it's as simple as a dog eating her food, then bringing it back up again real quick. But usually, the link isn't quite so obvious. The food could cause rashes, digestive difficulties, asthma-like symptoms, lots of itching and scratching or abnormal behavior, or all sorts of other problems that have absolutely nothing to do with mealtime— on the surface.

Suppose, for example, your dog has a history of recurrent ear infections. There's a possibility that a food allergy could be playing a role in her discomfort. An adverse reaction to food isn't an easy thing to detect, but it will be worth it, for your dog's health and happiness, if you can find out for sure. Then you can stop feeding her the usual and find a new diet that suits her better. Your vet will help you here.

Fixing Food Allergies

You can't cure a food allergy or intolerance, but you can fix the problem by finding out what food disagrees with your dog. To do this, you'll need the advice and guidance of your vet and the cooperation of your pet—not too difficult since her main role will be eating. Oh, and you'll need time and patience, since it can take

Food Allergies and Intolerance

weeks or even months to make the diagnosis. But the results can really make it worthwhile.

Do an elimination diet. The only way to know for sure what food gives your dog a bad reaction is to eliminate it from her diet for one to two months to see if she improves. But there are many ingredients in her food and you don't know which particular one has to go.

"The only way to find out is to take her off everything she usually eats and restrict her diet to something she's never been exposed to," says veterinarian Dr. Stephen Waisglass. This is based on the simple rule about allergies: You can't be allergic to something you've never eaten before—allergies build up over time.

So if your dog dramatically improves on her elimination diet and then she gets worse again when you start her back on the usual, you know the problem is in the food. Not the brand of food but the ingredients. And not the quality of the ingredients, just the actual ingredients. If she's allergic to beef, it doesn't matter if it's a sirloin steak or a fast-food hamburger—they'll both set her symptoms going again.

While tricky to track down, food allergies and intolerances are easy to treat—you simply eliminate the culprit food from your dog's bowl for ever more.

Feed her new foods. Your vet will recommend a diet specially designed for your dog. Her test diet will probably consist of a meat source such as lamb, rabbit or venison, combined with a carbohydrate like rice or potatoes. There's nothing magical about any of these ingredients, except that they must be new to your dog. If there's lamb in the food your dog normally eats, lamb is out and something else is in.

Your vet will also possibly explain to you that the best test diets are homemade. While there are commercially prepared foods that you could use—check with your vet about which ones—a home-made elimination diet has the advantage of giving you total control over what goes into your dog's stomach. She must be fed this for at least a month, preferably two, before you can be certain of the results.

Conducting an elimination diet can be hard work. The up side is that your dog will really appreciate your efforts—after all, there's nothing like a home-cooked meal to pique a dog's interest. And it will all be worthwhile when your dog improves on her special trial food, because you'll know for sure that it is food that is contributing to her problems.

If she doesn't improve, at least you know that food isn't the cause of her recurring complaint. With your mind set at rest on that score, you and your vet can set about tracking down clues and looking for other potential suspects.

Challenge the results. If your dog's symptoms have

cleared up while she's been on her elimination diet, you will know that food is the problem. But what kind of food? That is the 60-million-dollar question. To solve the mystery, you have to "challenge" the results. Reintroduce common foods to her diet, one at a time, to find out which one makes her react.

It could be beef, chicken, soy (add some tofu) or corn, so test for all of these individually, one every five to seven days. The food that makes her symptoms come back is the food that she has the allergy or intolerance to, and that's the food you'll want to ban from her bowl from now on.

Find the food for her. You've hit the jackpot when it comes to successful treatment, because you can fix her problem 100 percent, and no drugs are needed. If it turns out your dog is allergic to soy, for example, just buy a dog food that is soy-free. Got a problem with lactose? Give her a food that contains no dairy products, which are high in lactose. Or at least give her lactase supplements, which will help her digest the lactose found in dairy foods. There are plenty of

dog foods on the market, so once you know which ingredients you need to avoid, finding the food for your dog should be no problem.

Be careful with a home-cooked diet. If you want to continue feeding your dog home-cooked meals (minus the food she reacts to, of course), make sure you get a good recipe from your vet that is properly balanced to meet your dog's nutritional needs. The test diet isn't well-balanced and will cause deficiencies if she stays on it for too long.

Hip Dysplasia

Certain dogs have hips that don't fit together as snugly as they should. This is an inherited condition, called hip dysplasia, that can be pretty hard on a dog because it makes her hind legs sore and stiff, and getting about can be a real chore. Some breeds are more susceptible than others.

Although puppies aren't born with hip dysplasia, they may be born with a tendency to develop it. The changes can happen so gradually that sometimes

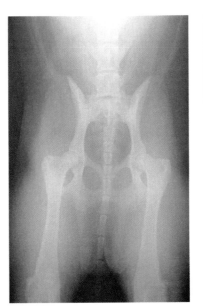 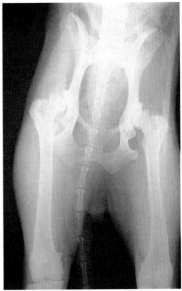

These x-rays show how the head of the thigh bone fits snugly into the socket of the hip bone in the normal dog on the left, and how prone it is to slipping out of place in the dog with hip dysplasia on the right.

Hip Dysplasia

they aren't evident until she is one to two years of age. Over time, the "loose" hip joints can cause the bones to wear, leading to a painful form of arthritis.

Any dog can develop hip dysplasia, and not just the large breeds, as is often thought— many smaller dogs get it, too. Veterinarians often treat it with drugs or even surgery. But there are a number of preventive strategies, as well as some effective home-care treatments, that can also be very helpful.

Helping the Hips

If your dog is one of those breeds that is particularly prone to hip dysplasia, it's important to do everything you can to prevent it. Here's what vets recommend you do while she is still a pup to improve the situation dramatically.

Keep her light on her feet. You want to feed your fast-growing pup well so she does not get hungry, but be very careful not to overdo it. A pup that is at risk for hip dysplasia will do much better if she is lean rather than plump. You don't want her to be carrying extra weight around, because that will put extra stress and strain on her hips.

Feed your pup small amounts of food several times daily. And don't leave the bowl on the floor for longer than 15 minutes, as this will just encourage her to overeat.

Provide low-mineral meals. If your dog is at risk for developing hip dysplasia, a low-mineral diet will be the best one for her because it will contain less calcium and may also have a better "balance" of electrolytes than usual. There are several such diets available by prescription. Your vet will typically recommend this type of food until your dog has finished all her growing.

Stay away from calcium supplements. Kids need calcium for growing bones, so they get to drink lots of milk. Puppies need calcium for their growing bones, too, but that doesn't mean they need calcium supplements. In fact, they are a definite no-no for young, rapidly growing, large dogs such as Doberman Pinschers, Great Danes and Retrievers.

Calcium supplementation actually interferes with cartilage and bones developing normally in large dogs. Puppy foods already contain lots of calcium, and additional supplementation only causes problems.

Give her easy exercise. Exercise is important because it strengthens muscles around the hip joints, which helps keep them stable. But don't overdo it because that could stress the

Swimming is very good exercise for dogs that are experiencing pain and problems with their hips, because the muscles are getting a workout while the water supports the body weight. Always make sure that your dog is warm and dry afterward, though.

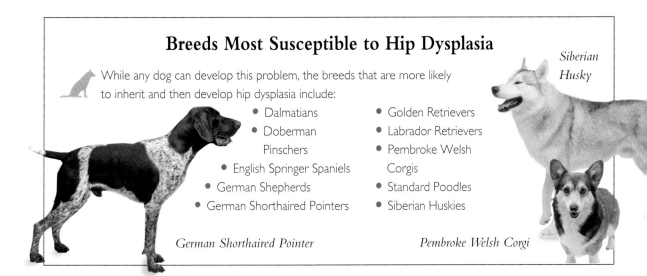

Breeds Most Susceptible to Hip Dysplasia

While any dog can develop this problem, the breeds that are more likely to inherit and then develop hip dysplasia include:

- Dalmatians
- Doberman Pinschers
- English Springer Spaniels
- German Shepherds
- German Shorthaired Pointers
- Golden Retrievers
- Labrador Retrievers
- Pembroke Welsh Corgis
- Standard Poodles
- Siberian Huskies

Siberian Husky

German Shorthaired Pointer

Pembroke Welsh Corgi

already abnormal hip joints and make matters worse.

Make her exercise sessions regular and aerobic, but not haphazard. Opt for a two-mile walk on a leash rather than catching Frisbees in the park. Swimming, too, is a great way of keeping her toned—the water supports her weight and reduces wear and tear on joints.

Easing the Aches

If your pet has already developed signs of hip dysplasia, then some of same things that help prevent it can also help relieve the aches. For a start, make sure you keep her lean, which will lighten the load on her hip joints. And do keep her moving, gently. A 20-minute walk twice a day will do her a lot of good. If she's actually hurting, take a day off. Rest as well as exercise can help the hips feel better.

Your vet may also recommend giving your dog over-the-counter medications to relieve pain and inflammation. Aspirin can be very effective, says Dr. Mandelker. So can carprofen, a prescription drug that tends to cause fewer side effects than aspirin does.

In addition, make sure that her bed is in a warm, dry place. Give her a gentle massage around the hip joints to relax the area and give her some pleasant relief. To learn more about help for sore hips, see "Arthritis" on page 298.

Avoiding Hip Dysplasia

Since hip dysplasia is an inherited problem, certain breeds of dogs are much more prone to it than others. And both large breeds and many small dogs can be affected.

Before you fall in love with an adorable ball of fluff, make sure she comes from a family with no history of hip dysplasia for at least three generations.

Good breeders will be able to provide certification—either from the Orthopedic Foundation for Animals or the Institute for Genetic Disease Control in Animals—proving that hip dysplasia doesn't run in your pup's family. This is the best insurance you can get that your pup won't ever be affected.

HOT SPOTS

The last time you looked, your dog had a full coat of fur. But all of a sudden, a bare spot has appeared and her skin looks sore and inflamed. Worse, the spot appears to be growing. What's going on?

Your dog could have a hot spot, a condition vets call pyotraumatic dermatitis. Hot spots are painful sores that appear suddenly on a dog's body, mostly behind the ears and around the tail.

Usually, they occur when a dog has been scratching, biting or licking because she's itchy from an allergy or some other irritation, says Dr. Waisglass. Why they appear the way they do is still a mystery. Pets with more dense coats seem more likely to get hot spots, especially in humid conditions, adds Dr. Waisglass.

Although hot spots look scary, only the top layers of skin are affected and they heal without leaving scars. They are rarely anything to worry about. Until they heal, however, they can be painful. The sooner you get rid of them, the happier your dog will be.

Healing Hot Spots

Your vet may recommend a short-acting cortisone spray or gel to relieve the itch of hot spots. In most cases, however, all you need to do is keep the area clean and use home remedies to ease the pain. With these simple treatments, most hot spots will heal by themselves within a week.

Begin with a trim. The first thing to do for hot spots is to trim the fur around the area, which will make it easier to keep clean. Trim away from the sore until you reach an area of normal skin. If you have an electric trimmer, you can shave the area completely. But keep in mind that hot spots are painful and your dog is likely to struggle a bit. You'll want to be careful not to cut or scrape her skin while giving the trim.

Give her a bath. A nice cool bath with some Epsom salts or Burow's solution will relieve the pain of hot spots and soothe away some of the itchiness. It will also get the area clean. Follow the instructions for how much to add to her

One very effective way to stop your dog from biting at a hot spot is to have her wear an Elizabethan collar until the wound has healed.

bath. And it's okay to give her a bath as often as she needs one to feel comfortable.

Apply an antiseptic. After cleaning the hot spot, gently apply an antiseptic, such as chlorhexidine or povidone-iodine. This will prevent the infection from spreading and help the hot spot to heal more quickly. Don't use isopropyl alcohol—it is excruciatingly painful on an open wound.

Avoid using any kind of ointment or moisturizer, as this could seal in the infection and force it to go deeper into the skin. Stick with water-soluble sprays or gels only, and the hot spot will soon be gone.

Keep it open. A hot spot that is exposed to air will dry up and heal on its own much better. Covering it with a bandage might seem like the obvious way to keep it clean, especially if your dog won't leave the hot spot alone, but in fact that's not the case.

If you've done everything you can to relieve the pain but your dog is still gnawing or scratching the sore, you may want to restrain her with an Elizabethan collar, a collarlike ring that goes around her neck, which will prevent her from reaching the hot spot, explains Dr. Waisglass.

You can get an Elizabethan collar from pet supply stores or veterinary offices. Or if you want to make your own, see "How to Make an Elizabethan Collar" on page 364.

ITCHING

When you think of things that make you itch, you possibly think of mosquito bites and poison ivy. While these itch-inducing entities do affect dogs, they are nowhere near as common a cause for dogs as they are for people.

Even without mosquitoes and poison ivy, there are plenty of reasons for a dog to itch—more than 500 different reasons, in fact. When your dog is scratching all the time, it's important to figure out what's bothering her. That's not always so easy to do. While there are some very common causes of canine scratching, it can sometimes take a lot of detective work to figure out what the problem really is.

Easing the Itch

Your dog doesn't really care what's causing the itching.

While you're figuring out how to stop the problem for good, all she wants is some immediate relief. Here's what the experts recommend you do.

Bathe her regularly. It may be a little labor-intensive, but frequent baths are the fastest way to give your itchy dog some relief when she needs it. It's best to use cool water—warm water will only make the itch worse. Adding some Epsom salts, colloidal oatmeal (like Aveeno) or baking soda to the water will increase the soothing effects.

Soaking your dog for five to ten minutes can provide temporary relief that will last from a few hours to a few days. After bathing, pat your dog dry with a fluffy towel. Don't use a hair dryer unless it has a cool setting. Warming the skin will only increase her desire to scratch, so keep things soothing by keeping it cool.

Give her fatty acids. Research has shown that special fatty acids found in either marine oils or evening primrose oil can be very effective for easing itching, so you could try her on some fatty acid supplements for a little relief. The supplements, available at pet

Itching

If, like this Beagle, your dog is being driven crazy with an itch, the first thing to do is to work out the cause. It's not always a flea. There are hundreds of other reasons why she may be scratching and biting herself to pieces.

supply stores, will usually need to be given for several weeks before your dog will start to feel the benefits. So they are more useful for easing long-term problems than for on-again, off-again irritations.

Try an antihistamine. Vets sometimes recommend giving itchy dogs an over-the-counter antihistamine. These are most effective for easing short-term itches—say from an insect bite or a flare-up of hay fever. Oral antihistamines that will do the job include clemastine (Tavist), chlorpheniramine (Chlor-Trimeton) and diphenhydramine (Benadryl). Your vet will tell you what dose to use.

Take fast action. Dogs will occasionally get itchy after contact with something that irritates the skin, like poison ivy. This is often on their bellies, where there isn't a lot of fur to protect them.

To ease this kind of itching, wash the area thoroughly with a gentle skin cleanser, then apply a mild cortisone ointment, explains Dr. Waisglass. "Select a product available over-the-counter with 1 percent or less hydrocortisone, such as Cortaid," he adds.

Stop bugs from biting. Like people, dogs can get very itchy from insect bites and stings. When you're visiting bug-filled areas, vets often recommend applying mosquito repellents containing DEET. Just be sure to follow your vet's instructions exactly because these products can be dangerous if not used in the right way, says Dr. Waisglass.

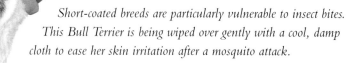

Short-coated breeds are particularly vulnerable to insect bites. This Bull Terrier is being wiped over gently with a cool, damp cloth to ease her skin irritation after a mosquito attack.

The Worst Offenders

There are literally hundreds of itchy things that can set your dog's hind leg in motion. Here are the ten most common reasons for a dog to have a good scratch.

1. Fleas
2. Airborne allergens like pollen, which result in hay fever
3. Parasites, such as ear mites, scabies or cheyletiellosis, also known as walking dandruff
4. Skin infections caused by bacteria
5. Ticks and lice
6. Food allergies
7. Fungal infections, including yeast infections
8. Seborrhea
9. Contact allergies
10. Whole-body illnesses, such as liver disease, immune-system problems and some cancers

When bites do occur, the ears and belly suffer the most because these are the areas where there is less hair to protect the skin from marauding insects. You can treat the bites by bathing them with cool water, following up with a soothing spray of witch hazel. In fact, witch hazel will make any kind of itch feel better. You can also use hydrocortisone ointment or try oral antihistamines to give your dog some immediate relief.

LICKING

Just as humans use a washcloth and soap, dogs will lick in order to keep themselves clean. But sometimes they go overboard and lick themselves for hours at a time. This can lead to hair loss, infection or damage to the skin.

There are many different reasons for excessive licking. The most common reason is that the skin is itchy or irritated and your dog is licking for a little relief—in a sense, it's just another kind of scratching. The second most common reason is behavioral—your dog could be stressed or upset and all this repetitive licking is her way of coping.

Licking for Relief

When your dog really starts to lick or chew at herself, the first thing you need to consider is if she has a pain, itch or irritation in that area. Pay particular attention to where she licks.

A dog that licks her front paws likely has allergies from inhaling dust or pollens—the canine version of hay fever. A dog with fleas often licks and chews at her hindquarters, which is a very popular flea meeting spot. This isn't hard science, but you will find it is borne out in most instances. The exception is the dog that licks his genitals—this is apparently just for recreation.

It's usually not difficult to stop the constant licking, once your vet has discovered the cause of the problem. If fleas or other parasites are the culprit, you'll need to mount a vigorous attack on the offending critters. Airborne allergens or food allergies will take time,

Licking

When to See the Vet

It doesn't happen often, but sometimes dogs will lick for so long that they create a large, open wound—a condition vets call acral lick dermatitis or lick granuloma. These wounds can be extremely serious and often get infected. So if your dog is licking a lot and starting to get a sore, you need to call your vet right away.

Why dogs do this isn't known—the condition has perplexed vets for years. Some believe it is a skin problem, others that it is a behavioral problem, and still others that there is a problem with the nerve endings that causes dogs to experience "phantom" pain.

Vets occasionally recommend that dogs with lick granulomas wear an Elizabethan collar, which will prevent them from worrying the wound. When the wound heals and you take the collar off, however, dogs will often go right back to licking. Bitter-tasting sprays aren't even a mild deterrent on your dog when it comes to a lick granuloma.

However, there are a number of medications that can help stop lick granulomas for good. A lot of different drugs seem to work for different dogs. Some dogs respond to long-term antibiotic therapy, some to cortisone and some to anti-anxiety medications. It may take a little time for your vet to find the solution that works best for your dog.

effort and careful monitoring to discover, but when you know what the allergen is, you can take steps so that she avoids it altogether or at least has minimal contact. Your vet will advise you on the best course of treatment.

And if your dog needs a little temporary relief while you're coming up with the long-term solution, try easing the irritation with cool-water baths, soothing witch hazel sprays, mild cortisone creams or anti-histamines—speak to your vet to see what he recommends. And for more information, see "Itching" on page 335.

Help for Stress

During stressful situations dogs will sometimes get into licking cycles, says Wayne Hunthausen, D.V.M., an animal behaviorist in private practice in Westwood, Kansas, and co-author of *Practitioner's Guide to Pet Behavior Problems.*

Maybe you've just moved to a new home and all your dog's familiar routines and haunts suddenly disappear. Or a new baby in the family means you can't give your dog as much attention as usual. She may cope by licking herself. In the future, she may start licking even when she's not truly upset but simply because her emotions are running high, explains Dr. Hunthausen. You really want to nip this negative behavior in the bud, before she decides it's the only way to get through the day.

Behavioral drugs such as fluoxetine (Prozac) have been found to be very helpful for treating licking, says Dr. Hunthausen. But whatever drug therapy your vet prescribes, it's also important to reduce the stress in your dog's life. If there have been sudden changes, spend a little extra quality time with her, reassuring her and making her feel okay.

Maybe she's licking herself just because she's got nothing better to do with her time. Take her out for at least two brisk walks each day and play a

Mange

favorite game—be it fetch, catch the Frisbee, running around the yard or whatever works for her—to help channel some of her excess energy away from licking.

As a last resort, you may want to try a little taste dissuasion. Get a bitter-tasting spray or anti-licking ointment from the pet supply store and apply it to the sites that attract all the tongue action. Your dog may decide that the bad tastes take all the fun out of licking and that it's better to leave her skin alone.

Licking Wounds

Dogs may lick sores on their skin, whether or not they are painful. "We assume that this licking is a way that dogs have of physically cleaning the wound and trying to keep it dry and parasite-free," says animal behaviorist Dr. Gary Landsberg. It could also help in soothing away any pain, although dogs will lick at sores that aren't painful, too.

Licking in moderation may be doing your dog's wound some good. "Recent research has shown that dog saliva does have some healing properties," says Lynn M. Harpold, D.V.M.,

If your dog gets a case of mange from scabies mites, she'll need more relief than a good roll in the grass offers. Scabies is a truly itch-inducing condition, but your vet will be able to treat it quite easily.

a veterinarian in private practice in Mesa, Arizona. But your dog's licking is no substitute for proper medical care, she adds. Indeed, your dog could be giving herself too much of a good thing.

Excessive licking and worrying at a wound can sometimes actually prevent it from healing, and you might need to stop her from getting at the wound by putting an Elizabethan collar around her neck. You can either buy one of these from a pet supply store or your local veterinary office, or you can make one yourself. To learn how this is done, see "How to Make an Elizabethan Collar" on page 364.

MANGE

Mange can make a dog look pretty sad and neglected, as if

she got into a fight with a closet full of moths—and the moths won. It might cause hairless patches, leave red open sores, look like dandruff, or it could be unbearably itchy, depending on the type of mange it is. Mange comes in many different forms—the most common are scabies, cheyletiellosis and demodectic mange. Ear mites cause another form of mange. In fact each type of mange is caused by different kinds of mites that dwell on or in the skin. However, your vet will need to first diagnose the type of mange that your dog has, and the treatment will be different depending on what type it is.

Scabies

This is the itchiest condition known to dogs—minuscule scabies mites that burrow into

Mange

the skin and lay their eggs are enough to drive a dog crazy. Dogs often develop a skin sensitivity to the mites, which makes the itching even worse. Scabies is highly contagious and the mites are easily passed from dog to dog.

Scabies is relatively easy to treat. Most dogs will be mite-free within six weeks and the itches will have eased off after 10 to 14 days, regardless of which treatment you opt for. Medicated dips are one easy solution. Washing your dog with lime and sulfur medications diluted with water not only kills the mites but also eases the itching.

However, your vet will probably give your dog a series of injections, as this is the most efficient way to eliminate these pesky critters. When they go, the itch goes. While not licensed for the purpose, some flea control products, such as Frontline, also seem to be effective against scabies.

Even when you successfully treat scabies, your dog can pick up a new infestation the next time she comes into contact with a dog with scabies on board. It pays to know who your dog's friends are—and to

keep her away from any balding or scratchy canines. It also pays to treat all your pets, not just the one with the infestation, because chances are if one pet has it, the others will also have it quite soon.

Be careful how close you get to your dog while she has scabies because it can be contagious to people, too. The mites can bite, especially if they come in direct contact with your skin. You might notice itchy patches between your fingers or around the belt line, but fortunately, biting is about all they can do to you.

The mites that cause scabies in dogs can't live and reproduce on people, so once your dog is successfully treated, the mites will be gone from you, too—no dips, shots or other treatments necessary.

Cheyletiellosis

This type of mange is courtesy of a white, crablike mite that goes by the name of Cheyletiella. It's just large enough to be seen by a keen eye and has been affectionately dubbed "walking dandruff." Although not as itch-provoking as scabies, cheyletiellosis will make most dogs scratch. And, like

scabies, it is passed from pet to pet—your dog will even share these babies with you if you don't keep a safe distance.

Treatment options are the same as for scabies. Either a medicated dip once a week or a series of injections administered by your vet will stop the mites in their tracks. The problem is usually resolved within two to six weeks. However, these mites can survive in the environment for a few days, so it's important to clean the house thoroughly and wash your dog's bedding in hot water to prevent any late-comers from getting on board.

As a parting shot, spraying her bedding and the house with a flea control spray will also help kill the mites.

Demodectic Mange

Demodectic mange, or demodicosis, is caused by a small, cigar-shaped mite that lives in the hair follicles. These mites are "residents" that normally live on a dog's skin—they live on people's skin, too, which means they're not contagious. The mites cause no problems for the dog while her immune system is functioning okay. But if she becomes run down or her immune system gets overloaded or develops some kind of defect, it can't keep things under control and there's a sudden explosion in the mite population. The mites crowd the hair follicles and eventually rupture them, causing her hair to fall out and her skin to become infected.

The good news is that once your dog's immune system is restored to health, the mite problem will disappear. In about 90 percent of cases, if you just give it time, the mange will cure itself. But in 10 percent of cases, the immune system doesn't recover unaided. So if the mange does not improve after a month or if you notice that it is actually getting worse, then you'll need your vet's help. Your dog will need treatment to kill the mites and control the infections.

And you can help her heal herself. "Your dog's immune system cannot be fully dedicated to getting rid of the mites if it has too many other tasks to address," advises Dr. Waisglass.

"Make sure that your pet is free of internal parasites, including heartworm, and that you are feeding her a balanced, wholesome diet," he advises.

In a similar fashion, you can offer her other supportive care—try to reduce her stress levels by eliminating situations that may be upsetting or unsettling to her, and make sure that she gets plenty of fresh air and exercise.

Frequent bathing with a gentle antiseptic solution, such as chlorhexidine, or a product like benzoyl peroxide, which flushes out the hair follicles, can be useful, too. However, always check this with your vet first, advises Dr. Waisglass, so you are aware of any special dosage or usage instructions. For example, treatments with dips that have amitraz (Mitaban) require that you don't get your pet wet between therapies. Used properly, these medications will help your dog to lighten her mange-mite load.

Some breeds shed heavily at certain times of year. Minimize the vacuuming by brushing your dog with a slicker brush at least once every day during her molting seasons.

SHEDDING

Do you sometimes feel as if your dog is shedding so much, you could knit yourself a sweater with her hair? When it comes to hair loss, dogs sure have a lot of hair to get rid of, but there's usually nothing abnormal about it.

Shedding is a normal part of the cycle of your dog's hair growth. "The amount of normal shedding that a pet does is very much dependent on the type of coat she has, genetics

Shedding

and the environment in which she lives," says Dr. Waisglass. Most outdoor dogs have a shedding season in the spring as their "winter" coats are lost. However, if your dog is an indoor pooch, she possibly won't be outside long enough for her body to register the change in seasons, so she will shed all year round.

All dogs shed, some more than others—unless they're one of the few hairless breeds with absolutely nothing to lose. Longhaired dogs might appear to shed more, but really it's just the length of their hair that gives that illusion. Dogs that really do shed the most include Collies, Dalmatians, German Shepherds and Samoyeds. If you want a dog that loses hair lightly, consider a Poodle, Bichon Frise or maybe an Old English Sheepdog.

Even though shedding is completely normal, occasionally dogs will begin losing much more hair than they usually do. When bald patches begin showing through the fur, there's probably something wrong and you need to visit your vet right away for diagnosis and treatment. There are physical problems that can cause dogs to lose abnormal amounts of hair, including mange, ringworm, skin infections, stress and even cancer. But just because your pet is getting older, she shouldn't be losing her hair. "It isn't normal for the coat to thin out as a pet ages," says Dr. Waisglass.

Help for Hair Loss

Nature intended for your dog to shed and there isn't anything you can do to stop it. But if your dog is a big shedder, you can make it less of a problem. Forget drugs or nutritional supplements. The best way to handle excessive shedding is simply to remove dead hair before it deposits itself on your clothes, carpets and furniture.

To get rid of the dead hair from your dog's coat, the thing to do is to brush her once a day, especially during the shedding season. There are a variety of grooming tools that you can use, from slicker brushes to combs specially designed to remove loose hair.

Your groomer or your vet will recommend the tools and techniques that will work best with your dog's coat. For more information about your dog's particular coat and its requirements, see "How to Groom" on page 398.

Don't be surprised if you fill a garbage bag or two with hair on your first serious salon session. You may well think there's more hair in the bags than there is left on your dog. But remember, if the hair loss is abnormal, she would have bald spots. Otherwise, keep brushing until her coat feels soft and clean.

SUNBURN

Most dogs, like most people, enjoy sunny weather. They're happy to walk, romp, play and take their afternoon siestas in the bright sunlight.

Dogs are less likely than humans to get sunburn because they have all that insulating fur to protect them from too much ultraviolet light. But there are places where the fur doesn't reach. Take a good look at your dog and you can probably guess where she is most likely to turn pink: the nose, the tips of the ears (especially if she has upright ears) and the belly. So be careful with these sparsely haired areas.

Also, those dogs with fair skin and short hair will need

extra protection from the sun's rays—Dalmatians, white Bull Terriers and American Staffordshire Terriers, German Shorthaired Pointers, white Boxers, Whippets and Beagles all need to be more sun-shy than other canines. And Australian Shepherds have a tendency to get sunburned on their pale noses.

Sun-damaged skin is not a trifling matter. It's not just the pain of feeling like a boiled lobster. There's also the possibility of skin cancer, and some diseases, such as lupus erythematosus, are aggravated by too much sun exposure. You don't need to go crazy with sun protection, but it pays to be safe, particularly if the furry sun worshipper in your household is a pale-skinned one.

Dealing with Sunburn

When you need to soothe your pet's heated skin or you want to make sure you protect her from the sun's rays, here's what vets advise.

Offer her relief. Spray her with a squirt bottle. The water will cool down her burnt bits. Mix in some witch hazel to give her a little bit of extra help. Or let her soak in a cool bath—if you dissolve some baking soda in it, she will find it especially soothing.

There are also over-the-counter sprays, such as Solarcaine and Lanacane, which contain a local anesthetic to cut out any pain she may be feeling. And don't forget the healing qualities of aloe vera. You can get a cream or lotion from your pharmacy and gently apply this, or if you have an aloe vera plant handy, simply break off a leaf and squeeze out the gel onto the affected area.

Spread on a sunscreen. Sunscreens are a definite plus, especially the kinds that don't wear off in the water—or get licked off. "Those dogs that are at risk for sunburn can really benefit from sun protection," says Dr. Waisglass. Even if

It's best to avoid direct sun during the middle of the day. Although your dog has a fur coat to protect her, certain areas, such as her nose, ears and belly, are still very vulnerable to sunburn.

Sunburn

your dog isn't fair-skinned, if she is going to spend a lot of time in the sun, you may want to give her ears and nose a little extra help.

There aren't any hard and fast rules when it comes to sunscreens, but look for one with an SPF (sun-protection factor) of at least 15—the higher the SPF, the more protection she gets. Also, it mustn't contain an ingredient called PABA, because if your dog licks the sunscreen off—and chances are she eventually will—the PABA can be dangerous. Human sunscreens are fine, although there are now some canine products available, too.

Cover her up. A T-shirt could be the answer for those canine sunbathers with pale skin or those that like to expose their sensitive bellies. So, if your dog will allow it, pop the neck opening over her head, put her front legs through the armholes and pull the T-shirt down over her body.

Offer the shady option. Make sure that when your pet wants to rest in the shade, she can—whether it be in the shade of a tree, fence or some other covering. If she spends her days outdoors, she should

always have access to her own insulated doghouse.

Remember, too, that during summer you should avoid having her out in the sun for very long during the hottest time of the day, when the sun is at its fiercest—from ten in the morning until about three in the afternoon.

TICKS

Ticks are one of life's little nasties. These ugly parasites latch on to whatever skin is going by, then dig their heads in and start sucking up blood—their food of choice. During feeding, ticks can swell up to more than 50 times their normal size. But that's not their only disgusting feature. They also carry diseases, such as Lyme disease, tick fever, Rocky Mountain spotted fever, encephalitis, tick paralysis and a new, potentially fatal, illness called hepatozoonosis.

There are lots of different kinds of ticks and not all of them spread the same diseases, but if you find a tick on your dog, you can bet it's up to no good. That makes tick control and tick patrol a must if you live in or visit a part of the

This eastern wood tick is just one of many species that attach themselves to warm-blooded animals for a free meal of blood. As if that weren't bad enough, they also pass some fairly nasty diseases on to their hosts.

country where ticks are common. It is important to remove all ticks as quickly as possible to reduce the risk of them spreading disease. It takes about 24 to 72 hours for ticks to transfer their diseases, so that gives you a good window of opportunity to intervene.

Tackling Ticks

Ticks are bad news, but there are ways to get rid of the pesky little suckers.

Do a tick check. Ticks like wooded or grassy areas, so whenever you come back from an outing through this type of vegetation, take the time to do a head-to-toe search through your dog's fur. Ticks tend to congregate in and around a dog's ears, between her toes and around her head and neck. But don't stop there—check her entire body.

Get rid of it quickly. When you come across a feeding tick, you want to remove it quickly but carefully. Quickly, because the longer the tick feeds, the more chance it has of infecting your pet with a disease. Carefully, because you want to pull out the whole tick, body and head, and not leave anything behind. And once you've got the beastie out, make sure you drop it in a bottle of rubbing alcohol and really finish the job off.

Collar the problem. A tick collar that contains amitraz (Preventic) will actually cause embedded ticks to pull up stakes and leave. It will also make new ticks think twice about taking a bite and can be relied upon to give protection for about four months. So if you want to ensure your dog is off-limits to ticks, put one of these collars around her neck. But because it doesn't totally deter ticks, it is still a good idea for you to check your dog over

Removing Ticks

The trick with ticks is to get rid of them quick. Once they're embedded and are feeding on your pet, here's what to do.

1. Wear surgical gloves or cover your hands with plastic wrap. You risk being exposed to any disease that the tick is carrying, so be very careful not to squeeze, crush or puncture its body. It is also possible to become infected by hand-to-eye contact after handling ticks.

2. Soak the tick with alcohol. (Don't use kerosene or gasoline because they will hurt your pet's skin.) Stunned by the alcohol, the tick will loosen its grip on your dog's skin and won't start trying to dig back in the minute you apply some pressure. This will make it much easier for you to pull out the entire tick, body and head.

3. Grasp the tick's body near its head with forceps, a tick-removing tool or tweezers (below right). Pull gently until you feel the tick pull away. Try your best not to leave the head in the skin. If you just get the tick's body but leave the head in, there's a higher risk for disease as well as infection. Your vet will need to take a look at it.

4. Dispose of the tick in a jar of alcohol.

5. Disinfect the area with cleansers such as povidone-iodine or chlorhexidine. Alcohol may be too irritating on the small wound.

6. Wash your hands with soap and water to make sure you kill any germs that could cause disease.

If you don't feel up to removing a tick by hand, you can simply spray it with fipronil (Frontline), which will kill it within 24 hours.

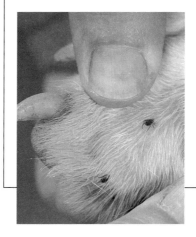

Ticks

A walk in the woods is a magical experience for your dog, but ticks also love this shady environment. Check your pet afterward in case any ticks have hitched a ride.

mowing the lawn and removing underbrush, leaf litter and extra foliage gets rid of any tick hiding places in your yard. Ticks need moisture, ground cover and contact with mice or other small animals to survive. Deprive them of those things and they're toast.

You really shouldn't need to use environmental insecticides to get rid of ticks in your yard, but chlorpyrifos (Dursban) is probably the most effective product to use if you have to cover large areas.

Be wary indoors. The brown dog tick is really the only member of the tick family that nests indoors and around kennels. The best way to prevent it is to remove debris from around your pet's kennel and make sure any crevices are sealed. If colonies of brown dog ticks set up house in your home, try treating them with a permethrin or chlorpyrifos spray. However, you are safest calling in a pest-control company to do the job for you.

after you've been in tick country. And while there are other flea and tick collars, they aren't as effective for deterring ticks.

Spray-on protection. Vets often recommend treating dogs with products such as Frontline, which contains fipronil and kills ticks within 24 hours of them attaching to your dog. Spray it on once a month and it will kill ticks (and fleas) for that entire period. And it is extremely safe—it can be used on puppies as well as pregnant females. Repellents like DEET and permanone are also effective, but the chemicals they contain may be somewhat dangerous for certain pets.

Patrol the yard. Most ticks are found on vegetation, so

URINARY TRACT PROBLEMS

It's not only humans that have problems with their urinary tracts. Dogs sometimes get urinary tract infections, urinary "stones" and even incontinence. Any urinary tract problem is potentially serious and should be treated by a vet. But there are things you can do at home to ease the discomfort and help prevent future problems.

Infections

Your dog used to be able to wait all day before asking to be let outside, but lately she's standing at the door every five minutes. And when you let her out, there's hardly anything to show for it. This means she probably has a urinary tract infection. It can be painful and gives a dog an urgent, frequent need to urinate what may be only small amounts.

Make sure you give your dog lots of opportunities to relieve herself. And make sure she keeps drinking lots of water, because this will help flush out her system, though it won't fix the infection. "Cranberry juice and vitamin C, remedies for people, have not proved effec-

tive in dogs," says veterinarian Dr. Lester Mandelker.

Apart from frequent toilet trips, there's not a lot you can do at home. To clear up your pet's urinary tract infection, it's a good idea to see your vet, says Dr. Mandelker. He will probably recommend oral antibiotics to treat the infection.

Bladder Stones

People get them in their kidneys. With dogs, most urinary stones are found in the bladder. Veterinarians typically call them uroliths, and the condition is known as urolithiasis.

Your vet will help you to implement a two-pronged attack on this problem. The first objective is to stop any crystals in your dog's bladder from developing into stones. To do this, make sure she drinks lots of fluids and has lots of opportunities to urinate. All this liquid in her system will flush out any crystals before

they have a chance to evolve into stones. Your vet may also recommend feeding her a special diet that makes the crystals less likely to form into stones.

The other goal is to dissolve stones that have already formed. There are different types of stones, and before you can help your dog out, your vet must run a test to determine which type she has. Some stones are more soluble in acidic urine; some in alkaline urine.

Once your vet has diagnosed the type of stone, he may recommend special diets or additives to change the pH of your dog's urine to help dissolve the stones, which will make them easier to eliminate.

Make sure your dog always has fresh, clean water to drink, and seek immediate veterinary help if you notice a problem with urination.

Urinary Tract Problems

Incontinence

It's normal for puppies to make messes, but when your older dog urinates when (and where) she shouldn't and doesn't know she's doing it, there's almost certainly something wrong.

This condition, called incontinence, is most common in older, neutered females, probably because they have low levels of the hormone estrogen, which the body needs to keep muscles in the urinary tract strong. It also tends to occur in pets that are overweight, which causes extra pressure on the bladder, and sometimes in dogs that are excited or under stress.

It isn't the same as when a dog loses her housebreaking and can't "hold it" as long as she used to be able to. With incontinence, the dog doesn't know she's doing it.

Incontinence can often be controlled, but you'll probably need help from your vet. A standard treatment is to give hormone supplements, along

Although there are many theories, we don't really know why dogs eat grass, as these Beagles are doing. Maybe they want to purge or soothe an upset stomach with the grass, or maybe they just fancy a little salad.

with other medications. And at home, the most important thing you can do is not to blame your dog for any accidents—she can't help it. The last thing you want to do is to make her feel more anxious or stressed because that can actually make things worse.

Instead, try to reduce stress in her life and spend more time with her outdoors, where a little dribbling doesn't matter at all. Also, the more chances she has to relieve herself, the less urine there'll be causing pressure on the bladder, and the less likelihood of accidents.

If you are going out and are afraid of what you might find on the carpet when you return, consider putting a diaper on

your dog or confining her to the bathroom or laundry where it's easier to clean things up later. For additional information, see "Aging" on page 290.

VOMITING

Few things are more unpleasant than coming home and finding the remains of your dog's breakfast in the middle of the living room carpet. But for your dog, it's just another day. Dogs vomit much more readily than people do. A lot of the time, there's a simple reason for it, like a raid on the garbage can or eating too much too fast. But if you're still unsure about the cause, give your dog a quick physical examination

Why Do Dogs Eat Grass?

What is it about grass, anyway? The moment your dog gets outside she seeks out a nice tuft of lawn and makes like a sheep. Why does a primarily meat-eating animal go for the green? Especially when there's a good chance she'll vomit up the grass she just ate.

The truth is, nobody knows for sure why dogs eat grass, although there are a few different ideas on the subject. The most common explanation is that dogs know when they've eaten something they shouldn't have and they graze on grass to purge themselves. Yet another theory is that grass has soothing properties for the canine stomach and dogs with an upset tummy know to eat some grass the same way we know to swallow an antacid. Finally, some people argue that dogs just like to eat grass—it's a taste thing. Although if they like it so much, you have to wonder why they often regurgitate it later on. Perhaps it's just because they're getting too much of a good thing.

and take her temperature before calling your vet for more specific instructions.

If your dog appears physically ill or the vomiting won't stop, you should call your vet immediately. It could be something poisonous or toxic that she's swallowed, in which case every second counts. Also, if she has been vomiting a lot, she may need intravenous fluids to replace the water and electrolytes she has lost.

Soothing Upset Stomachs

Most cases of vomiting will turn around within 24 hours. In the meantime, there are things you can do to help your dog feel better again.

Put her on a fast. Your dog will benefit from missing at least one meal after she's vomited. This will give her stomach a chance to rest and get back to normal again. If the problem is garbage-raiding or a bout with the flu, things should settle

down within a day. Until then, try to limit her food intake—this is not the time to worry that your pet is going hungry.

But let her have liquids. Make sure your dog has access to small amounts of water—just don't fill her bowl. Or give her ice cubes to lick. You don't want her to dehydrate, but at the same time you don't want her gulping down huge quantities of water, which will only make her feel queasy again.

Be bland. If your dog has fasted for 24 hours and the vomiting has stopped, you can get her back onto solid food again. Start by slowly reintroducing bland foods, such as boiled chicken, cottage cheese, rice or beef bouillon, until you're sure that her tummy has settled down and is able to cope with food again. Then gradually start giving your dog her regular food mixed with the bland foods until she's eating normally again.

Try a stomach soother. Pepto-Bismol coats the canine stomach and will give your dog some temporary relief. But always check with your vet first so you know it's safe and you get the right information on the dosage and frequency.

Weight Problems

Weight Problems

Perhaps we're pampering our pets too much, but obesity is a real problem in the canine population. In one study, more than 25 percent of dogs were found to be more than 15 percent above their optimal body weight. Sometimes it's because of a medical problem, but usually it's a case of too much food and not enough exercise. Regardless of the cause, being overweight can lead to diminished quality as well as quantity of life for your pet.

Dogs love to eat and, let's face it, food is a very convenient, and popular, reward to give them. It's not that dogs don't get signals from their intestines to tell them when they're full or when they're putting on enough fat.

"The problem is that the canine body's idea of enough fat and ours may be very different," says Cornell University animal behaviorist Dr. Katherine Houpt. But since you control the feed bag, you have ultimate power—and responsibility—when it comes to controlling her calories. Your dog will probably eat whatever you give her. So you are really

How to Weigh Your Dog

To know if your dog is getting close to her target weight, you are going to have to weigh her. Your vet will have a set of platform scales in his office, specifically designed for pets. But what about at home?

You may be able to get your small dog to stand still on your bathroom scale while you get a reading. The other method is to pick her up and stand on the scales to weigh the two of you. Then put your dog down and weigh yourself. Subtract your weight from that of the two of you together and you will arrive at your dog's weight.

the only one who can help her to lose those extra pounds.

Putting your dog on a weight-loss program is an act of love and caring. And you'll find most dogs don't mind a sensible program at all—it just takes some physical and behavioral planning on your part to accomplish it.

Losing Weight

You don't need to sign her up for Jenny Craig, get a prescription for Phen-Fen or join an expensive gym. Follow the suggestions outlined here and your dog will be healthier and happier, and you will be, too.

Know that she has a problem. Maybe your dog is solid but not overweight. Maybe she's a shade more than solid—she really is overweight. One way to tell if your dog is truly too big for her boots is to find out what her ideal weight is.

If she is a purebred, you will be able to get this information from a book about her breed. Compare this with her weight and you'll know whether dieting is in order.

An even better alternative, especially if your dog is a one-

Weight Problems

Why Do Dogs Lick Your Face?

It's so sweet when your dog greets you at the door with a wet kiss and a wagging tail. She must really love you. We should all have human partners who shows us so much affection.

However, that wet greeting at the door may not mean what you think it means. "When a dog licks you, she's begging for food," says Katherine A. Houpt, V.M.D., Ph.D., an animal behaviorist and director of the Behavior Clinic at the College of Veterinary Medicine, Cornell University, in Ithaca, New York. Apparently, this is exactly what a pup does to solicit food from her mother or another adult. You may not have realized that your dog licks you because she wants more food, not more of you. But now that you know, don't give in to her begging because it will likely turn your trim pooch tubby.

of-a-kind mixed breed, is to do a rib test. Feel her sides; if you can't find her ribs, it's diet time. **Try a change in diet.** It's important that you evaluate your current feeding practices. Your vet can help calculate how many calories a day your dog should be consuming compared to how many you're actually feeding her. It may simply be a question of changing the food she eats to meet the lower calorific target.

For example, if you are feeding your dog a premium or performance dog food, it is probably providing far too many calories, especially if she is sedentary a lot of the time. Such diets are typically high in meat protein and fat and provide more calories than your dog can use.

If she's Superdog or she's going for the world record in the animal Olympics, that's another matter—and she probably hasn't got a weight problem anyway. In most cases, you can safely switch your dog to a wholesome product with moderate amounts of protein and less fat and more fiber than she was previously getting. Most of the time, you won't even need to reduce the amount you feed her.

Feed her frequently. Feed your dog several small meals a day rather than one large meal at the beginning or end of the day. This will help keep hunger pangs at bay and convince her that her tummy is feeling okay. Just because you're feeding her more often doesn't mean you feed her more—simply divide the amount of food she is fed in one day into two to four servings and serve them up at more frequent intervals.

Switch her snacks. Snacking is the downfall of every dieter who finds it hard to resist those tempting in-between-meals moments. But you don't have to stop giving her snacks and treats completely, you just need to change her habits. Cereal biscuits tend to be very high in calories, so swap to something healthy. Try carrots, fruit or popcorn—without the salt and butter, of course.

Think again about high-fiber diets. Traditionally, high-fiber diets have been prescribed for dogs with weight

Weight Problems

Breeds that are accustomed to hard work, such as this Belgian Sheepdog, need plenty of vigorous exercise if they are to retain their lean lines.

problems. These slimming diets have lots of roughage that will fill up your dog's stomach.

"This produces one of the signals the brain uses to determine whether enough food has been eaten," says University of Pennsylvania veterinarian Dr. Kevin Byrne. However, recent research has suggested that fiber may not leave a pet feeling "full." Fiber can also interfere with the absorption of nutrients such as selenium and zinc, so discuss the benefits of high-fiber diets with your vet before deciding to put your hefty pet on one.

Get her moving. A regular exercise program is a great way for your dog to shed weight and start feeling taut, trim and terrific again. This doesn't mean the two of you need to enter a marathon. A good long walk or relaxing jog twice a day is the way to get the heart pumping and burn off some calories. If exercise is new to her, start off with short strolls and build up to longer, more vigorous workouts.

The Pudgiest Pets

Some dogs are more likely to pile on the pounds, and keep them on, than others—it's in the genes. If your dog is one of the following breeds, you're going to have to pay extra special attention to her weight and feeding needs:

- Basset Hound
- Beagle
- Cocker Spaniel
- Dachshund
- Labrador Retriever

Basset Hound

Labrador Retriever

Worms

Reward her differently. When your dog earns a treat, don't automatically reach into your pocket for a bit of food. Consider a social reward instead, such as playing fetch, tug-of-war or going for a swim. You might be surprised to learn that your dog prefers social rewards to food in most instances. Sure, dogs love to eat, but substitute play and exercise for food and most will think it's a fair trade.

Watch for the results. You don't want the weight to suddenly drop off your dog—that's not good for her. Your aim is for her to lose the extra pounds over a safe period of about 12 weeks. Keep in regular contact with your vet during this time, and if your dog hasn't reached her target by then, it's time for another veterinary visit.

WORMS

Nobody likes to hear that their dog has worms, but they are a common canine problem. The good news is that there are now more ways than ever before to eliminate internal parasites from your pet.

The most common worms are roundworms, hookworms, whipworms and tapeworms. Most puppies are either born with them or they get infected soon after birth by inadvertently consuming infected eggs or infected fleas during close contact with their mother.

The roundworms and tapeworms are the ones you can see in a dog's stool. They look ugly but they don't do a great deal of harm—usually nothing worse than a little diarrhea, vomiting or anal itching.

Hookworms and whipworms tend to keep a lower profile and do more damage, sometimes causing anemia, dehydration or nutritional deficiencies.

It's quite common for even the youngest of pups to have worms, simply as a result of contact with their mother. If the mother has worms, the pups will have worms. So it is important that you start treating your pup early—probably from when she is about two to three weeks of age.

But the bottom line is that no worm is a good worm, because they all put stresses on your dog as her immune system tries to cope with their presence. And they can all be spread to people, with the same unpleasant and sometimes dangerous consequences. So these parasites are an important human as well as canine health concern.

Controlling Worms

It is extremely important to control worms in your dog, for

Worms

The Most Common Worms

Worms aren't all the same, although they all cause the same shudder when you (or your vet) discover them in your dog's stool. Here are the most common offenders.

Roundworms. Adult roundworms live in the intestines after a dog has become infected by consuming something contaminated with larvae. You may see eggs in the stool, although in some cases you may actually see what look like wriggly strands of spaghetti. They can grow up to seven inches in length.

Hookworms. These latch onto the intestinal wall and consume large amounts of blood. Typically, the worms are three-quarters of an inch long, with a bend in one end—hence the name hookworm. The bodies are sometimes red from ingested blood. Dogs get infected when they ingest the hookworm larvae or when the larvae penetrate the dog's skin.

Whipworms. These worms will take up residence in your dog's colon after she has swallowed the eggs.

They can cause the colon to become inflamed. She won't start shedding new whipworm eggs into her stool until three months after being infected, which can make diagnosis quite difficult. The worms themselves, which can reach at least three inches in length, do not show up in the stool. They get their name because they look a bit like a whip; most of the body is slender and threadlike, while the end is thick, like the handle of a whip.

Tapeworms. Dogs are susceptible to several different types of tapeworm. The most common one is transmitted by infected fleas, which your dog accidentally swallows when doing her cleaning routine. This kind of worm is long, flat and made up of rectangular segments that each contain eggs. It can grow up to 32 inches in length. Individual segments are passed into the stool, and you may notice them on the skin and fur around the anus. They look innocent enough, rather like grains of rice.

---

her safety as well as your own. Fortunately, this isn't a difficult task so long as you treat the parasites, treat the premises, and also prevent new worms from developing. And worming products today are safer as well as more effective than their predecessors.

Start with a trip to the vet. If you suspect your dog has worms, a trip to the vet is in order. Once he knows which

worms your dog has, he will recommend prescription or over-the-counter medications that will eradicate the parasites from her body. Always use the product that is recommended by your vet; don't use an over-the-counter wormer. The reason for this is that most such wormers contain toluene or dichlorphen, which can actually be toxic to some dogs, so it's best to avoid them.

Start her young. If you have a puppy, you probably want to start treatment at two to three weeks of age and continue every two weeks until the pup is several months old. Most pups are infected but they won't actually have worm eggs turning up in their stool for a few weeks or months. The idea is to begin treating your pup before she starts showing signs of infection. That way, not

Your vet will recommend a worming product that is safe, effective and easy to administer, so there's no need to take chances with the health of either your dog or your family when it comes to worms. This Samoyed puppy is taking her medicine and getting off to a good start in life as a result.

only do you eradicate the worms from her system, you also make sure her toilet deposits don't become the source of infection for others.

Treat for fleas, too. The most common form of tapeworm is carried by fleas—a dog swallows an infected flea and the tapeworms get inside. "Flea control is critical if you hope to control tapeworms," says veterinarian Dr. Stephen Waisglass. For further information on ridding these external freeloaders from your pet, see "Fleas" on page 325.

Clean up after her. The best way to control worms in your dog's environment is to clean up after her. Removing stools promptly will help prevent reinfection. No infected feces hanging around means no dirt getting contaminated with eggs, so the cycle of reinfection can be kept to a minimum.

Take extra precautions. Prevention is now a lot more straightforward than it used to be, simply because some of the newer medicines that prevent heartworm have the added bonus of preventing intestinal worms, too. Heartworm medications that include pyrantel (Heartgard-30 Plus) control roundworms and hookworms in addition to heartworm. The ingredient milbemycin oxime (Interceptor) prevents hookworms from developing and controls roundworms and whipworms, as well as stopping heartworm. No one product directly kills tapeworms but a combination of milbemycin oxime and lufenuron (Sentinel) controls roundworms, hookworms and whipworms as well as helping to control fleas, which are carriers of tapeworm. So, since your dog will probably be taking heartworm medications anyway, why not give her one that also protects against worms?

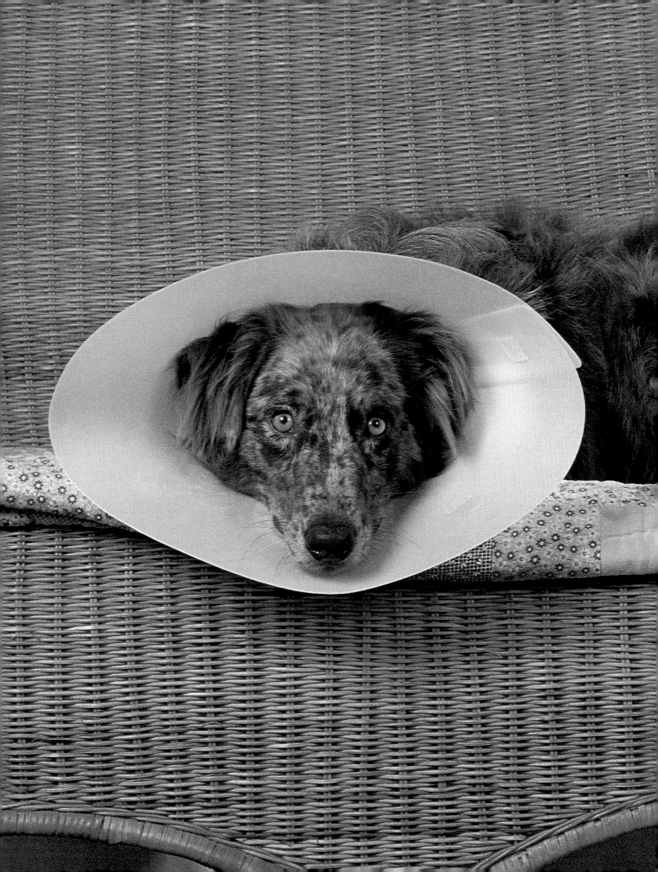

PART SEVEN

First Aid

At some time or other, nearly every pet owner's dog will get hurt, just because every dog is active, curious and isn't always thinking about the best or most obvious way to protect himself from injury.

Usually, the injuries are relatively minor and you'll be able to cope with them yourself using first aid at home. Other times, you will have to get him to a vet for some expert advice and assistance, but you'll need to do some things for him at home first, before you put him in the car and make the mercy dash.

The following solutions to common emergencies are easy to understand and administer—even for the weak at heart. Recognizing the problem and then carrying out these solutions quickly and efficiently are the most important factors in helping ensure that every emergency has a happy ending for your dog, and you.

Handling an Injured Dog

Your dog knows exactly how to be a well-behaved dog under normal circumstances. But being injured and in pain aren't normal circumstances, and your dog will need some special care and handling to keep him from further harm. You also want to make sure that you don't get hurt while trying to help.

Because your dog is in pain and doesn't understand what's going on, he will be scared. "No matter how gentle he normally is, the fear that accompanies an injury can turn him into an out-of-control biter," says Joseph Trueba, D.V.M., a veterinarian in private practice in Tucson, Arizona, who specializes in emergency pet care.

If your dog is injured you are going to have to get him to a vet, a shelter or an emergency treatment center as quickly as possible so he can receive the expert attention he needs. It may never happen, but just in case it does, you should be prepared because the quicker you act, the sooner you'll have your dog back with you and wagging his tail again. Have a first-aid box sitting at the ready in a cupboard in the kitchen or the laundry. Also, have an idea of how you plan to move your dog safely. That includes knowing ahead of time how you plan to keep him still and keep him from biting.

A Gentle Restraint

Your dog won't be able to understand that you are trying to help him. "A dog is afraid that your approaching touch will only worsen the agony," explains Dr. Trueba. If you look at it from his point of view, he's only trying to stop you and the pain he thinks you are causing him. The surefire way for him to stop you in your tracks is to give you a good bite. And the surest way to avoid being on the receiving end of his distressed teeth is to put a muzzle on him. That's the very first way you can help him. You can use one that you've bought from the store, or you can improvise if you're in a hurry.

You don't want to get bitten because you don't want a handful of pain. But there's another good reason for preventing him using his teeth. Once a dog bites someone— even if that person is his owner —the law requires that the dog be impounded (whether he's hurt or not) by the local animal control officer so he can be monitored for rabies. "This is necessary in all dog-bite cases, just to be sure the dog doesn't have rabies," says Dr. Trueba.

A dog that has been vaccinated has to be confined and observed for ten days; one that has not will be quarantined for six months. "Local authorities make the decision about where the pet is observed—at home or an animal control center," says Lisa Rotz, M.D., a doctor at the U.S. Centers for Disease Control and Prevention in Atlanta. "This is all the more reason to muzzle your injured dog before attempting to help him," says Dr. Trueba. "While it seems cruel, it's the kind thing to do. It's a way of ensuring that he'll recuperate in the comfort of his own home rather than in the strange surroundings of the dog pound."

How to Make a Muzzle

When your dog is injured, or you are trying to help someone else's injured dog, the first thing you need to do is muzzle him. If you don't have a shop-bought muzzle, fashion a makeshift version using your dog's leash, a pair of pantyhose, a necktie or a long strip of stretchable gauze. If none of these is handy, a dishcloth or a T-shirt will also work well.

A homemade muzzle is entirely safe, but make sure to leave your dog's nostrils free so that he can breathe easily. "Pantyhose work a little better than a stiff leash because they have some give to them—they also leave the leash for its intended job of controlling the dog," says Joan E. Antle, D.V.M., a veterinarian in private practice in Cleveland and a frequent speaker on pet emergency care. Even though it can be upsetting to see your pooch attempting to free himself from the muzzle, remember that the muzzle is there to help you both, not hinder you.

1 Make a noose by tying a loose knot in the middle of the strip of material, leaving a large loop.

3 Bring the ends downward and knot them under his chin. Carry the ends around his neck and tie them again behind his ears.

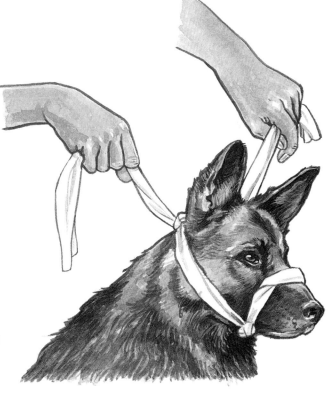

2 Approach your dog quietly from behind and slip the noose over his snout, pulling it taut about halfway up his nose.

First-Aid Kit

"A first-aid kit for your pet can literally spell the difference between life and death," says Joan E. Antle, D.V.M., a veterinarian in private practice in Cleveland and a frequent speaker on pet emergency care. So don't wait until after an accident has happened to prepare a first-aid kit for your dog.

Here's what you should include:

- Vital Information Card. This should list the name and phone number of your vet; the phone number, address and travel directions to the nearest emergency pet clinic; and the phone number of the local poison control office or the National Animal Poison Control Center
- First-aid manual, such as *Pet First Aid*, which can be ordered through the American Animal Hospital Association
- Pantyhose, a long strip of stretchable gauze or a spare leash (to make a muzzle)
- Blunt-tipped scissors
- Tweezers
- Eyewash (such as sterile contact lens solution or an eye rinse for dry eyes)
- Antibiotic ointment or powder
- Hydrogen peroxide
- Milk of magnesia
- Rectal thermometer
- K-Y jelly
- Bandaging materials:
  – one- to two-inch stretchable and nonstretchable gauze rolls
  – gauze pads in varying sizes, depending on your dog's size
  – bandage tape
- Cotton balls
- Strong packaging tape (for taping a broken leg to a firm surface)
- Soap
- Needle-nose pliers
- Beach towel, blanket or heavy cardboard (for a stretcher)

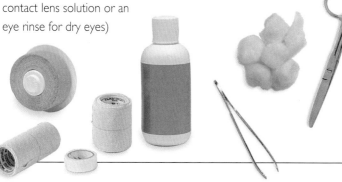

The only times you shouldn't muzzle your dog is if he has facial injuries or if he is having difficulty breathing. Similarly, avoid muzzling him if he is vomiting. And if he is very distressed, and is both vomiting and trying to bite you, don't attempt to either muzzle or move him. Instead, it's best if you call the animal control officer, who will help you move your dog safely, without being injured yourself.

Moving Him Safely

An injured dog must be transported to the vet quickly. But in your urgency to have him in the care of the experts, don't forget that the move involves more than speed. You also need to be very careful when you move him. "It's important to move an injured dog as little as possible when you have to transport him, and to protect him from further injury before moving him to safety or to be treated," says Dr. Trueba.

For example, if your dog has been hurt in a car accident, he may have broken bones but you probably won't know about them. Moving him in the wrong way could worsen the fracture or cause the broken bones to push through the

1 Lifting your dog as little as possible, gently slide the supporting surface under him. Talk to him throughout the move to calm and reassure him.

2 Bind your dog to the surface with whatever you have at hand—a sheet, towel or coat. When he is secured, carry him to the car.

skin. Even gentle movements may be too much, speeding up unsuspected internal bleeding.

"Keep one goal in mind as you're moving your dog," advises Joan E. Antle, D.V.M., a veterinarian in private practice in Cleveland and a frequent speaker on pet emergency care. "Try to move your dog as one unit." Before you think about moving him, immobilize his whole body.

Find an appropriate "body board"—a firm, flat surface that your dog can fit onto comfortably. This will reduce the risk of further disturbing the injury and make transporting him easier. "Depending on the size of your dog, this board could be an oven tray, a child's small

plastic sled, a wooden toboggan, a piece of cardboard or wood," says Dr. Antle. "Choose something totally flat, which will make the next step easier."

Lifting him as little as possible, slide the firm surface under him. If necessary, lift him slightly and gently at the front, then at the back, to slide it underneath. Now bind your dog to the supporting surface, advises L. R. Danny Daniel, D.V.M., a veterinarian in private practice in Covington, Louisiana. "While this might seem as cruel as muzzling him, it's the kind thing to do. You can't explain to your dog that he must lie still."

Using dish towels, bath towels, a coat or pieces of soft rag,

bind him gently but firmly to the support. Your familiar voice and calm manner will help to keep him as calm as possible. Once he's secured, lift him on his body board and carry him to the car for the trip to the vet.

If you don't have a firm surface handy, you will have to improvise. Use a coat, shirt or towel to make a sling in which to carry or drag your dog. To make up for the lack of a firm surface, try to find a second person to help you hold the sling as if it were a firm stretcher. To transport a small or medium-size dog, try using a cardboard box. Simply lift him into the box with one swift movement, then carry the box to the car.

Bites and Wounds

Even the mildest mannered dog can get himself into a scrape. Natural curiosity will cause him to investigate anything that moves or smells, and this can have painful consequences if the object of interest has a stinger, fangs or quills. He may even decide to stand his ground against a larger dog or other animal, regardless of personal danger. Chances are, at one time or another, your dog will come home with a wound and you'll have to make a dash for the first-aid kit.

Bandaging a Wound

"While many wounds heal just fine unbandaged, others do better covered," says Lori A. Wise, D.V.M., a veterinarian in private practice in Wheat Ridge, Colorado. Examples of wounds that should be bandaged include cuts on the foot pads and other areas that are likely to get dirty, large gashes and scrapes, and any wound that your dog licks excessively.

If the wound is deep, embedded with dirt or debris, or continues to bleed, take your dog to the vet immediately.

Don't attempt to dress these wounds yourself.

Before dressing a wound, it's important to clean it thoroughly. "As with your own cuts and scrapes, wash your dog's wound with gauze pads soaked in warm, soapy water," says Dr. Wise. Rinse with warm water, then dry the wound with gauze pads. Don't use cotton balls as the fibers may stick in the wound. Dry the surrounding fur with a clean cloth. Once the wound is dry, apply an antibiotic ointment. If the wound needs bandaging cover it with a sterile gauze pad. How you bandage the wound depends on its location.

Back Wounds

Because they are easiest to keep clean, back wounds rarely need bandaging. However, to prevent infection and give better access to the wound, you may have to clip some fur away.

To bandage a back wound, use a large rectangular piece of cotton fabric to secure the dressing in place. Slash each end of the cloth twice to make three tails and tie them under his belly.

Should Dogs Lick Their Wounds?

It's common to see your dog administering his own first aid by care-fully and meticulously licking his wounds. Because his mouth is full of bacteria, this doesn't do much to clean the wound, but it is a perfectly natural way for your dog to sooth himself. "Too much licking, however, can delay the healing process," says Joan E. Antle, a veteri-narian in private practice in Cleveland.

How much is too much? You'll know it's time to cover the wound and stop the licking if your dog licks his wound for more than a few moments a few times a day, chews at it or if the wound is getting worse instead of better.

The best way to stop your dog licking is to fit him with an Elizabethan collar. Or you can cover his wound with human clothing. For a wound on the paw or leg, tape on a snug-fitting sock. If the wound is on his hindquarters, slip a pair of men's or boy's underwear (depending on your dog's size) over his back legs. Ease his tail through the fly. For wounds on his chest or upper back, dress your dog in a snug-fitting T-shirt, with his front paws through the armholes.

1 A wound inside a long floppy ear needs air to circulate around it, so fold the ears on top of your dog's head.

2 Secure the ears in place with a bandage wrapped under his chin and tied on top of his head.

Sterilize a pair of blunt-tipped scissors by dipping them in rubbing alcohol, then use them to gently clip hair from around the wound.

"Monitor the wound regu-larly, cleansing it and applying antibiotic ointment twice daily," says Dr. Wise. If the wound is large or your dog won't leave it alone, cover it with a sterile gauze pad and keep the gauze in place with a large bandage. Find a piece of large, rectangular cloth the width of your dog's belly (from armpit to groin). It should be long enough to tie around his body. At each end cut two slits into the material to create three tails. Place the center of the cloth over his back to hold the gauze pad in place, then bring the ends under his belly.

Tie each pair of tails firmly but comfortably together under his belly. This bandage reversed will also work for chest and abdominal wounds.

Ear Wounds

"Unless they're severe, we rarely bandage wounds on the outside of the ears," says Dr. Wise. Wounds on the inside of the ears, though, may need a

How to Make an Elizabethan Collar

Named after the 16th century English fashion trend, these cone-shaped collars do a great job of stopping your dog from licking and biting at wounds just about anywhere on his body. You can purchase ready-to-wear collars at your vet's office and some pet stores, but you can also make one quite easily at home using a piece of firm cardboard. Some dogs won't eat or drink when wearing an Elizabethan collar, so remember to remove it at least three times a day to allow him to eat and drink freely.

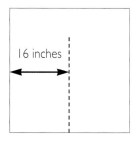

16 inches

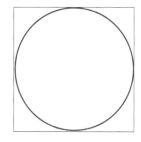

1 To work out what size cardboard you need, measure your dog's neck then add 6 to 16 inches, depending on his size. For example, if your dog's neck is 16 inches, as a large Labrador Retriever's would be, add 16 inches. You will need a piece of firm cardboard 32 inches square.

2 Cut out a circle the diameter of the square.

3 Cut a circle the same size as your dog's neck out of the middle. Make a V-shaped cut from the outer edge to the inner circle.

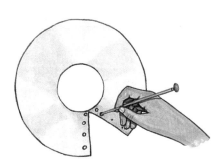

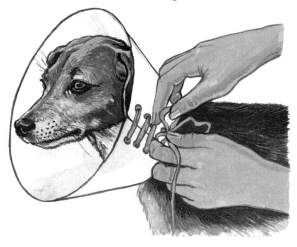

4 Use a knitting needle to punch out holes along either edge of the V-shaped cut.

5 Place the collar over your dog's head. Once the collar is in place, tie the punched edges together with a shoelace or piece of string.

special kind of bandage—one that opens the wound area to air. This is especially important if your dog has long floppy ears that lie close to his head. These create a warm, moist environment for infection to occur. Fold the ears over the top of your dog's head and hold them in place with a strip of cloth wrapped under his chin and tied in a double bow on the top of his head. Make sure the ear canals are open and your dog's eyesight is not blocked.

Leg and Paw Wounds

No matter where the wound is on the paw or leg, you'll need to wrap the entire leg. "This prevents swelling and speeds healing," says Dr. Wise. Hold the gauze covering the wound in place with one hand and use the other to wrap his leg. Starting at his paw, wrap his entire leg firmly but not too tightly, right up to the top. Tape the end of the gauze to the layer below. Finally, cover the entire paw and leg with bandaging tape, taping from the paw upward.

Change all bandages at least every other day, sooner if they get wet or dirty, or come loose. Gently clean, rinse and dry the wound, then apply antibiotic ointment each time you change the bandage. "Watch for redness, swelling, foul-smelling odor or discharge," says Dr. Wise. These are signs of infection and will require the prompt attention of a vet.

Dog Bites

Blind bravery often causes dogs to do battle with other dogs. Because of the way they defend themselves, dogs tend to be bitten on the neck, face, ears and chest. Although bites from other dogs don't look so bad, they can cause serious damage. A bite from long, sharp teeth damages the tissues under the skin and is often much deeper than it looks.

If you see your dog in a fight, the first task is to separate the

If your dog has been bitten, use a towel or blanket to keep him warm and stop him from going into shock.

animals. Never try to step into the scuffle because you might end up injured yourself. Instead, try splashing cold water on the fight, using either a hose or a bucket. Once your dog has settled down, take a good look at the wound. Clip the hair from around the area, wash the wound well with warm water and soap and pat dry. Apply an antibiotic ointment and cover with gauze.

If you see any indication of a puncture wound, or the bite seems unusually deep, take your dog to the vet for the expert care he needs.

Snake Bites

Instinctive curiosity drives dogs to investigate that moving hose on the ground, and it's also instinct that causes a snake to bite in self-defense when a dog gets too close. If you don't witness it happening, suspect a snake bite if your dog comes back from a jaunt through the woods or back country with a swollen, bleeding wound, especially if the wound is on his head or legs. If the snake was a poisonous species and the venom has already entered his system, your dog may be trembling, drooling, vomiting, have dilated pupils or collapse.

"If you can identify the snake with absolute certainty, treat the dog according to whether the snake is poisonous or not," says Dr. Wise. "If you have any doubt, though, always treat for a poisonous bite." When the snake is poisonous you have two goals: to slow the entrance of venom into your dog's system, and to get him to emergency care right away.

"Contrary to what you may have heard or read, do not lance the bite and try to suck out the venom," says Dr. Wise. This actually speeds blood flow to the area, causing venom to enter your dog's system faster. "Instead, keep your dog still and calm." If you can, carry him to the vet as this will slow his blood flow. Talk to him in a soothing voice. The calmer he stays, the slower his heart rate is and the slower the venom enters his system. Covering your dog with a blanket, coat or rug will keep him warm and help prevent or delay shock.

If you're absolutely sure the snake wasn't poisonous, you can take care of snake bites at home. Wash the bite area with warm soap and water, rinse with warm water, then apply antibiotic ointment. The bite area is usually small so it won't need to be bandaged.

Watch the area for three to four days, making sure it's getting better every day. If redness, swelling or weeping develops, take your dog to the vet promptly. "Sometimes, dogs have an allergic reaction to snake bites, even if the snake wasn't poisonous," says Dr. Wise. The reaction may cause swelling at the bite site, as well as of the lips, mouth, eyes and respiratory passages. These allergic reactions need veterinary attention right away.

Removing Porcupine Quills

What could be more fascinating to a dog than a moving pin cushion? But trying to get a good sniff of a porcupine often has a painful outcome.

If your dog has an encounter with a porcupine, use a pair of pliers to remove the quills, says L. R. Danny Daniel, D.V.M., a veterinarian in private practice in Covington, Louisiana. "Grasp each quill as close to the flesh as possible, working it out steadily but slowly." Porcupine quills are more than simple needles—their ends are barbed, which makes removing them from your dog's flesh a challenge. If you can extract the quills successfully, wash the wounds with warm, soapy water, then rinse

them with fresh warm water and apply an antibiotic ointment. Monitor the wounds for three or four days. "At the first sign of swelling, redness, weeping or other signs of infection, take your dog to the vet right away," says Dr. Daniel.

If any quills break as you try to pull them out, take your dog to the vet— the pieces will have to be removed surgically after the area is numbed. "Leaving them in may cause infection," explains Dr. Daniel. Sometimes, you'll have to seek the vet's help to remove the quills because it's often just too painful for your dog. Your vet will numb the area before removing the quills.

Bleeding

If you're like many people, the sight of blood might make you feel woozy. But when your dog is hurt and bleeding, you are his only lifeline. Take charge of the situation by talking to your dog in that soothing voice he knows and trusts—doing this will help you to stay calm as well.

Always act quickly if your dog is bleeding, but with even greater speed if the blood is pumping rhythmically from a cut. "Spurting blood generally indicates a cut artery, which bleeds more rapidly and causes heavier blood loss than a cut vein," says Dr. Wise. Blood from a cut vein will ooze more slowly and evenly.

There are three methods you can use to stop bleeding and they should be used in the following order: applying direct pressure to the wound, applying pressure on pressure points and applying a tourniquet.

Applying Directly Pressure

"This easy technique almost always stops bleeding within minutes," says Terri McGinnis, D.V.M., a veterinarian in private practice in San Francisco and author of *The Well-Dog Book.* Place a sterile gauze pad directly over the bleeding area and press down firmly. If you don't have sterile gauze, use a clean rag, cloth or your fingers until someone can get you bandages.

If blood soaks through the material, don't remove it. Just add layers of additional material to the pile. This way, if clots have started to form, you won't break them apart. Once the bleeding has stopped, remove the bandage and pile of cloths, then use clean material to bandage the wound. If the bleeding hasn't stopped after five minutes of applying direct pressure, bind the gauze pads in place with bandage tape so your hands are free to attempt the second strategy.

Applying Pressure to Your Dog's Pressure Points

The second technique you should attempt to reduce bleeding is clamping down on the artery that supplies blood to that area. There are five

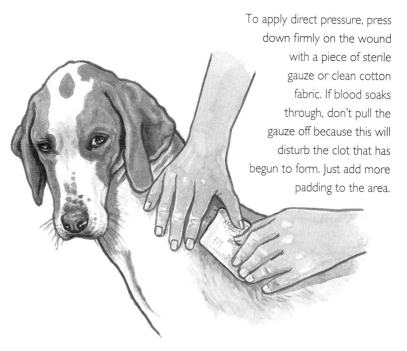

To apply direct pressure, press down firmly on the wound with a piece of sterile gauze or clean cotton fabric. If blood soaks through, don't pull the gauze off because this will disturb the clot that has begun to form. Just add more padding to the area.

main pressure points on your dog's body and, depending on where the cut is, you should apply firm pressure to whichever one of these areas is between the wound and the heart. Always choose the one closest to the wound. "If bleeding continues, let up on the pressure slightly for a few seconds every few minutes," says Dr. Wise. While you want to stop the bleeding, you must allow some blood flow to the surrounding area so that healthy tissues aren't damaged by being deprived of their blood supply.

- If the cut is on your dog's front leg, press your middle three fingers firmly and deeply into his armpit.

- If the cut is on his rear leg, place your middle three fingers deeply into the middle of the groin (the area inside the thigh where it meets the body) and press firmly.

- If the cut is on his tail, reach under it and place your three middle fingers where it joins the body. Keep your thumb on the top of the tail and apply gentle pressure.

- For a cut on the neck, feel for the round, hard windpipe just below his throat. Slide your middle three fingers to the side of it where the cut is until you find the soft groove next to his windpipe, and press firmly, but gently. If you suspect

Do Dogs Have Different Blood Types?

Just as dogs have different kinds of coats, they also have different blood types, which they have inherited from their parents. There are eight common blood types in dogs. But most of the time your vet won't test your dog's blood to determine what type it is.

"First of all, most dogs won't ever need to have a blood transfusion," says Joan E. Antle, D.V.M., a veterinarian in private practice in Cleveland and a frequent speaker on pet emergency care. In the rare event that they do, however, they have one big advantage over people. "Almost every dog can receive a first transfusion of any blood type," says Dr. Antle. For the second transfusion, they do need the correct blood. While vets always prefer to give dogs the correct blood type, it's faster to give whatever they have on hand—and in an emergency situation, time is of the essence.

Your Dog's Pressure Points

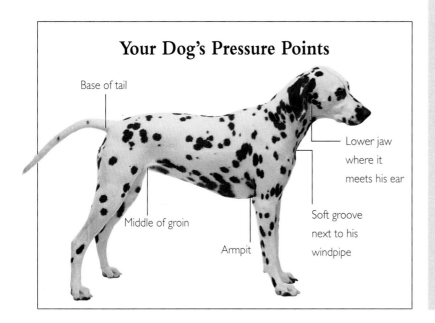

Base of tail

Lower jaw where it meets his ear

Middle of groin

Armpit

Soft groove next to his windpipe

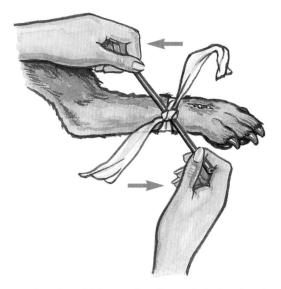

1 Apply a tourniquet only as a last resort. Wrap a strip of material twice around your dog's limb or tail, but don't knot it. Place a stick on top and tie it in place with the loose ends.

2 Turn the stick in one direction until the bandage is just tight enough to stop the bleeding. Loosen the tourniquet every five to ten minutes for a few seconds so that blood can circulate.

your dog has a head injury—perhaps he's dazed or disoriented—don't use this pressure point. Reducing blood flow to the brain could worsen a head injury. It's better to apply firm, direct pressure to the cut while you hurry him to the veterinarian.

- If your dog has a cut to his head, find the spot where his lower jaw angles up just below the ear, and press firmly with your middle three fingers. (This is also the spot where dogs love to be scratched.)

Applying a Tourniquet

If your dog is still bleeding heavily after you have applied pressure to his pressure points for more than ten minutes, apply a tourniquet. This is a bandage that constricts the blood vessels between the cut and the heart and stops the flow of blood. "Use a tourniquet only as a last resort to stop bleeding," says Dr. McGinnis. It should be used only for cuts to a dog's leg and tail, never to his body or neck. A tourniquet isn't really a home remedy and you should use it only when you are on your way to the vet.

Find a strip of material—a necktie, gauze strip or panty hose—and wrap it twice around the limb or tail above the cut, but don't knot it. Put a stick, pencil or other long and thin, sturdy object on top of the second layer of the material. Tie the stick in place with the two loose ends of material, then twist it so as to tighten the tourniquet just enough to stop the bleeding.

It's important to loosen it every five to ten minutes for a couple of seconds to allow some blood flow to the healthy tissues in the area.

Broken Leg

The most common cause of a broken bone is a dog getting into an argument with one of those metal boxes on four wheels that goes faster than anything he's ever seen. Sometimes it's hard to know that your dog's leg is broken. "Dogs are stoic," explains Dr. Daniel. "They generally don't whine when they're in pain."

Fortunately, they are also pretty smart about lessening the pain. A dog tends not to put any weight on a broken leg, especially if it is broken above the knee. Other telltale signs to look out for include a leg that has a lump in it, a paw that is facing in a slightly different direction or one leg looking slightly deformed in comparison to the others.

While all fractures will need veterinary care at some stage, some should be considered emergencies, in need of immediate attention. Fractures that have broken through the skin warrant a fast trip to the vet. These are called open, or compound, fractures, and as well as bleeding, they can very easily become infected.

Fractures that don't break through the skin, called simple fractures, can wait overnight for treatment, or even a day or two if his accident has happened on the weekend. "Bear in mind, though, that even simple fractures can be painful, and your dog will feel better after the vet has set his leg and put proper splinting material on it," says Dr. Daniel.

Immobilizing the Broken Leg

No matter what sort of fracture your dog has, the most important thing you must do is to stop him from moving his leg. "The aim is to prevent any further injury to the fractured area," says Dr. Daniel. "In order to do this, you have to prevent your dog from making any movement at the joint above and below the fracture."

Depending on the type of break, you can do this either by applying a splint to his injured leg or by completely immobilizing him. As soon as you've done this, take him to the vet for the expert care he'll need to restore him to full mobility.

A Fracture Below the Knee

A break below the knee is relatively easy to splint, because the joint above the break (the knee) is easily accessible. Choose a splinting material that suits the size of your dog. In most cases, an effective splint can be made by rolling a magazine or several sheets of newspaper around the fractured area. You could also use a large bath towel, rolled several times around the area. Depending on the size of your dog, sticks, pencils and yardsticks (broken in half and the sharp ends taped with masking tape) also make good splints.

Whatever you decide to use, make sure that the splint extends above the knee and below the end of the paw. Before you try to move your dog, secure the splint in place by tying several strips of cloth or gauze around it, or sticking down some bandage tape. Just be careful not to tie the splint too tightly as you could stop the blood supply to the leg.

"Sometimes, a restless dog will move so much that the

splint rubs into his skin and creates pressure sores that can be as bad as the fracture itself," warns Dr. Daniel. "If your dog is particularly restless or the area is difficult to splint, first pad his broken leg with a towel and then apply the splint."

A Fracture Above the Knee

A fracture above the knee is difficult to splint because the hip area (above the rear legs) or shoulder area (above the front legs) is difficult to immobilize. "If the joint above or below the fracture is left free to move, it's very dangerous," says

Dr. Trueba. People often splint the joint below the fracture properly, but don't immobilize the one above. "This adds weight to the fracture, pulling at and further damaging the fractured area. It can also cause extensive injury to soft tissues surrounding those bones."

The best approach is to use a piece of plywood, a piece of sturdy cardboard or even a large oven tray. "Place the dog on the flat surface, broken leg lying across the surface. Tape the broken leg in place securely, and then tape the whole dog loosely to the board before moving him," says Dr. Daniel.

Protruding Bones

When a broken bone pushes through your dog's skin, he has what is known as an open fracture. If this happens, you must first dress the wound. "Soak sterile gauze in contact lens solution, and then apply this moist material to the open wound," says Dr. Daniel. If you don't have any contact lens solution handy, soak the gauze in plain water. If you are in a situation where you don't have any of these things, wrap a thick, clean cloth around the wound. At least it is protected and your dog's broken leg is now ready to be splinted.

Splint a fracture below the knee by rolling a magazine or some newspaper around the limb and binding it securely in place.

A fracture above the knee must be immobilized above and below the break before your subdued or unconscious dog can be safely moved. Secure his body to a firm, flat surface, then tape the broken limb to the board. Your dog can then be transported as a unit on the board.

Broken Tail

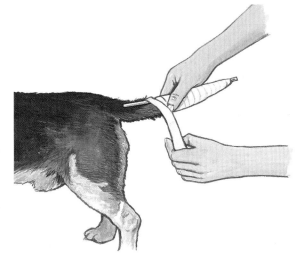

What's more of a welcome flag than your dog's wagging tail? Unfortunately, this excitable part of his anatomy often gets him into trouble. At some time or other, most dogs have their tail accidentally slammed in the car or house door. You can tell if your dog's tail is broken because he'll only have half a wag and won't be able to move it beyond the break. Until the fracture heals, he'll probably wag away as if nothing has happened, but he will need a little help and some loving care. "If the skin is broken, the tail will bleed heavily, and even more when your dog wags it," says Dr. Antle.

Treatment

First of all, you'll need to stop the bleeding. Gently grasp the tail where it's bleeding with a couple of gauze pads, or a clean rag or cloth. Remember, your dog's tail still hurts, even if he acts as if it doesn't, and grabbing at the point where it's broken may cause the most stoic of dogs to let out a yelp.

Press down on the area gently, but firmly, to stop the bleeding. Next, wash the wound with soap and water. Apply an antibiotic ointment, then tape sterile gauze pads over the wound.

Depending on where the fracture is, you may be able to immobilize your dog's tail without your vet's help. "If the tail isn't broken at the base, you can take care of the fracture at home," says Dr. Antle. Use a chopstick or thin stick as a splint and bandage it to your dog's tail, starting from the tip.

Use cloth first-aid tape and start at the tip of the tail. Wrap the tail snugly, working toward the body with closely overlapping layers. Once you reach the end, cut the tape and stick

If the break is not at the base of the tail, clean and dress the wound, then bandage a splint to your dog's tail. Start at the tip and overlap the layers closely to provide good support.

the end down to the layer below. This splint will also hold the wound dressing in place. Leave the splint on for a week or two, or until he can wag his whole tail and it moves as it did before the fracture.

If your dog's tail is broken at the base, you will need a little help from your vet. "With a break at the base, your dog may not be able to go to the toilet on his own, simply because he can no longer lift his tail," says Dr. Antle.

In addition, your dog may have suffered nerve damage and only your vet will be able to tell for sure. Keep him comfortable and take him to the vet as soon as possible.

Burns

Ever hopeful that you'll share a morsel of what you're cooking, dogs are often underfoot in the kitchen. While most kitchen beggars manage to stay out of trouble, some get a little too close to the action. As a result, they may suffer burns, especially from spattering grease or scalding water.

Dogs may also suffer chemical burns from splashed yard or household chemicals, and curious puppies who chomp into electrical cords often get the inside of their mouths burned. Whatever the cause, acting quickly and calmly can reduce a burn's severity and help your dog to recover faster.

Heat Burns

Quickly putting ice on a burn or holding it under cold running water will help to ease the pain and stop further damage, says Paul M. Gigliotti, D.V.M., a veterinarian in private practice in Mayfield Village, Ohio. "The coldness stops the heat of the burn from penetrating into the deeper tissues," he explains.

The easiest way to cool a burn is with the garden hose, provided you don't turn the faucet on full force. Your pooch may not cooperate if you turn the hose on too strongly. Worse, too much water pressure could also damage tissue if the burns are deep and have broken up the skin. Help your dog to remain calm by talking to him continuously in a soft, soothing voice and by stroking him with one hand as you wet him down with the other.

Alternatively, hold your dog in a gentle hug as you apply an ice pack to the burned area. "Apply cold water or an ice pack for a full 20 minutes," says Dr. McGinnis.

The next step depends on how badly he's burned. Burns are divided into three categories: first, second and third degree. With a first-degree

A gentle stream of cold water over the burned area will ease the pain and stop the heat from damaging deeper tissues. For severe burns, take your dog to the vet.

burn, the skin is red, tender to the touch and possibly swollen. Deeper burns that blister and swell are second-degree burns. The most serious, third-degree burns, are easy to recognize because the skin is white, charred or burned away.

"For first- and second-degree burns, apply a triple-strength antibiotic ointment twice daily," says Dr. Gigliotti. Each time you apply the ointment, check the skin carefully to make sure it's getting better, not worse. "If the burned area starts to weep, increase in size or become more tender to the touch, take your dog to the vet to make sure the burn has not become infected."

Third-degree burns require immediate professional care. Before you take your dog to the vet, place sterile gauze pads over the burned area, then apply an ice pack. Even if you don't have sterile gauze pads, still use an ice pack. Ice cubes in a plastic bag will work fine. At the same time, keep your dog warm to prevent shock.

"Severe burns can send a dog into shock, a condition in which his circulatory system slows right down," says Dr. Gigliotti. To preserve his body heat and prevent shock, wrap your dog in a blanket, sweater, coat or towel as you take him to the vet. As with all serious injuries, try to find someone to drive while you attend to your dog. On the way, keep him warm and continue to hold the ice pack on the burn.

Chemical Burns

There are a number of common household chemicals that can cause burns to your dog's body. If your dog suffers a chemical burn, dilute the substance by flooding the area with water. "Even though the skin may break open right away, flush the area with copious amounts of water to wash away any remaining chemical on the skin and to stop further burns," says Dr. McGinnis. Then take your dog to see the vet immediately.

Electrical Burns

Puppies chew through just about anything they can sink their teeth into, including electrical cords. "If he's lucky, he'll just get a nasty burn in or around his mouth," says Dr. Gigliotti. Fortunately, most dogs recover well on their own from these burns, although in some cases tissues in the mouth will flake off after a few days.

Keep Out of Reach

There are plenty of household products that can cause burns to your dog. Things to watch out for include:

- *Cleaning detergents*
- *Drain cleaners*
- *Weed killers and other garden sprays*
- *Paints*
- *Paint strippers*
- *Turpentine*
- *Battery acid*
- *Petroleum-based products*

If you haven't seen your dog eat a wire cord, you can suspect an electrical burn if he doesn't eat anything, despite appearing to be hungry. His mouth will be sore and tender so feed him on a diet of liquid or soft foods.

Chomping on an electrical cord can cause more serious injuries. It can damage lung tissue or even cause your dog to stop breathing. If he stops breathing, start CPR immediately. Lung injuries will cause your dog to drool, cough and have trouble breathing. If you notice any of these signs, even a day or two after he bites an electrical cord, take him to the vet immediately.

Car Accidents and CPR

It can happen so quickly. An open gate or a dropped leash, followed by an innocent dash into the road by your dog. "While leashing laws have dramatically reduced the number of dogs hit by cars, accidents still happen," says Dr. Trueba, a veterinarian who specializes in emergency care.

Minimize His Injuries

As soon as your dog is hit, immediately protect yourself and your dog from oncoming traffic, says Dr. Trueba. "Ideally, you should assess and possibly bandage the dog before moving him. But if he is lying on a busy street, you don't have that option." In heavy traffic, wave a white or brightly colored cloth to alert approaching cars, and enlist someone's help to move your dog to a safer spot.

Although your dog would never bite you deliberately, he may try to if he is in pain or shock. "If your dog is conscious, protect yourself from his frightened bite with a muzzle," says Dr. Trueba. (For more information, see "How

to Make a Muzzle" on page 385.) Then, grasp the fur along his backbone with both hands and drag him back out of harm's way. Pull him evenly and keep his body flat on the ground. Remember, talking to your dog in a soothing voice will help him through this difficult situation. This will also give you something to focus on and help to keep you calm.

The Three-Point Check

"After moving the dog out of traffic, or if you have the luxury of leaving him where he is for a few moments, you should check three things in the following order," says Erika de Papp, D.V.M., a veterinarian at the School of Veterinary Medicine at the University of Pennsylvania in Philadelphia.

First, check if your dog is breathing. Look for the rise and fall of his chest with each breath and place your hand near his nose to feel for any expirations. If there is no sign of breath, you will need to perform CPR.

Next, check whether your dog has a pulse. The easiest

place to check for his pulse is his inner thigh. This is where a major blood vessel, called the femoral artery, runs very close to the surface of the skin. To feel for his pulse, place your index and middle fingers on the middle of the inside of his rear leg, where it meets the body. If you can't feel your dog's pulse, you will need to perform CPR.

Finally, check for bleeding. "If you find a gash bleeding profusely, try to stop the bleeding by applying direct pressure to the wound or pressure to the relevant pressure point," says Dr. de Papp.

Keep Him Covered

Dogs can go into shock after an accident. This is especially true if he's bleeding severely. "You can buy valuable time by keeping your dog warm," says Dr. de Papp. Cover your injured dog with a coat, sweater, blanket, towel or rug.

"It's a good idea to cover him anyway, just in case he has internal bleeding," she advises. Possible internal bleeding is one good reason why any dog hit by a car should be checked over by a vet.

"Even if your dog seems to be uninjured after a car accident, only a vet can tell if he is bleeding internally, which can be life-threatening," says Dr. de Papp. "No matter when the accident occurs, take your dog to the vet or an emergency pet service immediately," says Dr. Trueba.

Life-Saving CPR

We all know that CPR—cardiopulmonary resuscitation—can bring a person back to life. It can also work for your dog. "If you know how to perform CPR, there's an excellent chance you can breathe life back into your dog and restart his heart after a serious accident," says Gabor K. Vajda, D.V.M., a veterinarian in private practice in Phoenix.

Your dog's brain will suffer from a lack of oxygen if he cannot breathe on his own or his heart stops beating. After about five minutes of not receiving enough oxygen, his brain could suffer irreversible damage. Since it often takes longer than five minutes to get your dog to the vet, it's always worth persisting with CPR, says Dr. Vajda.

How to Perform CPR

To remember the three rules of cardiopulmonary rescusitation, simply think ABC: Airway, Breathing and Circulation.

Open His Airway

A dog that's been hit by a car may not be able to breathe because something is blocking his airway. After a car accident, this could be blood, vomit or saliva. Make sure that his nostrils are not obstructed and use your index and middle finger to swipe the back of his throat clean.

In other cases, your dog might not be breathing because of the position of his neck. Placing him on his side, extending his head back and pulling the tongue forward will make breathing easier. "That may be all your dog needs to start breathing spontaneously," says Dr. Vajda.

Breathe Air In

Hold your dog's mouth shut, place your mouth over his nostrils and blow into his nose four times.

"Breathe into your dog's nose with enough force so you see his chest rise, feel resistance and hear air entering the lungs," explains Dr. Vajda.

Circulate Blood

Position your dog on his right side on a hard surface. Place the heel of one of your hands on the ribs over the heart, where his left elbow would touch his chest when bent. Place the heel of your other hand on top of the first and press down.

"Push down with enough force so that you press the chest about halfway to the ground or floor," advises Dr. Vajda. Compress 15 times, then breathe into your dog's nose twice. Repeat the process.

Ideally, you should be compressing the heart 80 to 100 times in one minute. To do this, count steadily out loud, "One and two and three and four," explains Dr. Vajda.

If you can enlist the help of someone else, one person can blow one breath into your dog after the other compresses the heart five times at a count of one thousand one, one thousand two, one thousand three, and so on.

It's a good idea to continue giving CPR while someone else drives you to the vet. If you're not able to get to a vet, continue CPR until your dog is breathing on his own, or for at least 20 minutes.

1 Open your dog's airway by swiping the back of his throat with your index and middle fingers. Extend his head back and pull the tongue forward. Also check that his nostrils are unobstructed.

2 With your dog's mouth held closed, place your mouth over his nostrils and blow into them with enough force so that his chest rises.

3 Lie your dog on his right side on a hard surface. Place the heel of one of your hands on his ribs over his heart. Place your other hand over the first and push down rhythmically and with reasonable force about 15 times. Blow into his nostrils and repeat the compressions.

Choking

Maybe your dog forgot to chew a large piece of food. (Remember, dogs once lived in packs where the fastest eater got the most food.) Or perhaps a toy slipped too far back in his mouth. Whatever the cause of choking, your calm and efficient actions can quickly restore the breath of life in your best friend.

"A choking dog may breathe very loudly, cough, become anxious or gasp for air," says Merry Crimi, D.V.M., a veterinarian in private practice in Portland, Oregon. To stop him choking, you will need to get the lodged object out of his mouth immediately.

If he's light enough for you to lift totally off the ground, put your arms under your dog's belly and slide them back until they catch him at the groin, just in front of the hind legs. Lift him into the air upside down and give him a gentle shake to try and dislodge the item. For heavier dogs, grasp them in the same manner, but let the front legs rest on the ground like a wheelbarrow.

If your dog is heavy, lift his back legs off the ground as if he were a wheelbarrow. Give his body a good shake to dislodge the obstruction.

To perform the Heimlich maneuver, wrap your arms tightly around your dog's belly just under his rib cage. Give one quick, forceful squeeze and the object causing the obstruction will usually be expelled.

With his head down, give his back legs a good shake.

Because he's not getting enough air, a choking dog may eventually faint. Fortunately, though, that makes helping him easier because you won't have to worry about him resisting your efforts.

If he does faint, open his mouth and pull his tongue out as far as you can. While a bare hand works, you can get a better grip on the tongue if you grasp it with a cloth. "With the other hand, reach into his throat and fish out the culprit that is blocking his airway," says Dr. Crimi.

The Heimlich Maneuver

If the object has slipped so far down his windpipe that you can't reach it or shake it out, you'll need to put some more first-aid measures into practice. "The Heimlich maneuver that works so well on choking people can also work on dogs," says Dr. Crimi.

If your dog is still conscious and standing, tightly wrap your arms around his belly just under the rib cage. For smaller dogs just use both your hands. Give one quick, forceful squeeze. Most of the time the object will pop right out.

If your dog is unconscious, lay him on one side and feel for the last rib. Place both hands, palms down, just behind this bottom rib and press down forcefully a couple of times.

"If none of these tricks work, pack up your dog and head for the vet or an emergency pet clinic," says Dr. Crimi. If your dog has stopped breathing or has no pulse, you should administer CPR.

If you can, get somebody to drive you to the vet. That way, you will be able to comfort your dog and give him CPR on the way.

Water Hazards

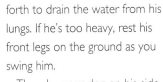 Although most dogs are good swimmers, some aren't. Dogs can get into trouble if they fall into a swimming pool, lake or river. And sometimes even great swimmers can go out too deep and not be able to make it back to shore. Or they may fall through ice or not be able to pull themselves out of a swimming pool.

If you find your dog floating unconscious in the water, pull him out, then suspend him in the air by his rear legs. Gently swing him back and forth to drain the water from his lungs. If he's too heavy, rest his front legs on the ground as you swing him.

Then, lay your dog on his side and place a towel, rug or pillow under his back haunches so that his head is slightly lower than the rest of his body. This will allow any additional water to drain from his lungs. If your dog is not breathing or there is no pulse, administer CPR. Then get him to a vet as quickly as possible.

Better safe than sorry—even dogs that are strong swimmers should wear a life jacket in a boat.

Heatstroke

Just one look at your dog's furry coat makes it easy to understand why he's so much better at preserving body heat in cold weather than he is at cooling down when it's hot.

Although dogs have sweat glands on their feet, these are almost useless and a dog must rely exclusively on panting to breathe off excess heat. "As you can imagine, this cooling-down system isn't efficient, which makes all dogs prone to heatstroke," says Dr. Wise.

Which Dogs Suffer Most?

Certain dog breeds are more susceptible to heatstroke than others. These include short-nosed breeds such as Pugs, Bulldogs and Boxers, who have small airways and even less ability to blow out hot air. Dogs with double coats, such as German Shepherds and Old English Sheepdogs, are more prone to suffer from heatstroke because they retain more heat than dogs with single coats, such as Poodles and terriers.

Leaving a dog in a parked car is the leading cause of heatstroke, says Dr. Crimi. "Contrary to what a lot of people think, even on relatively mild days, heatstroke can strike a dog in just minutes." On a 75° to 80°F day, the temperature inside a parked car—even with a window cracked open—quickly climbs to more than 100°F. And as you would imagine, this drives up your dog's body temperature fast.

Dogs can also suffer heatstroke if they exercise too heavily on a hot, humid day, or if they live outdoors and don't have shelter from the sun. If they are overweight or have heart or lung ailments they are also susceptible. An older dog is less tolerant of heat and will suffer heatstroke more rapidly than a younger dog.

Make sure your dog has access to plenty of drinking water and shade at all times. Dogs with double coats, such as Old English Sheepdogs, and short noses, such as Bulldogs, are particularly susceptible to heatstroke.

Preventing Heatstroke

Nearly every case of heatstroke is preventable, says Merry Crimi, D.V.M., a veterinarian in private practice in Portland, Oregon. Here's what you can do:

- Don't take your dog with you on errands if you plan on leaving him in the car. The five minutes you spend finding what you need and standing in line at the checkout can spell disaster.
- In all weather, but especially in hot weather, make sure he has unlimited access to cold water.
- If you're an avid exerciser, don't push your dog on exceptionally hot and humid days. If he drops behind, let him take a break.
- Keep older dogs and those with heart or lung conditions inside on hot days. If you don't have air conditioning, turn on a room fan.
- For dogs living outside, provide all-day shade, such as a doghouse, overhang or a large beach umbrella. Remember, as the sun shifts, so does shade, and trees may not offer protection all day.

How to Handle Heatstroke

The first sign of heatstroke is rapid, heavy panting, often with excessive salivation. Shortly after this, your dog will start gasping for air. His eyes will become glassy, his gums may turn deep red, and he'll become weak and unable to stand. "If heatstroke progresses, your dog may develop bloody diarrhea, vomiting or seizures," says Dr. Wise.

"As soon as you suspect heatstroke, cool down your dog as fast as possible," says Dr. Crimi. The easiest ways to lower your dog's body temperature is to immerse him in cool water in the bathtub, kitchen sink, a bucket or a child's swimming pool. Avoid icy water as a dramatic change in temperature can be dangerous.

You can also use the garden hose to cool him down. If the hose has been off for a while, let it run until the water becomes cool. Alternatively, place towels soaked in cool water on his head, neck, chest and abdomen. Take the towels off and re-dip them in cool water every five minutes because they will heat up fast. In addition to using cool water you can park your dog in front of an air conditioner or fan. If your dog is conscious and can drink, offer him cold or even ice water.

Sometimes, heatstroke leads to serious problems that only the vet can detect. For example, high body temperatures may damage the kidneys, brain, heart or lungs.

"After cooling him down, take your dog to the vet for a checkup, just to be on the safe side," says Dr. Crimi.

Poisoning

Dogs often eat before they think—and not just dog food. They may steal a plate of brownies or chomp into a bottle of medicine. They gulp down bitter-tasting household chemicals without a second thought and just love the taste of slug and snail poison.

"Suspect poisoning if he has trouble breathing, has seizures, has a slow or fast heartbeat, drools or foams at the mouth, has burns around his mouth and lips, or is bleeding from the anus, mouth or nose," says Dr. Antle, a veterinarian who specializes in emergency care.

Other symptoms of poisoing include your dog being drowsy, unconscious or acting as if he is out of control.

To help your dog, you should know how to make him vomit and when it's safe to do so (see chart at right). If you don't think it's safe to make him vomit, or you don't know what he's eaten, call your vet for advice right away. "Any dog who has ingested something poisonous should be checked by a vet, even if you've made him vomit," advises Steve Hansen, D.V.M., a veterinary toxicologist and vice-president of the American Society for the Prevention of Cruelty to Animals' National Animal Posion Control Center in Urbana, Illinois. Take the poison or pill container and a

Dogs are naturally curious animals so it is very important that you keep all household chemicals and other poisonous substances locked away out of reach. Medicines, cleaning supplies, gardening products and paints are just some of the harmful substances dogs have been known to eat with great abandon.

When to Induce Vomiting

Poisoning is an emergency that requires fast action. Often the best remedy is to get your dog to vomit, which will remove the harmful substances from his system. However, if he's swallowed caustic substances, such as drain cleaner, vomiting will make things worse. The following guide will help you know whether or not to induce vomiting.

POISON	INDUCE VOMITING?	POISON	INDUCE VOMITING?
Antifreeze	Yes	Nail polish	No
Arsenic (ant, rat and mouse poison)	Yes	Paint thinner	No
Aspirin	Yes	Paintbrush cleaner	No
Battery acid	No	Paste (glue)	No
Bleach	No	Pesticides (see arsenic, strychnine, warfarin)	
Carbolic acid (phenol)	No	Phenol (see carbolic acid)	
Crayons	Yes	Pine-oil cleaners	No
Drain cleaner	No	Plaster	No
Fertilizer	No	Putty	No
Furniture polish	No	Roach traps (see insecticides	
Glue	No	Shampoo	Yes
Household cleaners	No	Shoe polish	Yes
Insecticides (including flea and tick dips)	Yes	Sidewalk salt	No
Kerosene	No	Slug and snail bait	Yes (if bait has organo-phosphate carbamate, induce vomiting only if just eaten)
Kitchen matches	Yes		
Laundry detergent	No		
		Strychnine (rat and mouse poisons)	Yes
Lead (found in old linoleum, old paint, old plaster or old putty)	Only if eaten in last half hour	Toilet bowl cleaners	No
		Turpentine	No
Medications (antihistamines, tranquilizers, barbiturates, amphetamines, heart pills, vitamins)	Yes	Warfarin (rat poisons and medications)	Yes, but only if just eaten
Motor oil	No	Weed killers	Yes

sample of his vomit with you to the vet right away.

Inducing Vomiting

The best way to help your dog vomit is to give him hydrogen peroxide. Trickle one teaspoon of hydrogen peroxide for each ten pounds of body weight into his mouth. "If it doesn't work the first time, give him the same amount again in 15 or 20 minutes," says Dr. Hansen. You should also be making your way to the vet. If you don't have any hydrogen peroxide, use a mixture of one tablespoon of dry mustard and one cup of cold water. "While the most important step is to

get the substance out of your dog before it gets into his system, making him vomit is not always safe," says Dr. Hansen. Caustic substances, such as drain cleaner and petroleum-based products, can burn twice: once when they go down and again when they come back up. You still want to get the poison out of his stomach quickly, but only the vet can do so safely.

"That's why it's so important to know what your dog has eaten before acting," says Dr Hansen. If you don't know, assume it's something that might hurt him on the way back up, and get him to the

vet. Never induce vomiting if your dog is having trouble breathing, is having seizures, has a slow heart rate, is unconscious, has a bloated abdomen or the product label says not to.

Antidotes

Depending on the substance your dog has consumed, your vet can sometimes administer an antidote to dilute the poison in his body or reduce its absorption. Sometimes an antidote to a poison is simply milk or water, but you should always ask your vet to administer it as he will know the correct amount to give and the correct way to give it.

Chocolate—How Much is Dangerous?

For a dog, the smell of chocolate is almost as tempting as the smell of a big juicy steak. That's why you may find your dog ripping into a box of wrapped chocolates under the Christmas tree or nabbing baker's chocolate from the kitchen counter.

Although he loves it, chocolate doesn't agree with your dog's system. That's because it contains caffeine and a related chemical called theobromine. Both of these are stimulants that raise your dog's heart rate—occasionally to the point of being fatal. Fortunately, most dogs who overdose on chocolate just get an upset stomach, which may be accompanied by vomiting and diarrhea.

The amount of chocolate that can cause death depends on your dog's size and the kind of chocolate he steals. With baking chocolate, half to one ounce can cause death in small dogs such as Chihuahuas and Toy Poodles. In medium-sized dogs, such as Cocker Spaniels and Dachshunds, the amount is two to three ounces. In large dogs, such as Collies and Labrador Retrievers, the amount is four to eight ounces.

With milk chocolate, four to ten ounces may cause death in small dogs; one to one and a half pounds in medium-sized dogs; and two to four and a half pounds in large dogs.

Torn Nails

When your dog suffers a torn nail, it's usually because he's caught it in the carpet, on your clothing or in a crack on the sidewalk. Rather than stopping calmly to free the snagged nail, he tries frantically to pull it free and tears it in the process. "Injured nails are one of the most painful and bloody injuries a dog can suffer," says Dr. Trueba. Regular nail trimming and grooming greatly reduces the risks, but even well-trimmed nails get torn from time to time.

The first sign of a torn nail is bleeding around the toes. "Dogs' feet have a generous blood supply, which means they bleed quickly and extensively when injured," says Dr. Antle. This speeds up when your dog becomes frightened and starts moving around. And if he's outside and starts pawing in the dirt, this increases the risk of infection.

Treating the Nail

To stop the bleeding, apply firm pressure with gauze pads or a clean rag. Once the bleeding has stopped, wash the paw well with warm water and soap and examine the injury.

"If the nail is not dangling but has simply torn, it probably won't have to be removed," says Dr. Trueba. A torn nail will have come away slightly from the paw on the inner side of the nail and will need to be trimmed. If you usually do this for your dog, then trim it and dress the wound so it can heal. If you're not familiar with the nail-trimming process, this is not the time to learn. Apply ointment and clean, dry gauze pads, taped firmly in place, and take him to the vet.

If the nail is dangling, it will be hanging off the paw and will need to be extracted. This means that the nail must be cut off at the place where it has torn. Otherwise, it will grow back deformed—this can be uncomfortable and even result in your dog developing a permanent limp. "The procedure to cut or pull out your dog's dangling nail is incredibly painful for him," says Dr. Trueba. "That's why it's generally best for a vet to numb the area before she removes the nail." Concentrate on stopping the bleeding, washing the wound and binding it with sterile bandages, then get him to the vet right away.

Preventing Infection

Whether your vet has removed a dangling nail or you have trimmed back one that was torn, you must take great care to prevent any infection occurring around the damaged area. An infection can quickly become serious: it can travel to the bone above the nail, possibly requiring both nail and bone to be amputated and leaving your dog with a life-long limp.

"Wash the area thoroughly with soap and water and coat it with an antibiotic ointment," says Dr. Antle. Then wrap the affected paw securely in gauze and put a sock on it. Use first-aid tape to secure it in place.

Monitor the wound daily. If it becomes red, is warm to the touch or there is any type of discharge, it is probably infected. "Any of these signs warrants an immediate trip to the vet," says Dr. Trueba.

Emergency Quick Reference Chart

EMERGENCY	SYMPTOMS	WHAT TO DO
Bleeding		• Gently but firmly press sterile gauze or clean cloth over wound • Keep dog warm to prevent shock • If wound bleeds through pad, apply more cloth on top; do not remove soaked gauze or cloth • If bleeding continues beyond five minutes, apply pressure to pressure point (groin, armpit, neck, jaw or tail base) and take dog to vet • If bleeding continues another ten minutes, apply a tourniquet on the way to the vet—loosen it at five-minute intervals
Broken leg	Dog won't walk on leg; leg is deformed	• If bone protrudes through skin, cover wound with sterile bandage or clean cloth • For breaks below knee, splint with firm material (magazine, ruler), bind in place with cloth strips and take dog to vet • For breaks above knee, place dog on flat surface, secure him in place and take to vet.
Broken tail	Tail doesn't move below fracture	• For tail breaks not at base, dress open wound then tape entire tail with cloth bandage tape • For tail breaks at base, take to vet
Burns First and second degree Third degree	Red, swollen, blistered skin Red, swollen, blistered and charred skin	• Apply cold water or ice immediately for ten minutes • Apply antibiotic ointment. Dress and monitor wound • Cover and take dog to vet immediately • Apply ice to burn at once. Keep dog warm to prevent shock
Car accidents		• Protect yourself from bites with a muzzle • Check dog is breathing and has heartbeat. Move dog to safety • Start CPR as necessary • Stop bleeding • Take dog on flat surface to vet immediately
Choking	Dog gasping for air, coughing or unconscious	• Reach in and clear mouth of foreign objects • Pull tongue forward and extend head back to open airway • Grab dog by legs, suspend him in midair to shake foreign object from airway (with a large dog, rest front legs on ground)

EMERGENCY	SYMPTOMS	WHAT TO DO
Choking (continued)		• Grasp dog from behind, around his belly just before front legs, and squeeze firmly to expel foreign object from lungs • Take to vet, administering CPR as necessary
Drowning		• Clear mouth of any material • Pull tongue forward and extend neck back to open airway • Suspend dog by hind legs, swing gently to drain lungs • Start CPR as necessary as you take to vet
Heatstroke	Dog panting excessively, drooling, glassy-eyed, vomiting, unconscious	• Immerse in cool (not icy) water • Offer cold water to drink if dog is conscious • Place in front of fan or air conditioner • After cooling down, take to vet for examination
Poisoning	Dog has seizures; burns around mouth; low or fast heartbeat; trouble breathing; is drooling; foaming at mouth; bleeding from anus, mouth or nose; is unconscious; or displaying erratic behavior	• Induce vomiting only if you are certain what the dog has eaten and if vomiting is appropriate for that poison • Take to vet, taking container of poisonous substance along
Shock	Dog is weak, cold to the touch, has pale or gray gums and is breathing rapidly	• Keep dog warm • Try to control bleeding if this is the cause of shock • Take to vet immediately
Snake bite	Bleeding wound on head or legs, dilated pupils, trembling, drooling, vomiting, collapse	• Keep dog calm and still • Take to vet immediately • Don't lance bite or suck out venom
Unconscious dog	Motionless, but has a heartbeat	• Make sure dog is breathing. If not, clear mouth of foreign objects, pull tongue forward, perform mouth-to-nose resuscitation (hold mouth shut) • Take dog to vet on a flat surface to protect any broken bones
Wound Superficial Deep	 Bleeding, scrape or cut Bleeding, deep gash	• Stop bleeding with pressure direct to the wound • Wash with soap and water and apply antibiotic ointment • Try to stop bleeding • Monitor for signs of shock and take dog to vet

PART EIGHT

Looking Good

It's a good idea to get your dog into a coiff and clean routine. Grooming her is a perfect opportunity for the two of you to hang out together, even if it does involve a bit of work on your part. And the payoff for all your efforts with the brushes, combs, cotton balls and water is your happy, healthy, head-turning pet.

20 GROOMING

This isn't just about looking good, it's about feeling good, too. Start with the coat, move on to the eyes, ears and teeth, and wind up around the feet. You'll soon have your dog looking and feeling clean and pristine.

21 BATHTIME

With a little preparation and a no-nonsense approach, the dirt will be dispersed and your dog will be dry again in no time. It doesn't have to be an ordeal and you'll appreciate the results when you see her fresh, fluffy coat.

20 GROOMING

To keep your dog clean, healthy and looking her gleaming best, follow a grooming routine that suits her coat type. Grooming is easy to learn. No matter how much time it takes, both you and she will be proud of the results.

Ears and Eyes
page 405
Hair in the ears and eyes can be a nuisance. Here's how to make her look and feel good

Grooming Counts
pages 391–394
Grooming is not just a luxury. It keeps your dog healthy and nice to be near

How to Groom
pages 398–402
Learn the best grooming techniques for each type of coat

Keeping Feet Neat
pages 406–407
Feet take a lot of punishment, so pamper them regularly

Tools of the Trade
pages 395–397
Select the right brushes and combs to groom your dog's coat type

Clipping
pages 403–404
Clipping is an art. Learn when to do it yourself and when to call on the experts

Clean Teeth
pages 408–409
It takes only a few minutes a day to keep her breath sweet and her mouth healthy

Grooming Counts

Our canine friends love to romp through the grass, swim in lakes and roll in the mud. Unadulterated fun—that's what dogs are all about. But when they are done with all that frolicking, they also want to come back into the house and lie on the sofa like one of the family. And that's where good grooming comes in.

Grooming is more than just swiping a brush over your dog's coat. Regular grooming keeps your dog clean and looking pretty darn good. It also keeps shedding to a minimum and gives you the chance to inspect your dog to make sure her skin, teeth, ears, eyes and nails are healthy.

Because grooming is so important, it's vital that you teach your dog to tolerate it as soon as you

Dogs love to roll in all kinds of things to "clean" themselves. This Golden Retriever has been in the mud, but her owner might think that soap and water do a better job.

Staying Ahead of the Shed

One of many good reasons for grooming your dog is to cut down on the amount of loose hair that ends up on your floors and furniture. Shedding is a normal, healthy function of a dog's body, but that excess hair can drive you nuts. "To keep mess to a minimum, daily brushing is vital," says Michelle Pope Patterson, a professional groomer in Fayetteville, North Carolina. Much of your dog's loose hair should end up in your brush, not in your environment, and that alone makes it worth the time and energy you spend grooming your dog every day, especially during the shedding season.

bring her home. Even if she's only a fuzz ball right now, spend time brushing her coat. Practice lifting those puppy paws up and manipulating them. If she learns now that grooming is a part of everyday life, she will be more cooperative when she's an adult. If your new dog is already an adult, spend some time each day teaching her how to be handled. For more information, see "Hates Being Handled" on page 158.

To help you with the task, there are grooming tools galore that have been designed to tackle just about any kind of canine coat. And just like

Coat Types

There are so many different breeds of dogs, it's natural that there are different types of dog coats. To know how best to groom your dog, you will need to determine the type of coat she has. All dog coats fit into one of the following categories. If your dog is a mixed breed, she will also fit into one of these categories, depending on the type of breed that is most dominant in her genetic makeup.

Short Wiry Coat

Dogs with short wiry coats have hair that is thick and hard, and somewhat bristly to the touch. Wirehaired Dachshunds (right) and most terriers have this type of coat.

Short Smooth Coat

There is no undercoat on this type of coat. Pugs, Basenjis (left) and Dobermans have short smooth coats.

Short Double Coat

This is a flat coat with straight, coarse hair on the outside and a soft, thin undercoat beneath. Labradors and Rottweilers (left) have this type of coat.

Curly Coat

This coat has close curls that are thick and soft. Poodles (right) and Bichon Frises have curly coats.

Long Silky Coat

There is no undercoat with this kind of coat. Yorkshire, Maltese and Silky Terriers (below) have long silky coats.

Long Coarse Coat

Mixed into the long coarse coat is a softer undercoat. Examples of this coat type include the Shih Tzu (above), Lhasa Apso and Tibetan Terrier.

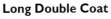

Hairless Coat

The Chinese Crested (below), Inca Orchid and Xoloitzcuintli are examples of hairless dogs. Despite having little or no hair, their sensitive skins still need regular grooming.

Long Double Coat

This is a long, straight and coarse outer coat, with a very thick undercoat all over the body. Samoyeds, Chow Chows (left) and Collies have long double coats.

humans, every dog has a different style. In fact, there's so much more to grooming than just brushing a dog's coat that thousands of professional groomers make a living doing nothing but coiffing dogs.

Different Techniques for Different Breeds

There is a basic technique for grooming each of the various coat types found in dogs. Each technique is designed to make the dog's coat look its best and the way it is supposed to look for the breed. Even if you don't have a purebred, your dog can still benefit from the proper treatment of her coat. Mixed breeds can be given attractive clips that make them look extra special.

There are three main aspects to grooming a dog's coat: brushing, combing and clipping. Your dog's breed will determine what technique you will need to use. For example, a Poodle will need an extensive workout with clippers, while a Labrador Retriever can happily get by with nothing more than a good brushing.

Professional groomers tend to divide dogs into the following coat types: short smooth coats; short double coats; short wiry coats; long double coats; long coarse coats; long silky coats; curly coats; and hairless coats. Each of these coats requires a different type of care, says Mary Allan, a professional groomer in Broken Arrow, Oklahoma. "Short smooth coats only require regular brushing to remove dead hair and shampooing to maintain good condition," she says. "Long coarse coats are probably one of the most labor-intensive types of coat, and need frequent, careful and thorough brushing."

Before you start to groom your dog, do some research on her breed. If your dog is a purebred, look at some photos of show dogs to see exactly

Does a Dull Coat Mean a Sick Dog?

A dog's coat is often a window to her inner health, says Jan Bellows, D.V.M., a veterinarian in private practice in Pembroke Pines, Florida. "A shiny coat usually signifies good health, and one that is dull indicates a problem."

If your dog's coat has been looking rather lackluster of late, take her to the vet for a checkup. One of the problems that can cause a less-than-glossy coat is internal parasites. "Very often, a dog with a dull coat is infested with worms," says Dr. Bellows. She could also be lacking certain minerals or other nutrients. A blood test will tell you if there's a problem with her protein, calcium or phosphate levels, or if something else is wrong.

If your dog is healthy in all other ways but simply lacks a glow to her coat, Dr. Bellows suggests adding some safflower oil to her diet. Mix one teaspoon per day into her regular food if your dog is less than 50 pounds, and a tablespoon a day if your dog is 50 pounds or more.

how that breed is presented. You could even attend some dog shows to see pets that are properly coiffed. If you purchased your pooch from a breeder, ask the breeder to give you a lesson in grooming. Most breeders are experienced in grooming dogs and their tips and expertise can be invaluable, especially if you want your dog to have an authentic look.

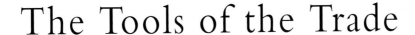

The Tools of the Trade

To keep your dog looking her best, you will need to have the right grooming equipment. There's a huge range of brushes and combs to choose from. Pick the ones that are appropriate for your dog's coat type and her grooming needs.

Bristle Brushes

These brushes are good for stimulating your dog's skin and spreading the natural oils that help to keep her coat shiny and her skin healthy. Bristle brushes are best used on dogs with short coats since they don't do a good job of penetrating longer coats. There are all kinds of bristle brushes, but Allan recommends the kind of "porcupine" or pincushion brush manufactured for humans by Mason and Pearson, with bristles set in a rubber base.

"These brushes separate finer hair well and the boar bristles distribute the natural oils throughout the length of the hair, which is a necessity for silky coats," she says.

Pin Brushes

The pin brush has long, straight metal pins attached to a rubber backing. Most pin brushes are oval-shaped and are used primarily on long-coated breeds. They are excellent for fluff-drying dogs with long hair.

Slicker Brush

This is the most versatile brush since it works with many different types of coats. The bent wire bristles of the slicker brush grasp and remove a dog's loose undercoat. Slickers come in many different sizes, shapes and stiffness of bristles. Dogs that are brushed regularly with a slicker brush seldom become matted.

Soft bristle brush

Slicker brush

Pincushion brush

Wide-toothed comb

Mat splitter

Hound Gloves

Some people prefer to groom their dogs with a hound glove instead of a brush. These brushes fit over the hand like a glove and feature a cloth base with rubber nubs that capture loose hair. Dogs enjoy being groomed with hound gloves because they like the feeling that they are being petted. The hair can be washed out or easily removed by hand.

Dematting Tools

These combs and splitters come in a variety of shapes and styles, all designed to saw through mats in your dog's coat without you having to cut them off. Some skill is required to use them properly—in the hands of a novice, your dog could end up looking like a shaggy dog story.

Combs

These come in different tooth sizes, and the spacing between the teeth varies. The larger-toothed combs are used to remove undercoat in some of the heavier-coated breeds, while other combs can be used to test the undercoat after grooming to see if there are still more loose hairs that need to be removed. Some combs have handles, while others are straight combs with one-half of the comb containing fine-spaced teeth and the other half wider-spaced teeth.

Double-sided grooming glove

Stripping Combs

These are commonly used on terriers and other breeds with wiry coats to tidy them up. There are certain stripping techniques that can transform your dog into a real star. Proper use of a stripping comb requires considerable skill and it's perhaps best that they be left in the hands of a professional groomer.

Hound glove

Dryers

Professional groomers use a dryer designed specifically for use on dogs. Called a force dryer, these feature convenient stands that make it easier to blow-dry your dog's coat. But because they cost between $150 and $500, you have to be pretty serious about grooming your dog if you buy one. There are some portable models manufactured for home use and these may be adequate and more affordable.

Removing Burrs and Mats

Sticky burrs and tangled mats are a pesky problem for canine coats, especially for those dogs who love to play hard. If your dog swims, then she will have the biggest problem with mats because water causes a dog's fur to stick together. If you own a dog with a long coat, silky coat or thick double coat, burrs and mats will be a recurring fact of her canine life, and you will need to know how to get rid of them.

"Burrs and mats should be removed with a dematting tool and a slicker brush," says Pat Field, a professional groomer in Markham, Ontario. "The burrs can usually be brushed out once the mats are broken up. The dematting tool will cut through the mats, separating them, and then a slicker brush can be used to brush the mat out." If the mats are too tight, use a mat-splitting tool. This cuts through the length of the hair instead of across it. Use a small slicker brush to brush a few hairs at a time gently from the tangle.

Some groomers recommend applying a chemical substance to a mat or burr before trying to remove it, and then patiently using old-fashioned elbow grease to work the mat out. "I first saturate the area with a silicone-based mat spray and let it sit for about 15 to 30 minutes," says Mary Allan, a professional groomer in Broken Arrow, Oklahoma. "Then I try to work out the mat or burr with my fingers by pulling and easing the hair apart a little at a time." This manual method takes time, but causes the least trauma to your dog's coat.

Whatever you do, don't bathe your dog until every mat has first been removed from her coat. "Putting a dog right into the bath without first removing the mats will only lead to more matting," explains Field. "Once a mat gets wet, it tightens and becomes harder to remove. Also, when a badly matted dog is bathed, the shampoo gets trapped in the mats and can't be rinsed out properly. This can result in skin irritation."

If all else fails, you'll need to get out your trusty scissors or clippers, says Michelle Pope Patterson, a professional groomer in Fayetteville, North Carolina. Sometimes dogs are so matted or covered in burrs that it's more practical to shave the coat and start over. "If a mat is touching the skin, it is usually best to shave the dog," she says.

How to Groom

If you groom your dog yourself in between visits to a professional groomer, you might be disappointed by her overall appearance. Let's face it—groomers are trained to do this, and they are real pros. "Most people don't understand why they can't maintain the same 'just groomed' look when they bathe their dogs at home," says Patterson. Unless you are especially talented and experienced in grooming, your dog is always going to look much better after a visit to a professional groomer. However, there are some grooming tips that will help you make your dog look as if she's spent the day at the beauty salon.

"The most important contribution to a well-groomed look is using the correct type of brushing technique and the right brush or comb for your dog's type of coat and hair style," says Allan.

"For the best results, blow-dry your dog, brushing and combing as you go. If you can't blow her dry, then towel her well, leave her inside to dry so she doesn't roll in the dirt, then thoroughly brush and comb her. Most dogs, especially Poodles, will have kinky hair when wet, and it will stay that way if not brushed out thoroughly after or during drying."

Grooming is bliss for this Labrador. Her short double coat is being finished off with a hound glove, and because it feels just like she's being petted, she'll happily sit still for hours. If you choose a double-sided glove, it can be used on either your right or left hand.

Short Smooth Coats

These are probably the easiest coats to groom. Use a bristle brush or a hound glove, and first brush against the direction your dog's hair lies. This will help to remove any excess hair from underneath. Then, using the same tool, brush in the direction the coat lies to pick up loose hairs on the surface. A once-a-week brushing will keep shedding under control.

Dogs with short smooth coats can benefit from a bath with a light conditioner after they have been groomed. Towel-dry her, then let her coat dry off naturally.

Short Double Coats

These coats require more care, since the double coat underneath sheds constantly, with an even greater loss of hair in spring and fall. Use a

slicker brush or pin brush, and start by taking sections of your dog's coat and separating it with your hand so there is a parting where her skin is visible. Then use the brush to comb out the undercoat, brushing outward from the skin as you do so. This is the best way to keep mats from forming in the thick undercoat. The undercoat will be thickest at the neck and hind legs, and you can brush it straight out with your slicker in these areas.

Once you have finished brushing the undercoat, use the same brush to go over the top coat, brushing with the lie of the coat. Brush your dog twice a week, but increase this to several times a week during the shedding season.

Depending on how dirty she gets, bathe your short double-coated dog as often as needed, but not more than once a month. Before you bathe her, make sure you have brushed her well. When you are done, towel her dry first, then use a hair dryer designed especially for dogs. If your dog is still damp, allow her coat to dry naturally. When it's completely dry, brush her coat with the slicker in the same way as before.

Short Wiry Coats

The characteristic wiry coat requires a different type of handling from the more traditional smooth and double coats. A slicker brush, medium-tooth metal comb and a stripping comb are needed to groom this type of coat. Start by running the stripping comb lightly along the back of the dog, thinning the overgrown wiry coat. Go easy at first—you can always remove more hair later, but you can't put it back if you thin out too much. This thinning does not need to be done at every grooming session, only when the hairs on the very top of her coat

This Wire Fox Terrier is being given a star makeover by having her coat stripped by a professional groomer. Even non-stars should have this treatment from time to time.

(called the guard hairs) begin to protrude along her back. Overgrown guard hairs will curl up above the rest of her hair and give her an unkempt look.

After thinning out, brush your dog's wiry coat in layers, from the skin outward, with the slicker brush. You can then comb in layers in the same way with the metal comb, which will pick up any loose hairs.

Your dog's wiry coat will also need to be carded and hand-stripped regularly. Carding is a technique whereby loose hair is removed by "brushing" the coat with a blade or stripping stone. "It's quite a long process and your dog needs to be well-trained," says Allan.

Hand-stripping is a technique in which the loose hairs are grasped between finger and thumb and tugged out. Take your dog to a professional groomer or her breeder so that the carding or stripping is performed by someone experienced in the technique, says Allan. While you can eventually learn to do it yourself, you should start by having it done by someone experienced—a poor carding or hand-stripping job can leave your dog looking and feeling terrible.

After your dog has been groomed, you can bathe her with a texturizing shampoo. This is a special shampoo that adds body and coarseness to wiry coats. Dry her carefully with a blow dryer, working in the direction the hair lies. She should then be brushed one more time.

Long Double Coats

With a thick undercoat as its trademark, long double coats are the ones that shed the most. If your dog has this type of coat you will need a slicker brush or pin brush and a large, wide-tooth comb to groom her.

Brush your dog's entire body with the slicker or pin brush first, taking sections of her hair and separating it with your hand. Brush outward from the skin to help

Although Afghans have long straight coats, the best technique to use for grooming them is the same as for long double coats. This groomer is parting sections of the Afghan's coat and brushing with a pin brush from the skin outward.

remove the loose hairs in the thick undercoat. After you have gone over her entire coat, take the wide-tooth comb and place it deep within the coat, parallel to the skin. Comb outward in this way to remove more loose undercoat. Since the undercoat is thickest on the back legs and around the neck, you may need to work through some mats here using a dematting tool.

Bathe your dog only after you have groomed her. Towel-dry her, then carefully dry her more with a blow dryer. If you use a high setting on the blow dryer, more of the shedding undercoat will be removed, so brush her again afterward.

Long Coarse Coats

The long, human-hairlike quality of this coat makes it one of the more time-consuming coats to groom. It easily gets tangled and matted, and most pet owners have their dog's long coarse coat clipped regularly to keep grooming to a minimum. If you have chosen not to have your dog's coat clipped, be prepared to make a big commitment in grooming time and energy.

Begin the grooming session by commanding your dog to lie down on her side. Remove any mats that you find, and be careful not to break the hairs as you do so. You can also sprinkle some cornstarch on the tangles to make them easier to separate. With a pin brush, brush the coat out gently in the direction that it grows. Once you have pin-brushed the entire coat, go over it again with a soft bristle brush.

Bathe your dog after you have brushed her. Squeeze the shampoo gently through the coat to prevent tangling. "Great care should be taken to rinse very thoroughly, as shampoo left in the coat can cause skin irritation that will lead to scratching and a tangled, matted coat in no time," says Allan.

These coats usually require a light conditioner as well, so use a shampoo with conditioner, or apply a cream rinse. When you towel your dog dry, squeeze the excess water from her coat with the towel. If you want the correct look for her breed, blow-dry her with a dryer designed for dogs, rather than letting it dry naturally.

If you want to trim the long hair that is sticking out of your dog's ears, do this before you bathe her. Don't clip it too close, and make sure to keep the cut hair from falling back into your dog's ear canal.

Long Silky Coats

Long silky coats are difficult to care for and they are usually clipped to keep grooming to a minimum. If you want to keep your silky-coated dog's coat long, you'll need to spend considerable time grooming it—at least two or three times a week, if not more.

The biggest challenge in grooming a long silky coat is dealing with the mats that often form around the legs, ears, side of the face or anywhere else where the hair is particularly long. To remove mats, use a dematting tool, then brush the entire coat with a slicker brush in the direction the hair lies. After grooming, bathe your dog with a conditioning shampoo or follow the shampoo with a cream rinse. Dry her coat with a hair dryer designed for dogs (don't hold the nozzle too close), then brush again.

Curly Coats

The typical curly coat needs regular brushing to keep its neat, curly look. Whether your dog is clipped in a modified show clip or a puppy clip (best done by a professional groomer), you will need to use a slicker brush to brush the coat against the way it grows to make it fluff up away from the body. If your dog's coat has started to look unruly, it may be time to go back to a professional groomer for another clip. Never attempt to do the job yourself unless you are experienced in this art.

A soft slicker brush is being used to fluff up the curly coat of this Bichon Frise. The coat has been rinsed with a body-building conditioner and blow-dried. It is now being brushed against the direction it grows, from the skin outward, to give it volume.

Professional Styling

If your dog has a longhaired, double-coated or curly-haired coat, you may have already considered paying for the skills of a professional dog groomer. Not only will a professional do all the work for you, but she can make your dog look absolutely terrific. As well as brushing, combing, clipping and washing your dog, a professional groomer will also trim her nails, clean her ears and prune the hair neatly between her toes.

Professional groomers are not used by clients just to spruce up show dogs. They are accustomed to dealing with all the different kinds of dogs with all the different kinds of lifestyles, and can usually accommodate most reasonable requests. On the other hand, don't think that a professional groomer can turn your Benji-look-alike into Rin Tin Tin. Groomers can do wonders with an unkempt dog, but they're not trained to perform miracles.

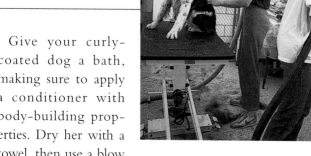

Give your curly-coated dog a bath, making sure to apply a conditioner with body-building properties. Dry her with a towel, then use a blow dryer to fluff-dry her, all the while brushing her with the soft slicker brush from the skin outward. When fluff-drying, be careful not to pull the brush through the hair too roughly, as this will irritate your dog's skin.

Hairless Coats

Dogs with no hair obviously don't need regular brushing, but they do need frequent baths. Use a gentle shampoo, preferably one with an antibacterial agent, to help ward off the skin problems that are common in these breeds.

"About every week or so, it is beneficial to give them a scrub with a gentle face puff while shampooing," says Allan. This will help their circulation and get rid of dead skin cells. As with other dogs, great care should be taken to rinse hairless dogs thoroughly after a bath.

After their bath, they'll need an extra beauty step. "They should always be moisturized with an oil-free moisturizer, and this should be applied daily," says Allan. Hairless dogs are also very prone to sunburn and you should apply an SPF (sun protection factor) 15 or higher sunblock all over, whenever they go outside.

Since not all hairless dogs are completely hairless, you can use a regular safety razor to remove any existing light body hair. On breeds where tufts of hair are found on the top of the head, legs and tail, such as the Chinese Crested, use a slicker brush to groom these areas.

Clipping

Although the mastery of the art of clipping belongs to the professional groomer, you too can use these instruments to groom your dog and make her look good. The extent to which you use clippers will depend on the type of dog you have and the kind of coat she sports, but almost any dog can benefit from some tidying up with clippers.

Need a Clip?

The breed that requires the most clipping is the Poodle. Whether it is one of the large Standards or a tiny Toy, the Poodle coat screams out for the clippers. Not only is this because of the stylishness of the breed, but also because a Poodle's coat grows continuously. The finely dolled-up Poodles you see at dog shows have their hair clipped down to the skin in places, and shaped and molded in others. This show clip is not practical for most pet Poodles because it is so difficult to maintain, but even the traditional puppy cut requires clipping.

Some of the other breeds that are clipped on a regular basis include the Bichon Frise, Bedlington Terrier, Kerry Blue Terrier, Bouvier des Flandres and Airedale Terrier. While these breeds don't call for as much clipping as a Poodle, they do need shaping to keep them looking like the breeds that they are.

Whether you have a Poodle or another breed that needs clipping, you will be better off keeping your pet in a simple clip that makes her look good but is relatively simple to maintain. "In the truest sense of the word, the only really dramatic show clip will be on a Poodle," says Patterson. "On all other types of dogs, say, a Scottish Terrier or a Schnauzer, it would be hard for the average pet owner to tell the difference between a show clip and a pet clip."

Practice Makes Perfect

If you want to do the clipping yourself instead of taking your dog to a professional groomer you will need to practice a lot—it takes quite a bit of skill to clip a dog's coat properly. You may even decide to take a course on dog grooming. This will give you plenty of opportunity to practice before you take the clippers to your pet.

If you decide to invest in your own clippers, make sure you choose a selection of blades. Different ones are appropriate for the different areas on your dog's body.

If you've been taking your dog to a professional groomer, ask her to teach you how to clip. "I encourage my clients who want to clip their own dogs to come and watch me work on their dog once. Then they can decide if it's something they want to do themselves," says Patterson.

One of the most important things to be aware of is that you must always cut with the hair, not against it. Cutting against the grain of the hair can result in cuts and burns on your dog's skin.

Clippers and Blades

If you decide to invest in your own clippers, narrow your selection down to the two basic types that professional groomers use: standard clippers and small clippers. "Standard clippers are used for all-around grooming," explains Beverly Latham, a professional groomer and instructor of a pet-grooming correspondence course in Coeur d'Alene, Idaho. "Small clippers, ones about the size of mustache clippers, are used on the face, ears and feet of some breeds."

The top two brands of clippers are Oster A-5 and Andis, says Patterson. These are available from pet supply catalogs and at a few pet supply stores. "The dog clippers that you find in department stores are worthless for most dogs," she says. "They come with a blade that is designed to only cut clean Poodle hair. They will not cut any dog hair that is dirty, and will bind up on Cocker Spaniels or any other thick-haired dogs."

Ask your groomer to help you purchase some decent clippers and blades. "A rep-

utable groomer would rather help you learn to clip your dog with a decent set of clippers than spend time repairing the damage you will do with a cheap pair. I am always glad to help clients purchase clippers and blades and to help them with the follow-up care that is required," says Patterson. Be sure to get a number 10 blade for the stomach, feet, face and genital area, and a number 7F blade for clipping the body. "The number 7F is good for everything from Poodles to Chows," says Patterson. The total cost for the clippers and blades should be about $150.

This Standard Poodle sports a sculpted "lion" clip. Such elaborate clips require lots of maintenance and are usually only given for show dogs.

Ears and Eyes

As well as making your dog attractive, grooming has a practical side as well. When you sit down to groom your dog, you have the opportunity to take a close look at her ears and eyes. Now is the time to check them for any signs of problems and to work at keeping them clean and healthy.

Clean Ears

Dogs with hairy faces tend to have hairy ears, and the more hair in your dog's ears, the more chance there is of dampness and possible infection. When you take your dog to a professional groomer, she will most likely pluck the excess hair from your dog's ears. "Dogs that accumulate hair in the ear canal, such as Poodles, Shih Tzus and Lhasas, need to have that hair removed by grasping a few hairs at a time with either fingers or forceps, and pulling gently," says Allan. "This can be made easier by the use of powders specially marketed for the purpose."

If you don't feel comfortable plucking your dog's ear hair, trim it with blunt-nosed scissors. Make sure you keep the cut hair from falling into her ear. If your dog won't sit still long enough for you to do this, take her to a professional groomer. You don't want to hurt her with the scissors while she is struggling.

Dogs with floppy ears are especially prone to ear problems because the design of their ears prevents good air circulation. If you own a Labrador Retriever, Bloodhound, Cocker Spaniel or any breed or mix with floppy ears, be

Clean your dog's ears regularly from the time she is a puppy. Like this young Bulldog, she will become accustomed to her ears being handled if it's part of the grooming routine. A wipe with a cotton ball dampened in mineral oil or water is all that's needed.

especially diligent about checking and cleaning the insides. While it's important to keep her ears clean, some wax needs to remain in the ears, so don't overdo it. If your dog's ears seem particularly dirty, dampen a cloth with mineral oil or use a cotton ball and a commercial ear cleaner to wipe the inside of the earflap clean. If the dirty appearance returns in a week or so, your dog may have an ear infection. In this case, it's best to take your dog to the vet for a checkup.

Clean Eyes

To keep your dog's eyes sparkling and clear, simply wipe them with a cotton ball dipped in lukewarm water. This will get rid of any discharge that may have built up in the corners. Never cut hair around the eyes. If your dog has hair that falls into her eyes, use a rubber band or clip to pull it back. When you clean your dog's eyes, take a close look at them to see if there is anything unusual. If you see any redness, cloudiness, swelling or tearing, contact your vet.

Keeping Feet Neat

Of all her body parts, your dog's feet probably take the biggest pounding. When she runs along the pavement, her pads endure the friction of hard cement. If it's really hot out, she can get blisters from contact with the heat-absorbing pavement, and if it's cold, she has to negotiate jagged ice and frozen snow. Dogs that live in the country aren't completely off the hook, either. She will be stepping on rocks, sharp pieces of wood and whatever other objects Mother Nature has strewn in her path.

Protecting the Paws

How can you protect your dog's delicate paws from damage during her daily workout? Rub vitamin E and juice from an aloe plant onto them, both before and after taking her out for a walk, says Jan Bellows, D.V.M., a veterinarian in private practice in Pembroke Pines, Florida. Inspect your dog's feet after each outing to make sure there are no sharp objects or injuries present. Examine the paws for blisters and redness on the webs between the toes. "Things can get caught in there, so look for objects that may have become lodged," says Dr. Bellows. If you find anything, remove it with a pair of tweezers.

Your dog might be showing signs of discomfort in her paws by the way she walks. "If she's a little

In some breeds, the hair on the feet can get so long that it looks as if your dog is wearing slippers. Because it can trap dirt and debris, it's a good idea to keep it trimmed.

gimpy on a certain leg, there could be a paw injury," says Dr. Bellows. If the problem persists or your dog is in obvious pain, Dr. Bellows recommends you see your vet. The problem could be something as simple as a foxtail caught between the toes, or something more serious.

Clipping Between the Toes

You may have noticed that your dog has an abundance of hair between the nails on her feet. If you take your dog to be groomed professionally, the groomer will snip those hairs off, giving your dog's feet a neat and orderly appearance. There's no reason you can't do the same at home, provided your dog is willing to cooperate.

"With most medium- to longhaired dogs, it is important to keep the hair between the toes cut," says Patterson. "The reason is that this space typically hides dirt, burrs, fleas and tiny mats. Your dog may take to chewing on her feet, which soon becomes a habit that is hard to

break." It's difficult to cut the hair between the foot pads but it's a good idea to keep this trimmed also. "Often, this hair is where dirt and debris end up after your dog has been outside," says Patterson.

The best way to trim your dog's feet is by using a pair of blunt-nosed baby fingernail scissors. Hold her foot up and separate the pads with one hand while carefully trimming the hair as close as possible to the pads with the scissors. "If the hair on the top of the foot is untidy, it can be slicked upward and the excess trimmed carefully with a thinning shear, a little at a time, until it looks right," says Allan.

Nail trimmers

Clipping the Nails

Imagine letting your fingernails grow unchecked for months or years. They would interfere with the use of your hands and look pretty darn strange. Now imagine having to walk on those out-of-control fingernails. Nail-trimming is not just something you should do for your dog's appearance. It's also vital for her health and comfort. The pain from walking on neglected nails is reason enough to trim your dog's nails regularly.

Avoiding the Quick

Trimming your dog's nails is not as difficult as it may seem, provided your dog cooperates. You can trim her nails with a hand-held cutting device or with an electric grinder. Whichever method you use, you need to cut the nail just at the point where it starts to curve downward. You want to avoid the quick, the area of the nail that contains nerves and blood vessels.

If your dog has white nails, it's easy to locate the quick. Simply look for the pink line that extends from the base of the nail down toward the tip. When you trim, clip below this pink line so you don't cut into it. For dogs with dark-colored nails, finding the quick is trickier. Hold a flashlight up to the nail to get an idea where the quick ends, then go by memory.

Be conservative in your cutting. If you cut the nail too short, you may cut into the quick. This will hurt her and cause bleeding, and she'll be reluctant to let you continue. Keep a container of styptic powder handy in case you cut into the quick. Sprinkling this over the cut area will quickly stop the bleeding.

The tool you use to trim your dog's nails should be the one you feel most comfortable with. An electric nail grinder lets you get nearer to the quick without actually hitting it. For owners who prefer to use a hand-held trimmer, go slowly. "Cut only a tiny amount at a time," says Allan. "If you look under the nail, you will see a groove running from the tip up toward the foot. The end of this groove is generally where the quick begins. If you cut no farther than that, you should not cut into the quick."

When clipping the nails, avoid cutting the quick, the sensitive part (shown at the right as the pink area). Cutting the quick will make her bleed a little and she'll remember the pain, which will make future nail trimmings more difficult.

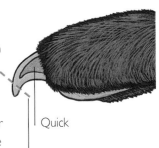

Quick

Cutting line

Clean Teeth

An important, but often overlooked, part of your dog's daily grooming routine is the brushing of her teeth. Dogs need to have clean teeth in order to have fresh breath and a healthy canine smile. But there are also some very serious reasons for cleaning your dog's teeth regularly. Poor dental hygiene can lead to a number of diseases. "Dogs with teeth that are not cleaned can suffer from diseases in the mouth as well as infections in the major organs," says Dr. Bellows.

Avoid Dental Decay

If you don't brush your dog's teeth regularly, plaque builds up on her teeth and under her gums, just as it does in humans. If the plaque is not removed, a bacterial infection, called periodontal disease, can develop. If left untreated, the bacterial infection can enter the bloodstream and spread to your dog's kidney, liver, heart or brain. Other problems, such as mouth abscesses and loose teeth, can also develop in dogs that don't have good dental hygiene. And dogs with dirty teeth and periodontal disease will have very bad breath. "Ninety-eight percent of dogs with bad breath are suffering from periodontal disease," says Dr. Bellows. "If a dog's breath doesn't smell good, then there's probably a problem with her teeth."

One way to avoid all these unpleasant problems is to brush your dog's teeth daily. Your dog should also be examined once a year by your vet, who may recommend a professional cleaning.

How to Brush

Thousands of dog owners brush their dog's teeth every day. And it's a lot simpler than you think. First, collect your supplies. You can either use a piece of gauze wrapped around your finger, a "finger" toothbrush (a nubby-surfaced rubber cap that fits over your index finger) or a toothbrush made especially for dogs. You'll also need special dog toothpaste. All of these items are available in pet supply stores.

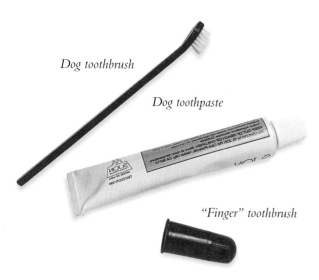

Dog toothbrush

Dog toothpaste

"Finger" toothbrush

It's really not as hard as you might think to brush your dog's teeth, particularly if you equip yourself with some of the specially designed tools shown here.

What's Wrong with Human Toothpaste?

There are so many different brands and types of human toothpaste available: special whitening formulas with baking soda; extra-strength fluoride toothpastes with exciting flavors, such as peppermint and wintergreen; even toothpastes packaged in nifty and convenient containers that make using toothpaste extremely easy.

Since human toothpaste has so many wonderful qualities, why can't we use it on our dogs? The answer is simple. "Dogs don't spit like people do," says Jan Bellows, D.V.M., a veterinarian specializing in dental care in Pembroke Pines, Florida. "They swallow the toothpaste, so that makes everything different."

As delicious as our human toothpastes are, they are not meant to be eaten. Instead, we rinse out our mouths and spit the paste into the bathroom sink. Dogs, on the other hand, will swallow after having their teeth brushed. This means their toothpaste must be edible. It also has to be appetizing because the better the toothpaste tastes, the more likely it is that your dog will sit still for you while you brush her teeth.

While some dogs might enjoy the minty taste of human toothpaste, the poultry and beef flavors offered in canine toothpastes are much more appealing to the majority of pooches. Keep experimenting until you find the one she likes best.

Brushing one or two teeth at a time, work your way round her upper jaw before moving on to the lower. It didn't take long for this Welsh Corgi to get used to the idea.

Start by sitting your dog in a comfortable position and lifting her upper lip. If your dog squirms, you may need a helper to restrain her. Once you have access to some of the top teeth, you are ready to begin. "Gently rub a couple of teeth at a time," says Dr. Bellows. "Be sure to brush where the tooth attaches to the gum."

Use a back-and-forth or circular motion when brushing, much the way you would to brush your own teeth. Make your way around your dog's upper teeth, being especially careful to clean the teeth at the back, since these are the ones most prone to periodontal disease. When you have finished with her top choppers, move down to the bottom.

If possible, perform this brushing routine on your dog once or twice a day. "If you don't have time, take a small towel and rub the outside of the upper teeth with it once a day," says Dr. Bellows. "This is where the salivary glands are and where dental problems are likely to begin."

21 BATHTIME

When your dog gets a little smelly and his coat starts to lose some of its shine, it's time to get out the cleaning gear and get him into the tub. Bathtime isn't going to be his favorite activity, although it will help if you can get him used to it from an early age. And the end result will make your efforts and his patience all worthwhile— your pristine pooch showing off his gorgeous, newly washed coat.

When to Wash Him
pages 411–413
Pay attention to the condition of your dog's coat and you'll know when he needs a bath

Bathing Step-by-Step
pages 419–420
A guide for cleaning the different dog coats—double-coated, non-shedding and shorthaired

The Best Bathing Techniques
pages 414–418
From brushing him down to lathering him up and drying him off

Shampoos and Conditioners
page 421
With so many bathtime products, you'll find one that works for him

When to Wash Him

Dogs don't need baths all that often, which is lucky for both of you, given most dogs' lack of enthusiasm for bathtime. But even the most fastidious dogs need regular baths and, depending on their coats, some dogs need them more often than others.

A dog that spends a lot of time outside, for example, tends to get grungier than an indoor dog. But every dog is different. The most obvious question you're going to have to ask yourself is—and be honest now—how dirty is he? Determining the frequency of your dog's dates with shampoo and water isn't so much a matter of his breed and size. It's mostly a question of what condition his coat is in.

How Dirty Does He Get?

Whether he's the biggest grub or he's always immaculate between the toes, it's the way your dog looks and smells that will be telling you when it's bathtime. If you have a tiny, apartment-dwelling dog who rarely frolics outside enough to get a hair out of place, you'll be fine bathing him every few months. Regular brushing will remove the dead hair and any accumulated dirt in between times.

However, if you live in a suburban or rural setting, where there are more opportunities for your dog to become one with nature, he's going to be a dirtier dog. "If your dog swims a good deal, or goes out and rolls in 'deer exhaust,' you are going to want to bathe him pretty frequently," says Pat Kansoer, a professional

This dog is having a blissful time, rolling on the grass. If your dog likes getting down and dirty like this, he'll need a bath more often than if he mostly plays indoors.

groomer and animal behaviorist in the Chicago area. Shoot for once a month, unless your nose and his coat demand more.

Naturally Self-Cleaning

While your dog needs an occasional bath, it's sometimes best to let nature take its course. Dogs with thick, double-coated hair, such as the Samoyed, rarely need washing. The main thing is to brush them regularly. This distributes the natural oils, gets rid of dirt and loose hair, and prevents matting.

Then there are dogs with waterproof coats. It's best not to bathe breeds like Great Pyrenees or Chesapeake Bay Retrievers too often because you could reduce the coat's ability to repel water—important in a dog that swims a lot or lives in a cool climate. It's the same with a mixed breed with a water-repellent coat. You'll know he has one when you try to get him thoroughly wet. It will take determination and extreme diligence—and several rounds of shampoo—to get him soaked right down to the skin.

Washing Away Allergies

"Minimizing the dog hair in the house and bathing your dog frequently can lessen allergic responses of family members," says Christine L. Wilford, D.V.M., a veterinarian in private practice in Seattle and a regular columnist for the *American Kennel Club Gazette*. "But dog hair is not the real culprit. It's tiny proteins in the dog's saliva that are the source of allergies. These cling to the dog's coat when he licks himself, and when the saliva dries they become dander." People and dogs can develop an allergic reaction to this dander.

Bathing your dog is the best way to remove the itch-causing, sneeze-producing dander. To make his bath even more effective, Eileen Gabriel, a professional groomer in Carmel, New York, suggests this trick: "Dilute a capful of fabric softener in a bucket of water and use it as a final rinse after you've bathed your dog. This works really well for holding down the dander."

Many things can make your dog itch and scratch and lick himself for a little relief. Bathing will remove dander as well as other possible allergens, such as pollens, molds and dust, from his coat. Rinsing him off with cool, clean water is especially soothing for him.

You don't have to put him in the tub every time he starts to itch, says Kansoer. In between baths, you can help control dander by simply wiping your dog's coat down with distilled water and a towel, he suggests.

The Bathtime Bottom Line

All dogs should be bathed at least two or three times a year, says Lois Friesen, a professional groomer and grooming instructor in Leduc, Alberta. "The skin is the largest organ on a dog's body and it's important to maintain cleanliness so as to keep his skin healthy."

Use your judgment when deciding if your dog needs a bath. If he looks or feels dirty, he probably is. If he's had a delightful time rolling in dung or other unmentionables, he definitely does. And if company is coming and you want him to look his best, a bath is certainly not going to hurt.

Sniffing Out Problems

If your dog starts smelling unpleasant, it may not be his coat that's causing the problem. Even if it is, a bath may not be the best solution. Make sure you give him the olfactory once-over to discover the source of the smell first.

- Check his ears, advises Kansoer. Drop-eared dogs, such as Basset Hounds and Cocker mixes, can start to smell simply because their ears are dirty. The warm, moist environment under the long, drooping ear flap is perfect for fungal or bacterial growth. Cleaning his ears may be all you need do to quell the smell.
- Another place for a sniff test is his mouth. A bad smell coming from your dog's mouth could signal canine dental disease. So don't worry about the mouthwash. It's time he was seeing the vet.

He Loves Swimming, So Why Does He Hate His Bath?

Even dogs that love to swim usually hate to take a bath. Why is it that they will happily plunge into a murky lake but hide in the closet when it's time to fill the tub? After all, it's the same thing, except that it's possibly a whole lot cleaner, so what is the problem?

Very simply, when your dog is swimming, he's in control. He's having fun and, more than likely, taking a dip was his idea anyway. Being bathed is most definitely somebody else's idea, and it is really not his notion of a good time.

"When a dog gets a bath, he is often in an unfamiliar environment," explains Pat Kansoer, a professional groomer and animal behaviorist in the Chicago area. "And when he's swimming, he's not worried about someone splashing him in the face, or getting water in his eyes or ears." You'll notice that even dogs that like to swim don't usually stick their heads under water. It's not called dog-paddling for nothing.

Not all dogs hate baths, of course. Those that are trained early on to take baths will often enjoy them. If you have a puppy, get him used to his bath as early as you can, suggests Lois Friesen, a professional groomer and grooming instructor in Leduc, Alberta. "Talk sweetly to him and teach him to stay while he's being washed," she advises. "And make it fun. If you see it as a chore, he'll pick up on your feelings."

- Certain foods your dog has eaten may make his coat smelly. "Garbage in, garbage out," says Kansoer. "Not everything a dog eats comes out in his waste." Some of it permeates and is exuded through the skin, just like when you smell of garlic two days after feasting on pasta with pesto. Feed your dog a high-quality food, making sure he stays away from garbage in all its forms—garbage cans, too many table scraps, or throw-away tidbits he finds during a walk.

- Many longhaired breeds can get that doggy smell because of mats or dead hair trapped in their coats. And a dog that is really matted may even smell of mold or mildew since the mats trap moisture. Always be sure to brush all the mats out before washing him. If you can't brush through the coat, don't wash it. Take your dog to a groomer instead, who will remove the mats, possibly by cutting them away. But prevention is always going to be the best policy. "I can't stress enough how important it is to regularly brush a dog's coat, especially double-coated breeds like Samoyeds," says Valerie Shoemaker, a professional groomer and grooming instructor in Cupertino, California. "Otherwise, that undercoat will mat, get wet and really start to smell."

- The hair around your dog's rear end can trap a lot of dirt that will undoubtedly give off a bad odor. Most groomers suggest you shave the hair in this area if you don't plan to show your dog. "It will save a lot of grooming time and make life easier for both of you," says Kansoer.

If your dog smells and you can't find any reason for it, especially if you haven't noticed the odor before, it's best to call your vet. Some odors can be symptoms of medical problems, such as a hormonal disorder, and he may need a checkup.

The Best Bathing Techniques

When it comes to bathing, the main consideration is the type of coat your dog has. Whether he's a Maltese or a Collie mix, he's got long hair and that will require the same type of preparation, cleaning and after-bath care. The shorthaired dogs are easier and need only a quick brush to loosen dirt and remove dead hair before their bath. Although dogs are often classified according to size, apart from the choice of tub and location, size is not so important in bathing.

Where to Wash Him

Smaller dogs are easy to accommodate when it comes to bathtime. Often, the kitchen sink will be adequate, although a laundry-room utility sink may be better if he's apt to make a jump for it. The high sides will deter any escape plans, and you might prefer dog hair in your laundry rather than your kitchen. Having your dog at this height is also easier on your back and knees.

Good bathing begins with a good brushing. It is crucial for longhaired dogs like this, and the combined brush and curry-comb his owner is using is just right for the job.

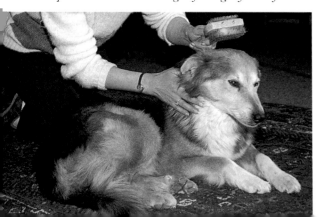

The kitchen sink is obviously not suitable for medium-sized or large dogs, but they will fit in your bathtub. However, if you think you'll be bathing your dog frequently, you might consider buying him a specially manufactured portable doggy bathtub, available at pet supply stores or through mail-order catalogs. Then you won't have to cope with skeins of dog hair in your bathtub's drain, and you can bathe your dog in a handy area of the house—or yard if the weather is warm enough—rather than being confined to the bathroom and having him track water all over the hallway carpet as he makes his way from the bathtub to the kitchen.

The Brush-Off

The most important step when bathing your dog comes before a drop of water touches his coat. First, you must brush him.

For shorthaired dogs, such as Labradors or Smooth Coat Chihuahuas, brushing is useful because it removes dead hair and loosens dirt, making it easier to wash away. For all other dogs, especially those with double coats, brushing before bathing is not simply useful, it's essential. You must brush the coat free of mats before starting to bathe him. And don't stop at the neck when brushing out his coat. The long hair on his face can mat as easily as the hair on his belly.

"If you can't get a comb all the way through your dog's coat, then don't get him wet," advises Kansoer. "You will never get his hair clean if you try to bathe a dog that has mats in his coat. You will also hurt him, since the mats will pull tighter as they dry, like an old felt hat." You also risk trapping moisture against your dog's skin, which can cause skin problems.

"Think of someone pulling on those little hairs at the back of your neck, and imagine them all over your body," says Laura Koerner, a professional groomer in Yorktown Heights, New York. "That's what it feels like if a dog hasn't been brushed regularly. Even a quick movement can hurt." If you've brushed and brushed and you can't get the mats out, it's time to seek professional help. Groomers have a lot of tricks for getting mats out without hurting your dog in the process.

After you've finished brushing your dog, go ahead and clip his nails. You can also remove the excess hair from inside his ears. You really only need to do this if his ears are infected and the hair could stop ear drops from getting down into the ears. You can use blunt-tipped tweezers to do this, advises Gabriel, or you can simply use your fingers to pluck out the hairs growing near the ear openings.

There's no need to plug his ears with cotton before bathing. "I know a lot of books recommend this, but in 20 years of grooming, I never have," Gabriel says. "We humans wash our ears and dogs' ears need to be washed, too." There's no need to worry about getting your dog's ears wet.

Suds Up

Now it's time to get wet—him, that is, not, hopefully, you. Lift or lead your dog into the tub, ready for the scrubdown. If he's apt to try to escape, make this a two-person endeavor. One of you holds his collar (you can remove it briefly to wash his neck area when you need to) while the other one wields the hose and shampoo.

Wash him outdoors on a warm, sunny day. When it's over, he can stand at a distance and shake himself dry.

If you're bathing him indoors, it's a good idea to attach a shower hose to the tap. Run the water, but take care with the temperature. Your dog's bath water should be about the temperature you'd use for a baby, suggests Friesen, and perhaps even a little cooler for larger dogs that prefer cool conditions, such as Saint Bernards, Malamutes or large, hairy mixed breeds. "Never make it too hot," she warns. "Dogs can easily become overheated."

Use a shampoo especially formulated for dogs, since the pH level of their skin differs from that of humans. In a pinch, use Palmolive or Ivory dishwashing detergent—they are very mild and have no added grease-cutters. Work the shampoo into your dog's coat with your fingers or a bathing mitt. Work it in all over his body, up onto his head—be careful not to get any soap in his eyes—under his chin and neck, under his belly and bottom, right down to his toes.

If your dog is going through a spell of profuse shedding, Shoemaker explains that a bath can be the best way to control the situation. "After soaping him up, pull a slicker brush through his coat," she says. "You'll pull off great clumps of hair. There'll be a lot but just keep at it until you're not getting any more."

The terrific thing about the versatile slicker brush, with its bent wire bristles, is that you don't have all that hair flying around your house. You can just put the wet, manageable clumps into a bag and throw it away.

Finally, after you've got your dog in a real lather, rinse him thoroughly. Any soap left on his skin will irritate him. After rinsing, some groomers recommend applying a conditioner to compensate for any loss of his coat's natural oils. There are a number of different kinds. The easiest conditioners are left in, while the others must be rinsed out.

Special Care Areas

Certain types of dogs require attention to certain areas when you're giving them a bath, notably those with particularly furry or creased faces, and those with weepy eyes. Also make sure you don't neglect your dog's ears and feet.

Face First

A dog with lots of hair on his face is like an old man who catches crumbs in his beard. If you have this kind of dog, you will need to be especially vigilant to make sure that his face stays clean. Accumulated food or saliva will stain his hair and can cause skin irritations, so this cleaning task isn't just for bathtime. In fact, if your dog has a tendency to save some crumbs for

later, you will need to wash and dry his beard and mustache after every meal.

For any dog with a Pug- or Boxer-type appearance, you will need to take extra precautions to keep his scrunched-up face in good condition. "Those wrinkles on his face are very tight and they need to be thoroughly cleaned and dried to prevent irritation from developing inside the folds," says Gabriel. During bathing, she suggests wrapping your finger in a paper towel or using a cotton-tipped swab to get inside the folds. Then go back over with a clean, dry towel or swab to remove any moisture.

In the Ears

Your dog's ears should be cleaned at least once a month, even if you don't bathe him quite that often. The best way to do this is to wrap your finger in a washcloth or other soft cloth moistened with either mineral oil or a commercial ear-cleaning solution. Rub the inside of his outer ear to remove any accumulated dirt and wax.

Around the Eyes

If your dog has weepy eyes, he may need this area bathed at other times in addition to when you wash him. Depending on your dog, you may

Dogs with large amounts of facial hair, such as this Standard Schnauzer, will need some special face care every day, as well as at bathtime.

have to clean under his eyes every day to stop any staining from becoming permanent.

Sometimes it's enough to just wipe his cheeks with a clean, damp cloth—tap water is fine, or you can use distilled. But you'll have to go a bit further to remove any matter that may have dried into his coat. "Use a baby's toothbrush for this," suggests Gabriel. "It is soft so it will do no harm if you accidentally touch your dog's eye, yet the bristles will remove more matter than a cloth because it will press in deeper."

Don't Forget the Feet

After working hard to make sure your dog's coat is thoroughly rinsed, it's easy to forget that his feet have been soaking in soapy water the whole time. "Remember that the shampoo, the water and the conditioner all run downhill," says Friesen.

If water and shampoo are left to dry between your dog's toes, his feet will feel itchy and irritated. When you're washing him, get your fingers between his toes to clean them thoroughly, and be just as fastidious about rinsing and drying there, too. Gabriel suggests that part of your pre-bath ritual should include clipping the hair between his toes and trimming the rest of the hair around his feet so that it's even with the pads. His feet will not only stay cleaner, they'll also be much easier to clean.

Drying Your Dog Thoroughly

Getting your dog completely dry is as important as getting him completely clean, especially if he has a long coat or is double-coated. "If you let him just dry naturally, you are asking for trouble," says Shoemaker. "The hair will mat right up."

While matting isn't a problem for shorthaired or hairless dogs, they will still need to be thoroughly dried so they don't get cold. Usually a good toweling off and several hours inside your warm house is enough to do the job.

With an older dog, whatever his coat type, make sure you dry him as well as you possibly

---

How to Stop Him from Shaking Water All Over

It's hard to fight nature, which is exactly what you're doing when you try to keep your dog from shaking after his bath. When a dog feels water tickling his skin, he's going to shake to try to make it stop. There are ways, however, you can minimize the water damage:

- Towel off as much water as possible before letting him out of the tub. The less water he has on his coat, the less he can distribute over you and the surroundings.
- Keep him in the room you bathed him in until he's finished shaking. This way you at least limit the number of rooms where you need to wipe up.
- If the weather is warm, bathe him outside. This is the best option of all because he can shake to his heart's content while you just step back and watch—from a safe distance.

can and keep him in a warm room for a few hours. You don't want him getting cold from a damp coat, and if he has an arthritic condition like hip or elbow dysplasia, it will only add to his discomfort.

Drying a double-coated or longhaired dog is not quite so simple. You will need more than just a towel, although Shoemaker says that you can get up to 70 percent of the water off your dog's coat with a towel if you are diligent. Pet supply stores and catalogs carry special super-absorbent towels that are even more effective.

But double-coated or longhaired dogs will also need a blow-dry. Using a hair dryer is the only way to remove the residual water. Your natural inclination may be to use your own dryer, but Shoemaker cautions against this. "Hair dryers for people get too hot and can burn a dog," she explains. "Plus they don't have the velocity to get the dog dry. You'll be there all day."

You can get a good portable hair dryer, ideal for home use, for a reasonable price. If your local pet supply store doesn't stock these dryers, check advertisements in dog magazines or mail-order catalogs. It's the best way you can ensure that your dog is high and dry after his bath. The alternative is to take your double-coated dog to a groomer for his wash and blow-dry—although the cost of a year's grooming fees will probably be the same as the amount you'll pay for a doggy hair dryer.

This shorthaired dog needs a good towel-down to get dry. If it's cold, keep him inside for a few hours, too.

Skunked!

One thing that strikes fear into the hearts of dog owners is the thought of their canine companion getting sprayed by a skunk. With good reason. You can be in for some long-term misery, says Eileen Gabriel, a professional groomer in Carmel, New York. "If you have a double-coated breed and don't remove the scent right away, you will smell skunk every time your dog gets wet for the next two years," she explains.

To avoid this olfactory horror, Gabriel says you must remove the skunk spray before it dries. The important thing is to bathe your dog right away with shampoo, while the scent is fresh. Then apply a deskunking preparation. As for the old tomato-juice remedy that you may have heard of, Gabriel is less enthusiastic about this. "It will simply stain your dog red," she says. If you're looking for an alternative, you can make up your own deskunking mixture. Pat Kansoer, a professional groomer and animal behaviorist outside Chicago, has a deskunking concoction he swears by:

2 tablespoons of Pet Preference Odor Eliminator
1 quart of 3 percent hydrogen peroxide
1/4 cup of baking soda
1 teaspoon of plain shampoo (no additives)

Stir this mixture together and bathe your dog with it as soon as possible. Rinse him thoroughly with water. Always make up the mixture fresh. Don't keep a bottle made up and ready, because the solution can build up pressure in the bottle, possibly causing it to break.

Bathing Step-by-Step

Since dogs have so many different types of coats, the way you bathe them will be different, too. Here are some tips for getting started. Choose the method given for the type of coat that most closely matches your dog's coat.

Bathing the Double-Coated Dog

Dogs such as Samoyeds or Malamutes can be a real challenge, because of their thick, double coats. Here's what groomers advise for double-coated dogs.

1. Remove all mats and as much loose hair as possible by brushing and combing your dog's coat thoroughly.
2. Clean his ears with an ear-cleaning solution.
3. Wet his coat, making sure the undercoat also becomes saturated. This can take a while, so keep at it. Sometimes it won't feel completely wet until after the first application of shampoo.
4. Apply the shampoo and work up a lather. Rinse, then apply more shampoo.

5. Comb the shampoo through your dog's coat, removing any dead hair.
6. Use your fingers to get between his toes.
7. Rinse, rinse and rinse again, starting at the head and working toward the back, using clean water until it runs clear.
8. Apply conditioner, making sure to comb it into his undercoat. Rinse it off according to the manufacturer's instructions.
9. Use towels to absorb as much of the water as possible. Then pat him dry—avoid rubbing back and forth, as this could tangle his long hair.
10. Dry your dog thoroughly, preferably with a high-velocity dryer designed for dogs. Brush or comb him while drying.

Bathing the Non-Shedding Dog

These guidelines are for longhaired canines that tend not to shed their dead hair. The Shih Tzu, for example, has a double coat, and the dead hair may become entangled with the live hair instead of falling away. You'll need to pay particular attention to brushing this kind of dog before

Given the tricky nature of washing a Samoyed, this owner is taking extra care as she wets her dog thoroughly and rubs the shampoo into his dense inner coat.

One Samoyed pup is being patted with towels, while the other pup receives the finishing touches with the help of a hair dryer made specially for dogs.

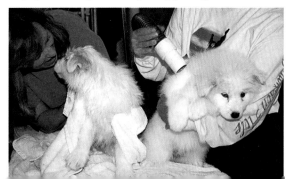

washing him. These guidelines will work for all longhaired breeds, including those with eyes that are prone to tearing, such as Maltese, Lhasa Apsos and Poodles, and for mixed breeds with similar coats and under-eye staining.

1. Remove all mats and as much loose hair as possible by brushing and combing your dog's coat thoroughly.
2. Clean under the eyes with a cloth dampened with distilled or tap water. Use a baby toothbrush to remove any dried matter.
3. Clean his ears with an ear-cleaning solution.
4. Wet his coat.
5. Apply the shampoo and work it into his coat with your fingers.
6. Use your fingers to get between his toes.
7. Rinse thoroughly, starting at the head and working toward the back, until the water runs clear.
8. Apply conditioner, then rinse it off according to the manufacturer's instructions.
9. Use towels to absorb as much water as possible. Pat him dry.
10. Dry your dog thoroughly with a dryer designed for dogs. Brush or comb him while drying. Don't forget to brush and dry his long facial hair.

Bathing the Shorthaired Dog

Smooth-coated, shorthaired dogs, such as Labrador Retrievers—possibly the ultimate "wash-n-wear" dog—German Shorthaired Pointers, Beagles, Weimaraners and Italian Greyhounds, are among the many breeds that are easy to clean and dry.

1. Give your dog's coat a quick brushing to loosen any dead hair and dirt.
2. Clean his ears with ear-cleaning solution.

3. Wet his coat.
4. Apply shampoo, working it into his coat with a rubber-bristled brush.
5. Rinse thoroughly, starting at the head and working toward the back, until the water runs clear.
6. Apply conditioner, then rinse it off according to the manufacturer's instructions.
7. Towel him dry. There's no need to use a hair dryer, but keep him inside in cold weather until he is completely dry.

Preparing for a Bath

Bathtime will go much more smoothly if you're well-prepared. First, make sure you're not rushed. No matter how small your dog, a bath is not a ten-minute job.

You must allow time for pre-bath brushing, the bath itself and the drying afterward. For a longhaired dog, the first and last steps will take the most time, and you'll need to allow for that.

If you are bathing him in winter, be sure to keep him inside until he is properly dry. A wet coat, whether short or long, will provide him with no warmth or insulation.

Once you know you have plenty of time to be able to do the job correctly, you can get your materials together. Here's what you'll need:

- Comb or brush
- Scissors
- Shampoo
- Conditioner
- Towels
- Hair dryer

Shampoos and Conditioners

The grooming products aisle of a pet supply store can leave any dog owner bewildered. Choices of shampoo alone rival those for humans, not to mention conditioners. Here's a quick look at what's available via mail order or at the pet store.

Choosing a Shampoo

An all-purpose dog shampoo might be fine for your dog, or you may decide to go for one that is designed to help with a particular condition.

- Conditioning shampoos work like all-in-one shampoos for people, eliminating the additional step of conditioning. With these, it should be relatively easy to comb through your dog's coat.
- To combat any dryness and to promote body and fullness in the hair, use a protein shampoo. This is probably of greatest interest to people who plan to show their dog.
- For a soothing and skin-friendly shampoo, you can try an oatmeal shampoo. It can also help reduce itching. This type of shampoo is recommended by Koerner, who uses it on all the dogs that visit her grooming parlor.
- Hypoallergenic shampoo is usually free from perfume and dye. It is useful for dogs that have shown a skin sensitivity to other shampoos.
- Flea-and-tick shampoo often contains an insecticide, pyrethrin, that kills parasites on contact. Some groomers caution against using any shampoo that contains insecticide, since even with careful rinsing, some will stay on the dog's coat and be licked off. However, it may be the best thing for your dog if he is really infested with fleas, says Dr. Wilford. "Pyrethrin is biodegradable in ultraviolet light, which means it will not stay on your dog's coat for long," she explains.
- Medicated shampoos are formulated to combat specific skin conditions. You should use these only on the recommendation of your vet.
- Herbal shampoos are products that contain "natural" herbal ingredients, such as tea tree extract, which will help with a range of things, from repelling fleas to soothing flaky skin.
- Color-enhancing shampoo is used primarily on white show dogs, and contains whitening agents. There are also shampoos formulated to enrich dark-coated breeds.
- Dry shampoo is sometimes a misnomer, since the product can be a liquid. In the powder form, it is dusted thoroughly through the coat, then brushed out. The liquid is a touch-up cleaner used by groomers or show enthusiasts to redo a small portion of coat. "You shouldn't use dry shampoo to clean an entire dog," says Kansoer. "That's not what it was designed for."

Getting Rid of Tangles

A conditioner isn't essential, but it can make brushing out a longhaired dog a little easier. Detanglers in particular will assist you if applied after shampooing.

Mink oil makes your dog's coat shine and offers some protection against the sun. And oatmeal conditioner works like oatmeal shampoo, to soothe itchy skin. It may also be combined with a detangling ingredient.

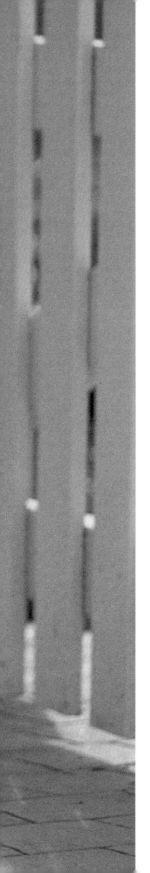

Further Information

It takes an enormous amount of patience, energy and information to raise a happy, healthy dog. It also takes the combined expertise of veterinarians, trainers and groomers, the folks who have made dogs their lives. Following, you'll find a list of organizations and clubs committed to caring for and having fun with dogs, along with all the experts who offered their advice for this book. The complete index makes locating all the information you're most interested in easy.

Organizations and Clubs

Kennel Clubs

The American Crossbreed Club
1847 Butson Road,
Platteville, WI 53818
This is an organization for lovers of
all dogs, not just purebreds. It aims
to promote population control and
humane training.

American Kennel Club
5580 Centerview Drive,
Suite 200,
Raleigh, NC 27606
Founded in 1884, the American
Kennel Club is the principal registry
of purebred dogs in the United States.
It is also the leading regulatory agency
for dog shows and performance events.

American Mixed Breed Obedience
Registration
P.O. Box 7841,
Rockford, IL 61126-7841
This group was formed in the 1980s
to promote the participation of mixed
breeds in obedience trials.

Canadian Kennel Club
100-89 Skyway Avenue,
Etobicoke, Ontario M9W 6R4,
Canada
This is the largest and most widely
used obedience and training
organization in Canada.

North American Mixed Breed
Registry
R.R. #1, Baltimore,
Ontario K0K 1C0,
Canada
This registry is open to all dogs that
aren't eligible for membership in the
American or Canadian kennel clubs.

States Kennel Club
P.O. Box 389,
Hattiesburg, MS 39403-0389
This registry of purebred dogs is most
active in the southern part of the
United States. It overlaps somewhat
with the American Kennel Club
(AKC), but also includes breeds the
AKC doesn't.

United Kennel Club
100 East Kilgore Road,
Kalamazoo, MI 49001
This club is a registry of purebred
dogs. Like the American Kennel
Club, it also organizes dog shows,
but places greater emphasis on
performance events than on
conformation.

Dog Obedience Organizations

American Kennel Club Obedience
Department
51 Madison Avenue,
New York, NY 10010
An arm of the AKC offering a wide
range of training, from puppy classes
to tracking. It also offers the Canine
Good Citizen (CGC) Certification
Test. It's open to purebreds as well
as mixed breed dogs.

National Association of Dog
Obedience Instructors
P.O. Box 432,
Landing, NJ 07850
This organization provides a list
of instructors in local areas. It is
committed to helping train others
by focusing on improved methods
of instruction. The Association is
strongly opposed to harsh training
methods.

Dog Sporting Organizations

Agility Association of Canada
R.R. #2, Lucan,
Ontario N0N 2J0, Canada
This group helps to promote and
regulate the sport of dog agility.

North American Dog Agility Council
H.C.R. 2, Box 277,
St Maries, ID 83861
This organization was created to
promote the sport of agility. It also
promotes the use of lower jump
heights and safer course designs.

United States Canine Combined
Training Association
2755 Old Thompson Mill Road,
Buford, GA 30519
This association promotes the sport
of Canine Eventing, the ultimate test
of teamwork between handlers and
their dogs. It requires precision,
elegance, obedience, courage,
stamina, jumping ability, endurance
and all-round versatility.

United States Dog Agility Association
P.O. Box 850955,
Richardson, TX 75085-0955
This association was started in 1986 to
promote international agility standards
as developed in the United Kingdom.

Humane Societies

American Society for the Prevention
of Cruelty to Animals
424 East 92nd Street,
New York, NY 10128-6804
This organization investigates and
prosecutes the mistreatment of
animals, and strives to educate about
humane interaction with animals.

British Columbia Society for the
Prevention of Cruelty to Animals
Provincial Office,
322-470 Granville Street,
Vancouver,
British Columbia V6C 1V5,
Canada
The Canadian counterpart to the
American Society for the Prevention
of Cruelty to Animals.

Humane Society of the United States
2100 L Street NW,
Washington, DC 20037
A nonprofit organization devoted
to making the world safe for animals
through legal, educational, legislative
and investigative means.

Ontario Society for the Prevention of
Cruelty to Animals
16640 Yonge Street,
Newmarket,
Ontario L3Y 4V8,
Canada
The Society investigates and prosecutes
the mistreatment of animals, as well
as striving to educate the general
public about humane interaction
with animals.

Progressive Animal Welfare Society
15305 44th Avenue W,
P.O. Box 1037,
Lynnwood, WA 98046
This organization provides services
in animal adoption, lost and found,
rehousing of companion animals, and
low-cost spaying and neutering.

Dog Rescue Clubs
All Breed Rescue Alliance
P.O. Box 2603,
Vincetown, NJ 08088
This is a nonprofit organization that
assists animal shelters and humane
societies by placing unwanted dogs in
appropriate homes.

American Kennel Club Companion
Animal Recovery
5580 Centerview Drive, Suite 200,
Raleigh, NC 27606
A nationwide pet identification
and recovery service with a central
database to record identification
numbers for dog owners using any
permanent form of identification
(microchip or tattoo).

The Animal Guardian Society
R.R. 2, Blackstock,
Ontario L0B 1B0, Canada
This all-breed rescue organization was
founded in 1987 and provides behavior
management training, along with pet
adoptions.

Pet Therapy Organizations
Animal Assisted Therapy
1140 Westwood Boulevard, #205,
Los Angeles, CA 90025
This group uses specially trained
dogs to help improve and further the
therapy of people with mental and
physical disabilities.

BC Pets and Friends
250-167 West 2nd Avenue,
Vancouver,
British Columbia V5Y 1B6,
Canada
This organization provides trained
dogs and other pets to interact with
people in nursing homes or who are
receiving professional medical care.

Canine Companions for
Independence
National Office,
P.O. Box 446,
Santa Rosa, CA 95402-0446
This nonprofit organization
provides highly trained assistance
dogs to people with disabilities and
to professional caregivers providing
pet-assisted therapy.

The Delta Society
289 Perimeter Road E,
Renton, WA 98055-1329
This group organizes programs to help
incorporate pets into the lives of
people who are ill and disabled, to
help improve their healing and gain
independence.

Pacific Animal Therapy Society
9412 Laurie's Lane,
Sidney,
British Columbia V8L 4L2,
Canada
Members of this society and their
trained pets visit retirement homes,
hospitals and other care facilities.

Medical Organizations
American Animal Hospital
Association
P.O. Box 150899,
Denver, CO 80215-0899
This association assists veterinarians
in providing quality medical care
of the highest standard, while at the
same time helping to promote
responsible pet ownership.

American Canine Sports
Medicine Association
P.O. Box 82433,
Baton Rouge, LA 70884
This is an association of veterinarians
who are devoted to the medical and
surgical needs of canine athletes and
the working breeds.

American Veterinary Medical
Association
1931 North Meacham Road,
Suite 100,
Schaumberg, IL 60173-4360
The role of this association is to
advance the science and art of
veterinary medicine, including
its relationship to public health,
biological science and agriculture.

Canadian Veterinary Medical Association
339 Booth Street,
Ottawa, Ontario K1R 7K1,
Canada
An association representing veterinarians throughout Canada.

Other Organizations

American Boarding Kennels Association
4575 Galley Road, Suite 400A,
Colorado Springs, CO 80915
A nonprofit trade association for the boarding kennel industry in the United States and around the world.

American Pet Association
P.O. Box 18869,
Boulder, CO 80308
A national organization dedicated to promoting responsible pet ownership. Founded in 1991, the Association helps people and their pets live together peacefully and safely.

National Association of Professional Pet Sitters
1200 G Street NW, Suite 760,
Washington, DC 20005
This is a nonprofit organization dedicated to promoting in-house pet care and expanding the pet-sitting industry.

National Dog Groomers Association of America
P.O. Box 101,
Clark, PA 16116
This association works with groomers throughout the world, promoting and encouraging professionalism and education.

National Pet Registry
USA:
5713 Corporate Way, Suite 100,
West Palm Beach, FL 33407

Canada:
339 Springdale Boulevard,
Toronto, Ontario M4C 2A3
An organization providing high-quality brass tags engraved with a 24-hour, toll-free number to help reunite lost pets with their owners.

Pet Supplies/Mail Order Catalogs

Doctors Foster and Smith
2253 Air Park Road, P.O. Box 100,
Rhinelander, WI 54501-0100

JB Wholesale Pet Supply
5 Raritan Road,
Oakland, NJ 07436

Omaha Vaccine Company
P.O. Box 7228,
Omaha, NE 68107

Pedigrees
1989 Transit Way, Box 905,
Brockport, NY 14420-0905

R.C. Steele
P.O. Box 910 DW 144,
Brockport, NY 14420

Magazines and Newsletters

American Dog Owners Association
6154 Columbia Turnpike,
Castleton, NY 12033
A bimonthly newsletter promoting responsible dog ownership.

American Kennel Club Gazette
5580 Centerview Drive, Suite 200,
Raleigh, NC 27606-0643
The official publication of the American Kennel Club.

Bloodlines
100 East Kilgore Road,
Kalamazoo, MI 49001
The official publication of the United Kennel Club, published six times a year.

Canine Review Magazine
S.S. 2, Site 4, Comp. 22,
Kamloops,
British Columbia V2C 6C3,
Canada
A publication keeping dog show exhibitors worldwide informed on what's happening in the show rings.

Dogs in Canada
Apex Publishing & Publicity Ltd.,
89 Skyway Avenue, Suite 200,
Etobicoke, Ontario M9W 6R4,
Canada
The official monthly magazine of the Canadian Kennel Club, reporting on the world of purebred dogs.

DogWatch
Torstar Publications, Inc.,
99 Hawley Lane,
Stratford, CT 06497
A monthly newsletter published by the Cornell University College of Veterinary Medicine.

Paw Prints
P.O. Box 150899,
Denver, CO 80215-0899
A newsletter published by the American Animal Hospital Association and the Delta Society for veterinarians to distribute among their clients.

Pets Quarterly
512 King Street E,
Suite 300, Toronto,
Ontario M5A 1M1, Canada
This is Canada's largest circulation pet magazine, published four times a year.

Your Dog
Customer Service,
P.O. Box 420272,
Palm Coast, FL 32142-0272
A monthly newsletter produced by Tufts University School of Veterinary Medicine for dog owners.

Advisers

PART ONE: GETTING
ACQUAINTED

Chapter 1: The Perfect Match
DIANE BAUMAN is a dog obedience
trainer in Sussex, New Jersey, who
lectures and writes on dogs and dog
training.
STEVE DILLER is a dog obedience
trainer in Elmsford, New York.
SUZANNE HETTS, Ph.D., is an applied
animal behaviorist in private practice
in Littleton, Colorado.
KATHALYN JOHNSON, D.V.M., is a
resident in animal behavior at Texas
A&M University's College of
Veterinary Medicine in College
Station.
JANET LALONDE, D.V.M., is a
veterinarian in private practice in
Alexandria, Ontario, and a Whippet
breeder.
LOUISE SANDERS is a Bullmastiff
breeder in Largo, Florida.
SUE STERNBERG is a dog trainer
and obedience instructor in Accord,
New York.
CHRISTINE L. WILFORD, D.V.M., is
a veterinarian in private practice in
Seattle, and a regular columnist for
the *American Kennel Club Gazette*.

Chapter 2: Joining the Clan
SUSAN BONHOWER is a Newfoundland
breeder in Cornwall, Ontario.
JAY GEASLING, D.V.M., is a
veterinarian in private practice in
Buffalo and president of the American
Animal Hospital Association.
WAYNE HUNTHAUSEN, D.V.M., is an
animal behaviorist in Westwood,
Kansas, and co-author of *Practitioner's
Guide to Pet Behavior Problems*.

JANET LALONDE, D.V.M., is a
veterinarian in private practice in
Alexandria, Ontario, and a Whippet
breeder.
GARY LANDSBERG, D.V.M., is an
animal behaviorist in private practice
in Thornhill, Ontario, and co-editor
of *Dog Behavior and Training*.
ROBERT LINNABARY, D.V.M., is
an instructor at the University of
Tennessee College of Veterinary
Medicine in Knoxville.
JEANINE MURPHY is a dog trainer in
Somers, New York.
PRISCILLA J. WHITTINGTON, D.V.M.,
is a veterinarian in private practice in
Yorktown Heights, New York.
CHRISTINE L. WILFORD, D.V.M.,
is a veterinarian in private practice
in Seattle, and a regular columnist
for the *American Kennel Club
Gazette*.

Chapter 3: Bringing Up Puppy
AMY AMMEN is the director of
Amiable Dog Training, host of
"Amiable Dog Training with
Amy Ammen" on MATA
Television in Milwaukee, and
author of *Training in No Time* and
Dual Ring Dog.
MARILYN BAIN is a breeder-handler
of English Springer Spaniels and
owner of Legacy Kennels in Kalispell,
Montana.
CAROLYN BROWN is a puppy
socialization instructor and
breeder-handler of American
Staffordshire Terriers in Thayer,
Missouri.
PAUL S. MCGRATH, D.V.M., is a
veterinarian in private practice in
Kalispell, Montana.

CHRIS WALKOWICZ is a Bearded
Collie breeder in Sherrard, Illinois,
and author of *The Perfect Match*
and co-author of *Successful Dog
Breeding*.
DAVE WEDUM is a professional
dog trainer and owner of Grizzly
Dog Obedience School and
Training Kennels in Choteau,
Montana.
BONNIE WILCOX, D.V.M., is a
veterinarian in private practice in
Preemption, Illinois, and co-author
of *The Atlas of Dog Breeds* and
Successful Dog Breeding.

Chapter 4: Canine Communication
AMY AMMEN is the director of
Amiable Dog Training, host of
"Amiable Dog Training with Amy
Ammen" on MATA Television
in Milwaukee, and author of
Training in No Time and *Dual
Ring Dog*.
MARY BURCH, Ph.D., is an animal
behaviorist in Tallahassee, Florida,
and author of *Volunteering with Your
Pet* and *The Border Collie*.
CAROL HOPWOOD is a psychotherapist
and owner-instructor at Grizzly Dog
Obedience School in Whitefish,
Montana.
JUDY IBY is a registered veterinary
technician and Cocker Spaniel
breeder-handler in Milford, Ohio,
and author of *The New Owner's Guide
to Cocker Spaniels* and *The Cocker
Spaniel*.
JOHN LOOMIS is the owner-instructor
of Alibi Obedience and Agility
Training School in Jacksonville,
Arkansas.

PART TWO: TRAINING

Chapter 5: Starting from Scratch

STEVE AIKEN is the owner of Animal Behavior Consultants in Wichita, Kansas, and the "Pet Shrink" on America Online.

CAROL LEA BENJAMIN is a professional obedience trainer in New York City, and the author of *Mother Knows Best: The Natural Way to Train Your Dog* and *Dog Training in 10 Minutes.*

TONY BUGARIN is an obedience instructor in Los Angeles.

DEENA CASE-PALL, Ph.D., is a psychologist and animal behaviorist in Camarillo, California.

SHARON CROWELL-DAVIS, Ph.D., is a professor of veterinary animal behavior at the College of Veterinary Medicine at the University of Georgia in Atlanta.

JANICE DeMELLO is an obedience trainer in Somis, California.

NICHOLAS DODMAN, B.V.M.S., is professor in the Department of Surgery and director of the Behavior Clinic at Tufts University School of Veterinary Medicine in North Grafton, Massachusetts, and the author of *The Dog Who Loved Too Much* and *The Cat Who Cried For Help.*

BENJAMIN HART, D.V.M., Ph.D., is a professor in the Department of Anatomy and Physiology at the School of Veterinary Medicine at the University of California in Davis.

LYNETTE HART, D.V.M., Ph.D., is a sociologist and director of the Human-Animal Program at the University of California in Davis.

WAYNE HUNTHAUSEN, D.V.M., is an animal behaviorist in Westwood, Kansas, and co-author of *Practitioner's Guide to Pet Behavior Problems.*

STEVE LINDSAY is a trainer and owner of Canine Behavioral Services in Philadelphia, Pennsylvania.

AMY MARDER, Ph.D., is an animal behavior consultant to Angell Memorial Animal Hospital in Boston, and the pet columnist for *Prevention* magazine.

SANDY MYERS is a behavior consultant and trainer in Naperville, Illinois.

JOHN C. WRIGHT, Ph.D., is an animal behaviorist, professor of psychology at Mercer University in Macon, Georgia, and a member of the adjunct faculty at the University of Georgia School of Veterinary Medicine in Atlanta.

JILL YOREY is the training consultant at the Society for the Prevention of Cruelty to Animals in Los Angeles.

Chapter 6: Bathroom Basics

PATRICK CONNOLLY, D.V.M., is a veterinarian in private practice in Thousand Oaks, California.

JANICE DeMELLO is an obedience trainer in Somis, California.

DENNIS FETKO, Ph.D., is an animal behaviorist in San Diego and host of "Animal Talk with Dr. Dog" on KFMB radio in San Diego.

SUZANNE HETTS, Ph.D., is an applied animal behaviorist in private practice in Littleton, Colorado.

SCOTT LINE, D.V.M., is an animal behaviorist at the Golden Valley Humane Society in Minneapolis, and staff veterinarian at the University of Minnesota Veterinary Teaching Hospital in Minneapolis.

KAREN MARTIN, D.V.M., is a veterinarian in private practice in Thousand Oaks, California.

Chapter 7: Basic Training

SUSAN ANDERSON, D.V.M., is a clinical instructor of outpatient medicine in the Department of Small Animal Clinical Sciences at the University of Florida College of Veterinary Medicine in Gainesville.

DAN ESTEP, Ph.D., is an animal behaviorist in Littleton, Colorado.

WAYNE HUNTHAUSEN, D.V.M., is an animal behaviorist in Westwood, Kansas, and co-author of *Practitioner's Guide to Pet Behavior Problems.*

SCOTT LINE, D.V.M., is an animal behaviorist at the Golden Valley Humane Society in Minneapolis and staff veterinarian at the University of Minnesota Veterinary Teaching Hospital in Minneapolis.

KATHY MARMACK is an animal training supervisor at the San Diego Zoo.

SANDY MYERS is a behavior consultant and trainer in Naperville, Illinois.

JILL YOREY is a training consultant at the Society for the Prevention of Cruelty to Animals in Los Angeles.

Chapter 8: Advanced Training

STANLEY COREN, Ph.D., is a professor of psychology at the University of British Colombia in Vancouver, and the author of *The Intelligence of Dogs.*

BOB JERVIS is an animal trainer and the director of training at the National K-9 Dog Training School in Columbus, Ohio.

CAPTAIN GARY SMITH, of the Ventura County Fire Department in Camarillo, California, is the owner and trainer of a Disaster Search Dog.

MARY KAY SNYDER is a professional animal trainer formerly with Birds and Animals Unlimited in Lake Forest, California.

Chapter 9: Correcting Unwanted Behavior

SUSAN ANDERSON, D.V.M., is a clinical instructor of outpatient medicine in the Department of Small Animal Clinical Sciences at the University of Florida College of Veterinary Medicine in Gainesville.

BONNIE V. BEAVER, D.V.M., is a professor and chief of medicine at the Texas Veterinary Medical Center at the College of Veterinary Medicine at Texas A&M University in College Station.

PETER L. BORCHELT, Ph.D., is an animal behaviorist in private practice in Brooklyn, New York.

STANLEY COREN, Ph.D., is a professor of psychology at the University of British Colombia in Vancouver, and the author of *The Intelligence of Dogs*.

DEBRA L. FORTHMAN, Ph.D., is an animal behaviorist and Director of Field Conservation at Zoo Atlanta in Georgia.

LINDA GOODLOE, Ph.D., is an animal behaviorist in private practice in Chester County, Pennsylvania.

SUZANNE HETTS, Ph.D., is an applied animal behaviorist in private practice in Littleton, Colorado.

KATHERINE HOUPT, V.M.D., Ph.D., is a professor of physiology and director of the Behavior Clinic at Cornell University College of Veterinary Medicine in Ithaca, New York, and author of *Domestic Animal Behavior*.

WAYNE HUNTHAUSEN, D.V.M., is an animal behaviorist in Westwood, Kansas, and co-author of *Practitioner's Guide to Pet Behavior Problems*.

SUZANNE B. JOHNSON, Ph.D., is an animal behaviorist in private practice in Washington, D.C.

DOROTHY LAFLAMME, D.V.M., is a veterinary nutritionist in the St. Louis area, and vice-president of the American College of Veterinary Nutrition.

KATHY MARMACK is an animal training supervisor at the San Diego Zoo.

MARY KAY SNYDER is a professional animal trainer formerly with Birds and Animals Unlimited in Lake Forest, California.

DAVID S. SPIEGEL, V.D.M., is a veterinarian in private practice in Wilmington, Delaware.

JILL YOREY is a training consultant at the Society for the Prevention of Cruelty to Animals in Los Angeles.

PART THREE: ESSENTIAL CARE

Chapter 10: Fun and Fitness

MIKE BOND is an agility judge and owner-instructor of Agility Ability School in Naperville, Illinois, and a regular columnist for *Front and Finish*, a dog obedience newspaper.

KEN MARDEN is a field trial and hunting test judge, and a breeder-handler of champion German Shorthaired Pointers in Titusville, New Jersey.

BOB MCKOWEN is a dog show and field trial judge in Leola, Pennsylvania.

GEE WEAVER is a boarding kennel owner, professional groomer and foster care coordinator for the Animal Relief Center in Whitefish, Montana.

M. CHRISTINE ZINK, Ph.D., is a veterinarian lecturing in pathology at Johns Hopkins University School of Medicine in Baltimore, Maryland, and author of *Peak Performance: Coaching the Canine Athlete*.

Chapter 11: The Best Accessories

AMY AMMEN is the director of Amiable Dog Training, host of "Amiable Dog Training with Amy Ammen" on MATA Television in Milwaukee, and author of *Training in No Time* and *Dual Ring Dog*.

MITCH RAPOPORT is executive director of the National Dog Registry in the United States.

BRYAN SIMPSON is manager of American Kennel Club Companion Animal Recovery.

SUSAN STRONBERG is the owner of Noah's Bark pet store in Kalispell, Montana.

KEITH WALL, D.V.M., is technical services veterinarian with Schering-Plough Animal Health, manufacturer of the Home Again microchip.

PENNY ZORN is a professional groomer and the co-owner of the Poodle Parlor in Kalispell, Montana.

Chapter 12: Caring for Latchkey Pets

CONNIE CLEVELAND is a professional dog trainer in Fountain Inn, South Carolina.

ROBIN KOVARY is a professional dog trainer and behavioral consultant in New York City, and president of the American Dog Trainers Network.

LARRY LACHMAN is an animal behaviorist in Laguna Hills, California.

LIZ PALIKA is a professional dog trainer in Oceanside, California, and author of *All Dogs Need Some Training*.

Chapter 13: Traveling in Comfort

ELIZABETH ALTIERI, D.V.M., is a veterinarian in private practice, New Jersey.

WENDY BALLARD is publisher of *DogGone: The Newsletter About Fun Places to Go and Cool Stuff To Do With Your Dog*.

MARIA GOODAVAGE is the author of *The California Dog Lovers' Companion* and *The Bay Area Dog Lovers' Companion*.

JOHN HAMIL, D.V.M., is a veterinarian in private practice in Laguna Beach, California.

JOANNE HOWL, D.V.M., is a veterinarian in private practice in Rochester, New York.

JIM KRACK is executive director of the American Boarding Kennels Association, Colorado Springs, Colorado.
LARRY LACHMAN is an animal behaviorist in Laguna Hills, California.
PRISCILLA K. STOCKNER, D.V.M., is executive director of the Center for Humane Education in Escondido, California.

PART FOUR: FOOD, GLORIOUS FOOD

Chapter 14: Nutrition for Life
JULIE CHURCHILL, D.V.M., is an assistant clinical specialist in small animal nutrition at the University of Minnesota's College of Veterinary Medicine in St. Paul.
EDMUND DOROSZ, D.V.M., is a veterinarian and nutrition specialist in Fort McCloud, Alberta, and author of *Let's Cook for Our Dogs*.
FRANCIS KALLFELZ, D.V.M., is a professor of nutrition at Cornell University's College of Veterinary Medicine in Ithaca, New York.
DOROTHY LAFLAMME, D.V.M., is a veterinary nutritionist in the St. Louis area, and vice-president of the American College of Veterinary Nutrition.
KATHY MICHEL, D.V.M., is a clinical assistant professor of nutrition at the University of Pennsylvania School of Veterinary Medicine in Philadelphia.
REBECCA REMILLARD, D.V.M., is an animal nutrition specialist at Angell Memorial Animal Hospital in Boston.

Chapter 15: Canine Cuisine
MARGARET DUXBURY, D.V.M., is a veterinarian in private practice in Amery, Wisconsin, and a contributor to *Dog Fancy* and *DOGS USA* magazines.

LISA FREEMAN, D.V.M., Ph.D., is clinical nutritionist and assistant professor at Tufts University School of Veterinary Medicine in North Grafton, Massachusetts.
JOHN HAMIL, D.V.M., is a veterinarian in private practice in Laguna Beach, California.
CHRISTINE L. WILFORD, D.V.M., is a veterinarian in private practice in Seattle and a regular columnist for the *American Kennel Club Gazette*.

PART FIVE: HEALTH WATCH

Chapter 16: Prevention
LYNN M. HARPOLD, D.V.M., is a veterinarian in private practice in Mesa, Arizona.
KATHERINE HOUPT, V.M.D., Ph.D., is professor of physiology and director of the Behavior Clinic at Cornell University College of Veterinary Medicine in Ithaca, New York, and author of *Domestic Animal Behavior*.
DAN LORIMER, D.V.M., is a veterinary ophthalmologist in private practice in Southfield, Michigan.
KENNETH LYON, D.V.M., is a veterinary dentist in private practice in Mesa and Tucson, Arizona, and the co-author of *Dog Owner's Guide to Proper Dental Care*.
LESTER MANDELKER, D.V.M., is a veterinarian in private practice in Largo, Florida, and co-author of *Burns Pharmaceutical Index*.
MIKE PAUL, D.V.M., is vice-president of the American Animal Hospital Association.

Chapter 17: Neutering
WAYNE CAVANAUGH is vice-president of communications for the American Kennel Club.

JAY GEASLING, D.V.M., is a veterinarian in private practice in Buffalo and president of the American Animal Hospital Association.
MARY BETH LEININGER, D.V.M., is president of the American Veterinary Medical Association.
ALLAN PAUL, D.V.M., is small animal extension veterinarian at the University of Illinois College of Veterinary Medicine in Urbana.
LESLIE SINCLAIR, D.V.M., is director of companion animal care at the Humane Society of the United States, Washington, D.C.
LORI TEHGTMEYER, D.V.M., is a veterinarian in private practice in Oak Park, Illinois, and a veterinary staff member of American Online Pet Care Forum.

Chapter 18: Birthing
GLENN CRAFT, D.V.M., is a veterinarian in private practice in San Clemente, California.
CHRISTINE DRESSER, D.V.M., is a veterinarian in private practice in Medina, Ohio, and a Pug breeder.
CAMILLE MCARDLE, D.V.M., is a veterinarian in private practice in New Hope, Minnesota.
BONNIE WILCOX, D.V.M., is a veterinarian in private practice in Preemption, Illinois, and co-author of *The Atlas of Dog Breeds* and *Successful Dog Breeding*.

Chapter 19: Caring for the Older Dog
STEVE AIKEN is the owner of Animal Behavior Consultants in Wichita, Kansas, and the "Pet Shrink" on America Online Pet Care Forum.
WENDY BROOKS, D.V.M., is a veterinarian in private practice in Los Angeles.

MICHELLE BROWNSTEIN, D.V.M., is a veterinarian in private practice in Rochester, New York.

JOHN HAMIL, D.V.M., is a veterinarian in private practice in Laguna Beach, California.

PETER SCHMITZ, D.V.M., is a veterinarian in private practice in Broken Arrow, Oklahoma.

PART SIX: EASING COMMON COMPLAINTS

KEVIN BYRNE, D.V.M., is an animal dermatologist and lecturer at the University of Pennsylvania School of Veterinary Medicine in Philadelphia.

GREGG DUPONT, D.V.M., is a veterinary dentist in private practice in Seattle.

LYNN M. HARPOLD, D.V.M., is a veterinarian in private practice in Mesa, Arizona.

KATHERINE HOUPT, V.M.D., Ph.D., is professor of physiology and director of the Behavior Clinic at Cornell University College of Veterinary Medicine in Ithaca, New York, and author of *Domestic Animal Behavior*.

WAYNE HUNTHAUSEN, D.V.M., is an animal behaviorist in Westwood, Kansas, and co-author of *Practitioner's Guide to Pet Behavior Problems*.

G. G. KELLER, D.V.M., is a veterinary radiologist and executive director of the Orthopedic Foundation for Animals.

GARY LANDSBERG, D.V.M., is an animal behaviorist in private practice in Thornhill, Ontario, and co-editor of *Dog Behavior and Training*.

DAN LORIMER, D.V.M., is a veterinary ophthalmologist in private practice in Southfield, Michigan.

KENNETH LYON, D.V.M., is a veterinary dentist in private practice in Mesa and Tucson, Arizona, and the co-author of *Dog Owner's Guide to Proper Dental Care*.

LESTER MANDELKER, D.V.M., is a veterinarian in private practice in Largo, Florida, and co-author of *Burns Pharmaceutical Index*.

GENE NESBITT, D.V.M., is an animal dermatologist in private practice in Standish, Maine, and a consulting staff dermatologist at Tufts University School of Veterinary Medicine in North Grafton, Massachusetts.

STEPHEN WAISGLASS, D.V.M., is a veterinarian in private practice in Thornhill, Ontario.

PART SEVEN: FIRST AID

JOAN E. ANTLE, D.V.M., is a veterinarian in private practice in Cleveland and a frequent speaker on pet emergency care.

MERRY CRIMI, D.V.M., is a veterinarian in private practice in Portland, Oregon.

L. R. DANNY DANIEL, D.V.M., is a veterinarian in private practice in Covington, Louisiana.

PAUL M. GIGLIOTTI, D.V.M., is a veterinarian in private practice in Mayfield Village, Ohio.

STEVEN HANSEN, D.V.M., is a veterinary toxicologist and vice-president of the American Society for the Prevention of Cruelty in Animals' National Animal Poison Control Center.

TERRI MCGINNIS, D.V.M., is a veterinarian in private practice in San Francisco and author of *The Well Dog Book*.

ERIKA DE PAPP, D.V.M., is a veterinarian at the School of Veterinary Medicine at the University of Pennsylvania in Philadelphia.

LISA ROTZ, M.D., is a doctor at the U.S. Centers for Disease Control and Prevention in Atlanta.

JOSEPH TRUEBA, D.V.M., is a veterinarian in private practice specializing in emergency care in Tucson, Arizona.

GABOR K. VAJDA, D.V.M., is a veterinarian in private practice in Phoenix.

LORI A. WISE, D.V.M., is a veterinarian in private practice in Wheat Ridge, Colorado.

PART EIGHT: LOOKING GOOD

Chapter 20: Grooming

MARY ALLAN is a professional groomer in Broken Arrow, Oklahoma.

JAN BELLOWS, D.V.M., is a veterinarian in private practice specializing in dentistry in Pembroke Pines, Florida.

PAT FIELD is a professional groomer in Markham, Ontario.

BEVERLY LATHAM is a professional groomer and instructor of a pet grooming correspondence course in Coeur d'Alene, Idaho.

MICHELLE POPE PATTERSON is a professional groomer in Fayetteville, North Carolina.

Chapter 21: Bathtime

LOIS FRIESEN is a professional groomer and grooming instructor in Leduc, Alberta.

EILEEN GABRIEL is a professional groomer and Alaskan Malamute breeder in Carmel, New York.

PAT KANSOER is a professional groomer and animal behaviorist in the Chicago area.

LAURA KOERNER is a professional groomer in Yorktown Heights, New York.

VALERIE SHOEMAKER is a professional groomer and grooming instructor in Cupertino, California.

CHRISTINE L. WILFORD, D.V.M., is a veterinarian in private practice in Seattle, and a regular columnist for the *American Kennel Club Gazette*.

Contributors

Consultant and Author

LOWELL ACKERMAN, D.V.M., Ph.D. (chapter 16 and part 6). Dr. Ackerman practices veterinary medicine in Arizona in the United States, and in Ontario, Canada. He is a diplomate of the American College of Veterinary Dermatology and also has a doctorate degree in nutritional counseling. He is the author of *Owner's Guide to Dog Health* and *Skin and Coat Care for Your Dog*, among other titles, and has lectured on canine medicine throughout North America and Europe.

Authors

KIM CAMPBELL THORNTON (chapters 15 and 18). Kim is the former editor of *Dog Fancy* magazine. She has written six books about dogs and cats, including *Why Do Dogs Do That?*, and is a contributor to the *American Kennel Club Gazette, Critters USA, Dog Fancy, Dogs USA, Pet Product News* and *Veterinary Practice Staff*. She is based in California and has been active in promoting the adoption of retired racing Greyhounds.

BETTE LAGOW (chapters 1, 2, 14 and 21). Bette is a freelance writer who has written about dogs, cats and horses for a number of national magazines and has worked as an editor for the *American Kennel Club Gazette*, where she covered numerous purebred dog shows. Bette resides in New York.

KRISTINE NAPIER (part 7). Kristine works as a freelance health and science writer. She has written a number of health books, and has contributed to *Prevention's Symptom Solver for Dogs and Cats* (Rodale Press). Kristine lives in Ohio.

JACQUELINE O'NEIL (chapters 3, 4, 10 and 11). Jacqueline is a former manager of special events for the American Kennel Club and the creator of the publications *AKC Hunting Test Herald* and *AKC Pointing Breed Field Trial News*. An award-winning writer, she is the author of six books on dogs. Jacqueline lives in Montana.

AUDREY PAVIA (chapters 12, 13, 17, 19 and 20). In her varied career, Audrey has been an editor at *Horse Illustrated* magazine, managing editor of *Dog Fancy* magazine and senior editor of the *American Kennel Club Gazette*. She is based in California and currently works as a freelance writer specializing in animals.

ELAINE WALDORF GEWIRTZ (part 2). Elaine is a professional journalist residing in California. She has written numerous magazine and newspaper articles about dogs and dog training. Elaine also breeds, trains and exhibits Dalmatians in both conformation and obedience events, and has produced many champions.

Index

Credits & Acknowledgments

The publishers would like to thank the following organizations for their assistance in the preparation of this book: Pets International Pty Ltd, Kra-mar Pet Supplies Pty Ltd, THF Publications/Nylabone®.

Photograph credits:
(All photographs are copyright to the sources listed below.)
t = top, b = bottom, l = left, r = right, c = center

Ad-Libitum: Stewart Bowey, ic, iiiitc, viiibl, xitr, 1t, 1bc, 1b, 2t, 3tr, 3b, 5tr, 10c, 12b, 13tr, 13tl, 18tl, 18tc, 18tr, 18cr, 19tl, 19tc, 19c, 20tl, 20tc, 20tr, 21tl, 21tc, 21tr, 21c, 22tc, 22tr, 22c, 23tl, 23tc, 23tr, 24tl, 24tc, 24c, 24tr, 25tl, 25tc, 25tr, 26tl, 26tc, 26c, 26tr, 27tl, 27cl, 27tc, 27c, 27tr, 28tl, 28cl, 28tc, 28cr, 28tr, 29tl, 29tc, 29cr, 29c, 29cr, 30tl, 30cl, 30tcl, 30tr, 30cr, 31tl, 31tr, 31cr, 32tl, 32cl, 32tc, 32tr, 33tl, 33cl, 33tc, 33tr, 34tr, 34tc, 34c, 34tr, 48b, 54t, 54tcl, 54bl, 54bc, 55tl, 57l, 61tl, 62tl, 64tl, 68t, 68br, 69tl, 71b, 75b, 79tl, 79b, 81b, 82cl, 83tl, 89tr, 92b, 98b, 104bl, 104bc, 107b, 108tl, 109b, 109t, 110t, 112tl, 112l, 112bl, 112br, 131tl, 136tc, 142bl, 149br, 162bl, 173c, 173cr, 185b, 186t, 186b, 187bl, 189b, 191b, 202c, 202b, 203t, 205t, 205b, 211b, 228t, 228cr, 229bl, 229bc, 234bl, 236b, 236tl 237b, 241tc, 242bl, 242c, 244tl, 246–247c, 248tl, 248tr, 264t, 280b, 284bl, 284bcl, 284bcr, 284br, 287tl, 304cl, 304c, 304cr, 306c, 313br, 316br, 319bl, 319br, 322bl, 328c, 333tl, 333tr, 333tcr, 352bl, 352br, 360bl, 360bc, 360br, 368b, 382bl, 390tl, 390bl, 390bc, 390br, 391tl, 392tl, 392b, 392tr, 393tl, 393c, 393bl, 393br, 395tl, 395bl, 395bc, 395br, 396tl, 396cl, 396cr, 396br, 400b, 403tl, 403br, 404br, 407t, 408tl, 408bl, 408br, 410br, 416bc, 420b, 421tl.

Animal Photography: R. Willbie, 128t.

Animals Animals: Renee Stockdale, 282b.

Animals Unlimited: 155b, 271b, 272b.

Auscape International:
Alexis/Cogis, 165c, 228bl, 238tl; Beroule/Cogis, xibr, 152bc, 267b; D.R./Cogis, 46b, 55r; Jean-Paul Ferrero, 16c; Francais/Cogis, 22tl, 42cr, 43b, 48tr, 54cr, 60tl, 82bc, 93tl, 100l, 206b, 401b, 406b; Gissey/Cogis, 42cl, 43tl; M. Grenet & A. Soumillard/PHO.N.E., 44b; Hermeline/Cogis, 6b, 15b, 45b, 47r, 84tl, 170bl, 170c, 173tl, 177tl, 209t, 273b, 326c, 336bl, 345br; Jean-Michel Labat, 25c, 60b, 211t, 212tc, 212bl, 224tl, 380bl, 389tl; Labat/Cogis, 217tr, 233t, 269t; Jean-Michel Labat/PHO.N.E., 158t, 213tr; Labat/Lanceau/Cogis, 200t, 278c; Lanceau/Cogis, 11br, 51b, 193b, 334bl, 348br, 390tr, 393tr, 405tl; Lili/Cogis, 69b, 238bl; François Varin/Cogis, 312r; Jean-Claude Revy/PHO.N.E., 325tr; Rocher/Cogis, 82cr, 88t; Vedie/Cogis, 14tl; Wara/Cogis, 87t.

Australian Picture Library:
Sharpshooters, vi–vii.

Bill Bachman and Associates:
80–81, 104cl, 104br, 105tl, 120tl, 122cr, 126tl, 147br, 203b, 343bl.

Walter Chandoha: ixbr, 74b, 81tc, 96t, 231b, 122bc, 129tl, 190bl, 210–211, 236bl, 410cl, 411tl.

Bruce Coleman Limited:
Adriano Bacchella, 41t; Jane Burton, 290; Bob Glover, 346bl; Kim Taylor, 174br.

Kent and Donna Dannen: 8b, 11tl, 42cr, 50tl, 71t, 77r, 78b, 108b, 122bl, 124b, 125r, 127r, 127tl, 129b, 160bc, 169b, 174tl, 184b 189tl, 192cr, 192b, 195tl, 197tl, 198t, 198tl, 199tl, 207t, 226bc, 242bc, 251tl, 270cr, 274tl, 274b, 275b, 276b, 324bl, 337c, 355tr, 402c, 419bl, 419br.

Davis/Lynn Images: Tim Davis, 172tl, 176cl; Renee Lynn, 170bc, 178bl, 180tl, 422–423.

FLPA: Hugh Clark, 59c; Foto Natura, 212cr, 223tl, 399t; Klein-Hubert/Bios/Foto Natura, 122br, 131tr, 131cl, 131bl; J. & P. Wegner/Foto Natura, 219br.

Matt Gavin-Wear: 166bl.

Robert Harding Picture Library: 148br; James Strachan, 353br.

The Image Bank: Bockelberg, xiv–1, 323c; Flip Chalfant, 389b, 410t; Gary S. Chapman, 104cr, 119tl; David De Lossy, 62b; Britt Erlanson, 2cl, 3tl; David Europe, 212cl, 213tl; Garry Gay, 212c, 217tl; Alfred Gescheidt, 197bl; Deborah Gilbert, 106t; Steve Grubman, 64b, 106t; G.K. & Vikki Hart, 99b, 169tc, 184t, 264bl, 265tl, 381tr, 423b; David W. Hamilton, 192cl, 193tl; Carol Kohen, 81c, 104tl; Chuck Kuhn, 170cr, 182tl; Ted Russell, 198cr, 206tl; Sobel/Klonsky, 56l, 88b; Frank Whitney, 161bl.

Ron Kimbal Studios: xii–xiiib, 2tc, 12tl, 37tl, 76b, 96tc, 102tl, 146tc, 167br, 180bc, 250bc, 280cl, 281tl, 339tr.

Ron Levy: 2bl, 8tl, 74t, 123b, 190br, 198br, 204l, 208tl, 296tr, 301tr, 332bl, 391b, 417b, 410cr, 419tl.

NHPA: Henry Ausloos, 142tr; Stephen Dalton, 397b; Gerard Lacz, 237br; Yves Lanceau, 68bl, 72tl, 414b; Elizabeth MacAndrew, 90b.

Norvia Behling: xbr, 1tc, 2br, 6t, 9t, 35b, 36c, 38tl, 40l, 42br, 52tl, 53b, 54c, 54br, 58tl, 59tr, 65tl, 67tl, 67b, 68cl, 69tl, 72b, 81t, 82t, 82bl, 82br, 85b, 91tl, 94tl, 95l, 96bl, 97tl, 104c, 110c, 111tl, 120b, 153tr, 157br, 170br, 183tl, 183bc, 184cl, 185tr, 185tl, 187br, 191t, 194b, 195b, 198bl, 201b, 204br, 204c, 215br, 235b, 240–241, 241bc, 242br, 249br, 252bl, 256bl, 257br, 260tl, 264br, 265tr, 267tl, 270t, 270cl, 270b, 271tl, 277tl, 279b, 283t, 291tl, 292tl, 293br, 302bl, 308bc, 309tc, 310cl, 311br, 314tc, 316tc, 336tl, 341br, 345bc, 356–357, 360bcl, 379bc, 388–389, 390c, 390cr, 398tl, 406tl, 409t, 410bl 411tr, 414tl, 418r.

Oxford Scientific Films: Alan & Sandy Carey, 352tl.

The Photo Library, Sydney:
iiic, 175tr; Lori Adamski Peek, 4t; Ian Cunningham, 170cl, 171tl; Tim Davis, 2bc, 17tl, 19tr, 31tc, 145tr; Renee Lynn, 104tr, 118tl, 131br, 169bc, 190t, 192t.

Polperro Picture Productions:
Brian Geach, 144bc.

Silvestris: Herbert Kehrer, ii; J.U.P. Wegner, 214tl.

Dale C. Spartas: 68cr, 77tl, 81bc, 122t, 122cl, 123tl, 163tc, 168–169, 177br, 184cr, 187tl, 188b, 222tl, 240b, 277b, 280t, 280cr, 285tl, 287b, 366b, 391r.

Stock Photos P/L: Jim Erickson, 102b; Stephen Green-Armytage, 169tr, 170t; TSM-Paul Barton, 58b, 159br, 171bc; TSM-Steve Prezant, 242cl, 243tl; TSM-Grafton M. Smith, 181tr; Herbert Sprichtinger, 2cr, 35tl.

Renee Stockdale: 5b, 38b, 119r, 126r, 138tr, 139bc, 140c, 141tl, 212br, 220tr, 226bl, 227tr, 228cl, 228bl, 229tl, 230b, 234tl, 235tr, 241t, 242tr, 242tl, 242cr, 243bc, 251br, 253t, 255tl, 257tl, 259t, 285b, 288–289, 295t, 299tl, 299br, 303bc, 328t, 330tr, 331bc, 331br, 344tr, 347br, 350r, 365b, 373br, 380br, 398b, 405tr, 412b, 415t.

TFN Publications: 311tc.

Wildlight Photo Agency:
Carolyn Johns, 156tr; Philip Quirk, 143tr.

Illustration credits:

Janet Jones: 18–34 (silhouetted figures), 113–117, 132–135, 196, 225.

Sue Rawkins: 18–34 (silhouetted dogs).

Keith Scanlon: 244, 260–262, 296, 359–387, 407.

Cover credits: Ad-Libitum/ Stuart Bowey, front flap, front t, spine, back c & b; The Image Bank/Benn Mitchell, back t; The Photo Library, Sydney, front c.